Handbook of Banking and Finance in the MENA Region

Transformations in Banking, Finance and Regulation

Print ISSN: 2752-5821
Online ISSN: 2752-583X

Presently, the banking and finance sectors evolve within a globalized and highly uncertain environment. Each business and financial decision requires careful consideration of country-specific and international factors due to high levels of shock transmission and volatility spillovers. Furthermore, it would be remiss to omit the COVID-19 health crisis, which caused harmful effects to all areas of the real economy and made profound changes in the way our firms, economies, and markets used to function.

Many other already well-known aspects, including the repercussions of quantitative easing policies, disruptive technologies in finance (e.g., FinTech, Big Data, Data Analytics, Artificial Intelligence, and Blockchains), as well as innovative financing instruments for startups (e.g., ICOs and crowdfunding) are currently revolutionizing banking and finance and posing numerous challenges to regulatory bodies and policymakers. Climate change emergencies also put pressure on governments and firms worldwide to improve policy on governance, corporate social responsibility, and sustainability practices.

This book series "Transformations in Banking, Finance and Regulation" attempts to address these issues by focusing on transformative perspectives in banking and finance. Accordingly, it provides evidence-based guidance, recommendations, and pathways to assist businesses and policy decision-makers through an interdisciplinary and in-depth understanding of ongoing changes in the behavior of economic agents.

Published

Vol. 13 *Handbook of Banking and Finance in the MENA Region*
edited by Khaled Hussainey and Tamanna Dalwai

Vol. 12 *Green Finance and Sustainable Development Goals*
edited by Sabri Boubaker and Thai-Ha Le

Vol. 11 *Handbook of Environmental and Green Finance: Toward a Sustainable Future*
edited by Sabri Boubaker and Thai-Ha Le

Vol. 10 *Banking Resilience and Global Financial Stability*
edited by Sabri Boubaker and Marwa Elnahass

For the complete list of volumes in this series, please visit
www.worldscientific.com/series/tbfr

Transformations in Banking, Finance and Regulation
Volume 13

Handbook of Banking and Finance in the MENA Region

Editors

Khaled Hussainey
University of Portsmouth, UK

Tamanna Dalwai
Nottingham Trent University, UK

World Scientific

NEW JERSEY • LONDON • SINGAPORE • BEIJING • SHANGHAI • HONG KONG • TAIPEI • CHENNAI • TOKYO

Published by

World Scientific Publishing Europe Ltd.
57 Shelton Street, Covent Garden, London WC2H 9HE
Head office: 5 Toh Tuck Link, Singapore 596224
USA office: 27 Warren Street, Suite 401-402, Hackensack, NJ 07601

Library of Congress Cataloging-in-Publication Data
Names: Hussainey, Khaled, 1972– editor. | Dalwai, Tamanna, editor.
Title: Handbook of banking and finance in the MENA region / editors, Khaled Hussainey, University of Portsmouth, UK, Tamanna Dalwai, Nottingham Trent University, UK.
Description: New Jersey : World Scientific, [2024] | Series: Transformations in banking, finance and regulation, 2752-5821 ; vol. 13 | Includes bibliographical references and index.
Identifiers: LCCN 2023028695 | ISBN 9781800614727 (hardcover) | ISBN 9781800614734 (ebook) | ISBN 9781800614741 (ebook other)
Subjects: LCSH: Banks and banking--Middle East | Banks and banking--Africa, North. | Finance--Middle East. | Finance--Africa, North.
Classification: LCC HG3256.A6 H36 2024 | DDC 332.10956--dc23/eng/20230705
LC record available at https://lccn.loc.gov/2023028695

British Library Cataloguing-in-Publication Data
A catalogue record for this book is available from the British Library.

For any available supplementary material, please visit
https://www.worldscientific.com/worldscibooks/10.1142/Q0435#t=suppl

Desk Editors: Sanjay Varadharajan/Ana Ovey/Shi Ying Koe

Typeset by Stallion Press
Email: enquiries@stallionpress.com

The editors dedicate this book to the book series editors, Sabri Boubaker and Duc Khuong Nguyen, for their ongoing effort in enlightening readers with various developments in the field of banking, finance, and regulations.

Khaled Hussainey dedicates this book to his wonderful family, who have supported his professional journey and have been the most important contributor to his success.

Tamanna Dalwai dedicates this book to her mom, Rubina Dalwai, and dad, Abdul Rahman Dalwai, who have been the pillars of her life.

The editors would also like to dedicate this book to the families of all the contributors, who have patiently compromised on their valuable time together during the process of writing the chapters.

https://doi.org/10.1142/9781800614734_fmatter

Foreword

I have been given the honor of writing the foreword of the *Handbook of Banking and Finance in the MENA Region.* It is a great privilege to have the opportunity to review the chapters in this book before its launch. I found this book to offer stimulating discussions on various areas affecting the banking sector of the Middle East and North Africa (MENA) as a whole or specific countries. Some of the developments are specific to countries such as Morocco, Egypt, Oman, Syria, and the United Arab Emirates, while other topics discuss the Gulf Cooperation Council (GCC) or the MENA region as a whole.

The advancements in the banking system are shaping the competitive advantage and attractiveness of the firms and the overall economy. Technological innovation and digital finance are increasing the productivity of services and enhancing customer experience. While Europe and Asian countries have developed as fintech hubs, the MENA region has, in recent years, embraced financial technology. During the COVID-19 pandemic, there was an enhancement in digital technologies, thus improving lending, payment, wealth management, and health insurance services. The banking sector is also playing an important role in supporting emission reduction programs and the sustainable development of countries. Thus, banks play an instrumental role in providing access to climate finance. Financial inclusion for the MENA region has seen a mixed response where the high-income countries are more successful than the low-income countries.

The MENA region is gaining momentum toward open banking and is trying to solidify its position as a go-to destination. This handbook edited by Professor Khaled Hussainey and Dr. Tamanna Dalwai provides similar directions in the growth of MENA's financial sector and makes significant contributions to the existing literature. The book comprises 15 chapters that are divided into three main themes. The first theme presents the new advancements in finance and banking that cover interesting topics such as the adoption and proliferation of digital technology, green finance, and the introduction of fintech in the financial systems. The second theme discusses the banking sector's contribution to the MENA region. It covers discussion on the determinants of banks' profitability, the impact of COVID-19 news in financial market volatility, financial development and corporate governance efficiency, and the banking system in Oman. The theme also presents banks' progress in implementing financial inclusion, independence of the central bank of Egypt, the impact of capital adequacy and non-performing loss on loan loss provisions, and the new Basel III liquidity ratio. The last theme covers macroeconomic factors and financial development that present financial accounting disclosures and investors' sentiments, IPO valuation, pricing setting and stabilization mechanism, the role of corruption in financial development, and determinants of financial inclusion.

I strongly believe that there is wide coverage in this book of issues, and it does justice to the title. The book enhances the readers' knowledge by providing insights into the micro and macro-level factors affecting the banking sector. I am confident the book will be an interesting and valuable reading experience for academics and practitioners.

I wish to congratulate the publisher, editors, and all the contributing authors on the publishing of this book.

Mahdi Salehi
Professor
Department of Accounting
Ferdowsi University of Mashhad
Mashhad, Iran
April 28, 2023

https://doi.org/10.1142/9781800614734_fmatter

Preface

Chapter 1 begins with an introduction of how the internet has spread its network to the remotest parts of the world. The availability of digital technologies, infrastructure, and devices like laptops, tablets, smartphones, and wearables has enabled a lot of commercial transactions online. Banking could not remain untouched by these transformations, as customer preferences in both their personal and professional lives have changed, as there is a great demand for digital banking services like mobile apps, internet banking, digital wallets, and electronic payment systems (Sardana and Singhania, 2018). The consumers in the Gulf are not far behind. A McKinsey Report indicates that in the UAE with, an internet penetration of 92%, at least 80% of these customers prefer to utilize banking facilities online and are willing to shift some part of their financial assets to banks that offer an extensive digital solution (Shirish *et al.*, 2016; Sharma, 2022). This chapter aims to comprehend the consumer's acceptance of digital banking in the Middle East, focusing largely on the current challenges (infrastructural, cultural, and behavioral) and the vast opportunities, considering that only a fraction of the Middle East's digital potential has been captured (Elmasry *et al.*, 2016). The research methodology includes an extensive literature review on digitization in banking, available fintech solutions, consumer behavior toward e-commerce, and the region's rapid transformation into a digital economy. A remarkable insight gained from this research is that, in the Middle East, there is a robust consumer adoption of digital solutions, but consumers would like multichannel options available to meet their complex financial needs. Other pertinent requirements from a digital banking experience are trust, security, and ease of usage. A major drawback is the lack of qualified digital talent and a strong IT sector that can complement the bank's journey toward digitization.

Chapter 2 aims to enhance knowledge of green finance in the existing literature and review the sustainable development activities in the Middle East and North African countries. The study has also identified the challenges of providing green finance activities around the MENA region and offers suggestions to overcome the hindrances with the help of literary evidence. Research studies revealed that green finance and its related elements are at the forefront of discussion around the world. The reason behind these extreme changes in green nature is due to political, economic, social, and environmental fluctuations, which are affected by a fiscal crisis. Researchers have used the latest methodology of PRISM 2020, which is an advanced version of PRISMA 2009, to conduct a systematic literature review by considering 10 years of literature studies between 2013 and 2022 from the Scopus Search Engine to meet the research objectives of the study. This study would help future research activities on green finance to learn from the initiatives of MENA nations to understand the practical difficulties and opportunities available in society. It has remarkable implications for academic researchers, officials making policies, and entities providing various services to practitioners in the field of green nature as it is unique in understanding the growth and development of green finance activities and its sustainable development around the MENA region. The study concluded that green finance initiatives are possible by focusing on implementing various carbon emission proposals as part of sustainable programs. Government and financial institutions must consider that green finance activities enhance sustainable financing.

Chapter 3 discusses how fintech or the application of new technologies to finance is revolutionizing the financial services sector and creating a break with traditional finance. In some countries, fintech start-ups, digital in nature, have been able to expand access to finance to unbanked people to enable better financial inclusion of households and businesses. In other countries, these start-ups are nibbling away at the market share of traditional financial actors, particularly banks, to create a disruptive effect insofar as their technological advantage allows them to offer alternative financing or investment solutions compared to traditional financial intermediaries. In this chapter, I will try to examine this process in the MENA region, particularly in Morocco, by adopting an exploratory and analytical methodology of the introduction and evolution of fintechs. Finally, I conclude that the regulations adopted in Morocco do not allow start-ups to compete with traditional financial actors, only to complement them in order to improve financial inclusion.

Using the fixed effects estimator, Chapter 4 examines the profitability of 11 private banks in Syria over the period 2007 Q1–2018 Q4. To evaluate the impact of the Syrian crisis (civil war), the sample is divided into a pre-crisis period and a crisis period. The profitability determinants include bank-specific characteristics and industry-specific and macroeconomic factors. Dividing the sample has a twofold purpose: what determines the profitability of private banks in Syria and how the behavior of these determinants has changed in the crisis relative to the pre-crisis. The findings assert the presence of behavioral changes in profitability determinants across the two periods and that a high extent of banks' time-varying profitability is captured by the factors included.

Chapter 5 examines the impact of COVID-19 news in the United States on the volatility of financial markets in the MENA zone. We examine the effect of surprises from financial markets announcements relating to new, confirmed, and death cases of COVID-19 in each country in the sample. We use the GARCH (1.1) specification by incorporating the surprise component in the estimated model during the period from January 1, 2019, until December 31, 2020. The empirical findings show that the evolution of the daily returns and volatilities of the stock indexes of the MENA zone used in our research shows very significant peaks, in particular in the first three months of 2020 during the most significant spread of the COVID-19 epidemic. We show that the announcements of new cases of COVID-19 in the United States (NCUSA) have a significant impact on the Lebanon stock index and on Tunisia's stock index. Announcements of confirmed cases (CCUSA) of COVID-19 present a relative and insignificant impact on all stock market indices of the MENA zone used in our research. Finally, the announcements of the death cases of COVID-19 in the United States (DCUSA) have a significant impact on the stock market index of Morocco, Saudi Arabia, and United Arab Emirates. This chapter is the first to examine the effect of surprises from financial markets announcements relating to new, confirmed, and death cases of COVID-19 on the volatility of financial markets in the MENA zone.

Chapter 6 discusses financial development and corporate governance efficiency in the Middle East and North Africa (MENA) region. Macroeconomic soundness is essential for developing financial sector services, and corporate governance is a substantial factor in determining firm performance. Insufficient corporate governance can harm shareholders' interests and lead to undesirable results such as business insolvency. In addition, firms face many business risks and challenges related to regulation, competition, market and customer trends, technology shifts, supply chains, cost management, financing, performance monitoring, business rescue from insolvency, and total value optimization. Therefore, we discuss the nature and level of financial development and corporate governance in the MENA region, the problems faced by institutions in the MENA region that hinder financial development, the adoption of best practices in terms of corporate governance, and the role of efficient corporate governance as a key to overcoming some of these challenges and achieving continuous improvement using the data envelopment analysis (DEA) approach.

Chapter 7 provides an understanding of the banking system's development and structure in the Sultanate of Oman. It reviews existing literature and reports on the banking system in Oman between 1970 and 2020, and it provides a brief history of the Omani banking system before 1970. It also highlights the recent banking sector performance and the important role played by technology and the Central Bank of Oman (CBO) during the COVID-19 pandemic. This review demonstrates that the Omani banking system and sector experienced substantial developments in the regulatory and institutional framework due to which the performance of the banking sector remained stable in recent years. However, like other countries, the COVID-19 pandemic and the economic downturn affected the performance of banks, reducing banks' profitability and increasing non-performing loans (NPL) and assets. Despite this, the Omani banking system remained resilient, and the measures and policy initiatives taken by the CBO and the application of technology helped mitigate the adverse influence of the COVID-19 pandemic.

Chapter 8 presents a proposed multidimensional framework for measuring the level of application of financial inclusion (FI) at the individual bank level based on international expertise and experience in the field of FI application by relying on a balanced scorecard, clarifying the advantages and disadvantages of FI for banks, and reviewing previous attempts to build an indicator to measure FI. After reviewing the literature and conducting a series of interviews with bank managers in Egypt, this study concludes that bank application of FI has many benefits, such as diversifying banking assets, attracting new customers, stabilizing deposits, and reducing liquidity risks as well as providing a large database to banks, which can contribute to the possibility of introducing new products that can satisfy customer needs and building credit evaluation models to facilitate access to financing. However, the application of FI may have negative effects on banks, as providing basic financial services at zero cost (or costs lower than actual bank costs) may lead to a low level of welfare for financial service users and providers. At the same time, service providers may refrain from providing financial services when they have little incentive to do so. In addition, this study finds that all the indicators for measuring FI are used at the state level, and no indicator exists for measuring FI at the individual bank level. Therefore, this study proposes a multidimensional framework for measuring the level of application of FI at the bank level based on four perspectives of a balanced scorecard to contribute to the development of bank performance by providing appropriate and accurate information that can help the bank management in identifying shortcomings and weaknesses as well as opportunities for improvement and strengths, which can be exploited to improve future performance.

In Chapter 9, we assess macroeconomic independence using the prices of goods and services and short-term interest rates throughout a range of time periods categorized by alternative exchange rate regimes. To assess how well-floating exchange rates have increased Egypt's macroeconomic independence from the European Union (EU) and the United States (US), the ARDL model (autoregressive distributed lag) or Bounds Test has been devised. We examine a number of hypotheses concerning global transmission, interest rate and price movement, and international trade using this empirical methodology. According to the findings, Egypt's products market and monetary policy are, over the long term, completely independent from those of base regions like the EU and US. Because of this, the Central Bank of Egypt (CBE) may decide its plan of action (policy direction) and define its goals without being impacted by shocks from the EU and the US.

Chapter 10 examines the impact of capital adequacy ratios (CARs) and non-performing loans (NPLs) and the application of IFRS 9 on loan loss provisions (LLPs). It also analyzes the impact of LLPs and NPLs and the application of IFRS 9 on CARs for a sample of Gulf banks during the period 2012–2021. Panel data analysis was adopted to reach an appropriate model to study the effect of independent variables on dependent variables. The results of the study showed that the majority of Gulf banks did not find statistically significant differences in the performance of the CAR and NPL indicators before and after applying IFRS 9. However, there were statistically significant differences in the performance of the LLP indicator before and after applying IFRS 9 in favor of applying IFRS 9 (after 2018). The study also found that there was a difference in the performance of the indicators. The study also found that there is a negative impact of CAR on LLP, and vice versa. On the other hand, the effect of NPL was positive on both CAR and LLP, while there was no effect of IFRS 9 adoption on both CAR and LLP. The importance of studying CAR and LLP is highlighted by the importance of financial solvency that may be affected after obligating banks to apply IFRS 9 in January 2018; therefore, the results of this experimental study can add to the limited knowledge about the behavior of CAR, LLP, and NPL before and after IFRS 9 adoption in developing countries. This chapter contributes to the limited literature on CAR, LLP, and NPL before and after IFRS 9 adoption in developing countries in general and GCC countries in particular. A review of previous literature revealed limited or no studies measuring the impact of CAR on LLP and effect of IFRS 9 adoption on GCC banks. Very limited research has been conducted in developing countries in general. This is important taking into consideration the environmental factors in developing countries, which can give a different view on the issue of CAR, LLP, and the extent to which they are affected by the application of the IFRS 9 standard.

Chapter 11 examines the role of bank liquidity in ensuring financial stability. Based on the Basel III liquidity framework guidelines, the authors calculated the NSFR for 124 banks operating in the Middle East and North Africa (MENA) region during the period 2014–2021. The findings of this study show the following: first, the

NSFR has a positive impact on financial stability; second, the results highlight that NPLs, diversification, bank size, and the business cycle have a negative impact on stability, while the ROE and business cycle have a positive impact; and third, these results support the efforts of the Basel Committee on Banking Supervision (BCBS) in developing guidelines for the NSFR to enhance the liquidity risk management. These results will be useful for authorities and policymakers seeking to clarify the implications of adopting the liquidity requirement on banking behavior.

Chapter 12 aims to critically review the existing theoretical and empirical literature on financial accounting disclosures, investors' reactions toward bad financial news, and the moderating effect of the individual investor's sentiments (particularly the termination of loss-making projects, fluctuation of share price, and firm's image) in project-based organizations (PBOs). To achieve this, the authors have reviewed extensive research work from reputed and highly cited databases across developed and developing countries, particularly focusing on the UAE. Based on the reviewed literature, it is concluded that there is a solid connection between intention and behavior reaction in a manner that enlarges the possibility of the action to be performed. However, investors' perception of bad financial news has not been empirically examined to date through various information channels. Hence, further investigation is required to determine investors' reactions toward bad news using the dimensions determined in previous reviews.

Chapter 13 discusses the Egyptian regulatory framework of the IPO process as well as its listing on the Egyptian Exchange (EGX). We will examine the most recent IPOs executed in the Egyptian capital market during the period of 2016–2022 to identify the valuation, pricing, and stabilization mechanisms used by investment banks in light of Egyptian laws and regulations. We use descriptive analysis for the IPO structure data to implicitly identify the incentives to go public. Interestingly, all shares offered in the Egyptian IPOs during the period of concern are secondary offerings, so Egyptian IPO firms use the capital market as an exit strategy rather than to finance expansion. A discounted cash flow model and trading multiples are the techniques most applied in the IPO valuation. The book-building pricing mechanism is widely used by investment banks in the Egyptian IPO market.

Chapter 14 aims to assess the effect of corruption on the relationship between financial development and economic complexity in MENA. To this end, we estimate a panel data model on 21 MENA countries between 1995 and 2020 using the double least squares method. Overall, the analysis shows significant heterogeneous results conditional on corruption. Specifically, corruption worsens the effect of financial access, and the depth and efficiency of economic complexity over the sample period. In contrast, it improves the effect of financial stability on economic complexity in the region. The results appear to be robust to an alternative estimation technique.

Chapter 15 begins with an introduction on how the financial crisis, the accumulation of sovereign debt, shocks to commodity prices, and pandemics are just a few of the recent economic crises that have affected the world and had a major effect on economic activities. In this context, the financial sector must fully contribute to encouraging economic growth in order to achieve equitable economic growth and reduce poverty. To that end, access to affordable and secure financial services is crucial. The main goal of financial inclusion, which allows people to take advantage of saving and investing opportunities, is to provide basic financial services to society's poor and excluded groups. This chapter aims to identify the factors that promote financial inclusion in the MENA region. It specifically examines the impact of GDP per capita, the money supply as a percentage of GDP, the number of internet users as a percentage of the population, and consumer price inflation. The International Monetary Fund and the Global Development Indicators provided secondary data for the study, which covers the period 2004–2020. The dynamic panel was conducted using Stata 17 software to obtain the coefficients of such variables that affect the levels of financial inclusion in six MENA countries. The results reveal that income level, measured by GDP per capita, financial sector development, measured by the money supply, and the number of internet users all have positive effects on financial inclusion in the MENA region, while consumer price inflation has no impact. The Financial Inclusion Index (FII), according to Sarma's (2008) approach, has not been employed in any relevant studies, despite the theoretical and empirical literature offering a range of perspectives on which factor can determine financial inclusion. This study uses this index to measure financial inclusion and then applies dynamic panel estimation to identify the factors that promote financial inclusion in MENA countries. Consequently, this chapter strives to enrich the literature by comprehending the determinants of financial inclusion in the MENA region, covering the period 2004–2020.

https://doi.org/10.1142/9781800614734_fmatter

About the Editors

Khaled Hussainey is a Professor and Research Lead of Accounting and Financial Management at the Faculty of Business and Law, University of Portsmouth, UK. He has over two and a half decades of teaching and research experience at both undergraduate and postgraduate levels. He has a growing research reputation in the field of accounting and finance. He has been featured in the 2021 database (published on October 19, 2021) created by experts at Stanford University, USA, for "World Ranking of Top 2% Researchers". He has published about 150 articles in peer-reviewed journals, has written a number of book chapters, and edited a textbook on corporate governance in emerging economies. He also won the best paper award from the *British Accounting Review* in 2007 and the *Journal of Risk Finance* in 2012. He has supervised more than 60 Ph.D. scholars and has examined more than 120 Ph.D. theses. He has received research grants from the Economic and Social Research Council (ESRC), the British Academy, the Qatar National Research Foundation (QNRF), the Financial Reporting Council (FRC), Plymouth University, the University of Portsmouth, and Abu Dhabi University. His research papers are published in top-ranked journals, such as *Accounting and Business Research*, *British Accounting Review*, *Journal of Accounting and Public Policy*, *International Review of Financial Analysis*, *Journal of International Accounting, Auditing and Taxation*, *Review of Quantitative Finance and Accounting*, and *International Journal of Finance and Economics*. He is Co-Editor of the *Journal of Financial Reporting and Accounting* and

Journal of Contemporary Issues in Accounting. He is an Associate Editor of the *Journal of Applied Accounting Research*, *International Journal of Accounting, Auditing and Performance Evaluation*, and *International Journal of Emerging Markets*, and a Guest Editor for the *Journal of Risk and Financial Management and Green Finance.*

Tamanna Dalwai is a Senior Lecturer in the Accounting and Finance Department at the Nottingham Business School, Nottingham Trent University, UK. She has been working in the higher education sector for more than 15 years. She previously worked as an Assistant Professor and Deputy Director of Quality Assurance at Muscat College, Sultanate of Oman. As the Deputy Director of Quality Assurance, she supported the development and continuance of quality management and played an instrumental role in the Institutional Accreditation of Muscat College. She has a Ph.D. in Accounting from Universiti Teknologi Malaysia and an MBA (Finance and Accounting) from California State University, East Bay; she is also an Associate Fellow of the Higher Education Academy, UK. On completion of her PhD, she was awarded the Best Student Award by the International Business School UTM. She has published more than 25 articles in peer-reviewed journals and has written a number of book chapters. She was awarded the Best Researcher Award at Muscat College in 2022. Dr. Tamanna has conducted several seminars and workshops for national and international higher education institutions. She is an external reviewer for the Ministry of Higher Education, Research and Innovation (MoHERI) for externally funded research grants and an ad hoc reviewer for various Scopus-indexed journals. She has been awarded four externally funded research grants by MoHERI. She is an avid researcher in the fields of intellectual capital, bank stability, capital structure, accounting education, corporate governance, corporate social responsibility, managerial ability, digitalization, financial theories, international accounting standards, cost of capital, quality assurance, and Islamic finance. She also has an upcoming edited book to be published by Palgrave Macmillan.

https://doi.org/10.1142/9781800614734_fmatter

About the Contributors

Abdelkader Mohamed Sghaier Derbali is an Assistant Professor of Finance at the Department of Finance and Accounting, Higher Institute of Informatics and Management, Kairouan University, Kairouan, Tunisia, and at the Department of Administrative and Financial Sciences and Techniques, Applied College, Taibah University, Saudi Arabia. His research interests include risk management, systemic risk, international finance, and capital markets and institutions. He has published articles, among others, in journals, such as *Research in International Business and Management*, *Finance Research Letters*, *International Journal of Critical Accounting*, *International Journal of Economics and Business Research*, and *The Chinese Economy*.

Ahmed Mohamed Habib is an Independent Researcher in accounting and finance. He is an Editorial Board Member in many prestigious scientific journals indexed in Scopus. He has published numerous articles in high-ranking journals and conferences. He has reviewed many journals indexed in the Web of Science and Scopus. His research interests include accounting and finance science, corporate governance, intellectual capital, corporate social responsibility, ESG criteria, working capital management, corporate narrative reporting, corporate finance, earnings management, corporate investment efficiency, performance optimization, continuous improvement, frontier analysis, data envelopment analysis (DEA), DEA applications, Malmquist index analysis, managerial ability, knowledge management, business strategies, decision support systems, and econometric analysis.

Ali Zagoub works as an Associate Professor in the Accounting Department at the University of Benghazi. He teaches intermediate accounting, cost accounting, corporate governance, and accounting research methods. He also works as the Director of a cooperation program with SDA Bocconi University to implement specialized postgraduate programs for the University of Benghazi. Dr. Zagoub has several papers and books published, such as *An Overview of the Corporate Governance Framework in Libya*, *Barriers of Environmental Management Accounting Practices in Developing Country*, and *Intermediate Financial Accounting*.

Amer Alaya is an Assistant Professor of Business Management and the Head of Student Administration at the British University in Dubai (BUiD). He started his career as a part-time lecturer at Aleppo University before moving to different academic institutions in Saudi Arabia and the UAE. He holds an MBA and Ph.D. in Business Management. Having worked for three well-known universities in the Middle East, he has intensive experience in quality assurance, quality monitoring, enhancement processes, examination procedures, and strategies for improving students' experience and administration.

Amira Houaneb is currently an Assistant Professor at the College of Business Administration, Prince Sattam Bin Abdulaziz University, Alkharj, Saudi Arabia. She has a Ph.D. in Finance from the Higher Institute of Management of Tunis, University of Tunis. She received her Bachelor's degree and her Master's degree from the Faculty of Economics and Management of Tunis, University of Tunis El Manar. Her research activities are threefold: the first is to explore corporate governance and conflicts of interest between shareholders and debtholders; the second major theme is accounting earnings management, and real earnings management; and finally the third research axis concerns banks' profitability and banking risks.

Asma S. Abdelhamid Alzwi works as a Lecturer in the Finance and Banking Department at the University of Benghazi. She teaches financial management, introduction to finance, risk management, bank credit, and quantitative methods in finance. Dr. Alzwi has many interests in contemporary issues in finance. Dr. Asma has several papers and books published, such as *Measuring the Financial Stability of Arab Banks: A Comparative Study* and *The Reality of Capital Adequacy in Arab Banks: A Comparative Study*.

Hala Fadheel Elfergani works as a Lecturer in the Accounting Department at the University of Benghazi. She teaches financial accounting, cost accounting, and auditing. In addition to being interested in financing issues in the banking sector, Dr. Hala has several papers and books published, such as *The Impact of the Predictive Ability of the Incurred Lose Model on the Quality of Accounting Profits: An Applied Study and Evaluating the Quality of Loan Loss Allowances Prepared According to the Expected Loss Model: An Applied Study*. Dr. Hala has participated in many scientific conferences related to accounting and finance, the quality of accounting education, and digital transformation in accounting education.

Hamada Elsaid Elmaasrawy Elsayed Ghazi is an Assistant Professor at the Department of Accounting at Tanta University, Egypt. He has many articles published in the fields of accounting, auditing, and corporate governance. He is a Reviewer for a number of journals listed in the Scopus database. He has co-authored several books related to Islamic finance, taxation, corporate governance, and financial accounting.

Husam Basiddiq is a Senior Lecturer at the College of Economics and Business Administration, the University of Technology and Applied Sciences, Oman. He completed his Ph.D. in Business (Accounting and Corporate Governance) at Nottingham Trent University. He obtained an M.Sc. in International Accounting and Finance from the University of Stirling and a B.A. with honors from the University of Bedfordshire. His research interests are in the areas of corporate governance, ownership structures, dividend policy, corporate reporting, and corporate social responsibility and sustainability. Most recently, Husam's research has focused on understanding the board decision-making processes and the factors affecting board processes.

Koumis Ngagni Agathe Cassandra holds a Master's Degree in Monetary and Banking Macroeconomics. She is currently pursuing her doctoral studies at the Faculty of Economics at the University of Douala. Indeed, the issues of finance, structural transformation, inequality, natural resources, and political concentration are very important to her. She is therefore working hard on her doctoral thesis with the support of her family. However, apart from her studies, she is busy playing sports and reading.

Krishna Murthy Meesaala holds a Ph.D. in Commerce and a Master of Business Administration in Finance and International Business, with over 20 years of expertise in accounting and finance education. He has presented more than 20 research papers at national and international conferences and has published more than 25 research articles in peer-reviewed journals, UGC Care-listed journals, SCOPUS, and Springer Nature. He has conducted several research and academic workshops. He has been awarded four Block-Funded research projects (Ministry of Higher Education, Sultanate of Oman).

Mahmoud Otaify has been working as an Assistant Professor of Finance at the Egypt-Japan University of Science and Technology (EJUST). He obtained a B.Sc. of Finance and Investment with excellent/honor grades from the College of Business Administration and Economics, Misr University for Science and Technology. Dr. Otaify earned M.Sc. and Ph.D. degrees in Financial Economics from the Faculty of Economics and Political Science, Cairo University, in 2012 and 2018, respectively. The topic of his M.Sc. thesis involved the determinants of the initial public offering of stocks, while his Ph.D. thesis investigated the response of volatility of characteristics-sorted portfolios to macroeconomic volatility. Dr. Otaify has taught several undergraduate courses, such as portfolio management, corporate finance, financial markets, and investment banking. Moreover, Dr. Otaify is working as an MBA Director at E-JUST University and has established a finance simulations hub as a training center for finance students. On the practical side, he is working as a Non-Executive Director at Horizon Security Brokerage Company. His research interests include corporate finance, market microstructure, asset pricing models, and investment banking.

Mazen Diwani is an Economist with 7 years of full-time working experience within the banking and economic consultancy sectors and more than 9 years in academia. He was awarded earned a Ph.D. Fellowship of Excellence for Foreign Nationals Educated Abroad at the Sapienza University of Rome and a Ph.D. in Models for Economics and Finance. He obtained a B.Sc. in Economics from Damascus University in Syria (2008) and an M.Sc. in Finance from Lund University in Sweden (2010). He has recently accepted a position at De Montfort University in the city of Almaty (Kazakhstan). His research interests involve applied microeconometric methodologies in labor market research, measuring individual and social well-being, and analysis of the effects of socio-economic and demographic factors on an individual's life course.

Mondjeli Mwa Ndjokou Itchoko Motande is a Professor of Economics. He wrote his thesis in Monetary Macroeconomics on "The properties of the monetary aggregates of the Central Bank of African States". In addition to his specialization, he has great interest in subjects related to development economics. This interest is manifested through his numerous publications on aspects such as fiscal policies, entrepreneurship, natural resources, economic growth, institutions, and inequalities. Currently, he holds the position of Dean of the Faculty of Economics and Management at the University of Maroua.

Moufida Ben Saada is an Associate Professor in Accounting and Finance at the Department of Finance and Accounting, Higher Institute of Informatics and Management of Kairouan, Kairouan University, Kairouan, Tunisia. His research interests include accounting, auditing, reporting, banking and market microstructure, and Islamic finance. He has published articles, among others, in the *International Journal of Financial Engineering*, the *International Journal of Finance and Banking Studies*, and *International Journal of Critical Accounting*.

Mustafa Kasim research interests involve macroeconomics, with a particular focus on fiscal and monetary policy, financial markets, foreign exchange, and international capital markets. In addition, he is interested in the instability of financial markets and the dynamic interrelationship between interest rates and macroeconomic policy objectives. He has researched exchange rate regimes, independence of macroeconomics, response of monetary policy, and economic growth. He has used a number of techniques in his research, including structured vector auto regression and the autoregressive distributed lag model. He is interested in supervising in the areas of macroeconomics, international financial markets, banking and risk management, and foreign exchange and trading strategies. He has experience in time series econometrics and the use of Eviews and SPSS.

Najib Mrabet is a qualified Professor and Teacher at the Higher School of Technology in Oujda, an institution of the Mohammed Premier University, Oujda, Morocco. A Moroccan national, married and father of one child, he obtained his doctorate in economics at the Faculty of Law at the Sidi Mohamed ben Abdeallah University in Fez. He also taught accounting and finance at the National School of Commerce and Management in Settat. He is the author and co-author of several articles and books on economics and finance.

Omar Ikbal Tawfik has earned a Ph.D. in Accounting from Iraq. He has worked as an Associate Professor at the College of Commerce and Business Administration at the University of Dhofar since 2015. He worked at the University of Abb in Yemen from 2005–2008, the University of Jerash in Jordan from 2008–2013, the University of Applied Sciences in Jordan from 2013–2015. He has interests in financial accounting, corporate governance, and auditing. He has published more than sixteen research papers in different journals (five of them are Scopus and Web of Science indexed), four chapters, and two books.

Oumayma Elbach is a Ph.D. Student in Finance at the Department of Finance and Accounting, Higher Institute of Informatics and Management of Kairouan, Kairouan University, Kairouan, Tunisia. His research interests include risk management, systemic risk, international finance, capital markets and institutions, banking and market microstructure, and Islamic finance.

Rachida El Yamani is a Professor of Economics at the Faculty of Law, Economic and Social Sciences, Mohammedia City, (Hassan II University, Casablanca). Her current studies focus on factors that influence economic growth, financial inclusion, financial innovation, and financial development. She started her career as a Professor Researcher at Hassan II University, where she also conducted a number of studies on the development of the financial market. She graduated from Hassan II University in Casablanca with a Master's degree in Economic Modeling Techniques and Econometrics in 2015 and a Ph.D. in Economics in 2019.

Rima Solanki is a Lecturer in the Department of Business Administration at the University of Technology and Applied Sciences, Ibri, Sultanate of Oman. She has completed her M.Com., PGDBA, and CISA (USA). She has around 22 years of experience in Oman in teaching various courses related to accounting and management in the bachelor's degree program.

S. Varalakshmi works in the Business and Economics Department at Mazoon College, Muscat, Sultanate of Oman. She has more than 15 years of experience teaching business-related curriculum and in research. She has a Ph.D. in Commerce and a Postgraduate Diploma in Personnel Management and Industrial Relations from MSSW, University of Madras. She is an Associate Fellow of the Higher Education Academy and has a Postgraduate Certificate in Learning and Teaching in Higher Education from the University of Stirling, United Kingdom. She has presented more than ten research articles at national and international conferences and published more than fifteen research articles in peer-reviewed journals, SCOPUS, and Springer Nature.

Seemab Rana is a Lecturer at the University of Technology and Applied Sciences. She has completed her M.Phil. degree in Economics from Bahauddin Zakarya University with a specialization in Econometrics. Her areas of expertise are banking development, economic fluctuations, and quantitative empirical analysis. She is the author of *Optimal Exchange Regime & Pakistan's External Sector: Basket Peg or Flex* (ISBN-13: 978-3659209253). Her publications also include research articles in well-known journals, such as *IJRCM* and *JDSS*. Her recent projects involve eco-financing, curriculum development, inflation, and unemployment trends.

Shatha Hussain is a Finance and Accounting Lecturer at City University College of Ajman. Her research interests primarily focus on corporate governance, behavioral finance, and information quality. She has extensive experience and knowledge relate to individual investors' challenges and solution development for managing their behavior. She has published 5 articles in refereed journals and conferences.

Sweetline Sujee is a Lecturer in the Department of Business Administration at the University of Technology and Applied

Sciences, Ibri, Sultanate of Oman. She has completed her M.Com, MBA (Finance), and PGDCA qualifications. She has around 25 years of experience in Oman in teaching all accounting and management subjects in the bachelor's degree program.

Syeeda Shafiya Mohammadi is currently a Senior Lecturer at Muscat College at the Faculty of Business and Accounting. She obtained her Master of Commerce degree from Osmania University, Hyderabad. Syeeda Shafiya has more than 13 years of proactive teaching experience at an international level. She is an Associate Fellow of the Higher Education Academy, UK, and an approved member of the faculty of finance and accounting for the University of Stirling programs. She also has broad experience in teaching professional courses, such as FIA and ACCA. Syeeda Shafiya has upgraded her career development through research in the fields of intellectual capital, corporate governance, corporate social responsibility, and international accounting standards. She has co-authored book chapters, published work in journals, and participated in international conferences. Syeeda Shafiya also has exceptional experience in accounting software, course advising, and career counseling. She is a good team player who achieves success with sincere dedication. She thrives on new challenges and believes that work should be fulfilling and rewarding.

Valentine Soumtang Bime is a Cameroonian Researcher who believes in the ability of developing countries, and African economies in particular, to emerge from instability. She is interested in issues of financial development, quality of governance, and the cultural aspects of economic development. She holds a Ph.D. in Monetary and Banking Macroeconomics from the University of Yaounde II-SOA (Cameroon). She has been an Assistant Lecturer at the same university since 2021.

Wassim Ben Ayed holds a Ph.D. in Accounting and Finance from the Higher Institute of Management (ISG) of Tunis and a Master's degree in Accounting from the Higher Institute of Accounting and Business Administration (ISCAE), University of Manouba. His doctoral thesis and a majority of his research explore the implications of banking regulation with respect to the dual system, risk management, bank efficiency, and accounting. He possesses a good research profile with several research articles published in Scopus-listed journals. He has worked at the Faculty of Law, Economics and Management, University of Jendouba, Tunisia. Currently, he is a fixed-term Assistant Professor of Accounting at the Military Academy, Fondouk Djedid, Tunisia.

https://doi.org/10.1142/9781800614734_fmatter

Acknowledgments

May Almighty Allah SWT grant success to this book. This book compilation was completed under the complete guidance and blessings of Almighty Allah.

We would like to thank the Book Series Editors, Professor Sabri Boubaker and Professor Duc Khuong Nguyen, for their faith in us and providing us with their valuable expertise while undertaking this journey to complete the *Handbook of Banking and Finance in the MENA region*. We are grateful to the Acquisitions Editor, Dr. Natalie K Watson, for her helpful support. A shining element of this book is the foreword written by Professor Mahdi Salehi, Department of Accounting, Ferdowsi University of Mashhad, Iran, who kindly agreed to contribute. We offer our sincere thanks to all the contributing authors who expressed their interest and were successful in publishing their chapters in this book.

All views expressed in the chapters remain the sole responsibility of the authors.

https://doi.org/10.1142/9781800614734_fmatter

Contents

https://doi.org/10.1142/9781800614734_fmatter

List of Figures

https://doi.org/10.1142/9781800614734_fmatter

List of Tables

https://doi.org/10.1142/9781800614734_fmatter

Introduction

Over the past few decades, banking in the Middle East and North Africa (MENA) region has witnessed considerable changes. These changes have been sparked by a confluence of economic, social, technological, and globalization issues. As a result of these adjustments, the MENA banking industry has grown more diversified and competitive, with a variety of banks and financial institutions providing cutting-edge goods and services to satisfy clients' changing needs. However, the MENA banking sector continues to encounter a number of difficulties and barriers, including political unpredictability, economic turbulence, and regulatory limitations. In addition, recent studies in the MENA region have looked at the development of the banking sector's sources and uses based on its overall balance sheet.

The low ratio of private credit to GDP provided by deposit money banks, is the lowest in comparison to other areas, and is one significant issue that the MENA countries face. Furthermore, the COVID-19 outbreak and the drop in oil prices have both had a negative impact on the MENA region. The MENA banking industry is anticipated to maintain its growth trajectory in the near future despite these obstacles, thanks to developments in fintech and the rising demand for Islamic banking products. Previous research suggests that the absence of market contestability and inadequate understanding of the financial and credit environment are to blame for the relative lack of competitiveness of the MENA banking and financial markets. As a result, many businesses in the private sector lack access to banking and credit institutions, which restricts their ability to expand. The MENA banking industry has advanced significantly in recent years, but there are still a number of issues that need to be resolved.

This handbook provides a wide coverage of banking and finance in the MENA region and enlightens the readers of various developments in the field. There are a total of 15 chapter contributions using theoretical and empirical research on regional or country-specific advancement and achievements in banking and finance. The 29 co-authors who have written chapters for the edited book represent 10 countries (Cameroon, Egypt, Libya, Morocco, Oman, Saudi Arabia, Syria, Tunisia, the United Arab Emirates, and the United Kingdom).

The chapters are assigned to three parts of the handbook. Part 1 entitled New Advancements in Finance and Banking addresses the adoption and proliferation of digital technology in the banking sector of the Middle East (Chapter 1); a systematic literature review of green finance in the MENA region (Chapter 2); and a case study approach of the introduction of fintech in the financial systems of the MENA region (Chapter 3).

Part 2 entitled Banking Sector Contribution to the MENA Region presents the empirical investigation of banks' profitability determinants for Syria's banking sector (Chapter 4); the impact of COVID-19 news on financial market volatility in MENA countries (Chapter 5); financial development and corporate governance efficiency of the MENA region (Chapter 6); a literature review of the banking system in Oman (Chapter 7); an exploratory study for measuring Egypt's banking sector progress in implementing financial inclusion (Chapter 8); a review of the independence of the Central Bank of Egypt and exchange rate regimes (Chapter 9); an econometric study of the impact of capital adequacy (CAR) and non-performing loans (NPLs) on LLPs for GCC banks (Chapter 10); and evidence from the MENA banking system on the new Basel III liquidity ratio (Chapter 11).

Part 3, entitled Macroeconomic Factors and Financial Development, covers financial accounting disclosures and investors' sentiments in the UAE (Chapter 12); IPO valuation, pricing setting, and stabilization mechanism in the Egyptian capital market (Chapter 13); investigation of the role of corruption in the relationship between financial development and economic complexity of the MENA countries (Chapter 14): and, lastly, determinants of financial inclusion in the MENA region (Chapter 15).

Part 1

New Advancements in Finance and Banking

https://doi.org/10.1142/9781800614734_0001

Chapter 1

Adoption and Proliferation of Digital Technology in the Banking Sector of the Middle East

Sweetline Sujee and Rima Solanki

Abstract

The internet has spread its network to the remotest parts of the world. The availability of digital technologies, infrastructure, and devices like laptops, tablets, smartphones, and wearables has enabled a lot of commercial transactions online. Banking could not remain untouched by these transformations as customer preferences in both their personal and professional lives have changed as there is a great demand for digital banking services like mobile apps, internet banking, digital wallets, and electronic payment systems (Sardana & Singhania, 2018). The consumers in the Gulf are not far behind. A McKinsey Report indicates that in the UAE, with an internet penetration of 92%, at least 80% of these customers prefer to utilize banking facilities online and are willing to shift some part of their financial assets to banks that offer an extensive digital solution (Shirish *et al.*, 2016; Sharma, 2022). The research aim was to comprehend the consumer's acceptance of digital banking in the Middle East, focusing largely on the current challenges (infrastructural, cultural, and behavioral) and the vast opportunities, considering that only a fraction of the Middle East's digital potential has been captured (Elmasry *et al.*, 2016). The research methodology includes an extensive literature review on digitization in banking, available fintech solutions, consumer behavior toward e-commerce, and the region's rapid transformation into a digital economy. A remarkable insight gained from this research is that, in the Middle East, there is a robust consumer adoption of digital solutions, but consumers would like multichannel options available to meet their complex financial needs. Other pertinent requirements from a digital banking experience are trust, security, and ease of usage. A major drawback is the lack of qualified digital talent and a strong IT sector that can complement the bank's journey toward digitization.

Keywords: Middle East, digital banking, fintech, consumer adoption, e-payment, multichannel banking option

1.1. Introduction

The sun has set on the era when a client has to visit a bank to withdraw or deposit money, update personal details, or conduct any other form of financial transaction. The combination of information technology, specialized human capital, and volumes of data has revolutionized banking to a point of disruption (Sujee *et al.*, 2022). Modern financial institutions involve fewer banks and more technology businesses that tirelessly work toward providing sustainable digital financial solutions to retail as well as corporate clients. Fintech is the new buzzword that has brought in user-friendliness and increased customer reach, especially for communities untouched by traditional banking.

Innovation is a constant, be it obstructive or disruptive (Christensen *et al.*, 2015). Fintech is one such solution that has proved its disruptiveness by engaging with selective solutions for few customers and has today spread across the world wherein the demand for fintech products far surpasses that of traditional banking products. The western part of the globe has been involved in research, development, and deployment of fintech solutions since the economic crisis in 2008, resulting from an understanding of the fact that the banking systems were over-regulated, preventing them from innovating and delivering services to suit the market needs (Krstić & Banka Ad Beograd, 2016).

The setting up of a digital environment, be it for the banking industry or the economy in general, requires certain enablers like infrastructure, a digital marketplace with digital goods and services, and a regulatory framework. The paradoxical situation in the Middle East is that it has the digital infrastructure and social media usage that compares and in some cases surpasses countries with similar GDP, but the utilization of digital solutions for payments and other transactions is comparatively poor (Cusolito *et al.*, 2022).

The objective of this research is to identify the issues that have created a bottleneck or an obstruction to the proliferation of the digital economy in the Middle East through one of its key indicators — digitization in the banking sector.

This research adopts a funnel structure, aiming to understand the larger picture in the form of banking, its norms and procedures, digital interventions and solutions available, adoption of these solutions in other parts of the world, and the impact following a closer study of the Middle Eastern banking sector. The findings clearly indicate the large-scale activities being undertaken toward the development of a sustainable digital economy and a robust digitized banking system.

1.1.1. *Traditional banking*

In the past, where customers would visit brick-and-mortar establishments to fulfill their financial needs of depositing or withdrawing money, seeking loans or transferring funds, and so many other monitory activities (Golden, 2016). The real existence of these financial institutions gave customers a sense of safety and comfort with respect to storing their hard-earned money. The customer's financial data were highly protected due to limited internet usage. Moreover, customers enjoyed the human connection they experienced despite having to travel to the bank for all their needs. The global financial crisis that unfolded in 2007–2009 caused extreme misery to the customers across the US and Europe, with a great deal of indirect impact on nations worldwide owing to globalization of products and services. Smaller banks suffered the most, turned insolvent, and required government bailout to survive. As a result, not only did the corporate customers face huge financial challenges but it also led to high levels of distress among the retail customers (Chiorazzo *et al.*, 2018). This crisis showcased the pitfalls of the traditional banking system and raised questions about its ability to survive. Incorrect financial planning and wrong strategic decisions are the two prominent reasons for the traditional system to have been overtaken by dynamic e-solutions. Customers have raised questions regarding banking charges, the time it takes to complete transactions, the inertia experienced in the banking process, the lack of customized solutions, especially during hours that clash with their work schedules, and the primary objective of banks, which is to create value for their customers. The banks, with their legacy technologies and extensive networks of branches, caused the digital disruption to gain a foothold in the financial services sector.

For banks to compete with the newer solutions available in the financial environment today, they need to constantly evolve and innovate in line with consumer tastes and demands using the voluminous amount of data that are available and monetize the same.

1.1.2. *Internet based banking*

With the advent of the internet, the overall business landscape changed. Smartphones penetrated the market, making the customer extremely knowledgeable. It gave them control to search for apt solutions, get better deals owing to the vastly competitive e-commerce ecosystem, and access solutions anytime from the comfort of their homes. From the business perspective, IT has helped bring in new players in the financial sphere looking to displace the traditional banking sector at least to some extent and hold an important role in the lives of people. Technology has helped deconstruct the entire banking system into small activities that are reasonably profitable, and new players are entering this market providing lucrative solutions in these factions. Technology-based service providers are customer centric and allow comparisons of products and services for ease of choice, allocate fund managers and advisors, and provide customized solutions. Social media platforms have been effectively used for crowdfunding and P2P lending. The advent of social insurance and virtual currencies is an innovative impact of technology-based finance. Digital wallets, banks, and insurance are some of the conveniences that the new-generation banking customer experiences (Indra, 2014).

Technology has fueled a new segment in the financial markets — fintech, an innovative combination of automation, highly specialized human resources, and large amounts of information in the field of financial services.

1.1.3. *Digital disruption*

Heather Cox, Chief Client Experience, Digital & Marketing Officer, Citi, said, "People need banking, but they do not need banks".

Digital disruption in financial services occurred due to the changes in customer expectations of services and products, and, on the supply end of the spectrum, due to smartphones, blockchain technologies, and the development of application programming interphases and AI. Payment services have become faster as a result of the APIs, which have collated customer data to aid in reducing switching costs, accessing credit scores, showcasing offers from various sources, and bringing out the overall efficiency in the consumers experience. Mobile devices, reach of the internet in remote locations, cloud computing, digital wallets, payment solutions, digital currencies, online shopping, and money transfer are some of the key outcomes of the digital disruption. Additionally, P2P, blockchain decentralized ledger technology, chatbots, cryptocurrencies, and robo-advisors are some of the other outcomes of the digitization process (Dermine, 2017). Bank of America is said to have more than 18 million customers using the mobile platform as the primary means of conducting financial decisions (Alkema & Jen Chen, 2020). The global market is witness to innovative payment systems like PayPal, Venmo, and M-Pesa. Western Union today faces high levels of threat from digital companies like TransferWise and WorldRemit in the transfers and remittances segment. On the credit side, brands like Prosper and SoFi in the US, the British Zopa and Funding Circle, or Alibaba in China are competing with established banks to provide residential loans as well as loans to SMEs.

Fintech is enhancing efficiency by utilizing big data analytics to evaluate customers and granting them quicker access to financial services, diminishing the necessity for collateral. This has resulted in a substantial decrease in the need for human resources and, as a result, a reduction in associated uncertainties (Berg *et al.*, 2018). Price discrimination is easier to perform as analytics can identify price-sensitive and time-sensitive clients and the high versus low risk borrowers. The advent of fintech has allowed the permeation of financial services to those target segments that remained unserved, especially in LDC and underdeveloped countries. Fintech has made the financial operators lean, fast, and flexible with high returns on equity, and it has the potential to attract specialist talent, making the overall concept and its application more robust and constantly evolving (OECD, 2020).

Blockchain technology has been heralded as a path breaker by the IT and financial world. It was first applied to Bitcoin, the popular cryptocurrency. Based on a decentralized and distributed ledger algorithm, it facilitates money transactions between people/entities without the involvement of a bank. Customer data are safe and it is impossible to erase transaction trails. Cloud computing has revolutionized the performance of the financial businesses. Storage, transmission, and aggregation of data happen in specialized places called the "cloud". Speedier and cost-effective solutions using DevOps are the norm, and there are data that indicate that the use of DevOps practices has reduced failure by 60 times, made recovery rates faster by 168 times, with made delivery time of services shorter by 200 times (Alkema & Jen Chen, 2020).

The use of artificial intelligence and robo-advisors is revolutionizing the financial services market. Peer-to-peer lending began as people financing other people. Today, it has developed into marketplace lending with large investors such as hedge funds or pension funds as participants. Looking at the plethora of benefits that technology has brought into the banking and financial services domain, the legacy institutions see the benefit of accepting and accommodating the new innovations with the aim of developing those into capabilities and competencies.

1.1.4. *Open banking*

Closed banking deals with legacy banking institutions, where innovation of financial products was internal and one-sided. Open Banking represents a shift from the traditional closed banking model, where innovation in financial products was limited to internal efforts. It now embraces a more comprehensive approach that includes both internal and external ideas integrated into a technology-based architecture, fostering innovation and digital inclusion in the retail banking sector. New entrants into the financial sector have created business models that offer enhanced personalized services to both individuals and commercial institutions alike. Open banking has been defined as "reliable, personalised financial advice, precisely tailored to your particular circumstances delivered securely and confidentially" (Competition & Markets Authority, 2016). Open banking has been instrumental in providing customers the opportunity to migrate from a single bank to a platform that is replete with competing offers. Open banking has introduced innovative revenue streams and different financial models deployed in the unserved and underserved markets, with a keen focus on enhancing customer experience (Brodsky & Oakes, 2017).

Open banking has come into existence due to the advent of Application Programming Interfaces or APIs as they are commonly known. APIs allow different software systems to exchange data with regard to customers' published open data, for individuals, business, financial institutions like banks, which are reservoirs of a variety of data, and finally technology companies (fintech) that can source and analyze the data and create an ecosystem providing a multitude of offerings to customers.

The open banking platforms have been accepted globally in two formats:

- The use of API to connect customers with financial solution providers like aggregators, banks, and fintech firms.
- The use of a central API connecting all possible players in the finance field as seen in Singapore.

The common aim remains the same — to create and accelerate the development of a digital economy.

The core objective of open banking is the creation of value for different stakeholders — value for the customer by understanding where they are, what do they need, and how to provide the necessary access; value for the business by developing an integrated and interlinked network of suppliers and customers. To do so, one needs to engage in the right human capital and a combination of assets that are capable of innovating new financial products and services using superior technological competence (Al-Debei & Avison, 2010; Kiron *et al.*, 2013).

Open banking comes in different forms depending on the stage of the current banking scenario. If this disruption is new, then the industry experiences the novelty factor with the setup of an entirely new architecture. If some headway has been made, then the changes developed may be modular. However, the process is that of constant evolution and fine-tuning till it arrives at products and services conducive to the needs of the customers (Ramdani *et al.*, 2020).

Digital banks across the globe have been successful in weakening the existing retail banking scenario by building upon the existing activities to deliver a more customer-centric digital option.

Open banking can be competitive only when used in addition to the usual products like accounts, mortgages, etc. Over and above that, they need to offer digital/cryptocurrency trading options, customized financial solutions, expert inputs, and round-the-clock support through an easy-to-use platform.

1.2. Use Cases in Open Banking

The Open Banking system is beneficial in several ways with newer possibilities developing each day.

A major advantage of open banking is the availability of customer data in a secure manner so that all parties that require the said data can access the same without asking the customer to do an independent KYC each time. Open banking will allow the customers to access all their holdings in one place by allowing the API to connect all relevant portfolios. Another benefit that will arise out of this situation is that fintech companies and third-party financial service providers can analyze a customer's portfolio, study the products invested in, investigate their risk potential, ascertain the amount of growth achieved, and suggest alternatives or changes to the current commitments that could help the customer achieve better realization from their investments. Such personalized recommendations will garner loyalty and satisfaction from customers (Mathew & Reppel, 2021).

APIs have helped in making the financial ecosystem secure and robust by constantly monitoring available assets, maintaining their quality, and reducing the risk of fraud.

New revenue streams have gotten developed with the use of open banking. The banks need to understand the potential of open banking and leverage its possibilities to sell their products efficiently and effectively. While a dedicated ecosystem can be developed, banks stand to gain much more by participating in existing ecosystems. Their access to customers will widen and they will be able to achieve higher levels of customer satisfaction than before.

1.3. Retail and Commercial Banking in the Middle East

For decades, Middle Eastern countries have had Islamic banks that followed the Sharia principles and largely focused on providing basic banking services to achieve an economic balance (Ahmad, 1985). According to Scriptures, the Islamic banking institutions date back 1400 years with facilities like deposits and loans available to the community from the start. Besides, on the commercial front, there existed commercial papers, promissory notes, and currencies (Chachi, 2005). These methods continued till the Western influence took over, and foreign banks started to open branches in the Middle East. Gradually, Islamic banks developed themselves and began to gain a stronger foothold in the financial markets. In 1974, the first international was established, the Islamic Development Bank. This institution has been credited as the sole financial institution that led to widespread economic and social development in the Gulf region. In 1977, the International Association of Islamic Banks was formed to further strengthen the cooperation and coordination among the existing Islamic banks. Even today, Islamic banks flourish. They are concentrated in the Gulf Cooperation Council region and account for more than half of all Sharia-compliant assets in the world (Timewell & DiVanna 2008).

1.4. Challenges Faced by Banks in the Middle East

Most banks in the Middle East have been around for years and they have a lot of constraints, owing to the nature of the banking business in the region. The IT platforms on which they operate are functional but incapable of integration with the newer software on which digitization is possible. Another challenge is that there is a paucity of local talent with the expertise to guide the transformation of the legacy banks into modern digital avatars. This has impeded their capabilities of developing a sound digital transformation strategy. Additionally, the Middle East has small and irregular IT service providers. As a result, the rate at which start-ups in the digital domain are emerging is 30 times slower than anywhere else in the world. The new models of banking are swift and innovative with the capability of developing and deploying new and customized solutions in very little time. Competitively, this poses a huge challenge to these legacy institutions.

There is a presence of foreign banks in the Middle East. However, their role is currently limited to serving the import activities rather than participating in the entire range of banking activities otherwise available to them. These banks can be instrumental in changing the financial ecosystem. A partnership with western origin banks that are digitized in their activities will help the traditional banks in the Middle East gain the required transformation (Arezki & Senbet, 2020).

1.5. Opportunities & Key Insights of Digital Banking in the Middle East

The region has immense potential for transformation, both in terms of its economic outputs and operational outputs. While a transformation to cleaner energy sources for self-use and as a supplier to the world is being worked upon, simultaneously digitization and conversion into a digital financial economy need to be prioritized with investment to compete with the changes in other parts of the world (Arezki, 2019). A report published by McKinsey indicates the opening up of the economy toward digitization, although the rate is uneven across the different countries in the Middle East.

McKinsey's survey on urban customers in the United Arab Emirates and in the Kingdom of Saudi Arabia indicates the change in the mindset of the customer with affiliation toward using e-commerce platforms and shopping for wearables, tablets, and above all smartphones. There is a great deal of interest in experiencing the fully immersive mobile banking options currently available. Internet penetration in the UAE is 92% and in the KSA is 65%, out of which 80% of consumers are keen to experience digital technology-driven banking services. E-commerce has had a distinct penetration in the Gulf market. Out of the population that has internet access, at least 80% have been engaged in some form of e-commerce exposure. Owing to the convenience, ease, and transparency with which digital financial institutions have positioned themselves, around 80% of the respondents were willing to store some of their funds in digital options. However, the draw toward a physical entity like a branch or an ATM is extremely strong, which would not see a decline or replacement by the digital options (Shirish *et al.*, 2016). However, on the business front, the inclusion of digital technologies is low. Around 18% of SMEs in the UAE, 15% in the KSA, and 7% in Egypt are presently online (Elmasry *et al.*, 2016).

The COVID-19 pandemic contributed significantly to spearheading digital banking in Middle Eastern countries. Customer behavior has been evolving since the past decade and the pandemic has provided the impetus for escalated provision of solutions. While the non-banking players are not as established in the Middle Eastern market if compared to the US, Europe, or other developed nations, the banks in the GCC have understood the consumer requirements and are working toward enabling themselves to serve digitally enhanced customers. The regional governments and regulatory authorities are also extremely supportive toward the digital initiatives of the banks and the establishment of fintech solutions in the Middle East via sandboxes and innovation labs (Joshi, 2022). Digital banking in the Middle East has increased by 17% annually from 2016 until 2020 as indicated by data presented by IBS Intelligence SalesVision.

The adoption rate of online banking and mobile banking in the Middle East compares to that in Asia. While these adoptions are fueling the e-commerce penetration, buying financial products online has not reached anything close to its potential. The adoption rate of digital banking solutions is closely tied to customers' expectations of user-friendliness, akin to the ease experienced on social networking sites that millennials and Gen Z are well-acquainted with. Further, customers want financial products to be available in a manner that they can browse and purchase without the involvement of a support team. Moreover, they are now looking at customized solutions and not the usual mass-deployed ones.

The GCC landscape is becoming a hotbed for fintech innovations. It is estimated that by the end of 2022, a market capture of over $2 billion is expected in the fintech arena. The UAE-based Mashrek bank has launched its digital-only arm. Similarly, the Commercial Bank of Dubai has partnered with NOW Money to transform itself into providing digital banking solutions. Other noteworthy achievements include the use of RFID-enabled cashless prepaid fueling at gas stations in Dubai and the use of Novot — a humanoid robot at bank Audi in Lebanon which welcomes guests and appraises them of various products and services offered by the bank. From the customer perspective, this is a big success as it has increased overall satisfaction levels. Souq.com is another example of the success of digitization in the Middle East. It was the first unicorn that has, since its launch, become the fastest-growing e-commerce venture with more than 75,000 vendors online.

The regulatory bodies in the Middle East have opened up and are offering licenses to fintech establishments to commence operations. The Saudi Central Bank is known to have issued 16 licenses to fintech institutions to initiate services in the areas of microfinance, insurance, and payments (Joshi, 2022).

Multichannel mode is observed as a preferred method of digital product adoption. Consumers are keen and trust the content available online, and thus conduct their research of products available, choose the right product, and finally procure the same through a bank branch. For complex products like loans and credit cards, banks are preferred. For any product that requires advice/consultation, banks are a favored channel. Also, many banks in the Middle East are not yet developed enough in terms of digitization, compelling customers to visit the branches to close deals.

Certain regulatory requirements mandate that the client visit the branch for the closure of certain deals. For example, banks in the Middle East are very stringent about KYC done in person to prevent any form of fraud.

The main reason that has prevented the otherwise digitally open-minded customers from becoming more digital for their banking needs is their security concerns with online offers.

However, the number of people buying banking products digitally after conducting online research is increasing (between 25% and 30% of the people who conduct research procure financial products like savings, term, and insurance digitally). The McKinsey report indicates that consumers in the Middle East are willing to migrate to digital-only solutions for products like credit cards and personal loans, and about 50% of the respondents were willing to migrate their savings or term deposits. The survey identified three key expectations that customers have in the Middle East with regard to digital banking solutions — (1) simplicity in financial products that reduces the need for a person to explain all features, (2) security, and (3) knowledge concerning digital banking solutions.

Country-wise trends in the adoption of digital services and establishment of fintech include the following (Joshi, 2022):

- *Kingdom of Saudi Arabia*: The adoption of Blockchain technology seems to be swiftly gaining a foothold in the KSA. They have introduced open banking, contact-free payment options, and chatbots to emerge as a digital economy by 2030.

- *Qatar*: The focus is similar in Qatar, with mobile banking, development of a fintech hub, and the legacy institutions using machine learning and AI to enhance customer satisfaction and build greater business advantage.
- *Kuwait*: Kuwait has provided a sandbox environment to facilitate the fintech establishments to research and gauge the market to finalize apt solutions conducive to the needs of their population. They are also working toward establishing a payment and settlement system infrastructure.
- *United Arab Emirates*: Digitization in the UAE has already taken major steps. Abu Dhabi's Islamic banks conduct over 90% of their transactions through online platforms. The government has provided innovation hubs for the development of fintech solutions.

1.6. Open Banking Adoption in the Middle East

Throughout the world, open banking has established its importance for customers, government agencies, and banks. It has grown multidimensionally in first-world countries in the West largely due to regulatory interventions and actions.

In the Middle East, open banking is at its nascent stage. Most banks believe that open banking options are best suited for fintech companies and digital banks. The flip side to that is that if these banks do not wake up to the changing financial ecosystem, they stand to lose a lot of market shares. Coupled with lowered oil prices and the impact of COVID-19 on other businesses, the overall business environment requires solutions that allow for the optimization of costs. Open banking or digital banking is a solution that is not only functional and integrated but can also be attuned to all needs in the future.

The fintech strategy is one of the pillars of the Financial Sector Development Program (FSDP) under the government plan to reduce dependence on oil and diversify the economy — Saudi Vision 2030 — and aims to transform the Kingdom into a global fintech hub to improve the financial services offered to its population. As everywhere else in the world, open banking in the Middle East is expected to witness overwhelming participation from government bodies, regulatory authorities, banks, third-party aggregators, and consumers, both individuals and organizational.

The COVID-19 pandemic provided a big thrust toward the need for rampant digitization of financial services in the Middle East. Moreover, a major advantage is the fact that the population is extremely open toward digitization and the infrastructure of internet penetration and mobile usage is very high. A World Bank report puts mobile phone usage in Bahrain at 200% and internet penetration at 99%. The numbers for Saudi Arabia are not far behind, with 96% internet penetration and 120% mobile usage (World Bank, 2022).

From the perspective of the Middle East, open banking would mean 4 lines of development:

- Develop the possibility for corporates to initiate and undertake payments any time of the day or night, especially aimed at SMEs which form a large segment of the business ecosystem.
- Banks could provide e-commerce acceptance to their account holders and acquire merchants that support the same and accept payments through account-to-account transfers.
- Partner with technology providers to run the payment services — possibly white labeled.
- Deploy an instant payment service allowing a beneficiary to request payment from a payer.

Some amount of digitization has happened. In March 2021, YAP, a Dubai-based bank initiated in partnership with RAK Bank, was launched that offers digital financial services like remittances and portfolio analytics to communicate customized investment solutions. Likewise, "Zand" is a completely digital bank launched in the UAE (Mathew & Reppel, 2021).

1.7. Key Insights

Digitization in the Middle East is growing at the behest of consumers. Countries like Qatar and Bahrain have 100% smartphone penetration and 70% social media presence. However, this number evens out to less than the global average as many regions in the Middle East have poor infrastructure and lowered adoption rates.

Business digitization is also very varied. GCC is far ahead in this segment than countries like Lebanon or Egypt. The firms have a low adoption rate for technology and technology-based products as well as their online presence, which is very low.

Some governments like the UAE and Bahrain have been seen as forerunners in digitization. Other countries like Oman and the KSA are very keen to digitize their offerings but are facing challenges due to the absence of structured governance.

In terms of ICT innovation, the Middle East is lagging. Qatar and Bahrain lead in this segment, owing to the compact geographical size of the nations.

There is a substantial gap between the digitization efforts undertaken by companies, governments, and regulatory bodies and the adoption of the available solutions by the end users. This indicates that the region with its young population has a huge potential in terms of digitization of financial solutions (Elmasry *et al.*, 2016).

1.8. Digitization Strategies Currently Underway

In several countries around the globe, it has been witnessed that digital inclusion has had a multitude of societal benefits. Some of the direct impacts include improved operational efficiencies in the governmental and private organizations, increased knowledge and awareness among the population, thrust toward education, social inclusion of the segments that were previously unserved, development of entrepreneurship, and rise of the SMEs leading to enhanced job creation and strengthening of the microeconomy of the region. The countries in the Middle East have a similar vision for themselves, and, although uneven, most countries in the region have embarked on the journey toward a digitized economy.

The KSA has formulated Vision 2030 in which digitization of services is the prime focus. Its National Transformation Program enlists digital transformation as one of its top four priorities.

The UAE has formulated the UAE Vision 2021, which primarily focuses on ICT development through the creation of tech labs with the aim of developing smart cities enabled by machine learning and artificial intelligence. This visionary document also showcases the country's interest in developing industries based on nanotechnology, assisted printing, and semiconductor technology.

Qatar and Egypt have vision documents that showcase their clear understanding of digitization as the backbone of developing competitive values and for any future development that the countries envisage for themselves. The development of transparent governance, better education facilities that include digital knowledge, a focus on entrepreneurship, and a strong digital economy is what the documents propose for these countries.

In the present scenario, only 1% of the ICT companies are based out of the Middle East among the top 1000 globally known companies. Also, among the digital unicorns, which have registered a digital capitalization of more than $1 billion, there is only one company from the MENA region — souq.com, an e-commerce enterprise. Moreover, in the Middle East, only 1.7% of the workforce is employed in digital jobs (Elmasry *et al.*, 2016).

1.9. Conclusion

Digitization in all spheres has the potential to bring huge benefits both for society and the economy of a region (Scafarto *et al.*, 2023). The processes become streamlined and efficient, unbiased and timely, and error-free and productive. Digitization has positive social impacts through increased employment potential and direct and indirect job creation, sound healthcare even in the remotest location through telemedicine options, improved educational outputs and student retention, and reduced business travel due to online meeting options, further leading to reductions on global emissions (Arezki & Senbet, 2020).

The countries in the Middle East have set up digital goals to be achieved in the following seven to 8 years. At the moment, this region is a consumer of digitization, but to savor the real benefits of a digitized economy, it must transform itself into a technology-based economy and a digital creator by developing human capital and related technologies. For digitization to take place, there must be equal participation and enthusiasm from the consumers, government, regulatory authorities, technology creators and distributors, and businesses, both public and private.

Consumer or retail banking has witnessed a major shift from reliance on traditional banking to a modern digitized format bringing financial products to the mobile phones, tablets, and laptops of consumers, complete with alternatives, comparisons, investment options, and advice, available 24 × 7 at the consumer's convenience. The COVID-19 pandemic arrested people's mobility and further accelerated the need for such transformation. Banks around the world have had to innovate as they began facing unusual competition in the form of fintech companies.

The banking sector in the Middle East is currently in a variety of stages depending on the governments' intentions, regulatory impositions, or resources available. However, in the countries where digital transformation has been factored in, adoption rates are high with an increase by 15% in average spends. In countries like the UAE, Bahrain, and Qatar, there is strong governmental support, and banks are responding to the same by innovating in their product designs and making themselves competitive through the deployment of financial products and services that are at par with those being offered by the new-age digital enterprises. They have streamlined their processes for higher customer satisfaction, and it is advisable that they align themselves to the needs of their huge customer base so that they do not lose market share.

Digitization of banking and financial services would be incompetent if some aspects were included, and some left out. The process implementation must be cross border and every element and aspect must come within the ambit of digitization. The top management and the senior government officials must be completely immersed in this process of transformation.

Digitization is dependent on human talent and the Middle East currently has a very weak base of the same. Encouraging the youth to get into digital education to develop and nurture in-house talent and build a corpus of human capital is a strategic move that must be made.

Banks have always been treated as an essential service that consumers require for the safety and security of their finances. However, the banking needs of the consumers go way beyond that. Their needs are no longer restricted to saving money; instead, they are looking for avenues that help them invest the saved money so that it can further grow. Once the digital capabilities are built, it becomes essential for banks to market themselves, their products, and adopt a persona that is more like an e-commerce site than a bank.

An extensive literature review has brought forth the various perspectives presented in this research. However, the authors feel that this research is limited by the fact that it has been conducted on the banking sector in general. A comparative study between the initiatives taken by the governments and large banking institutions in the different countries in the Middle East and the derived impact could be a very interesting area of study, substantiating the findings of the current one.

The way forward for traditional banks in the Middle East is to partner or collaborate with the new entrants like fintech companies that bring with them swift and efficient banking models that reduce operating costs, enhance consumer satisfaction, and drive in revenues. Using an omni-channel strategy would attract new customers and gain the loyalty of the retail customers.

Digitization in the Middle East is in its infancy and faces strong threats from agile fintech solutions that are extremely attractive to the digitally enhanced customers. In order to survive this wave, transforming to make themselves attractive is the need of the hour. Technical competence, capable human capital, and the right environment for the development of a digitally competent banking system will give the region a huge socio-economic boost and bring it up prominently on the global map of ICT activities.

References

Ahmad, A. (1985). Banking Structure and Sources of Finance in the Middle East and Arab and Islamic Banks: New Business Partners for Developing Countries. https://papers.ssrn.com/sol3/papers.cfm?abstract_=3115946 (Accessed 8 October 2022).

Al-Debei, M. M. & Avison, D. (2010). Developing a unified framework of the business model concept. *European Journal of Information Systems, 19*(3), 359–376.

Alkema, P. & Jen Chen, J. Y. (2020). Digital Disruption Perspectives from the Banking Industry New Imperatives for Leadership and Innovation. https://www.academia.edu/31366324/Digital_Disruption_Perspectives_from_the_banking_industry_New_imperatives_for_leadership_and_innovation (Accessed 17 October 2022).

Arezki, R. (2019). A Shifting Development Paradigm for the Middle East and North Africa. Middle East Institute. https://www.mei.edu/

publications/shifting-development-paradigm-middle-east-and-north-africa (Accessed 16 October 2022).

Arezki, R. & Senbet, L. (2020). Transforming Finance in the Middle East and North Africa. https://documents1.worldbank.org/curated/en/935611593023039875/pdf/Transforming-Finance-in-the-Middle-East-and-North-Africa.pdf (Accessed 24 October 2022).

Berg, T., Burg, V., Gombović, A., & Puri, M. (2018). On the Rise of the FinTechs — Credit Scoring using Digital Footprints. Federal Deposit Insurance Corporation, Humboldt University Berlin, Duke University, Center for Financial Research WP 2018-04.

Brodsky, L. & Oakes, L. (2017). Data Sharing and Open Banking. McKinsey & Company. https://www.mckinsey.com/industries/financial-services/our-insights/data-sharing-and-open-banking (Accessed 11 October 2022).

Chachi, A. (2005). Origin and development of commercial and Islamic banking operations. *Islamic Economics, 18*, 3–25.

Chiorazzo, V., D'Apice, V., DeYoung, R., & Morelli, P. (2018). Is the traditional banking model a survivor? *Journal of Banking & Finance, 97*, 238–256. DOI: 10.1016/j.jbankfin.2018.10.008.

Christensen, C., Raynor, M. E., & McDonald, R. (2015). *What is Disruptive Innovation?* Boston: Harvard Business Review. https://hbr.org/2015/12/what-is-disruptiveinnovation (pristup 6.1.2016).

Competition & Markets Authority (2016). Making Banks Work Harder for You. https://www.agefi.fr/sites/agefi.fr/files/fichiers/2016/08/cma_overview-of-the-banking-retail-market_9_aout.pdf (Accessed 8 October 2022).

Cusolito, A. P., Gévaudan, C., Lederman, D., & Wood, C. A. (2021). *The Upside of Digital for the Middle East and North Africa: How Digital Technology Adoption Can Accelerate Growth and Create Jobs.* Washington, DC: World Bank. DOI: 10.1596/978-1-4648-1663-5. License: Creative Commons Attribution CC BY 3.0 IGO.

Dermine, J. (2017). Digital Disruption and Bank Lending. https://european-economy.eu/wp-content/uploads/2018/01/EE_2.2017-2.pdf (Accessed 9 October 2022).

Elmasry, T., Benni, E., Patel, J., & Moore, Peter aus dem Moore, J. (2016). Digital Middle East: Transforming the Region into a Leading Digital Economy. https://www.mckinsey.com/~/media/mckinsey/featured%20insights/middle%20east%20and%20africa/digital%20middle%20east%20transforming%20the%20region%20into%20a%20leading%20digital%20economy/digital-middle-east-final-updated.ashx (Accessed 5 July 2022).

Golden, S. A. (2016). Users preference towards traditional banking versus e-banking — An analysis. *International Journal of Computational Research and Development*, *1*(1), 177–182.

Indra (2014). From the Traditional Banking System to Customer Centric Financial Ecosystem, pp. 1–27. https://www.indracompany.com/sites/default/files/banking_trends_october_2014_v._pc.pdf (Accessed 9 October 2022).

Joshi, M. (2022). Digital Banking Adoption in the Middle East — Present State and the Road Ahead. Tagit. https://www.tagitmobile.com/digital-banking-adoption-in-the-middle-east-present-state-and-the-road-ahead/ (Accessed 20 October 2022).

Kiron, D., Kruschwitz, N., Reeves, M., & Goh, E. (2013). The benefits of sustainability-driven innovation. *MIT Sloan Management Review*, *54*(2), 69.

Krstić, N. & Banka Ad Beograd, P. (2016). Digital disruption of the banking industry — Threat or opportunity. *Bankarstvo*, *45*(2), 13–31. DOI: 10.5937/bankarstvo1602012K.

Mathew, R. & Reppel, O. (2021). Time is of essence (Part 1 of 3). https://bankingblog.accenture.com/wp-content/uploads/2021/04/Accenture-Open-Banking-In-The-Middle-East-Part-1.pdf (Accessed 10 October 2022).

OECD (2020). Digital Disruption in Banking and its Impact on Competition. http://www.oecd.org/daf/competition/digital-disruption-in-financial-markets.htm.

Ramdani, B., Rothwell, B., & Boukrami, E. (2020). Open Banking: The emergence of new digital business models. *International Journal of Innovation and Technology Management*, 1–13. DOI: 10.1142/s0219877020500339.

Sardana, V. & Singhania, S. (2018). Digital technology in the realm of banking: A review of literature. *International Journal of Research in Finance and Management*, *1*(2), 28–32.

Scafarto, V., Dalwai, T., Ricci, F., della Corte, G. (2023). Digitalization and firm financial performance in healthcare: The mediating role of intellectual capital efficiency. *Sustainability*, *15*(5), 4031. https://doi.org/10.3390/su15054031.

Sharma, A. (2022). Majority of Middle East Customers Prefer Digital Banking, Survey Finds. *The National*. https://www.thenationalnews.com/business/technology/2022/03/10/majority-of-middle-east-customers-prefer-digital-banking-survey-finds/ (Accessed 12 July 2022).

Shirish, K., Jayantilal, S., & Haimari, G. (2016). Digital Banking in the Gulf Keeping Pace with Consumers in a Fast-moving Marketplace. *mckinsey.com*. McKinsey & Co. https://www.mckinsey.com/~/media/McKinsey/Locations/Europe%20and%20Middle%20East/Middle%20East/Overview/Insights/Digital%20banking%20in%20the%20Gulf/Digital%20Banking%20in%20the%20gulf%20161116%20DIGITAL.ashx (Accessed 10 July 2022).

Sujee, S., Solanki, R., & Dalwai, T. (2022). Technology innovations for business growth–impact of AI and blockchain on financial services. In *Explore Business, Technology Opportunities and Challenges After the Covid-19 Pandemic* (pp. 1283–1292). Cham: Springer International Publishing.

Timewell, S. & DiVann, J. (2008). Top 500 Islamic financial institutions. *The Banker*. https://www.thebanker.com/Top-500-Islamic-Financial-Institutions-1225670400.

Vives, X. (2019). Digital disruption in banking. *Annual Review of Financial Economics*, *11*(1), 243–272. DOI: 10.1146/annurev-financial-100719-120854.

Wilson, R. (1983). *Banking and Finance in the Arab Middle East*. London: Macmillan.

World Bank (2022). Mobile cellular subscriptions (per 100 people) — United Arab Emirates Data. https://data.worldbank.org/indicator/IT.CEL.SETS.P2?locations=AE (Accessed 10 October 2022).

https://doi.org/10.1142/9781800614734_0002

Chapter 2

Green Finance in the MENA Region: A Systematic Literature Review

Krishna Murthy Meesaala, Syeeda Shafiya Mohammadi, and S. Varalakshmi

Abstract

This chapter aims to enhance knowledge of green finance in the existing literature and to review the sustainable development activities in the Middle East and North African countries. The study has also identified the challenges of providing green finance activities around the MENA region and offers suggestions to overcome the hindrances with the help of literary evidence. Research studies revealed that green finance and its related elements are at the forefront of discussion around the world. The reason behind these extreme changes in green nature is due to political, economic, social, and environmental fluctuations, which are affected by a fiscal crisis. Researchers have used the latest methodology of PRISM 2020, which is an advanced version of PRISMA 2009, for conducting a systematic literature review by considering 10 years of literature studies between 2013 and 2022 from the Scopus Search Engine to meet the research objectives of the study. This study would help future research activities on green finance to learn from the initiatives of MENA nations to understand the practical difficulties and opportunities available in society. It has remarkable implications for academic researchers, officials making policies, and entities providing various services to practitioners in the field of green nature as it is unique in understanding the growth and development of green finance activities and its sustainable development around the MENA region. The study concluded that green finance initiatives are possible by focusing on implementing various carbon emission proposals as part of sustainable programs. Government and financial institutions must consider that green finance activities enhance sustainable financing.

Keywords: MENA region, green finance, sustainable development, ecofriendly and carbon emission

2.1. Introduction

Green finance is an essential part of the ethical financing system. When financial institutions aim to reduce the risks related to the environment, the concept of green finance comes into being. Green finance includes a significant part of the eco-friendly elements of various financial services, such as providing loans and establishing investments of various financial institutions. It is essential to focus on green environment business activities of financial institutions in the society as part of green economy creativities (Sahoo & Nayak, 2007; Shaumya & Arulrajah, 2017; Shakil, 2014). Environmentally driven approaches are possible through the global banking industry by adopting green banking (Ahuja, 2015). Financial facilities, environmental strategies, and socio-economic progress entail a major concept, namely, green banking. Banks are naturally approachable and have insulation for the future. Every financial institution has social responsibility to make sure the financing project complies with environment policies and is cognizant of the consequences for the prospective future (Ahmad *et al.*, 2013).

The MENA region has issued around twelve debt bonds relating to green nature and sustainability, with Saudi Arabia accounting for 63% and the United Arab Emirates accounting for 33%. The concept of green finance has different meaning in the MENA region, as the old green projects carried out based on hydrocarbon are preferred less when compared to green finance projects around the world. A very modest set of banking institutions carry on green finance projects in the MENA region, only few groups concentrate heavily on green finance projects but the rest do not emphasis on the participation of green environment. The Saudi National Banking Company, namely, Al-Rajhi Banking & Investment Corporation, and NBD PJSC Emirates Banking Company contributed around five hundred and eighty-three million US dollars toward green finance projects in the MENA region, compared to USD 300 million contributed by the rest of the globe. Islamic Banking institutions have contributed around USD 2.5 billion toward sustainable green finance projects in March 2021. Saudi Vision 2030 and Abu Dhabi Vision 2030 foster economic growth and sustainability in the MENA region. By the year 2050, the UAE plans to reduce the emission of carbon dioxide by 70% by replacing clean energy techniques by 25% to 50%, and aims to provide natural energy for household and company consumption amounting to 40%. The aim of this specific study is to realize the concept of green finance, describe the existing development in green finance in the MENA (Middle East and North African) region, and its challenges in the implementation of associated pursuits.

2.2. Background of the Study

Green finance consists of three important segments, namely, green finance related to a supportive system, green finance related to a preventive system, and green finance related to an integrated hybrid system. Green Finance related to a supportive system refers to financial aid offered for lower carbon emission industries and those dealing with goods and services which enhance energy factors by developing a safe environment for industries and people. A green finance preventative system refers to preventing those services which are polluting the environment that harm industries and humankind. Green finance related to a hybrid system refers to the services offered in support of green industries as well as preventive services (Choi, 2011).

Preserving the environment is one of the significant agendas of most of the nations around the world as part of sustainable growth and development to comply with the requirement of safe living for humankind. Green building activities are conducted with the intention of advocating and persuading people to embrace a green building approach. A majority of the Gulf Cooperation Council nations have focused very little on issues relating to environmental activities, such as emissions (Powmya & Abidin, 2014).

The term green finance occupies center state in financial markets. It is hard to understand and identify green finance activities in particular, but can be named any sort of monetary support that shifts into green and changing the society in a state of ensuring sustainability. Green finance is known through various tasks carried out by the entities but cannot be identified just by the nature of the investments and technology used. The challenge of green finance activities is to provide financial assistance to small and medium enterprises, and various plans and projects of infrastructure that create social benefit with very less profit for the investors. It is challenging to attract investment related to the public works that include various opportunities with a competitive nature. It is also difficult to identify various conflicts and inadequacies of green finance projects. It is challenging to have a sustainable economic environment that requires trillions of dollars to bring new infrastructure in the future. Financial institutions form the basis of change in the monetary system and in the economy that affects both savers and investors, which may result in loss and threat to earnings. It is also evident the maximum earnings are realized through the riskiest projects that include innovative ideas and potential technological investments with a high scope of growth in the economy. It is challenging to have a sustainable economic environment that requires trillions of dollars to bring new infrastructure in the future. It is also not easy to focus on the implementation of green finance projects that requires integrity and reliability. It is more important to produce potential policies and regulations and invest in various projects related to green finance, namely, equity or debt, which may be huge or small projects relating to private or public entities. It is also challenging from the viewpoint of the government to intervene by motivating green investments as it requires subsidies and various guarantees and tax concessions. It is more challenging to attract private entities to invest in projects relating to high carbon emissions, namely, infrastructure relating to energy or roads.

Sustainability and green nature were not discussed before the past two decades as part of any financial project (Cooper, 2019). Community groups and various philanthropic societies that have concentrated on green growth and social economic activities have existed, but they were few and far between. They motivated many social groups and eco-friendly communities to focus on capital markets and their governance; at the same time, social issues and environmentally sustainable activities were not given priority (Aller *et al.*, 2018). Unexpectedly, in the recent past, green nature and green inclusive activities have come to the forefront of the discussion around the world. The reason behind these extreme changes is due to political, economic, social, and environmental fluctuations, caused by fiscal crisis. The most crucial change took place in public behavior and opinions on economic, social, and environmental issues (Netopia, 2021). Undoubtedly, the debate on green finance is familiar to people, especially those who invest in various projects, borrow financial commitments, banking and financial institutions, corporate entities, and different ministries across the world (Zhang, 2019). Remarkable conversations on green finance studies and its implications are brought out to safeguard the ecosystem. The study emphasized the challenges faced by various users of green finance. Moreover, future studies on the same topic would help communities participating in green finance and other institutions to focus more on the topic of green finance and its activities in the budding stage. Different types of investors or borrowers are not familiar with various schemes of green finance, and it is believed that the participation in green finance will increase in the future. Various financial institutions offer marketing and promotional practices to bring awareness among corporates and reduce the barriers to green fiancé activities in the future. Climate change is one of the key factors urging investors to focus on the various green bond investment opportunities to foster awareness and to provide financial assistance for low-emission fiscal systems (World Bank, 2019). Green bonds would ensure awareness among public and private financial institutions regarding green finance activities and climate change. There was much growth in the recent past in green finance activities. A greater number of research activities have been carried out on green finance and green bonds. Research scholars were able to differentiate and analyze the term green finance and its related activities. Numerous studies have been conducted on green finance and its activities to determine and support the latest trends and research gaps. This study conducts a comprehensive analysis on green finance literature to collate results and compare the existing studies (Pham & Huynh, 2020; Pham, 2016).

Gulf countries must concentrate on different rules and approaches to retrieve financial assistance, as the regulation among neighboring nations are dissimilar. International institutions offer significant ideas and options to explore green finance resources in Arab regimes, but it requires serious capabilities to prepare proposals, justify the reasons for selection of projects, and offer guarantees for the proposed projects. The green finance elements are available in vast numbers toward green investments in terms of collaborations of various financial bodies offering possibilities on different projects related to green finance (Bentouati, 2019; Rahman *et al.*, 2022).

NAFASA International offers various suggestions to protect the environment in the Arab region by inviting foreign collaborations for green finance instruments. Private institutions should be guided, activated, motivated, and encouraged by facilitating administrative activities, providing tax subsidies as part of encouragement, and offering guarantees on borrowed funds. There should be proper coordination between the ministries related to finance and environment to grow green finance projects. Native green finance activities should be motivated and implemented to raise strong awareness for green finance projects. Such projects need coordination for various financial institutions among intraregional societies on the basis of cost benefit investment opportunities (Fisher, 2019).

2.3. Literature Review

2.3.1. *Development of green finance*

The financial industry plays a significant role in assisting companies secure the necessary financial resources, which is a critical factor in the success of any firm (Ji *et al.*, 2021). In addition to this, the financial industry offers potential profit-making chances to investors. There is a necessity to develop and increase green financing in this industry as standard or traditional financing choices are likely to have a negative impact on the environment (Kim *et al.*, 2020). Green financing is on a massive increase as investors are becoming more conscious and recognize the importance of green energy to environmental health and sustainability (Gagnon *et al.*, 2020; Miralles-Quirós & Miralles-Quirós, 2019). Green financing carries a reduced financial load than traditional financing since businesses that are more sustainable have less earning volatility (Umar *et al.*, 2021). Loan loss provisions and capital requirements for lenders can be reduced when borrowers possess less of a risk financially. This contributes to the accomplishment of environmental goals. The performance of green financial assets is higher than that of non-green ones according to studies (Ji *et al.*, 2021). However, extreme caution is advised as studies have also indicated that there are disincentives for investors who would wish to make use of environmentally green options (Naqvi *et al.*, 2021).

There have been three pathways identified by relevant research connecting economic growth with ecological decline. First, economic expansion can influence environmental degradation, which can be a result of financial development. The development of the financial sector draws in foreign direct investment (FDI), which in turn stimulates economic expansion. The consumption of more and higher energy caused by increased economic expansion will lead to the deterioration of the natural environment (Shahbaz *et al.*, 2018). Second, when the economy and the stock market are doing well, customers have access to more credit. As a result, there will be more disposable income and demand for energy-intensive goods. Increased purchases and usage of these products leads to more environmental damage (Agbloyor *et al.*, 2016). Third, the expansion of the financial sector drives up investment, which in turn results in a rise in power consumption. The production of electricity is the primary factor in the deterioration of the environment (Marrasso *et al.*, 2019). When the economy expands, energy consumption and demand both rise (Taghizadeh-Hesary *et al.*, 2020). Evidence suggests that economies with a high dependence on non-renewable resources tend to develop slowly (Umar *et al.*, 2021).

More specifically, strong institutions are more likely to advance societal goals through pushing for environmentally friendly legislation and regulation. Accordingly, Azhgaliyeva & Liddle (2020) recommended budgetary measures that would incentivize green projects for positive impact on the environment. Chen & Feng's (2019) research stated that authorities have a significant impact on the policies governing green investing. A study by Ntow-Gyamfi *et al.* (2020) stressed the importance of high-quality institutions in restricting environmental degradation over time.

2.3.2. *Green finance and sustainable development*

Green finance, as its name implies, is used for fund initiatives that are mindful of the environment. Even though there is no generally accepted definition of "green" projects, many different types of initiatives related to clean energy, energy conservation, and carbon emissions avoidance fall under this category. Green bonds are increasingly used for financing energy efficiency initiatives (Azhgaliyeva & Liddle, 2020). According to Raberto *et al.* (2019), transitioning to more energy-efficient production can be encouraged through green investment opportunities. The development of green economies is aided by green finance that encourages investment in renewable energy projects and contributes to the expansion of the green economy (Peng & Zheng, 2021).

Green finance, an innovative economic model, emphasizes effective resource allocation and transfer of environmental risk through macroeconomic policies (Liu *et al.*, 2019). These policies include financial investment and financing activities based on respect for sustainable development (Lee *et al.*, 2021). Green finance capital guarantee may further optimize the quality and efficiency of the supply system, reducing carbon emissions and speeding up the transition to a low-carbon circular economy (Lee *et al.*, 2022). To achieve environmental sustainability, the "green concept" can direct the transition to low-carbon industrial structures and the development of green technologies (Abbasi *et al.*, 2021b; Wang *et al.*, 2022).

Using Lee & Lee's (2022) framework for green financial development as a reference, one can see an index system with four tiers (green credit, securities, insurance, and investment) to solidify the partnership between ecology and finance, which is, without a doubt, beneficial to the development of both financial reform and low-carbon economic growth (Lee *et al.*, 2020). The anticipated benefits of sustainable financing to the economy and society are also discussed in the literature. Green finance, according to Lee & Lee (2022), may further enhance steady economic expansion. He *et al.* (2019) and Abbasi *et al.* (2021a) asserted that green finance helped to promote renewable energy technology, which in turn helped to control the output of carbon emissions. Abbasi & Adedoyin (2001) and Ren *et al.* (2022) stated that polluting businesses and environment preferences can be compensated by fostering efforts on green finance initiatives. Wen *et al.* (2021) indicate that green credit regulations effectively solve the challenges that energy-intensive firms have in converting and upgrading their operations when they are constrained by credit. Their findings are based on quasi-natural trials and micro data. The importance of green finance initiatives is accelerating for creating a low carbon economy without disturbing the environment through sustainable production practices.

2.3.3. *Impact of green finance and green technology innovation on low-carbon economy*

In essence, for Arab countries to satisfy their urgent sustainable development needs and tackle rising social demands and climate change issues, they can make use of innovative financing tools to scale up sustainable finance and climate finance. To raise the necessary funds, a variety of different funding techniques have been utilized on a global scale and specifically in the Arab region. These types of investments include blended finance, green bonds, green Islamic bonds known as "green sukuks", debt for climate swaps, and results-based financing (UNEP, 2021). The National Bank of Abu Dhabi of the United Arab Emirates issued the first green corporate bond in the Arab area in 2017 (ESCWA, 2019). The Egyptian Ministry of Finance announced in September 2020 that Egypt would be the first Arab country to issue sovereign green bonds to finance its sustainable development needs, with a focus on environmentally friendly projects like renewable energy and energy efficiency, pollution reduction and control, sustainable water, and waste management (*Arab News*, 2020).

Egypt's Integrated Sustainable Energy Strategy (2035) intends to increase energy efficiency and increase the percentage of renewable energy sources in the overall energy mix to achieve the goal of diversifying the country's energy sources to provide a stable and secure energy supply. It is projected that by the year 2022, renewable energy will supply 20% of the nation's electricity requirements, and that by the year 2035, the proportion of renewables used in power generation would be increased to 42% (International Renewable Energy Agency (IRENA), 2018). The Egyptian Ministry of Finance has issued the first ever sovereign green bonds in the Middle East and North Africa (MENA) region to accelerate the country's transition to a green economy. Egypt can use the bonds as a creative funding tool for its green and environmentally friendly initiatives like clean transportation, renewable energy, energy efficiency, pollution reduction and control, sustainable water and wastewater management, and adaptation to climate change. Initially scheduled for a five-year maturity,

Egypt's first green bond initiative has grown to a value of $750 million (Egypt, 2020). The Ministry has also mentioned that it intends to issue sukuks-Islamic bonds to meet its budgetary requirements (Waheesh, 2020).

Jordan is receiving assistance in expanding its green finance sector from international financing organizations. This assists the federal government to achieve its objectives for sustainable growth, increasing investment in renewable energy, energy efficiency, and other environmental and social projects to foster long-term economic prosperity. For instance, the French development agency AFD has provided a $53 million soft credit line to two Jordanian banks, the Cairo Amman Bank and the Capital Bank of Jordan, so that they might in turn lend to local businesses and consumers. The Sustainable Use of Natural Resources and Energy Finance (SUNREF) program of the AFD has been responsible for this work. The primary goal of this initiative is to increase accessibility to sustainable energy that is also cheap (SUNREF, 2020).

Bahrain endorsed the National Energy Efficiency Action Plan (NEEAP) and the National Renewable Energy Action Plan in 2017, in keeping with its regional and global commitments — the League of Arab States Energy Framework, the UN 2030 Sustainable Development Agenda, and the Paris Agreement (2015) (NREAP). While NREAP seeks to establish a renewable energy mix of solar, wind, and waste-to-energy technologies with goals of 5% by 2025 and 10% by 2035, NEEAP adopts an energy efficiency objective of 6% by 2025 (Bahrain, 2017a, 2017b). In order to promote the banking industry's contribution to sustainable development and economic growth in accordance with the UN 2030 Sustainable Development Agenda, the Bahrain Association of Banks (BAB) created a permanent sustainable development committee in 2018 (BAB, 2018). Sustainable finance is promoted by the committee by boosting funding and investment in areas including education, healthcare, socio-economic development, renewable energy, infrastructure, transportation, and green financing (Bahrain, 2018).

Sustainability and the United Arab Emirates' national policy framework led to the creation of the Green Economy for Sustainable Development Initiative in 2012, and the country's national policy framework for sustainable development was finalized and implemented in 2015. The United Arab Emirates Green Agenda

(2015–2030) is a collaborative effort between federal and local governments that builds on the UAE Vision 2021, which sought to integrate green growth into national strategies, establish the country as a role model for a low-carbon, green economy, and transform it into a global hub for sustainable development. Various facets of the transformation to the green economy are fundamentally based on five broad objectives such as knowledge-based economy that is competitive, renewable energy that helps mitigate climate change, green life and sustainable use of resources, sustainable environment and valued natural resources, and social development and quality of life.

The Green Diversification Program is one of the 12 programs that back the UAE Green Agenda. It has several sub-programs, such as the Green Finance and Investment Support Scheme, which are designed to help businesses and investors make greener financial decisions. The goal of this plan is to encourage more investment in green and renewable energy projects and the development of promising green financing mechanisms by the financial sector. This includes creating domestic green finance models and products such as energy performance contracts and green sukuks. Additionally, the program aims to connect entrepreneurs with funders and promote policy development and capacity development (UAE, 2017). The environmental, social, and governance (ESG) guiding principles established by the UAE are meant to assist national banks in better managing ESG-related risks that have an impact on their credit profiles. Financial institutions in the United Arab Emirates showed a willingness to include ESG factors into their business decision-making processes after being surveyed on green finance practices. The primary reason behind it is that entrepreneurs have the belief that incorporating ESG issues would result in cost reductions and increased efficiency, as well as more revenue, a better reputation in the market, and an improved competitive advantage (UAE, 2016). The Securities and Commodities Authority of the United Arab Emirates (SCA) released its Capital Markets' Sustainability Plan in the first quarter of 2019 (UAE, 2019). To promote green and responsible investment and safeguard the stability and growth of national financial markets, it acts as a comprehensive road map driving SCA's sustainability goal.

Saudi Arabia established a public investment fund to foster the growth of a green economy in line with the country's Vision 2030 goals. In 2016, the KSA government initiated the National Renewable Energy Program. It emphasizes renewable energy as a sector with significant potential to produce job opportunities and to transform the country toward more service- and knowledge-based sectors. This initiative is a key component of the National Transformation Program that is part of Vision 2030. The energy mix strategy for the Kingdom seeks to produce 70% of its power-producing capacity from natural gas by the year 2030, with the remaining 30% originating from renewable sources. To encourage private investment in the renewable energy sector, the government wants to spend \$30–50 billion on the industry by 2023 (International Renewable Energy Agency, 2016). It was announced in 2019 that Saudi Arabia would increase its renewable energy goal from 9.5 GW by 2023 to 58.7 GW by 2030 (Climate Transparency Report, 2019).

2.4. Research Methodology and Discussion

A specific pursuit engine, namely, the Scopus database, has been used by referring related keywords in this study to access the related literature, elaborate the concept of green finance, and identify the challenges in the MENA region. The study has included different phrases which are related to the topic (Lindenberg, 2014). Background of the research on green finance in MENA region has been investigated and analyzed with backup studies. Owing to major similarities in the topic proposed for the study, the keywords "Green Finance in MENA region" OR "Green Loans in MENA region" OR "Green Bonds in MENA region" OR "Green Credit in MENA region" AND "Finance relating to Climate in MENA region" were investigated based on various research articles and their usage. Quest engine applied to plot existing literature studies on green finance in MENA region in the different specialization namely business studies, economics, social sciences, environmental sciences and other multi focused areas (Hafner *et al.*, 2020).

Research authors used a very important technique to extract and prevent the duplication of quality articles without mixing and those articles listed in Microsoft Excel spreadsheet for determining a particular article and exploring similar kind of articles as part of literature review. This practice helped the researchers completely avoid duplication of similar articles from the database and find, handle, and spot the significant and related research studies. In the early stage of the study, the researchers limited the study period of the relevant articles to a period of 10 years between 2013 and 2022, and the rest were removed. Search process has been used on the green finance to understand and conceive the opinion and reviews of various studies around MENA period and all the articles were in English language. PRISMA 2009, which is used by researchers, was unable to help to produce comprehensibility of the published research studies, and was replaced by a newer version, PRISMA 2020 (Page *et al.*, 2016, 2018).

Latest approach of PRISMA 2020 version (Preferred reporting items for systematic review and meta-analysis) which is significant research technique has been used to choose and execute to determine and assess the progress in this study and to invite and attract new research studies from various researchers to support the concept of green finance in MENA region (Iqbal *et al.*, 2021; Panic *et al.*, 2013). PRISMA 2020 enhances reporting clarity. The agenda includes different phases, such as introducing the statements, formulating methods, determining the results, and interpreting discussions on systematic literature review. PRISMA 2020 consists of a flow diagram that portrays the knowledge over numerous stages of organized review. The technique also represents the total number of research studies found in the first stage and the number of studies included and excluded, along with the logic and reason behind the exclusion. The flow diagram helps the researchers draw the diagram automatically by defining the process on the selected topic. PRISMA 2020 also includes different extensions that accelerate the literature review for different elements in the study (Monash University, 2022).

The researchers used the Scopus indexed database with the help of titles to extract the number of articles related to Green Finance in the MENA region, and in total 136 research articles were explored. 34 articles were removed, as they were duplicates, before the second stage of screening. The second step in PRIMSA 2020 was to screen the records with the titles and abstracts explored by the researchers, which involved thoroughly reading the articles extracted through the search engine. A total of 102 articles were screened from the identified articles. Around 31 articles in the study were excluded, as they did not fulfill the criteria of the selected topic for the study. Around 71 articles were screened and sought for retrieval and 4 articles were not retrieved. Around 67 research articles were investigated by the researchers for eligibility (Page *et al.*, 2020). The study finalized 62 articles after following all the steps as prescribed by PRISMA 2020, and excluding 5 articles that were of low quality, poor clarity, and irrelevant (see Figure 2.1).

The study has been conducted by combining various research studies from the Scopus database by following the familiar search technique of PRISMA 2020 used for conducting a systematic literature review. The study emphasizes the growth and development of green finance in the MENA region. The study has also listed the information of author's contribution, country of corresponding author, nature of respective journals used related to green finance in MENA region. This study acts as a procedure for benchmarking the specific articles in green finance in the MENA region. The study also motivates researchers to explore more related topics to fill the research gap in the green finance field. It is the responsibility and accountability of every individual as a stakeholder to understand the need for a financial aid which arises due to irregularities in the monetary elements and policies relating to the atmosphere. It is also crucial to encourage the growth and development of green finance in the MENA region. One requires perfect guidelines and rules on various issues in green finance. It is the responsibility of the government to understand and suggest different policies to safeguard the environment by performing a key role to aid financial institutions and support finance markets to bring about sustainability. The present topic has been used to accelerate and identify the growth and development of green finance in the MENA region between 2013 and 2022. The researchers missed exploring the research contents of other periods. Further studies could be conducted to facilitate knowledge on green finance of different periods in the MENA region from more research database engines. Researchers can access wide range of articles on the green finance in the MENA region to fill the gap and foster light on the green investment which influence the growth on the green environment. The motivation of private investors should be identified and suitable incentives should be offered to welcome supporters of green finance. Future research activities on green finance would reflect the current situation of every nation, which

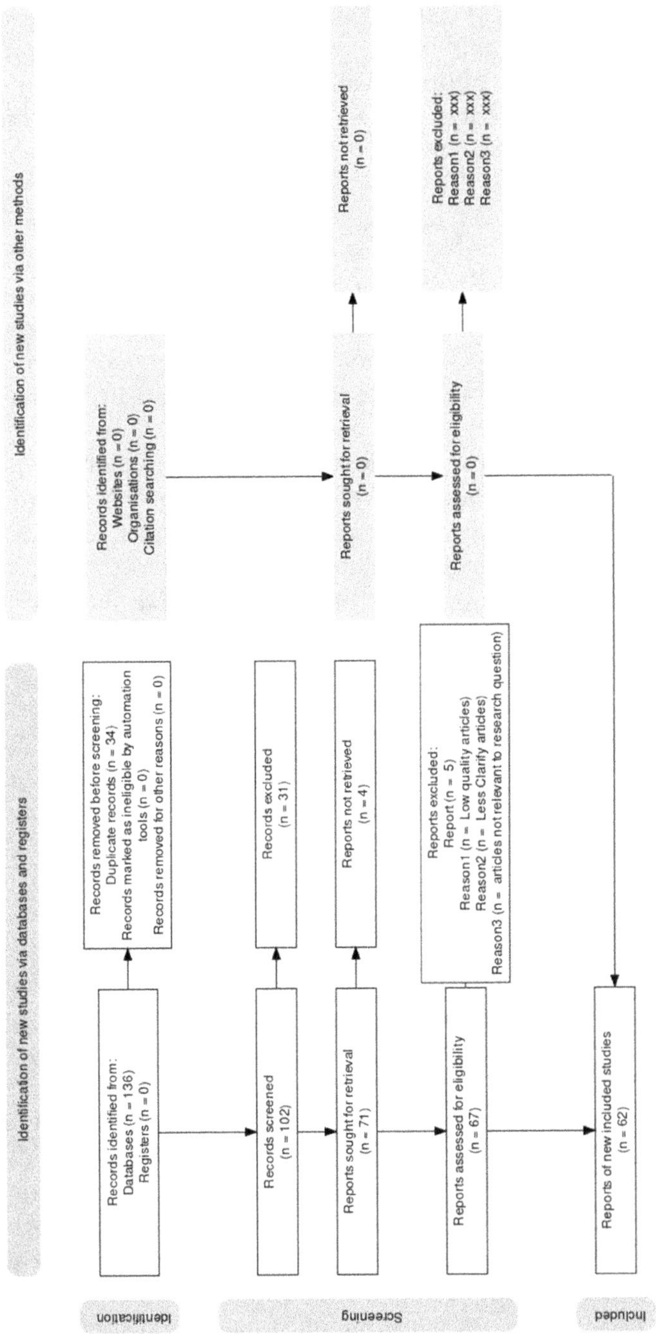

Figure 2.1. Literature review research strategy.
Source: Research methodology process.

mobilizes and invests in green finance activities and helps to learn from the initiatives of neighboring nations to understand the practical difficulties and opportunities available in society. The study also helps us facilitate knowledge of green finance in the MENA region.

2.5. Conclusion

There is renewable power all around the MENA region (Griffiths, 2017). The Gulf Cooperation Council nations are situated exactly under the "global sunbelt" with ample solar energy fit for implementation of solar power (IRENA, 2016). Green finance is an initiative of every country around the world as part of the latest approach toward sustainable development goals and inclusive green growth (Dmuchowski *et al.*, 2021). Socio-fiscal scenarios are the major criterion for the green environment which are useful for different people in the society and different societies to save the nature from vulnerability to ensure social justice, ecosystem, integrity and political multiplicity (Debrah *et al.*, 2021). It is observed from the study that the concept of green finance has acquired much attention around the world in general and the MENA region in particular. Gulf countries and North African countries have made fewer research contributions to green finance. Different approaches for the growth and development on the concept of green finance ultimately guarantee the prospective future in the society. A vast number of MENA nations focus on poverty alleviation and finding a substitute for natural resources to safeguard the environment. MENA nations should reconsider the green finance pledge to balance out fiscal pursuits. Harmonizing systematic barriers in the society on green finance projects is key factor to ensure green environment. The present study has remarkable repercussions for academic researchers, officials making policies, and entities providing various services to practitioners in the field of sustainability. This specific study is unique in understanding the growth and development of green finance activities and its sustainable development around the MENA region. Challenges in green finance in the MENA region were comprehensively studied to identify the remedial measures to enhance the activities and performance. Green finance initiatives are possible by focusing on implementing various carbon emission proposals as part of sustainable programs. Government and financial institutions must consider green finance activities that would enhance sustainable financing.

References

Abbasi, K. R. & Adedoyin, F. F. (2021). Do energy use and economic policy uncertainty affect CO_2 emissions in China? Empirical evidence from the dynamic ARDL simulation approach. *Environmental Science and Pollution Research International, 28*(18), 23323–23335.

Abbasi, K. R., Adedoyin, F. F., Abbas, J., & Hussain, K. (2021a). The impact of energy depletion and renewable energy on CO_2 emissions in Thailand: Fresh evidence from the novel dynamic ARDL simulation. *Renewable Energy, 180*, 1439–1450.

Abbasi, K. R., Adedoyin, F. F., Radulescu, M., Hussain, K., & Salem, S. (2021b). The role of forest and agriculture towards environmental fortification: designing a sustainable policy framework for top forested countries. *Environment, Development and Sustainability, 24*(6), 8639–8666.

Agbloyor, E. K., Gyeke-Dako, A., Kuipo, R., & Abor, J. Y. (2016). Foreign direct investment and economic growth in SSA: The role of institutions. *Thunderbird International Business Review, 58*(5), 479–497.

Ahmad, F., Nurul, M. Z., & Harun, M. (2013). Factors behind the adoption of green banking by Bangladeshi commercial banks. *ASA University Review, 7*, 242–245.

Ahuja, N. (2015). Green banking in India: A review of literature. *International Journal for Research in Management & Pharmacy (IJRMP), 4*, 11–16.

Aller, C., Herrerias, M. J., & Ordonez, J. (2018). The effect of financial development on energy intensity in China. *The Energy Journal, 39*(11), 25–38.

Arab News (2020). Egypt issues first green bonds in MENA. arabnews.com/node/1741946/business-economy.

Azhgaliyeva, D. & Liddle, B. (2020). Introduction to the special issue: Scaling up green finance in Asia. *Journal of Sustainable Finance & Investment, 10*(2), 83–91.

Bahrain (2017a). National renewable energy action plan. sea.gov.bh/nreap/.

Bahrain (2017b). National renewable energy action plan. sea.gov.bh/nreap/.

Bahrain (2018). First voluntary national review on the implementation of the 2030 sustainable development agenda and the sustainable development goals.

Bentouati, S. (2019). *Green Investments in the Arab Region.* NAFASA International LLC, Jordan.

Chen, Y. & Feng, J. (2019). Do corporate green investments improve environmental performance? Evidence from the perspective of efficiency. *China Journal of Accounting Studies*, *7*(1), 62–92.

Choi, S. P. (2011). legal and institutional study on green finance. *KLRI Journal of Law and Legislation*, *1*, 177–185.

Climate Transparency Report (2019). Climate transparency: Brown to green G20 transition towards a net-zero emissions economy: Saudi Arabia-country profile 2019.

Cooper, S. (2019). The evolution of sustainable finance. The Asset Standard Chartered Bank.

Debrah, C., Chan, A. P. C., & Darko, A (2021). Green finance gap in green buildings: A scoping review and future research needs. *Building and Environment*, *207*, 108443.

Dmuchowski, P., Dmuchowski, W., Baczewska-Dąbrowska, A. H., & Gworek, B. (2021). Green economy Growth and maintenance of the conditions of green growth at the level of polish local authorities. *Journal of Cleaner Production*, 301–306.

Egypt (2020). Ministry of finance, MENA's first sovereign green bonds sees strong demand for Egypt. mof.gov.eg/English/Pages/Green-BondDocumentation.aspx.

ESCWA (2019). Climate finance in the Arab region, technical report E/ESCWA/SDPD/2019/TP.10.

Fisher, P. (2019). *What are the Challenges of Green Finance.* The London Institute of Banking and Finance, United Kingdom.

Gagnon, M. H., Manseau, G., & Power, G. J. (2020). They're back! Post-financialization diversification benefits of commodities. *International Review of Financial Analysis*, *71*, 101–515.

Griffiths, S. (2017), A review and assessment of energy policy in the Middle East and North Africa. *Energy Policy*, *102*, 249e269.

He, L., Liu, R., Zhong, Z., Wang, D., & Xia, Y. (2019). Can green financial development promote renewable energy investment efficiency? A consideration of bank credit. *Renewable Energy*, *143*, 974–984.

International Renewable Energy Agency (2016). *Renewable Energy Market Analysis: The GCC Region.* Abu Dhabi: International Renewable Energy Agency.

International Renewable Energy Agency (2018). *Renewable Energy Outlook: Egypt.* Abu Dhabi: International Renewable Energy.

Ji, X., Zhang, Y., Mirza, N., Umar, M., & Rizvi, S. K. A. (2021). The impact of carbon neutrality on the investment performance: Evidence from the equity mutual funds in BRICS. *Journal of Environmental Management*, *297*, 113–228.

Kim, D. H., Wu, Y. C., & Lin, S. C. (2020). Carbon dioxide emissions and the finance curse. *Energy Economics*, *88*, 104–788.

Lee, C. C. & Lee, C. C. (2022). How does green finance affect green total factor productivity? Evidence from China. *Energy Economics*, *107*, 105863.

Lee, C. C., Lee, C. C., & Li, Y. Y. (2021). Oil price shocks, geopolitical risks, and green bond market dynamics. *The North American Journal of Economics and Finance*, *55*, 101309.

Lee, C. C., Wang, C. W., & Ho, S. J. (2020). Financial innovation and bank growth: The role of institutional environments. *The North American Journal of Economics and Finance*, *53*, 101195.

Lee, C. C., Wang, C. W., & Ho, S. J. (2022). Financial aid and financial inclusion: Does risk uncertainty matter? *Pacific-Basin Finance Journal*, *71*, 101700.

Lindenberg, N. (2014). *Definition of Green Finance.* Bonn, Germany: German Development Institute, p. 3.

Liu, R., Wang, D., Zhang, L., & Zhang, L. (2019). Can green financial development promote regional ecological efficiency? A case study of China. *Natural Hazards*, *95*, 1–2.

Marrasso, E., Roselli, C., & Sasso, M. (2019). Electric efficiency indicators and carbon dioxide emission factors for power generation by fossil and renewable energy sources on hourly basis. *Energy Conversion and Management*, *196*, 1369–1384.

Miralles-Quirós, J. L. & Miralles-Quirós, M. M. (2019). Are alternative energies a real alternative for investors? *Energy Economics*, *78*, 535–545.

Monash University (2022). Systematic Review PRISMA 2020. monash.edu/ systematic review.

Naqvi, B., Mirza, N., Rizvi, S. K. A., Porada-Rochoń, M., & Itani, R. (2021). Is there a green fund premium? Evidence from twenty seven emerging markets. *Global Finance Journal*, *50*, 100656.

Ntow-Gyamfi, M., Bokpin, G. A., Aboagye, A. Q., & Ackah, C. G. (2020). Environmental sustainability and financial development in Africa; does institutional quality play any role? *Development Studies Research*, *7*(1), 93–118.

Page, M. J., Shamseer, L., & Altman, D. G. (2016). Epidemiology and reporting characteristics of systematic reviews of biomedical research: A crosssectional study. *PLoS Medicine*, e1002028. https://doi.org/ 10.1371/journal.pmed.1002028.

Panic, N., Leoncini, E., de Belvis, G., Ricciardi, W., & Boccia, S. (2013). Evaluation of the endorsement of the preferred reporting items for systematic reviews and meta-analysis (PRISMA) statement on the quality of published systematic review and meta-analyses. *PLoS One*, *8*, e83138. https://doi.org/10.1371/journal.pone.0083138.

Peng, J. & Zheng, Y. (2021). Does environmental policy promote energy efficiency? Evidence from China in the context of developing green finance. *Frontiers in Environmental Science*, *2*, 299.

Pham, L. (2016). Is it risky to go green? A volatility analysis of the green bond market. *Journal of Sustainable Finance & Investment*, *6*, 263–291.

Pham, L. & Huynh, T. L. D. (2020). How does investor attention influence the green bond market? *Finance Research Letters*, *35*, 101533.

Powmya, A. & Abidin, N. Z. (2014). The challenges of green construction in Oman. *International Journal of Sustainable Construction Engineering and Technology*, *5*, 32–37.

Raberto, M., Ozel, B., Ponta, L., Teglio, A., & Cincotti, S. (2019). From financial instability to green finance: The role of banking and credit market regulation in the Eurace model. *Journal of Evolutionary Economics*, *29*(1), 429–465.

Rahman, S., Moral, I. H., Hassan, M., Hossain, G. S., & Perveen, R. (2022). A systematic review of green finance in the banking industry: Perspectives from a developing country. *Green Finance*, *2*, 347–363.

Ren, S. Y., Hao, Y., & Wu, H. T. (2022). How does green investment affect environmental pollution? Evidence from China. *Environmental and Resource Economics*, *81*(1), 25–51.

Sahoo, P. & Nayak, B. P. (2007). Green banking in India. *The Indian Economic Journal*, *55*, 82–98.

Shahbaz, M., Nasir, M. A., & Roubaud, D. (2018). Environmental degradation in France: The effects of FDI, financial development, and energy innovations. *Energy Economics*, *74*, 843–857.

Shakil, M. H., Azam, K. G., & Hossain Raju, M. S. (2014). An evaluation of green banking practices in Bangladesh. *European Journal of Business and Management*, *6*, 8–16.

Shaumya, K. & Arulrajah, A. (2017). The impact of green banking practices on banks environmental performance: Evidence from Sri Lanka. *Journal of Finance and Bank Management (JFBM)*, *5*, 77–90.

Sustainable Use of Natural Resources and Energy Finance (2020). Sustainable Use of Natural Resources and Energy Finance, Green Lending Program: Supporting sustainable Energy and Environment protection in Jordan.

UAE (2016). Ministry of Environment and Water MOEW, UAE Green Agenda (2015–2030): State of Green Finance in the UAE, the First National Survey on Contributions of Financial Institutions to Green Economy.

UAE (2017). Ministry of Climate Change and Environment MOCCAE, The National Climate Change Plan of the United Arab Emirates (2017–2050).

UAE (2019). Securities and Commodities Authority, The Securities and Commodities Authority Master Plan for Sustainable Capital Markets.

Umar, M., Ji, X., Mirza, N., & Rahat, B. (2021). The impact of resource curse on banking efficiency: Evidence from twelve oil producing countries. *Resources Policy*, *72*, 102080.

UNEP (2021). Promoting Sustainable Finance and Climate Finance in the Arab Region, Africa & Middle East Climate Change.

Waheesh, N. (2020). Egypt Goes for Green, Ahram Online, https://english.ahram.org.eg/NewsContent/50/1202/364639/AlAhram-Weekly/Economy/Egypt-goes-for-green.aspx.

Wang, R., Zhao, X., & Zhang, L. (2022). Research on the impact of green finance and abundance of natural resources on China's regional eco-efficiency. *Resources Policy*, *76*, 102579.

Wen, H. W., Lee, C. C., & Zhou, F. X. (2021). Green credit policy, credit allocation efficiency and upgrade of energy-intensive enterprises. *Energy Economics*, *94*, 105099.

World Bank (2019). *10 Years of Green Bonds: Creating the Blueprint for Sustainability Across Capital Markets*. Washington, DC: World Bank.

Zhang, D., Zhang, Z., & Managi, S. (2019). A bibliometric analysis on green finance: Status, development, and future directions. *Finance Research Letters*, *29*, 425–430.

https://doi.org/10.1142/9781800614734_0003

Chapter 3

Introduction of Fintech in the Financial Systems of the MENA Region: The Case of Morocco

Najib Mrabet

Abstract

Fintech or the application of new technologies to finance is revolutionizing the financial services sector and creating a break with traditional finance. In some countries, fintech start-ups, digital in nature, have been able to expand access to finance to unbanked people to enable better financial inclusion of households and businesses. In other countries, these start-ups are nibbling away at the market share of traditional financial actors, particularly banks, to create a disruptive effect insofar as their technological advantage allows them to offer alternative financing or investment solutions compared to traditional financial intermediaries. In this chapter, I will try to examine this process in the Middle East and North Africa (MENA) region, particularly in Morocco, by adopting an exploratory and analytical methodology of the introduction and evolution of fintechs. Finally, I conclude that the regulations adopted in Morocco do not allow start-ups to compete with traditional financial actors, only to complement them in order to improve financial inclusion.

Keywords: Fintechs, financial actors, blockchains, cryptocurrency, crowdfunding, banking law

3.1. Introduction

The introduction of fintechs in the financial sphere is a phenomenon that is experiencing strong growth worldwide. It has been able to attract hundreds of billions of dollars in money transfer, peer-to-peer lending, or blockchain operations. Because of their simplicity and low cost, the financial services offered by fintech companies are rapidly becoming a part of the global financial universe. These companies, which are digital in nature, have been able to expand access to financing to unbanked people and are nibbling away at the market share of traditional financial actors, especially banks, every day.

On the other hand, since the 2008 financial crisis, fintechs have developed at the interface between the technology and financial sectors, paralleling the restructuring of the financial landscape and the tightening of prudential regulation. In doing so, they present a design challenge to legislators and researchers.

Morocco, which has just completed the texts of its new 2015 banking law, seems reluctant to clear the way for fintechs and facilitate their development process like many African and Asian countries (Nigeria, Kenya, India, China, etc.). Indeed, the texts on peer-to-peer financial operations (notably crowdfunding proposed in 2018) were not ratified until early 2022. Similarly, there is still a regulatory vacuum regarding blockchains and companies operating in big data.

In this chapter, I will describe the evolution of fintechs in the Middle East and North Africa (MENA) region and in Morocco and show that putting in place an appropriate regulatory architecture allowing for the control and supervision of fintechs could maximize their benefits and reduce the related risks. At the same time, I deduce that any reluctance to react accordingly could severely shake the business model of traditional financial actors and make them lose an important part of their profit sources.

Therefore, the following chapter intends to make the following contributions to the existing literature:

- First, I'll start with a theoretical overview of fintechs, including definition, components, environment and evolution.
- Second, I shed light on the Moroccan banking and financial landscape and its regulation in which fintechs will be integrated.

- Third, I show that the new Moroccan financial regulation inaugurated in 2015 does not fully open the way to the flourishing of fintech operations even if the financial authorities want to make Morocco a regional financial center; moreover, the current objective is only to promote financial inclusion among the populations.
- Finally, I will review the position of fintechs in Morocco and other MENA countries.

3.2. Background

Currently, the world has more than 1.7 billion people who do not have access to formal financial services such as bank accounts (Demirgüç-Kunt *et al.*, 2018), which is 31% of the world's adult population. Fueled by the meteoric rise of cell phones, financial actors are taking advantage of new technologies to offer new forms of financial services with secure options to store, transfer, and accumulate money. Through banking regulatory reforms, countries are reducing barriers to financial account ownership and allowing new forms of savings, credit, and insurance services for underserved populations.

Regarding the MENA region, more than half of the population is "unbanked", having no secure means to store, save, borrow, or make payments (Demirgüç-Kunt *et al.*, 2018). As cell phone services become more prevalent, those with cell phone accounts account for more than those with bank accounts. New information and communication technologies have the potential to expand access to financial services in the region. The concept of financial inclusion recognizes that increasing access to formal financial services can improve economic security and stimulate economic growth.

In Morocco, the banking penetration rate reached 53% at the end of 2021. According to Bank Al-Maghrib, this percentage defines the number of residents with at least one active bank account as a proportion of the resident adult population. In other words, 47% of Moroccans do not have a bank account and do not have access to the financial services offered by traditional banks and financial actors.

On the other hand, the expansion of Moroccan banks abroad is part of Morocco's ambition to position itself as a regional financial center, according to the repeated statement of the governor of Bank

Al-Maghrib since 2010. To achieve this goal, several reforms have been carried out, including the reform of the banking law in 2015, the revitalization of the Casablanca Stock Exchange and the creation of Casablanca Finance City.

Thus, "Casablanca Finance City" (CFC), dedicated to the new financial professions, plans to become a true regional platform for these professions and will position itself as a financial gateway for investors wishing to access the rapidly growing markets of the African continent. This international financial center project opens promising prospects for the attraction of capital and the development of new businesses.

The new banking law has allowed the entry into the financial sphere of the country, so far, of so-called participatory banks, payment institutions or neo-banks, and crowdfunding platforms or collaborative finance. While waiting for permission of cryptocurrencies and online insurance, which are still prohibited, the country seems to be allocating the introduction of major financial innovations that combine finance and technological innovation.

The introduction of this combination of finance and technological innovations called fintech to the financial landscape of Morocco seems to create a dilemma for the regulatory authorities:

- To totally liberalize the creation of fintechs and allow them to raise large amounts of funds, which can have a disruptive effect and dominate financial services at the expense of traditional financial actors.
- Authorize their creation while limiting their size and evolution in order to avoid any rupture with traditional financial actors, which would put them in a position of complements rather than competitors.

3.3. Definition of the Concepts

3.3.1. *Definition of the "fintech" concept*

According to the International Organization of Securities Commissions (IOSCO), "the term Financial Technologies or 'Fintech' is used to describe a variety of innovative business models and emerging technologies that have the potential to transform the financial services industry." A somewhat more elaborate definition has been provided by the Financial Stability Board (FSB), which defines fintech as "technological innovation in financial services that could lead to new business models, applications, processes or products that have a material effect on the provision of financial services" (FSB, 2022).

The term emerged with information technology and has evolved since its origin. The concept represents the emergence of early information technology in bank management services such as wealth management software for financial advisors. Some authors like Coughlan & Coglan (2002) see the emergence of fintechs as the result of the interaction between financial organizations, consumers, and markets. The rapid development of the fintech ecosystem is causing structural changes within the financial system with the migration of some services to innovative non-financial companies.

On the other hand, Pushmann (2017) brings the concept of fintech closer to that of "financial innovation", which is defined as "the act of creating and then popularizing new financial instruments as well as new financial technologies, institutions, and markets." Thus, Pushmann does not see fintech as an ecosystem but as a major innovation process in the financial world. It is constantly evolving and keeps pace with the development of new information and advanced technologies. Fintechs represented archaic software in computers in the late 1990s, then mobile applications after the appearance of smartphones in the late 2000s, and finally advanced technologies such as artificial intelligence since the mid-2010s.

The segmentation of services in the financial sector and the specialization of new actors in each of these services are the main drivers of fintechs' growth and competition to the products and services of traditional financial actors. As a result, traditional actors are being challenged on their product and service offering; for example, traditional banks propose standardized offers covering all segments of the banking market, while fintech start-ups propose much more restricted but specialized and personalized offers on a particular segment.

The concept of fintech is therefore defined by these authors as a financial innovation that allows for incremental and especially radical changes in the financial sector. Fintech relies on new information technologies to bring new products and services, change business models, reorganize structures, optimize processes, and improve systems. The fintech concept is constantly in motion because it is based on technology that is constantly evolving.

3.3.2. *Fintech start-ups: Definition and emergence*

The concept of fintech start-ups is often used in the literature to refer to technology-intensive non-financial start-ups entering the financial sector; this concept is different from the set of traditional actors such as banks that integrate new financial technologies. Overall, Lee & Shin (2017) refer to a larger "fintech ecosystem" that includes five major actors:

- Start-ups
- Technology providers operating in artificial intelligence, Big-Data, cloud computing, or cryptocurrencies
- Financial market regulators
- Customers
- Traditional financial actors (banks, investment funds, stock exchange companies, etc.)

Fintech start-ups are companies that provide financial products and services using a digital marketing and sales approach and rely on a targeted product offering. Fintech companies are in direct competition with banks and insurers in almost all areas of the financial sector.

Currently, the number of fintech start-ups is increasing every year in almost all regions of the world as shown in Figure 3.1.

By the end of November 2021, there were 10,755 fintech start-ups in the Americas, 9,323 such start-ups in the EMEA (Europe, Middle East, and Africa) region, and 6,268 in the Asia-Pacific region.

The business model of these start-ups has shown very significant growth opportunities worldwide. Thus, the amounts invested in these fintech start-ups have almost doubled between 2018 and 2022 as shown in Figure 3.2.

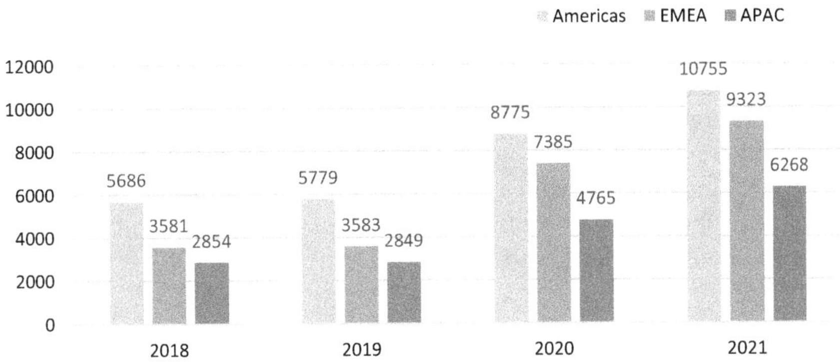

Figure 3.1. Number of fintech startups worldwide by region from 2018 to 2021. *Source*: Data adapted from *Statista*, https://www.statista.com/statistics/893954/number-fintech-startups-by-region/.

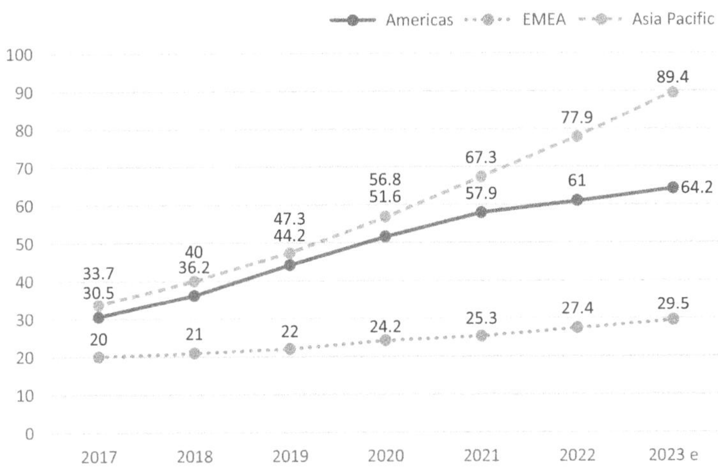

Figure 3.2. Fintech industry size over the world in USD million.

3.4. Digitalization of Financial Services: Theoretical Framework

Digital start-ups, all over the world, are putting a lot of pressure on banks and traditional financial actors by offering fast, secure, and cheaper financial services. With the generalization of smartphones and the development of smart contracts, these start-ups propose applications that allow the entry of the customer, the offer of services, and the conclusion of the contract in a few minutes. Thus, the opening of accounts, the exchange of values, payments, and their management are accessible on a cell phone. This digitalization of financial services has only been possible thanks to the digital revolution materialized by blockchain, smart contracts, and big data combined with artificial intelligence.

3.4.1. *The digital revolution and the rise of fintechs*

Currently, there are 272 neo-banks in the world; the value of transactions in the neo-bank segment is expected to reach $1.49 billion in 2022 with an annual growth rate of 24.68% to reach a total amount of $4.49 billion by 2027. The number of users is expected to reach 124.28 million by 2027. On the other hand, web giants are increasingly positioning themselves in the banking sector with fintechs (such as Apple Card, Facebook Pay, and Uber Money), which are characterized by reduced rates, specific and innovative services, and better customer knowledge.

This rapid development has only been possible thanks to the emergence of blockchain technology, big data, and artificial intelligence.

3.4.2. *Blockchain technology and smart contracts*

Blockchain is probably the most revolutionary technological invention of recent years. Indeed, the blockchain, when associated with cryptocurrencies such as Bitcoin, functions as a system for the exchange and transfer of totally digital money. This system provides an online payment method on an international level, while developing independently of any supervisory or control authority, and thus positioning itself as a new currency escaping regulatory influences and completely decentralized.

Each time a person makes a transaction, he or she goes on the network and computer algorithms determine the authenticity of the transaction. Once the transaction is verified, this new transaction is linked to the previous one to form a chain of transactions.

Blockchains can be used not only for transactions but also as a registry and inventory of all goods and services (energy, health, and finance including cryptocurrency). Indeed, one of the most popular blockchain technologies is Bitcoin, which hosts a large ledger (digital book). Bitcoin provides the platform to mine, store, and exchange bitcoins via a complex computer algorithm that is linked to a distributed network.

Since 2008, the volume of cryptocurrency transactions has been steadily increasing, showing the growing confidence and security of Blockchain technology. This represents a major innovation in fintech and may cause the next big disruption in the global financial sector (Pollari, 2016) by changing the nature of transactions even though it is still in the exploration phase. Lee and Shin (2017) rule that Blockchain will revolutionize many traditional financial services by speeding up money transfers, securing transactions, and lowering the cost of services.

On the other hand, according to Cai (2018), the banking and financial sector will be able to take advantage of blockchain through the use of smart contracts, where all financial elements such as securities, loan borrowing, and guarantees are trying to explore blockchain, especially by including rating/scoring companies to reference companies, their turnover and profitability to prevent defaults. Similarly, in terms of cash flow, smart contracts could certainly increase the banked population, facilitate access to financing, and reduce its cost.

3.4.3. *Big Data and artificial intelligence: Levers of fintech*

The term "Big Data" encompasses all the data emitted by users of Internet networks and collected by companies to exploit for commercial purposes. Big Data are unstructured and very varied, and often require computerized algorithms to process and analyze them. Fintech start-ups rely on financial, behavioral, and social data to offer innovative tools, products, and services that leverage structured data about their customers.

According to Dapp (2014), banks will need fintech start-ups and their technological know-how, particularly in terms of data algorithms, to facilitate financial services based on the exploitation and analysis of data to score operations and check the solvency of customers, for example.

Big data represent the second technological revolution in fintech. Indeed, fintech start-ups are using artificial intelligence and cloud computing to make better use of the data they collect and to offer personalized services to their customers. These technologies allow start-ups to automate the prediction of behaviors on the use of financial services and to innovate their products and services (Dapp, 2014).

Therefore, fintech start-ups as well as large web companies (Google, Facebook, etc.) that have developed a significant big data infrastructure and collect personal data on their customers are more apt to offer personalized products/services and thus gain decisive competitive advantages over banks that reacted late to the use of big data.

AI algorithms are currently present in the financial advice offered by fintechs, such as retirement savings plans, since they allow us to considerably reduce the cost for this type of services compared to traditional banks.

3.5. Fintech and the Transformation of Financial Services

By creating a new business model, and thanks to these digital innovations that have followed one another for more than 20 years, fintechs have been able to impose themselves in front of banks and traditional financial actors, on the one hand, through products and services constituting the core of the banking business (creation of money, loan borrowing, and portfolio management) and, on the other hand, through new products capable of facilitating e-commerce, the transfer of money, and participatory investment (Buchak *et al.*, 2018).

3.5.1. *Neo-banks: Money transfer and portfolio management*

The term neo-banks can be confusing because it does not mean the term bank in the classical sense, but rather means payment management institutions. Indeed, as they are not deposit banks and not authorized to receive funds from the public for a period of less than 2 years, neo-banks face many barriers to entry among credit institutions.

Among these neo-banks are banks accessible only through mobile applications, exclusively online banks, and digital spin-offs of traditional banks. They stand out for their ease of use where customers can manage their bank accounts directly from their mobile devices in real time and anywhere in the world. Their main features are as follows:

- The ability to open accounts in minutes with a simple ID document.
- The possibility of managing money for the customer through the sending of payment notifications, making virtual savings for a project or for vacations, and defining a budget or financial goals.
- The distribution of payment cards for online purchases or e-commerce around the world and benefiting from more favorable interbank currency rates.
- The possibility of withdrawing cash from ATMs free of charge or under advantageous conditions.

In the investment sector, the emergence of trading platforms connected to social networks has marked a real change in the business model of traditional investment banks. These platforms use "Advisor-Robots" or algorithmic programs to develop an investment portfolio and make investment recommendations tailored to individual clients, while taking advantage of the experiences shared in social networks (Deloitte, 2015).

In most fintechs using big data analytics and artificial intelligence, the "Advisor-Robots" are becoming increasingly efficient and require almost no human intervention. The combination of fintechs on simple investment advice and human expertise on complex investment advice generates optimized financial services for clients.

3.5.2. *Peer to peer: Cryptocurrency and crowdfunding*

Peer to peer (peer to peer or machine to machine) is a term applied to any direct exchange between two or more computers. It started with file sharing (movies, software, digital books, etc.) before being applied to finance in several forms, the most important of which are value exchange (cryptocurrency) and crowdfunding.

A cryptocurrency is a dematerialized (totally virtual) and decentralized currency (having no central authority to regulate it, nor legal tender in any country) combining blockchain technology and cryptography to validate transactions. It allows money to be transferred without any physical medium and without using an intermediary (Nakamoto, 2008).

Several cryptocurrencies have emerged since the 2008 crisis, such as Bitcoin, Ethereum, Peercoin, and Facebook's Diem (previously called Libra). Today, these cryptocurrencies allow businesses and other e-commerce users to make instant, secure, and low-cost transactions.

However, despite much publicity, cryptocurrency is not yet ready to replace real money as it cannot yet fulfill the function of a stable exchange of value or that of a store of value due to its high volatility.

Crowdfunding can be defined as (Schwienbacher & Larralde, 2010) "a public appeal, mainly peer to peer, for the provision of financial resources either in the form of a donation or in exchange for the future product or some form of reward and/or voting rights." It has experienced an impressive boom since the financial crisis of 2007 in terms of the volume of capital used.

The development of collaborative actions via internet platforms and social media has facilitated contact between agents in need of funding and small investors or donors. Initially, these participatory financing platforms were mainly directed toward donations, but then they quickly began to offer project holders the opportunity to raise funds from a large audience of Internet users either in the form of equity participation (crowd equity) or in the form of loans (crowdlending).

The following Table 3.1 shows the different types of crowdfunding:

- Some platforms only allow donations. In exchange for his generous contribution, the donor receives various symbolic rewards depending on the amount donated (a thank you message, a T-shirt, a free copy, etc.).
- Others offer a loan with or without interest. Borrower and lender agree on an interest rate and a repayment period. In this case, we sometimes speak of "crowdlending" to distinguish it from a donation.
- Finally, some campaigns called "equity crowdfunding" consist of real capital openings. Each contributor acquires shares in the company.

Table 3.1. Type of crowdfunding.

Donation	Equity crowdfunding	Debt-based
Financing by donation consists of the Internet user providing financial support to a project leader who retains all of his or her intellectual property. Donation-based financing can take two forms: donation-based, also known as a donation without consideration to finance a project led by a social entrepreneur or a charity, and reward-based, also known as a donation with consideration, which consists of giving consideration to Internet users when the fundraising is completed. The consideration, determined according to the amount of the donation, can be financial or symbolic (non-financial).	Equity crowdfunding involves an innovative start-up raising funds by issuing shares (i.e., equity) to a "crowd" of non-qualified individual investors via an online platform. The number of investors who can potentially invest in the company through equity crowdfunding can reach hundreds. In contrast to other forms of crowdfunding, crowd investing is subject to strict regulation, as it involves the issuance of financial securities to the general public in the form of a general solicitation.	Debt-based, crowdlending or peer-to-peer lending, consists in borrowing from a crowd to finance a project or a start-up with or without interest. This possibility depends on the conditions of the investment.

This method of financing has rapidly satisfied the growing need for financing of SMEs that are unable to access bank credit conditioned by guarantees. It has also proven itself in terms of speed compared to traditional credit. Indeed, crowdfunding platforms allow SMEs to get financed in a very short time (on average, three weeks against three months for bank loans). In this sense, participatory financing could provide a real alternative to bank financing on which SMEs are still heavily dependent and, in some cases, replace it (Agrawal *et al.*, 2013).

However, if the speed of financing is its strong point, the cost of crowdlending operations seems to be much higher than bank credit, which makes it a complement to traditional bank financing in most cases, not a substitute. Indeed, even if the beginning of crowdfunding made it a strong competitor to bank financing during the 2007 crisis, in which companies suffered from severe rationing of bank credit, its current cost represents a complement and not an alternative. Thus, operations financed by crowdfunding in France and in the United States parallel bank credit and have multiplied to cover the majority of financing needs such as working capital, research and development, intangibles, and even inventories.

Crowdfunding is currently booming all over the world and especially in the United States and France. Statistics at the global level are not provided by international organizations but mainly by websites interested in this mode of financing.

For an SME, crowdfunding de-complexes the act of financing the creation or launch of new projects, especially for young SMEs. It is therefore a tool for simplifying financing for those for whom traditional financing is inaccessible. It is the same for the other party, i.e., the subscriber, who will spread his adhesion to the project, even by small sums, to his network and thus help to multiply the number of members, donors, investors, and supporters. Thus, a simple saver becomes an actor of the economic activity, a grower of companies, and a creator of employment, and can even participate by technical advice when it is animated by the will of success of the project.

3.6. Methodology and Research Questions

The methodology adopted for this exploratory study integrates both the examination of the position of fintechs in Morocco in the face of technological innovations and the examination of the degree of penetration of fintechs in the banking and financial sector through financial regulation and the new banking law. Thus, I have developed the following research questions.

3.6.1. *Are fintech start-ups in the MENA region and in Morocco the result of technological innovations that favor their penetration in the banking and financial sector?*

In most cases, technological innovation creates a break with any traditional business, often due to the entry of new small factors that allow them more agility and operational speed (Macher & Richman, 2004). Dan & Chang (2010) explain the difficulties of large traditional companies in developing and exploiting disruptive technologies because of the weight of the heritage and the heaviness of their organization. The literature symbolizes the appropriation of technological innovations by fintech start-ups.

We have seen in the literature review that the integration of cutting-edge technologies, such as big data, artificial intelligence, and blockchain into the business model of actors in the banking and financial sector, has enabled them to reduce their costs and create new sources of productivity.

On the one hand, fintech start-ups have been able to build significant competitive advantages by adopting these technologies, which have allowed them to offer innovative and personalized products and services to their customers.

On the other hand, banks and other traditional financial actors have lagged behind in the integration of new technologies (Big Data in particular). Traditional banks have not considered the importance of these technologies, both from an operational and economic point of view (Trelewicz, 2017). This reinforces the competitive advantages of fintech start-ups.

However, the use of technological innovation by start-ups poses several challenges, including the financial risk in addition to the security and privacy challenge.

According to Lee & Shin (2017), the very nature of fintech start-ups can bring up issues related to these technological challenges because they are less financially sound and less armed in the event of major difficulties.

3.6.2. *In an inadequate legal and regulatory environment, can fintech start-ups flourish and compete with traditional financial structures?*

In the literature review, a majority of authors agree that new fintech actors are successfully renewing financial service offerings in important and historical segments, such as deposit collection, payment and money transfer, financing, and investment banking services. According to Anagnostopoulos (2018), these fintech start-ups are gaining market share over traditional financial actors because they are developing innovative business models that match the new expectations of customers:

- Traditional deposit banks strongly compete with new actors such as online banks or neo-banks that offer completely dematerialized, online, fast, and personalized bank account management services.
- Some start-ups offer merchants omnichannel payment solutions based on customer data.
- Crowdfunding allows some fintech start-ups to reach out to the crowd and bring them closer to the financial activities of investment and debt while allowing certain projects, considered "risky" by traditional banks, to be financed.

However, the evolution of regulation following the rapid developments of fintech is necessary to allow the multiplication of start-ups and investment in these technologies. This regulation should not pose quantitative or qualitative barriers to entry for these start-ups. Some authors (Dapp, 2015) point out that new fintech actors become very competitive only on simple financial services and limited to favorable regulation. Many non-banking start-ups do not have a financial license or a banking license, which restricts them in their service proposal and forces them to form partnerships with traditional actors. Thus, traditional actors retain significant competitive advantages in complex financial services due to their expertise and the difficulty faced by start-ups in complying with the regulatory requirements of offering such services.

3.7. Empirical Findings

Many research and financial reports (Mueller & Piwowar, 2019) (MAGNiTT & ADGM, 2019) estimate that the fintech industry in the MENA region is still in its infancy and the diffusion of fintech operations is limited to a few countries. Compared to fintechs globally, fintech investments in the MENA region only account for about 1% of global investment (Mueller & Piwowar, 2019). However, despite this slow start, these same reports estimate that the sector is evolving at an unprecedented rate, especially with the COVID-19 pandemic reinforcing the importance of integrating all aspects of a digital and contactless customer experience.

Morocco, which aims to become a regional financial hub, is not considered a pioneer in the field. Although it is directly behind countries like the United Arab Emirates, which has annual fintech operations exceeding 1 billion dollars, and Saudi Arabia, it is far ahead of countries like Algeria and Libya, whose field is almost totally untapped (Sekak, 2020).

3.7.1. *MENA — A diversified but growing fintech ecosystem*

The fintech market in the MENA region offers a majority of fintech services, including money transfer and payments, savings and investment, peer-to-peer exchanges, and online insurance and insurance marketplaces. The most active countries are the United Arab Emirates, Saudi Arabia, Morocco, Bahrain, Qatar, Egypt, and the rest of the MENA region including Tunisia. Countries that are completely absent are Algeria and Libya. The fintech market is therefore very diverse and cannot be considered a homogeneous group. Compared to the rest of the world, this region is still very weak compared to fintech hubs like Europe, Asia, and North America, but fintech adoption rates are increasing very fast. While people were looking to make less physical contact, the demand for contactless payment services has increased sharply in 2020. That said, neo-banks have begun to appear throughout the Gulf Cooperation Council. Traditional banks have ventured into payment solutions in addition to independent companies. Clear examples of these include Liv Bank (owned by Emirates NBD in Dubai) and Bahrain-based Ila Bank and Bank ABC.

Thus, the COVID-19 pandemic and corresponding health measures have hugely changed customer behavior in GCC countries, even though fintech founders have reported difficulties when applying for a banking license and navigating the strict regulations to enter the market.

Available statistics for this region related to 2019 showed that \$26 million was invested in insurtech start-ups, the highest amount ever recorded in history, with the total insurance premium market being \$57 billion in 2018, providing a vast market full of opportunities for insurtech start-ups. The top five funded insurtech companies were all based in the UAE, which has helped insure a significant portion of the low-income workforce in the country.

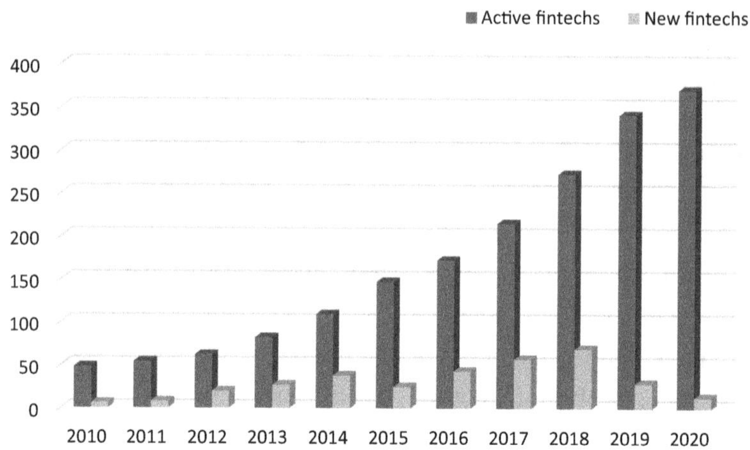

Figure 3.3. New fintech solutions per year, fintech across the Arab World, 2020. *Source*: Adapted from Consultative Group to Assist the Poor (CGAP), https://www.cgap.org/.

According to Figure 3.3, fintech creation is accelerating in the Arab world, which has counted over 20 new fintech solutions per year between 2012 and 2019, reaching a total of 400 in 2020.

The fintech sector in the Middle East is growing at a compound annual growth rate (CAGR) of 30%. For 2022, estimates predict that 465 fintech companies in the Middle East will raise more than \$2 billion in venture capital investments, compared to 30 fintech companies that raised nearly \$80 billion in 2017 (Figure 3.4).

In terms of the outlook for fintech in the MENA region, the sector is expected to grow and expand over the next few years. Countries with different models and attitudes are the United Arab Emirates, with Dubai being the most proactive municipality in this field, Saudi Arabia, with its huge NEOM project that is building a fully connected city, and to a lesser extent Morocco, Qatar, and Bahrain, which are expected to be leading competitors in the "fintech race" due to the various regulatory and incentive measures and initiatives they have taken in recent years.

3.7.2. *Fintech in the new Moroccan banking system*

The new banking law, which enacted new texts from 2015, has allowed the entry of some fintechs into the Moroccan banking

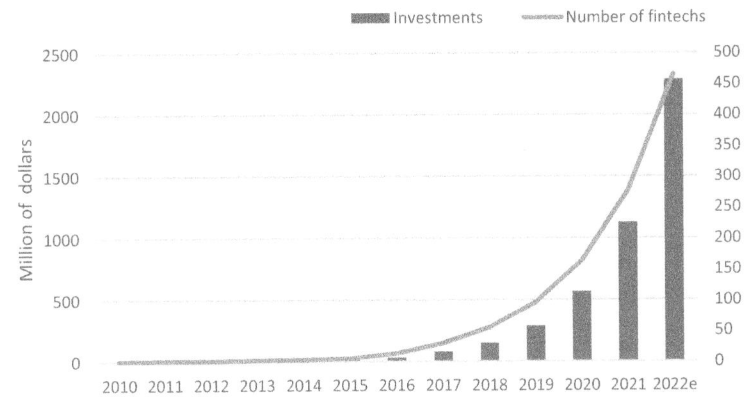

Figure 3.4. Venture capital investment into Middle East fintech companies.
Source: Adapted from DIFC FinTech Hive and Accenture, https://fintechnews.ae.

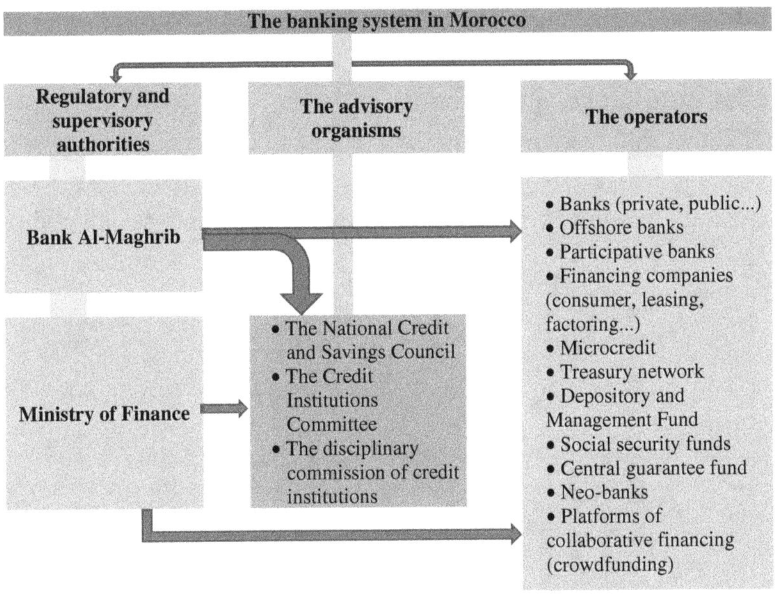

Figure 3.5. Banking system in Morocco.

landscape, notably neo-banks (see Figure 3.5). Other fintech solutions are still taking their first steps (peer to peer, crowdfunding) and some have not yet seen the light of day, like online insurance. However, some articles of the banking law concerning these fintechs seem to be concerned, first of all, by financial inclusion and, second, by the protection of the traditional banking and financial system. Indeed, many barriers to entry seem to restrict the emergence of fintechs, notably the convertibility of the dirham, the banking law (2015), and legal restrictions.

Figure 3.5 shows the diversity of operators governed by banking law, of which fintechs are the newcomers. In fact, neo-banks and crowdfunding platforms have been added to many operators that make up the majority of the Moroccan financial landscape.

With such a variable financial system, Morocco's openness to the fintech world through neo-banks and crowdfunding platforms has positioned it as the third largest fintech hub in the MENA region by 2020, hosting 40 fintech solutions, or 13% of the 400 active fintech solutions, according to research from the Consultative Group to Assist the Poor (CGAP) about financial inclusion (Figure 3.6).

3.7.2.1. *Neo-banks in Morocco*

The new banking law has allowed the establishment of neo-banks in Morocco under the name of "payment institutions". These institutions are authorized to open payment accounts only and to

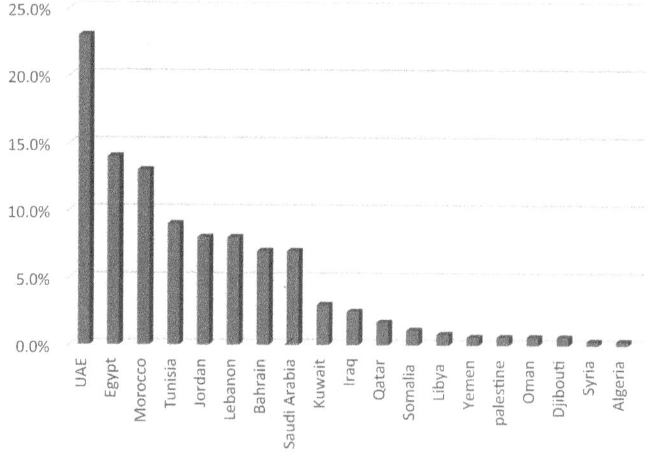

Figure 3.6. Fintech solution geographical distribution, fintech across the Arab World, 2020.

offer payment services on the basis of these accounts, but not to provide portfolio management services. Indeed, since they are not depository banks or authorized to receive funds from the public for a period of less than 2 years, some of the products that can be offered by neo-banks are subject to barriers to entry and remain monopolized by credit institutions.

Even though the process of obtaining approval for these payment institutions is done through the Comité des Établissements de Crédit, these payment institutions are considered as non-banks.

The services offered by these payment institutions to individuals, in addition to money transfer, payment of remote purchases from eligible merchants, and payment of bills, include money withdrawal and deposit via a traditional bank account and payment of imports for merchants.

To promote these payment institutions, Bank Al-Maghrib, in cooperation with the ANRT, has set up the national mobile payment solution within the framework of an ecosystem bringing together all the relevant actors (banks, payment institutions, mobile switch, and telecom operators). The bank has ensured the operationalization of interoperability between the mobile payment actors by

- Supporting the market in the identification of technical specifications.
- Setting up the mobile switch (managed by HPSS).
- The publication of the regulatory framework governing this new means of payment.
- The creation of a governance structure dedicated to "mobile payment".

By the end of 2021, the number of payment institutions increased to 18, a majority of which are subsidiaries of existing banks and the country's three telephone operators. The number of M-Wallet created exceeds 1.5 million.

3.7.2.2. *Crowdfunding and the difficult start*

In Morocco, Law 15–18 on crowdfunding (under the name of collaborative financing) came into effect in May 2022. After an impatient wait on the part of many economic operators, this law came to respond to a demand that is becoming increasingly apparent among young entrepreneurs capable of creating SMEs, some of whom are already clients of foreign platforms. It also intends to complement the banking legislation, under construction since 2015, which has integrated participatory finance (Islamic) and micro-credit associations to be able to give a breath of fresh air to financing of a social nature.

Law 15–18 on crowdfunding proposes the following definition: "Collaborative financing, known internationally as "Crowdfunding", is a mode of financing projects by the public. It makes it possible to collect funds, generally of small amount, from a large public, mainly in order to finance entrepreneurship and innovation or to support the emergence of social, cultural and creative projects." Thus, the legal framework for collaborative financing should contribute to

- The mobilization of new sources of financing for the benefit of very small, small, and medium-sized enterprises and young people with innovative projects.
- The active participation of the Moroccan Diaspora in the country's development projects via a simple, secure, and transparent financing mechanism.
- The support of civil society in financing projects with a strong social impact and human development.
- The release of the creative and cultural potential of young people.
- The reinforcement of the attractiveness and the influence of the financial market of the country.

The said text includes, also, a set of provisions defining the regime of contributing investor, the guarantees related to the organizational and technical means as well as the human resources that the collaborative finance companies must provide to carry out their activities.

The first reading of this definition focuses on low-amount financing that supports entrepreneurship of VSEs and SMEs, innovation, and social, cultural, and creative projects. Many limitations to the competition with banks may appear in the bill, especially Article 5 which clearly explains that

- crowdfunding operations cannot be considered as a public call for savings, and the provisions of Law No. 44-12 relating to persons and organizations making public calls for savings are not applicable to crowdfunding operations;

- the funds paid by contributors during a collaborative financing operation are not considered as funds received from the public within the meaning of the provisions of Law No. 103-12 relating to credit institutions and similar organizations;
- collaborative financing operations of the "loan" category are not considered as credit operations or operations assimilated to credit operations within the meaning of the provisions of the aforementioned Law No. 103-12;
- collaborative financing operations in the "donation" category are not subject to the provisions of Law No. 004-71 relating to the call for public generosity.

This barrier to entry to the credit market also appears in Articles 45 and 55, which show that it is up to Bank Al-Maghrib to set the conditions and modalities for the realization of remunerated loans whose applied interest rate cannot exceed in any case a ceiling rate set by Bank Al-Maghrib.

In Article 46, this limitation of financing to small amounts becomes clearer when it limits the accumulation of contributions of a natural person for each project to an amount fixed by regulation, within the limit of 250,000 dirhams.

The same article limits the cumulative contributions of a natural person, at the end of a calendar year, to collaborative financing operations, to an amount fixed by regulation, within the limit of 500,000 dirhams.

3.8. Fintechs in Morocco: What Prospects?

To clarify the prospects for fintechs in Morocco, I will try to determine the elements that could impact the development of these startups in the future. I will also discuss the results of a survey conducted among a hundred people whose questions were mainly about the knowledge of the products offered by fintechs.

3.8.1. *Factors impacting fintechs in Morocco*

We have seen that the legislative texts governing fintechs, either those for payment institutions or for crowdfunding, oblige these new startups to go through the banking infrastructure. Payment institutions, for example, have a duty to permanently reconcile the funds placed in payment accounts with those in an approved credit institution and must ensure complete traceability of the funds collected and set up a joint information system with the partner credit institution. In addition, the banks participate heavily in the equity of these payment institutions. Indeed, out of 18 payment institutions currently operating, 3 belong to telephone operators, 4 are subsidiaries of financial groups, 4 are independent, and the rest were created by traditional banks.

In addition to the mandatory passage through the banking system, many quantitative barriers to entry have been established for new fintechs to enter the national financial credit circuit and the financial services market. Indeed, these quantitative limitations affect both financing operations in the form of credit and equity participation and money transfer operations.

It can therefore be deduced that the main objectives of the legislation are

- Increasing financial inclusion.
- Decreasing the amount of cash in circulation.
- Financing of the social sector.

3.8.2. *The place of banks between cryptocurrency and digital currency*

Although Bank Al-Maghrib (the central bank) has formally prohibited the use of cryptocurrency, it has announced that it is studying the creation of a digital currency, taking into consideration its advantages and disadvantages, its development at the national and international level, as well as its impact on monetary policy and stability. To this end, a special committee has been formed to consider the creation of a Central Bank Digital Currency capable of avoiding the risks associated with cryptocurrency.

Moroccan banks, on the other hand, have been able to mark the development of digital currency only through the Payment Institutions of which a majority are their subsidiaries. These banks have stayed away from cryptocurrency until now due to the ban on their creation or use of their wallets. However, this has not prevented Moroccan traders from using international OTC platforms that ensure a certain confidentiality of transactions. This development of cryptocurrency is close to 1 million dollars of transactions per month (according to data from Usefultulips), and this despite the prohibitions of the monetary authorities (including the communiqué of Bank Al-Maghrib and the foreign exchange office of November 21, 2017) which recalled that transactions made in cryptocurrencies constituted "an infringement of foreign exchange regulations, subject to sanctions" in addition to the related risks:

- The lack of regulatory protection to cover losses in case of failure of exchange platforms.
- The absence of a specific legal framework for the protection of users of these currencies in relation to the transactions carried out, in addition to the non-compliance with foreign exchange legislation.
- Use of these currencies for illicit or criminal purposes, in particular money laundering and terrorist financing.

3.9. Conclusion

Traditional financial actors in Morocco as in the MENA region are lagging behind in the adoption of fintechs but still maintain a dominant position in the banking and financial sector due to quantitative and regulatory barriers and the authorities' inclination to prefer risk control to the total opening of markets to fintechs.

Do the new strategies of digital transformation and cooperation with start-ups allow traditional actors to maintain a dominant position in the sector? With fintech start-ups, blockchain, big data, and new risk management techniques, the traditional banking profession risks disappearing completely. Indeed, the need for banks to invest in blockchains and enter the field of cryptocurrencies and crypto assets is no longer to be demonstrated. The reluctance of the Moroccan banking system to do so is apparent in the legislation that will regulate the financial landscape in the coming years. The barriers to entry and the mandatory passage through banks in crowdfunding and cryptocurrency operations have not prevented the use and acquisition of virtual assets by Moroccans — a situation seen as a stopgap solution to overcome the restrictions imposed by the cap on the e-commerce allocation.

In general, there are many reasons for the use of new financial technologies in Morocco, such as low transaction costs, contribution to economic growth, and financial inclusion. However, their escape from the control of a government entity, the volatility of fintech assets, and the high risk of failure of the platforms that manage them give Moroccan authorities understandable arguments to remain cautious about their adoption.

The new balance of power in the banking and financial sector has forced traditional actors to consider fintech start-ups as potential partners and not just as threats. Therefore, beyond the necessary digital transformation strategies, traditional financial actors have initiated alliance strategies with fintech start-ups in order to take advantage of their technological lead to catch up on fintech integration and offer new financial services (Lee & Shin, 2017). In addition, traditional actors are forced to get closer to new Regtech actors to stay compliant with the new regulations and not lose market share to fintech start-ups using their technology to comply very quickly.

References

Agrawal, A.-K., Catalini, C., & Goldfarb, A. (2013). *Some Simple Economics of Crowdfunding.* National Bureau of Economic Research Cambridge.

Anagnostopoulos, I. (2018). Fintech and regtech: Impact on regulators and banks. *Journal of Economics and Business*, Elsevier, *100*(C), 7–25.

Bank Al-Maghrib (2022). Virtual currency, Virtual Currency. https://www.bkam.ma/en/Find-information-about/Virtual-currency (Accessed 14 July 2022).

Buchak, G. *et al.* (2018). FinTech, regulatory arbitrage, and the rise of shadow banks. *Journal of Financial Economics*, *130*(3), 453–483.

Cai, C. W. (2018). Disruption of financial intermediation by FinTech: A review on crowdfunding and blockchain. *Accounting & Finance*, *58*, 965–992. https://doi.org/10.1111/acfi.12405.

Cgap (2022). Empowering the poor through Financial Services, Making financial services meet the needs of the world's most vulnerable. https://www.cgap.org/ (Accessed 19 October 2022).

Dan, Y. & Chang, C. H. (2010). A reflective review of disruptive innovation theory. *International Journal of Management Reviews*, *12*, 435–452.

Dapp, T. (2014). FinTech — The digital (r), evolution in the financial sector. Editor: Lars Slomka Deutsche Bank Working Paper. Part 1, Frankfurt am Main Germany.

Deloitte (2015). Making an impact that matters 2015 Global Report: Executive Summary. https://www2.deloitte.com/content/dam/Deloitte/global/Documents/About-Deloitte/about-deloitte-global-report-full-version-2020.pdf (Accessed 20 October 2023).

Demirgüç-Kunt, A., *et al.* (2018). The Global Findex Database 2017: Measuring Financial Inclusion and the Fintech Revolution. Overview booklet. Washington, DC: World Bank. http://documents.worldbank.org/curated/en/332881525873182837/The-Global-Findex-Database-2017-Measuring-Financial-Inclusion-and-the-Fintech-Revo lution (Accessed 13 July 2022).

FSB (2022). FinTech and Market Structure in the COVID-19 Pandemic: Implications for financial stability. https://www.fsb.org/work-of-the-fsb/financial-innovation-and-structural-change/fintech/ (Accessed 15 August 2022).

Howarth, J. (2023). 57+ incredible fintech stats (2023–2025), exploding topics. https://explodingtopics.com/blog/fintech-stats (Accessed 06 November 2023).

Lee, I. & Shin, Y. J. (2017). Fintech: Ecosystem, business models, investment decisions, and challenges. *Business Horizons*, *61*, 35–46. https://doi.org/10.1016/j.bushor.2017.09.003.

Legalvision (2022). Types of crowdfunding. https://legalvision.com.au/types-of-crowdfunding/ (Accessed 18 October 2022).

Macher, J. T. & Richman, B. D. (2004). Organizational responses to discontinuous innovation: A case study approach. *International Journal of Innovation Management*, *8*(1), 87–114.

MAGNiTT and ADGM (2019). Mena Fintech Venture Report, MENA. https://www.adgm.com/documents/publications/en/adgm-mena-fintech-venture-report-2019.pdf (Accessed 06 November 2023).

Mueller, J. & Piwowar, M. S. (2019). *The Rise of FinTech in the Middle East: An Analysis of the Emergence of Bahrain and the United Arab Emirates.* Abu Dhabi: Ilken Institute.

Nakamoto, S. (2008). Bitcoin: A Peer-to-Peer Electronic Cash System. www.bitcoin.org (Accessed 13 July 2022).

Pollari, L. (2016). The rise of Fintech opportunities and challenges. *JASSA*, *3*, 15–21.

Pushmann, T. (2017). *Fintech. Business & Information Systems Engineering*, *59*(1), 69–76.

Schwienbacher, A. & Larralde, B (2010). Crowdfunding of small entrepreneurial ventures. *Handbook of Entrepreneurial Finance*, Oxford University Press, Forthcoming, https://ssrn.com/abstract=1699183; https://dx.doi.org/10.2139/ssrn.1699183; http://dx.doi.org/10.2139/ssrn.1699183.

Sekak, R. (2020). Perspectives de développement de la FINTECH en Algérie: Sortir de l'archaïsme bancaire. https://arab.news/r3c4a (Accessed 14 July 2022).

Statista Research Department (2023). Number of fintech startups globally by region 2023, Statista. https://www.statista.com/statistics/893954/number-fintech-startups-by-region/ (Accessed 06 November 2023).

Trelewicz, J. Q. (2017). Big data and big money the role of data in the financial sector. *IT Professional*, *19*(3), 8–10. Deutsche Bank Technology Centre.

Part 2

Banking Sector Contribution to the MENA Region

https://doi.org/10.1142/9781800614734_0004

Chapter 4

Determinants of Banks' Profitability in a War-Torn Banking Sector: Evidence from Syria

Mazen Diwani

Abstract

Using the fixed effects estimator, this chapter examines the profitability of 11 private banks in Syria over the period 2007 Q1–2018 Q4. To evaluate the impact of the Syrian crisis (civil war), the sample is divided into a pre-crisis period and a crisis period. The profitability determinants include bank-specific characteristics, industry-specific and macroeconomic factors. Dividing the sample has a twofold purpose: what determines the profitability of private banks in Syria and how the behavior of these determinants has changed in the crisis relative to the pre-crisis. The findings assert the presence of behavioral changes in profitability determinants across the two periods and that a high extent of banks' time-varying profitability is captured by the factors included.

Keywords: Banks' profitability, return on assets (ROA), return on equity (ROE), financial crisis, Syrian baking sector

4.1. Introduction

During the last three decades, banking has undergone considerable far-reaching changes in its operating environment. Despite the evolution that occurred in worldwide financial markets, caused by a process of bank disintermediation and the impact of new technologies which have been introducing more competition in the provision of financial services also enhanced by the emergence of new players such as fintech[1] companies, the role of banks remains central in financing economic activity. A sound and profitable banking sector is better able to withstand negative shocks and contribute to the stability of the financial system (Athanasoglou *et al.*, 2008). Hence, identifying the factors that are relevant to bank performance is a common goal for academic research, bank management, financial markets, and supervisory authorities.

While there has been extensive literature examining the profitability of banking systems in developed countries (i.e., USA and Europe), empirical works on factors that influence the profitability of banking systems in developing economies are relatively scarce due to the scarcity of data available to conduct a meaningful analysis. Studies on bank profitability (e.g., Al-Jafari & Alchami, 2014; Al-Qudah & Jaradat, 2013; Ben Naceur & Kandil, 2009; Bourke, 1989; Demirgüç-Kunt & Huizinga, 1999; Dietrich & Wanzenried, 2014; Goddard *et al.*, 2004; Masood & Ashraf, 2012; Molyneux & Thornton, 1992) differ with respect to estimating the impact of various factors that may be important in explaining profitability. Although analysis of bank profitability was proven to be conducted meaningfully in some studies, few econometrical issues are yet to be addressed properly. First, some studies consider factors that explain banks' profitability only at the bank and industry levels; however, a plausible thorough investigation of the effects of the macroeconomic environment on profitability is sometimes missing, and this is partially due to the small panels used in the estimation. Second, in some of the studies on bank profitability, the econometric methodology is neither adequately chosen nor appropriately designed to capture the properties of a banking sector in a certain country such as political crises or newly introduced private banks in a state-dominant banking sector (e.g., the case in the Syrian banking sector). Third, some studies presented their empirical results based on the econometric models selected without considering some of the tests that confirm the suitability of their models in capturing the relationships between bank profitability and the hypothesized factors, such as accounting for heteroskedasticity,

[1]Financial Disintermediation and the Future of the Banking Sector; Report on a conference jointly organized by Banco de España and SUERF. Madrid, 30 October 2018.

auto-correlation and cross-sectional dependence in the residuals, testing for the endogeneity of some of the variables considered, dealing with the non-stationarity of some the variables considered in modeling bank profitability, the problems of multicollinearity due to the simultaneous inclusion of certain variables, and finally the poor behavior of some of the estimators considered (such as the Arellano & Bond, 1991) in finite samples when the cross-section dimension of the data is small (i.e., small N), especially if the variables under analysis are persistent over time (Williams *et al.*, 2018).

Although few studies have analyzed the profitability of the banking sector in Syria, the past literature on the profitability of the Syrian banking system is no exception to the aforementioned econometrical issues. Therefore, this chapter aims to investigate the determinants of banks' profitability in Syria and, more specifically, attempts to examine profitability drivers before the crisis and seeks to explain to what extent these determinants have changed after the crisis.

This chapter builds on the works of Athanasoglou *et al.* (2008), Dietrich & Wanzenried (2011), and García-Herrero *et al.* (2009). Using data from 11 private commercial banks for the longest relevant period (48 quarters from 2007:Q1 to 2018:Q4), I hypothesize some factors that explain profitability and then capture the changes in their behavior. My econometric model is estimated through a fixed effects estimator. I apply several tests to account for potential endogeneity problems, panel data unit roots, and structural breaks. The results show that profitability is, for the most part, explained by five factors: bank capitalization, credit risk, cost efficiency, non-traditional activity (non-interest income), and banking sector development. Bank capitalization affects bank profitability positively in the pre-crisis and crisis periods. I find that the impact of credit risk is in line with the past literature reflected by its negative influence during the pre-crisis and crisis as well. Cost efficiency is found to enhance the profitability of banks during the whole period of study; hence, the less expenses incurred by banks, the more profits banks would achieve. Also, banks — whose income is more diversified — achieve lower bank profitability (measured by Return on Assets, ROA), and this is reflected by the negative relationship between non-traditional activity and ROA during the whole period of study. However, non-traditional activity seems to have a boosting impact on the shareholders' equity return reflected by its positive relationship with banks' profitability (measured by Return on Equity, ROE) during the pre-crisis and post-crisis periods of the study.

The chapter is organized as follows. Section 4.2 discusses the existing literature on bank profitability from which hypotheses on the impact of the determinants are developed; then, I present an overview of some stylized facts in the Syrian banking sector. Section 4.3 presents the methodology. Section 4.4 identifies data sources and presents my sample as well as the empirical results. Section 4.5 concludes the chapter.

4.2. Literature Review, Hypotheses Formulation, and Stylized Facts

The determinants of banks' profitability can be divided into two main categories, namely, those that are management controllable and those that are beyond the control of the management (Guru *et al.*, 2002). The first category, which is within the control of the bank's management, is referred to as "internal determinants" or "bank specific" and the name simply implies that these are the factors that the management of a bank can control. Bank-specific determinants show the differences in policies and decisions across banks' management, such as the heterogeneity in managing sources and uses of funds, capital and liquidity management, and cost management.

On the contrary, the external determinants (macro and industry-specific determinants) of banks' profitability are variables that are not controlled by the bank's management; however, they capture the contexts (economically and legally) that affect the operation and performance of financial institutions.

There are many bank-specific factors which have been previously used by other studies such as bank capital (capitalization), liquidity, credit risk, cost efficiency, and non-interest income ratio. I will summarize — for the sake of brevity — the findings in the literature on the impact of each of the profitability determinants — that are used in this chapter — on chosen measures of bank profitability.[2]

[2] An extensive account of the literature on the determinants of bank profitability was presented in a paper by Diwani & D'Ecclesia (2022).

Capitalization (CAP) — measured as the book value of equity to total assets — is found to have a positive impact on profitability in several studies such as Ameur & Mhiri (2013), Jabbar (2014), and Saeed (2014). Few studies reveal a negative relationship between capitalization and bank profitability such as Ali *et al.* (2011) and Chronopoulos *et al.* (2012). Since CAP indicates how financially sound a bank is and signals the bank's ability to resist economic shocks, more capital indicates seeking less external funding and a lower cost of capital when it is sought. Also, higher levels of CAP are associated with lower implied levels of leverage and risk; hence, I expect that CAP will be positively related to bank profitability (Hypothesis H_1).

Credit Risk (CR) — measured as loan loss provisions (LLPs) over total loans — indicates the quality of a bank's credit facilities. Credit risk is critical since the default of a small number of important customers can generate large losses, which can lead to insolvency (Bessis, 2011). This measure was found to have a negative impact on profitability in Staikouras & Wood, (2011), Poposka & Trpkoski (2013), and Trujillo-Ponce, (2013). Based on theory, when banks face troubles with their assets' quality, they are usually assumed to report lower profitability and, hence, I expect a negative relationship between ROA (ROE) and CR (Hypothesis H_2).

The indicator of a bank's liquidity (LIQ) — measured as total loans to total assets — may vary across countries, but generally includes cash, government securities, interbank deposits, and short-term marketable securities (Dalwai *et al.*, 2022; Golin & Delhaise, 2013). Findings regarding the impact of liquidity (LIQ) are mixed. This variable is found positively related to bank profitability by Shen *et al.* (2009), Sufian (2010), and Poposka & Trpkoski (2013). Since lower liquidity means higher risk, and, in accordance with the portfolio theory which suggests that higher risk leads to higher profitability, some studies have found LIQ to be negatively related to profitability, such as Sufian (2009, 2011), Lee & Hsieh (2013), and Al-Qudah & Jaradat (2013).

Given the contradictory results of past studies, I have no prediction regarding LIQ's relationship with profitability (Hypothesis H_3).

According to the literature, cost efficiency (COSEFF) — measured as the ratio of operating expenses to total assets — is reported to be an essential determinant of bank profitability, which is associated with the notion of efficient management. The more expenses a bank incurs, the less efficient the bank would be in managing its costs; therefore, a higher cost-to-income ratio is always associated with lower cost efficiency. The relationship between COSEFF and profitability is almost uniformly negative (e.g., Almumani (2013), Ameur & Mhiri (2013), and Turgutlu (2014). A decreasing ratio of these expenses to total assets is expected to be positively associated with increasing profitability; it is due to the notion that an improvement in the management of these expenses will increase efficiency and therefore increase bank profits that I expect COSEFF to be positively related to ROA (ROE) (Hypothesis H_4).

Non-interest income ratio (NTA)[3] is an important factor which — according to the literature — influences bank profitability. When the activities of banks are more diversified, this would lead to more income being generated from different resources, leading to a situation where banks are less reliable on interest income, which is easily affected by the adverse macroeconomic environment. In some studies, NTA was found to be positively related to profitability such as Alper & Anbar (2011) and Van Ommeren (2011) while negatively affecting profitability in Agustini (2011), Chronopoulos *et al.* (2012), and Raza *et al.* (2013). Given the juvenile nature of the banking sector in Syria, it is unknown whether this variable would exert a positive or negative impact on bank profitability; hence, I expect its impact to be in both directions (Hypothesis H_5).

Studies dealing with external determinants employ two sets of variables: industry variables, such as banking sector development, and macroeconomic variables, such as inflation rate and GDP growth rate. The role of banking sector development (BSD) — which represents financial structure and is measured as total assets of banks to GDP — in affecting bank profitability has been investigated in many studies in banking literature. I would expect a negative impact of BSD on profitability because the larger the banking sector, the more competitive it becomes, leading to lower levels of profitability. This was confirmed in Demirguc-Kunt & Huizinga (1999), Ayadi & Boujelbene (2012), and Ameur & Mhiri (2013). Conversely, a positive and significant effect of banking system development on

[3] I refer to it in this study as "non-traditional activity". The two terms are interchangeable.

bank profitability has been found in certain studies such as Tan & Floros (2012) and Raza *et al.* (2013). Since private banks in Syria are relatively new, and as time progresses, more development implies a convergence toward efficiency and better policies for managing costs, I expect that BSD would exert a positive impact on bank profitability (Hypothesis H_6).

The issue of the relationship between bank profitability and inflation rate (INF) — measured as quarterly CPI change rate — was introduced by Revell (1979). One of his findings is that the extent to which INF affects profitability depends on the speed rate at which wages and other operating expenses increase compared to inflation. Additionally, Perry (1992) finds that the impact of inflation on bank profitability is associated with the degree to which expectations of inflation are fully anticipated or not. An inflation rate fully anticipated by bank management implies that banks can appropriately adjust interest rates to increase their revenues faster than their costs, thus acquiring higher economic profits. However, if inflation is not expected and banks are idle in adapting their interest rates, then costs incurred by a bank may increase at a higher rate compared to the revenues, hence, adversely affect profitability. INF was negatively related to profitability across several studies such as Ali *et al.* (2011), Francis (2013), and Ayaydin & Karakaya (2014). However, it positively affected profitability in Tan & Floros (2012), Trujillo-Ponce (2013), and Raza *et al.* (2013). Since anticipating INF by banks' managements in Syria is questionable — due to the nature of ambiguity of government's policies and given the approach of Perry (1992) — I expect INF to be negatively related to ROA (ROE) (Hypothesis H_7).

The GDP growth rate (GGDP) — measured as the quarterly real change in gross domestic product (GDP) for the nation the bank is located within — proxies economic growth in which it affects bank profitability favorably by increasing the loan demand, decreasing their default rates, and granting banks the capability of charging more for their services. GGDP is positively related to profitability in Dietrich & Wanzenried (2011), Chronopoulos *et al.* (2012), and Vejzagic & Zarafat (2014). However, a negative association between GGDP and profitability is evident in Khrawish (2011), Ayaydin & Karakaya (2014), and Al-Jafari & Alchami (2014). The negative impact of GGDP on profitability might reflect the increased ease of entry and consequent fierce competition which was the case for private banks in Syria competing between themselves and with the established state-owned banks, hence I expect this variable to be negatively related to ROA (ROE) (Hypothesis H_8).

Figures 4.1 and 4.2 show the profitability of Syrian banks (study sample) over the examined period (2007:Q1–2018:Q4) represented by ROA and ROE, respectively. In Figure 4.1, and before the war (2013:Q1), most banks have almost a similar value of ROA which is attributable to the fact that until the year 2009, some new competitors kept entering the market and were able to sweep some of the market shares from other established banks to their favor (because of the new products and services launched with the takeoff of newly established banks); hence, ROA across the sector witnessed somehow a rebalancing position among the sample banks until the end of the year 2011. The war has taken its toll on the sector, specifically after 2013:Q1, when ROA witnessed a sharp increase across the sector (for most banks). This is due to the devaluating Syrian Pound (hereafter SYP) against the US Dollar (hereafter USD) which has paved the way for banks to make profits based on their possessions of the USD. To measure profitability, I adopt the standard approach in the literature using two alternative ratios: the ROA[4] and the ROE.[5]

In Figure 4.2, ROE had a modest value (above zero) among banks before the year 2010, since banks possessed — on their balance sheets — more than the minimum capital requirements (SYP 5 billion for commercial banks and SYP 10 billion for Islamic banks)[6] and at the same time they were achieving modest net income. This has inflated the denominator (equity) and the resulting low ROE ratios among banks. After 2013:Q1, as banks were enjoying higher incomes due to the devaluating SYP, equity — for all banks — was dropping in real value, and this has inflated the nominator (net income) and results in a higher ROE among banks in the crisis period.

---

[4]According to Golin & Delhaise (2013). ROA is one of the most common measures of banks' profitability in today's banking literature.

[5]For a detailed account on ROE, see: European Central Bank (2010). Beyond ROE — How to measure bank performance: Appendix to the report on EU banking structures. Frankfurt am Main: ECB.

[6]SYP 5 billion is equivalent to USD 106.4 million, while SYP 10 billion is equivalent to USD 212.8 million at a rate of USD/SYP = 47.

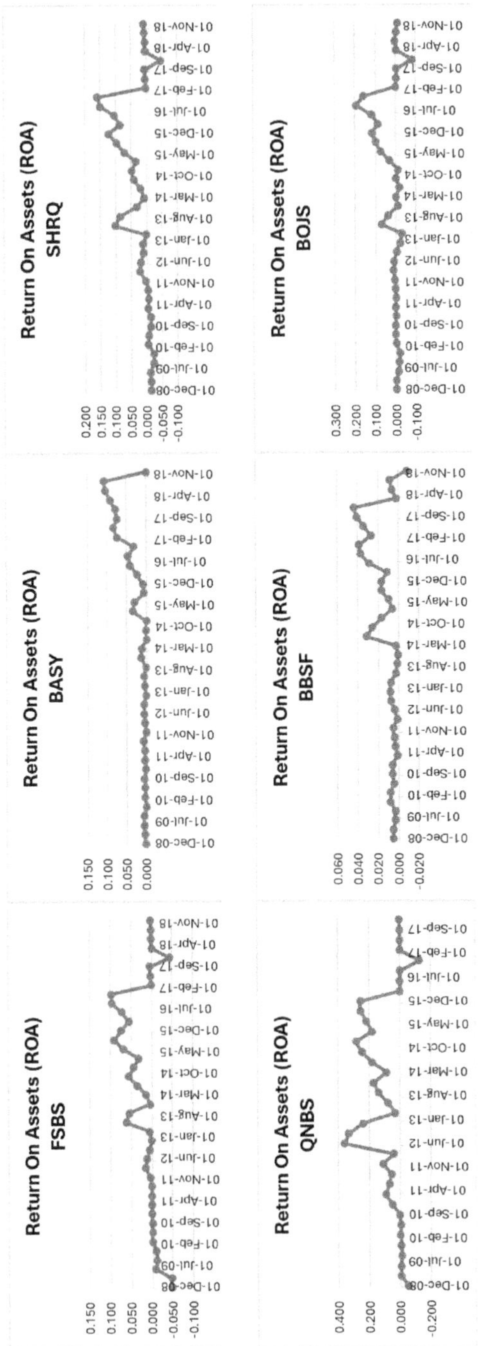

Figure 4.1. ROA of the sample banks over 2007:Q1–2018:Q4.
Source: Own calculation.

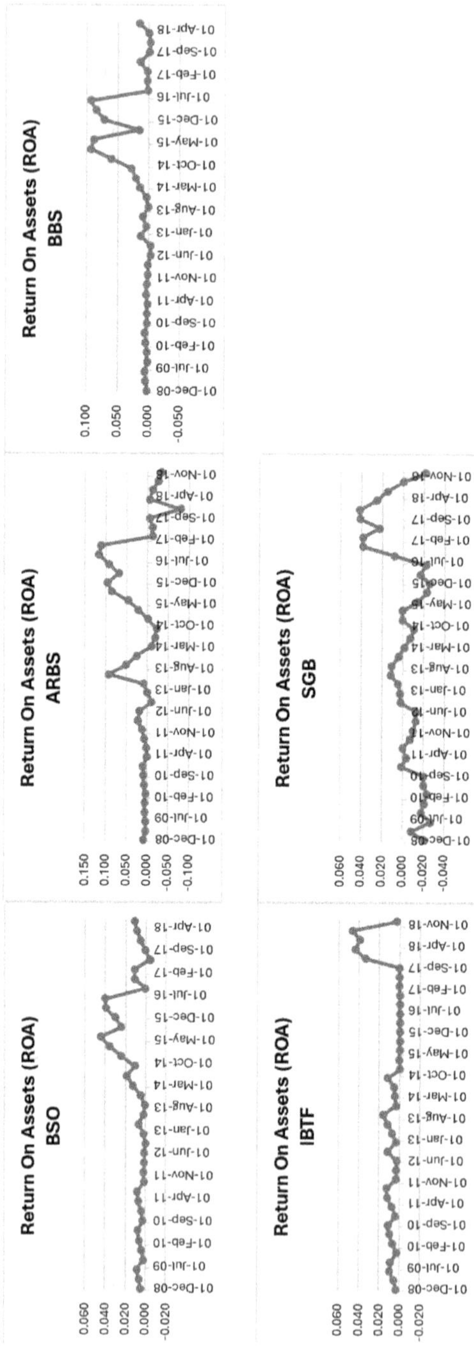

Figure 4.1. *(Continued)*

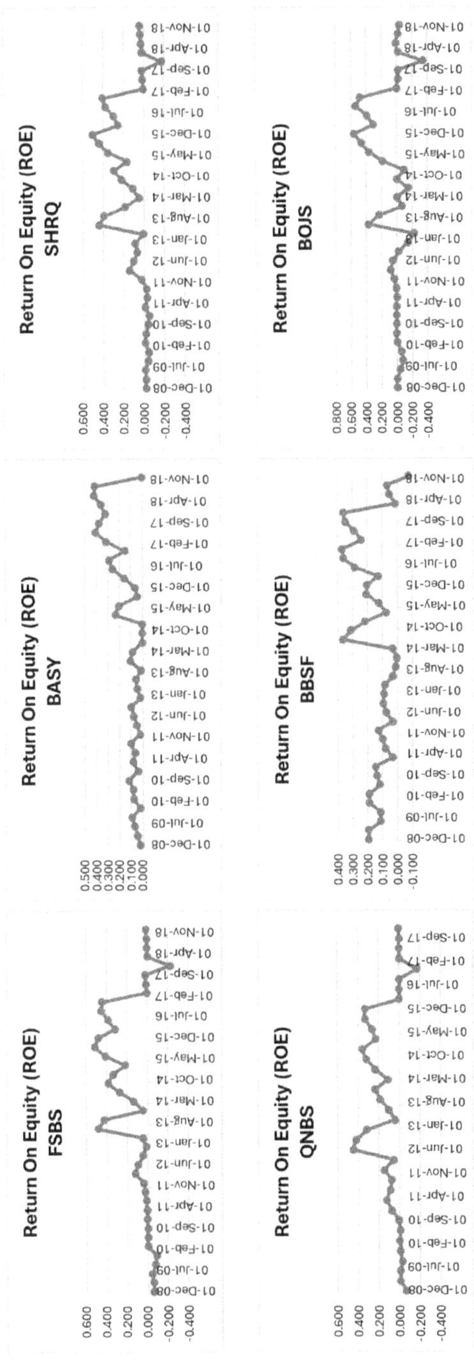

Figure 4.2. ROE of the sample banks over 2007:Q1–2018:Q4.

Source: Own calculation.

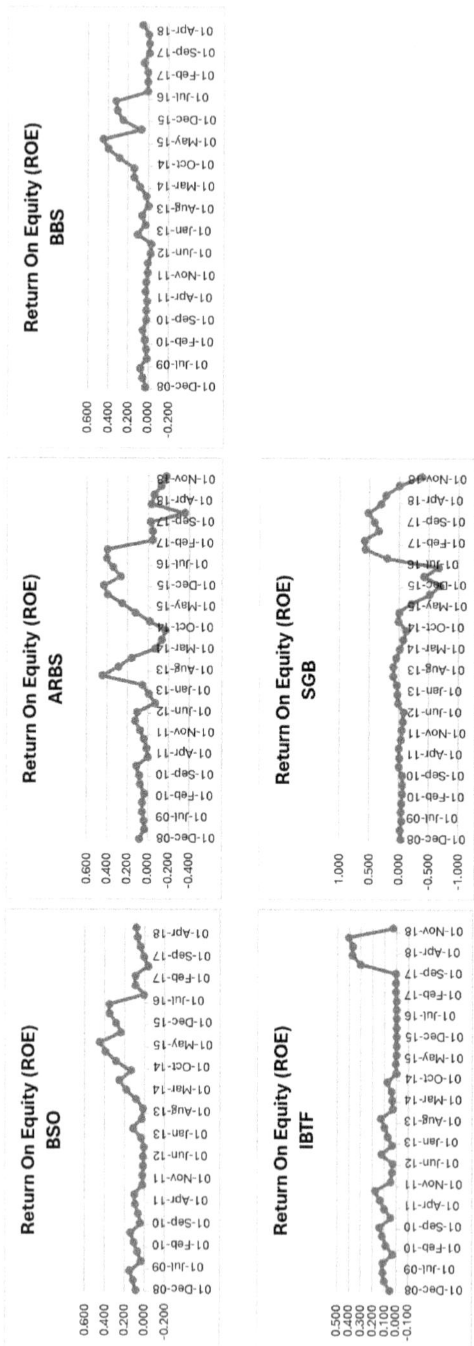

Figure 4.2. (Continued)

4.3. Methodology

Given the differences in operating strategies adopted by private banks in Syria, unobserved heterogeneity may be present which might cause a high degree of variability among the chosen regressors. Hence, I use panel data techniques to test my assumptions. However, some challenges still exist; when estimating bank profitability, measured by either the ROA or ROE, endogeneity might be an issue since more profitable banks could increase their equity more easily by retaining profits. Relaxing the perfect capital markets assumption produces the opposite causation because an increase in expected earnings will allow capital to raise the capital ratio; thus, I need to test for endogeneity in this study to find out whether the CAP is endogenous or not.

I favor the use of either fixed effects or random effects estimators over the use of GMM estimators for three reasons: (i) GMM estimators might behave poorly in finite samples when the cross-section dimension of the data is small (i.e., small number of banks, N), which applies to my case (11 banks). (ii) The use of System GMM (Arellano & Bover, 1995) estimator might also lead to some problems, specifically in young panel datasets such as mine. According to Williams *et al.* (2018), using the Arellano & Bover (1995) estimator entails a further checkup for consistency since it depends on the assumption of stationarity in the mean which has proved to be controversial in most empirical settings. To reach this consistency, the variables spotted in the dataset should be produced by dynamic processes initiated in the distant past which characterize their steady-state distribution. Due to the use of a juvenile panel dataset such as mine, it is hard to justify using GMM since most of these banks began operating in 2007; hence, GMM seems inappropriate. (iii) Finally, as indicated by Bazzi & Clemens (2013), an escalated concern was evident in recent years regarding the weakness or invalidity of the many instrumental variables of the type considered in panel GMM estimators such as Arellano & Bond (1991) and Arellano & Bover (1995). As recently illustrated by Kraay (2015), the effects of this concern may be substantial in practice.

Following Athanasoglou *et al.* (2008) and Dietrich & Wanzenried (2011), I use the following model:

$$\pi_{it} = c + \sum_{j=1}^{J} \beta_j X_{it}^{j} + \sum_{l=1}^{L} \beta_l X_{it}^{l} + \sum_{m=1}^{M} \beta_m X_{it}^{m} + u_{it}, \tag{4.1}$$

where

$$u_{it} = \mu_i + v_{it}. \tag{4.2}$$

π_{it} measures the profitability of bank i at time t(using ROA or ROE), with $i = 1 \ldots N$ and $t = 1 \ldots \mathrm{T}$; $\boldsymbol{N}$: represents the number of cross-sectional observations; $\boldsymbol{T}$ represents the length of the sample period; $\boldsymbol{c}$ is a constant term; $\boldsymbol{\beta}$ is the sensitivity coefficient for all explanatory variables; $\boldsymbol{X^j}$ represents the bank-specific variables; $\boldsymbol{X^l}$ represents the industry (market)-specific variables; $\boldsymbol{X^m}$ represents the macroeconomic variables; $\boldsymbol{u_{it}}$ refers to the disturbance error; $\boldsymbol{\mu_i}$ refers to the unobserved heterogeneity (the fixed effect); and $\boldsymbol{v_{it}}$ refers to the idiosyncratic error.

Equation (4.1) is a one-way error component regression, where μ_i is IIN (0, $\sigma^2_{\mu_i}$) and independent of v_{it}, which is IIN (0, $\sigma^2_{v_{it}}$). To decide between utilizing the fixed effects (FE) or random effects (RE) estimators, I apply the Hausman test. Afterward, my econometric analysis of Eq. (4.1) confronts the following issues. To tackle heteroskedasticity in error terms, I run all regressions adjusting the standard errors for heteroskedasticity and within-bank clustering. To ensure that my panel is immune to cross-sectional dependence in the errors which may arise because of the presence of common shocks and unobserved components that ultimately become part of the error term, I run all regressions using the estimator of Driscoll & Kraay (1998).

To examine how bank profitability determinants might have changed due to the Syrian crisis, and following Dietrich & Wanzenried (2011), I divide the sample into two sub-samples: a pre-crisis sub-sample (2007:Q1–2012:Q4) and a crisis sub-sample (2013:Q1–2018:Q4). To identify the precise threshold date for the beginning of the crisis, I perform a structural break test, assuming that the date for the break is 2013:Q1. For this purpose, I use the Chow (1960) test. Also, I perform the Variance Inflation Factor (VIF) test to check for multicollinearity between independent variables and dependent variables. Finally, this study employs the Fisher test — according to Maddala & Wu (1999) — to examine stationarity in panel data.

4.3.1. *Data sources and sample*

To collect the data, I had to be present physically in Syria at different times during the years 2017 and 2018. It was a very hectic mission as Syria, and more specifically Damascus, was being bombed as the result of the flights on the ground between state forces and opposing forces. Additionally, since Damascus International airport was closed for any flights from the rest of the world (except a few Arab countries), each time I had to go to Syria, I would travel from Italy to Turkey, transit there, then resume the flight to Lebanon, and then take a car from Beirut to Damascus in a 5–6-hour journey, not to mention the difficulties I faced on the road trip where tens of road blockades would exist, before I finally made it to Damascus. I went through countless bureaucratic procedures and sought permissions from the state to get the data. As for the bank-specific variables, they were collected from Syrian banks' annual reports and, most often, by visiting some branches in-person to work out some accounting-based issues to assure consistency across all the reports. I also visited both Damascus Securities Exchange and the Syrian Securities and Exchange Commission to obtain any missing data. As for the Macro variables, they were obtained from several sources such as the Central Bank of Syria, the Syrian Central Bureau of Statistics, and the Statistical Abstract Database, which is a joint database between the Syrian Central Bureau of Statistics and two ministries (i.e., finance and economy). Kindly refer to Table 4.1 for definitions, notation, and the expected effect of the explanatory variables on bank profitability measures (ROA, ROE).

My sample is composed of quarterly figures from 11 Syrian private banks over the period 2007:Q1–2018:Q4. I adjust the data to be in real 2018:Q4 terms using the GDP price deflator. These banks are all listed on Damascus Securities Exchange following its establishment in 2009. Since not all banks have available information for all years, I utilized an unbalanced panel to avoid losing degrees of freedom. In total, my sample contains 528 observations.

Table 4.1. Definitions, notation, and the expected effect of the explanatory variables on bank profitability measures (ROA, ROE).

Dependent variables	Measure	Notation	
Return on assets	Net profits before taxes/Assets	ROA	
Return on equity	Net profits before taxes/Equity	ROE	
Independent variables	**Measure**	**Notation**	**Expected effect (Hypothesis)**
A. Bank-specific			
Bank capital	Equity/Assets	CAP	Positive (H_1)
Credit risk	Loan loss provisions/ Total loans	CR	Negative (H_2)
Liquidity risk	Total loans/Assets	LIQ	Positive/Negative (H_3)
Cost efficiency	Operating expenses/ Assets	COSEFF	Positive (H_4)
Non-traditional activity	Non-interest income/ Net profits after taxes	NII	Positive/Negative (H_5)
B. Industry-specific			
Banking sector development	Total assets for banks/GDP	BSD	Positive (H_6)
C. Macro-specific			
Inflation rate	Quarterly inflation rate	INF	Negative (H_7)
GDP growth rate	Growth in quarterly GDP	GGDP	Negative (H_8)

4.4. Data Analysis and Empirical Results

4.4.1. *Descriptive analysis*

Table 4.2 reports descriptive statistics for the whole period covered in this study (2007:Q1–2018:Q4), pre-crisis sub-sample (2007:Q1–2012:Q4), and crisis sub-sample (2013:Q1–2018:Q4). ROA has increased in the crisis period compared to the pre-crisis by ten times due to the increase in most banks' profits as the result of the devaluating of the SYP against the USD. Similarly, ROE has increased in the crisis period by 197% due to (i) the improvement in USD/SYP

Table 4.2. Summary statistics for the independent and dependent variables.

	Whole sample (2007:Q1–2018:Q4)				Pre-crisis sub-sample (2007:Q1–2012:Q4)				Crisis sub-sample (2013:Q1–2018:Q4)			
	Mean	Std. dev.	Min.	Max.	Mean	Std. dev.	Min.	Max.	Mean	Std. dev.	Min.	Max.
Dependent variables												
A. Bank profitability measures												
ROA	0.0200	0.0510	−0.1260	0.3630	0.0030	0.0160	−0.0510	0.1140	0.0330	0.0630	−0.1260	0.3630
ROE	0.0830	0.2110	−2.0670	0.5880	0.0390	0.0620	−0.1390	0.1940	0.1160	0.2710	−2.0670	0.5880
Independent variables												
B. Bank-specific												
CAP	0.2080	0.1980	0.0120	0.8910	0.1930	0.2080	0.0280	0.8910	0.2190	0.1890	0.0120	0.8170
CR	0.3840	0.4510	0.0000	2.0360	0.0280	0.0460	0.0000	0.2510	0.6410	0.4360	0.0610	2.0360
LIQ	0.2690	0.1500	0.0000	0.6260	0.3640	0.1480	0.0000	0.6260	0.1960	0.1040	0.0180	0.5080
COSEFF	0.0220	0.0240	−0.0730	0.1420	0.0180	0.0140	0.0020	0.0940	0.0260	0.0290	−0.0730	0.1420
NTA	0.0260	0.1450	0.0000	2.8060	0.0110	0.0230	0.0000	0.2660	0.0370	0.1890	0.0000	2.8060
C. Industry-specific												
BSD	1.3580	0.5290	0.2210	2.8850	1.0350	0.4200	0.2210	1.6560	1.6800	0.4180	1.2410	2.8850
D. Macro-specific												
INF	0.0550	0.0790	−0.0870	0.3430	0.0370	0.0590	−0.0480	0.1790	0.0720	0.0910	−0.0870	0.3430
GGDP	−0.0150	0.0730	−0.2090	0.1560	−0.0140	0.0670	−0.1600	0.1060	−0.0160	0.0780	−0.2090	0.1560

from 517.43 in 2016 to 436 in 2017, which has negatively affected the financial results of the Syrian banks. The operating profits of banks have turned into a loss after adding the loss resulting from the reevaluation of the USD/SYP positions in banks, which has adversely affected the equity (the denominator in the ROE ratio) in Syrian banks. (ii) The accumulation of LLPs taken from the equity in most banks to account for the due loans has also contributed to a decrease in the levels of equity, which has artificially increased ROE as well.

To see whether the means of coefficients in the pre-crisis sub-sample are significantly different from their values in the crisis sub-sample, I perform Welch's t-test. Table 4.3 reports the p-values of Welch's t-test of significant differences between the means of the two sub-samples. These t-tests are based on the assumption of unequal variances between the two periods. Accordingly, all the coefficients of my variables proved to be significantly different between the

Table 4.3. Welch t-test for the means of dependent and independent variables between the pre-crisis and the crisis periods.

	Pre-crisis sub-sample (2007:Q1–2012:Q4)		Crisis sub-sample (2013:Q1–2018:Q4)		Welch t-test
	Obs.	Mean	Obs.	Mean	p-value mean differences
Dependent variables					
A. Bank profitability measures					
ROA	203	0.0030	264	0.0330	0.0000***
ROE	203	0.0390	264	0.1160	0.0000***
Independent variables					
B. Bank-specific					
CAP	203	0.1930	264	0.2190	0.1631
CR	191	0.0280	264	0.6410	0.0000***
LIQ	203	0.3640	264	0.1960	0.0000***
COSEFF	203	0.0180	264	0.0260	0.0001***
NTA	190	0.0110	264	0.0370	0.0258***
C. Industry-specific					
BSD	264	1.0350	264	1.6800	0.0000***
D. Macro-specific					
INF	264	0.0370	264	0.0720	0.0000***
GGDP	264	−0.0140	264	−0.0160	0.7716

Note: The p-values which are marked with *** represent significance differences at 99% confidence interval.

Table 4.4. Variance Inflation Factor (VIF).

Dependent variable ROA			Dependent variable ROE		
Variable	Coefficient variance	VIF	Variable	Coefficient variance	VIF
CAP	0.0021	2.5400	CAP	0.4958	2.2400
CR	0.0010	1.2600	CR	0.0470	1.6200
LIQ	0.0009	4.4000	LIQ	0.1995	4.1200
COSEFF	0.1249	2.7600	COSEFF	1.8264	2.4700
NTA	0.0014	1.2400	NTA	0.0308	1.8800
BSD	0.0004	2.0800	BSD	0.0045	2.6100
INF	0.0141	6.6100	INF	0.2320	5.4300
GGDP	0.0000	3.2000	GGDP	0.0000	3.4400

sub-crisis and crisis samples (except CAP and GGDP). Table 4.4 reports the Variance Inflation Factor (VIF) for ROA and ROE as dependent variables. All the values are less than ten, suggesting that multicollinearity is not a problem in this study (Kennedy, 2008).

Table 4.5 summarizes my findings regarding the test for a unit root in panel variables and time series variables by using the Fisher-type test. For each panel variable (except CR), all four of the tests strongly reject the null hypothesis that all the panels contain unit roots. The only exception for panel variables is credit risk (CR) where the four tests do not reject the null hypothesis at the 10% level. Therefore, if a panel variable has a unit root problem, the first difference of such variable is "stationary". Therefore, I took the first difference of both CR; hence, I transform the non-stationarity of CR by obtaining the first difference as the literature suggests. For the time series variables (BSD, INF, and GGDP), only GGDP is found to be non-stationary; therefore, I also transform the non-stationarity of GGDP by obtaining the first difference. Accordingly, the first differences of CR and GGDP become FCR and FGGDP, respectively. The dependent variables (ROA and ROE) are stationary. Table 4.6 summarizes the findings for FCR and FGGDP which are now evidently stationary.

To test for a structural break in my dataset, I assume that the breakpoint exists in the 25th quarter (i.e., 2013:Q1). Since $F_t > F_{0.05,\,\text{critical}}$, I reject the null hypothesis that the parameters are stable over time; hence, the implication of the presence of a structural break in my estimated model is evidenced.

Table 4.5. Results for panel unit root test.

Fisher-type test*	ICS		INZ		ILL		MICS		
	Statistic	p-value	Statistic	p-value	Statistic	p-value	Statistic	p-value	Status
Dependent variables									
ROA	69.9025	0.0000	−5.3841	0.0000	−5.7017	0.0000	7.2216	0.0000	Stationary
ROE	50.6439	0.0005	−3.8381	0.0001	−3.8343	0.0002	4.3182	0.0000	Stationary
Panel regressors									
CAP	251.5503	0.0000	−10.2924	0.0000	−20.6794	0.0000	34.6060	0.0000	Stationary
CR	15.9631	0.8177	0.6603	0.7455	0.6130	0.7288	−0.9101	0.8186	Non-stationary
LIQ	72.5046	0.0000	−3.7447	0.0001	−4.9075	0.0000	7.6139	0.0000	Stationary
COSEFF	84.5676	0.0000	−6.1951	0.0000	−6.9613	0.0000	9.4324	0.0000	Stationary
NTA	121.9223	0.0000	−8.6612	0.0000	−10.1957	0.0000	15.0639	0.0000	Stationary

	Statistic	1% Critical value	5% Critical value	10% Critical value	p-value	Status
Time series regressors						
BSD	−2.9000	−3.6070	−2.9410	−2.6050	0.0453	Stationary
INF	−4.5460	−3.6070	−2.9410	−2.6050	0.0002	Stationary
GGDP	−1.0820	−3.6070	−2.9410	−2.6050	0.7222	Non-stationary

Note: *ICS: Inverse chi-squared (22) p, INZ: Inverse normal Z, ILL: Inverse logit t (59) L, MICS: Modified inv. chi-squared Pm.

Table 4.6. Results for panel unit root test after differencing non-stationary variables.

Fisher-type test*	ICS		INZ		ILL		MICS		
	Statistic	p-value	Statistic	p-value	Statistic	p-value	Statistic	p-value	Status
Panel regressors**									
FCR	156.2737	0.0000	−9.8179	0.0000	−13.0672	0.0000	20.2425	0.0000	Stationary
	Statistic	1% Critical value		5% Critical value		10% Critical value		p-value	Status
Time series regressors***									
FGGDP	−1.0820	−3.6070		−2.9410		−2.6050		0.7222	Stationary

Notes: *ICS: Inverse chi-squared (22) p, INZ: Inverse normal Z, ILL: Inverse logit t (59) L, MICS: Modified inv. chi-squared Pm. **After differencing the panel regressors. ***After differencing time-series regressors.

4.4.2. *Determinants of Syrian banks' profitability: Results*

First, I need to test whether individual effects are fixed or random and, second, whether the capital variable (CAP) is endogenous. The choice between a fixed effects estimator (FE) and a Random effects estimator (RE) is based on the Hausman test results. The results are in favor of using an FE estimator.[7] Furthermore, it is possible that time effects are present in the error component of the model in Eq. (4.1) (due to the developments that took place in the Syrian banking sector during the sample period), as follows:

$$u_{it} = \mu_i + v_{it} + \lambda_t, \tag{4.3}$$

where λ_t is the unobservable time effect (t represents the year). To perform this exercise, I add the years 2007–2018 as additional regressors in Eq. (4.1). The joint significance of the unobservable time effects is tested by the $\mathrm{H_0}$: $\lambda_{07} = \lambda_{08} = \cdots = \lambda_{18} = 0$, where λ_{07} represents the effect of the year 2007; λ_{08} represents the effect of the year 2008; and λ_{18} represents the effect of the year 2018. The estimation results show that $\mathrm{H_0}$ is rejected at the 95% confidence level, hence time effects are present since the relevant F-statistic is significant at the 5% level [$F(11, 201) = 15.46$]. Additionally, the relevant LM test shows that $\mathrm{H_0}$ is rejected at the 95% confidence level [$\chi^2(11) = 142.87$, p-value $= 0.000$], implying that I should include year-specific dummy variables to account for λ_t. After examining the dummies for year effects, as it turns out, the only significant coefficients are that of the years 2009, 2010, 2011, 2012, 2013, 2014, 2015, 2017, and 2018 dummies. Therefore, I introduce dummies to Eq. (4.1):

$$\begin{aligned}\pi_{it} = c + \sum_{j=1}^{J} \beta_j X_{it}^j + \sum_{l=1}^{L} \beta_l X_{it}^l + \sum_{m=1}^{M} \beta_m X_{it}^m + \xi_1 D_{09} + \xi_2 D_{10} \\ + \xi_3 D_{11} + \xi_4 D_{12} + \xi_5 D_{13} + \xi_6 D_{14} + \xi_7 D_{15} + \xi_8 D_{17} \\ + \xi_9 D_{18} + u_{it},\end{aligned} \tag{4.4}$$

where $D_{09}, D_{10}, D_{11}, D_{12}, D_{13}, D_{14}, D_{15}, D_{17}$ and D_{18} are the dummy variables for the years 2009, 2010, 2011, 2012, 2013, 2014, 2015, 2017,

[7]The relevant value of the χ^2 test is $\chi^2(9) = 16.93$, with a p-value $= 0.0498$.

and 2018, respectively. The LM test for Eq. (4.4) does not reject H_0: [χ^2 (2) = 1.77, p-value = 0.4132] and thus I proceed with the estimation of Eq. (4.4). Furthermore, to test whether capital is better captured as an exogenous variable, I use the Durbin Wu-Hausman (DWH) test. First, the OLS estimates of regressing the potentially endogenous variable (CAP) on the remaining hypothesized determinants of bank profitability are obtained and then I include an instrumental variable for CAP. To instrument for CAP, I use corporate governance (GOV). Banks that choose to list their stocks on Damascus Securities Exchange (DSE) need to report a certain amount of capital, which is USD 6,382,979.[8] Therefore, GOV is a dummy variable which takes 1 if the bank's stocks are listed and 0 otherwise. I added the GOV as a regressor in Eq. (4.4), and recast CAP as the dependent variable instead of the profitability variable:

$$\begin{aligned}\mathrm{CAP}_{it} = c + \sum_{j=1}^{J}\beta_j X_{it}^{j} + \sum_{l=1}^{L}\beta_l X_{it}^{l} + \sum_{m=1}^{M}\beta_m X_{it}^{m} + \mathrm{GOV} + \xi_1 D_{09} \\ + \xi_2 D_{10} + \xi_3 D_{11} + \xi_4 D_{12} + \xi_5 D_{13} + \xi_6 D_{14} + \xi_7 D_{15} \\ + \xi_8 D_{17} + \xi_9 D_{18} + u_{it}. \qquad (4.5)\end{aligned}$$

I run Eq. (4.5) through OLS. I then rewrite Eq. (4.4) with an additional variable $\hat{v}_1$ that is the fitted residual vector from estimating Eq. (4.5) excluding GOV:

$$\begin{aligned}\pi_{it} = c + \mathrm{CAP}_{it} + \sum_{j=1}^{J}\beta_j X_{it}^{j} + \sum_{l=1}^{L}\beta_l X_{it}^{l} + \sum_{m=1}^{M}\beta_m X_{it}^{m} + \xi_1 D_{09} \\ + \xi_2 D_{10} + \xi_3 D_{11} + \xi_4 D_{12} + \xi_5 D_{13} + \xi_6 D_{14} + \xi_7 D_{15} \\ + \xi_8 D_{17} + \xi_9 D_{18} + u_{it} + \boldsymbol{\rho\hat{v}_{1i}}. \qquad (4.6)\end{aligned}$$

Under the null hypothesis that CAP_{it} is exogenous, $E\left(\hat{v}_{1i}u_{it} \mid \mathrm{CAP}_{it}X_{it}^{j}X_{it}^{l}X_{it}^{m}\right) = 0$, then the test of exogeneity would be the test of H_0: $\rho = 0$ in Eq. (4.6). After running Eqs. (4.5) and (4.6), the DWH test fails to reject the nulls hypothesis that CAP_{it} is exogenous at 10% level since Prob > F = 0.5522 on the coefficient ρ of

[8]When USD/SPY = 47, the equivalent is SYP 300,000,000 according to Decision Nr. 190 in the year 2009.

$\hat{v}_{1i}$. Therefore, I conclude that CAP_{it} is exogenous. Hence, I proceed with the estimation of Eq. (4.4) since the exogeneity of CAP is established.

Table 4.7 summarizes the findings for ROA. The first two columns report the results when including all quarters in my sample. To investigate the impact of the Syrian crisis on the banks' profitability determinants, I further split up the sample: columns 3 and 4 report the estimates for the pre-crisis period while columns 5 and 6 report the estimates for the crisis period. To identify the stability of the coefficients and their significance, I first include only the bank-specific determinants in the model (columns 1, 3, and 5). In a second step, I report the estimates of the full model with all variables (columns 2, 4, and 6). Overall, I observe some significant differences between the estimation results of the different periods, both with respect to the significance and the size of the coefficients. CAP has a significant and positive impact on ROA before the crisis and during the crisis (with a much larger impact). One of the main reasons for this increased impact (during the crisis) is that before the crisis — when Syrian private banks were newly established — they were considered by a large group of Syrians as being safer than banks in Lebanon where a large portion of Syrians were depositing their funds due to the existence of only state banks in Syria; hence, private banks in Syria were attracting additional saving deposits (mainly from Lebanese banks) before the crisis. Therefore, these banks were able to convert the substantially increased amount of deposits into significantly higher income earnings as the demand for lending increased in this period. However, during the crisis, and even though total earnings for these banks often largely decreased during this time of turmoil, a majority of Syrian banks raised their capital bases, which was perceived by the market as a signal of trustworthiness and the soundness of financial position. This has led to larger inflows of funds from Lebanese banks into Syrian banks.

CR is negative and highly significant for all different periods. The negative impact is due to, first, the lack of credit risk management before 2009 (i.e., banks were not obliged to set provisions against their defaulting loans). This had a far-fetched impact on banks' profitability whereas, in reality, some banks were incurring losses on their income statements as a result of the low degree of experience in dealing with insolvent borrowers. Second, before the crisis, there existed some banks which were dedicating LLPs "internally", and this had

Table 4.7. Regression results when ROA is the dependent variable.

	Whole sample (2007:Q1–2018:Q4)				Pre-crisis sub-sample (2007:Q1–2012:Q4)				Crisis sub-sample (2013:Q1–2018:Q4)			
	(1) ROA Bank-specific variables		(2) ROA All variables		(3) ROA Bank-specific variables		(4) ROA All variables		(5) ROA Bank-specific variables		(6) ROA All variables	
Dependent variable	Coeff.	Std.E	Coeff.	Std.E	Coeff.	Std.E	Coeff.	Std.E	Coeff.	Std.E	Coeff.	Std.E
CAP	0.1361*	0.0760	0.1187**	0.0348	0.0277*	0.0125	0.0255**	0.0109	0.1827**	0.1322	0.1986**	0.1311
CR	−0.1087***	0.0278	−0.1049***	0.0186	−0.0785**	0.0303	−0.1346**	0.0460	−0.0934***	0.0253	−0.0799***	0.0192
LIQ	−0.0279	0.0734	0.0385	0.0440	0.0227	0.0126	0.0136	0.0143	−0.0866	0.0763	0.0077	0.0695
COSEFF	−0.4583**	0.1302	−0.4780**	0.1838	−0.3771**	0.0571	−0.3869**	0.2309	−0.5616**	0.2468	−0.5801**	0.3390
NTA	−0.0477*	0.0394	−0.0611*	0.0336	−0.0419*	0.0101	−0.0486*	0.0186	−0.0834*	0.0451	−0.0894*	0.0434
BSD			0.0670***	0.0171			0.0069	0.0039			0.1038**	0.0428
INF			−0.0492	0.0721			−0.0227	0.0166			−0.1777	0.1744
GGDP			−0.0130	0.0150			−0.0094**	0.0132			−0.0170	0.0000
D09	−0.0488	0.0293	−0.0454***	0.0140	−0.0018*	0.0009	−0.0049*	0.0025				
D10	−0.0448	0.0325	−0.0608***	0.0184	−0.0032*	0.0015	−0.0064**	0.0027				
D11	−0.0423	0.0303	−0.0493***	0.0140	−0.0048	0.0028	−0.0082**	0.0028				
D12	−0.0460*	0.0252	−0.0510***	0.0115	−0.0015	0.0029	−0.0058	0.0033				
D13	−0.0331*	0.0169	−0.0762***	0.0170					−0.0145	0.0109	−0.0593*	0.0270
D14	−0.0400**	0.0129	−0.0500***	0.0099					−0.0358**	0.0146	−0.0258**	0.0094
D15	−0.0149	0.0118	−0.0234**	0.0096					−0.0161	0.0155	−0.0014	0.0090
D17	−0.0959***	0.0268	−0.0806***	0.0211					−0.1095***	0.0294	−0.0667**	0.0233
D18	−0.0754***	0.0217	−0.0680***	0.0162					−0.0775***	0.0237	−0.0455*	0.0218
Constant	0.0500**	0.0217	−0.0466**	0.0159	−0.0006	0.0043	−0.0009	0.0044	0.0216	0.0428	−0.1577**	0.0649
Number of Obs.	233		233		104		104		129		129	
R-squared	0.6879		0.7604		0.6608		0.7422		0.6551		0.6965	
Number of banks	11		11		11		11		11		11	

Notes: Coeff.: Value of the coefficient, Std.E: Robust standard errors. $^{***}p < 0.01$, $^{**}p < 0.05$, $^{*}p < 0.1$.

negatively impacted their ROAs. Finally, during the years 2009–2012, banks began to set provisions against their non-performing classified loans, which negatively have impacted banks' ROAs. However, after the crisis, LLPs have significantly increased. Interestingly, the negative impact of CR has decreased during the crisis period by approx. 38%. This indicates that managers of private banks, attempting to maximize profits, seem to have embraced a risk-averse strategy based on policies that aim to improve screening and monitoring of credit risk which translated (during the crisis) into a less negative impact on ROA.

COSEFF is negative and highly significant for all different periods. Its impact is larger in the crisis period which indicates the larger impact of prudent screening and monitoring during crisis times compared to normal ones Hence, the more efficient a bank is, the higher its profitability especially when the sector is experiencing severe conditions. Overhead costs mainly imply the non-interest expenses incurred by banks. As an important element, advertising expenses account for a large part of non-interest expenses. Hence, private banks in Syria should extend more efforts in advertising their products and services to attract more clients conditional on higher revenues exceeding the increasing advertisement expenditure.

NTA is negative and significant at 10% for all different periods. However, it has a much larger impact during the crisis period. In general, the negative effect implies that Syrian private banks which derive a higher proportion of their income from non-interest sources, such as fee-based services, dividend income, securitization, and trading profit/loss, are less profitable. As for the larger impact in the crisis period, there are two reasons for this result. First, developing non-traditional activities might be set to attract new customers rather than backing banks' profit; hence, the fee charged would be very low, and in some cases this leads to a larger decrease in profitability. Second, banks' employees are less experienced in dealing with non-traditional activities, adding up to the previously realized losses on these transactions and further leading to decreases in bank profitability.

BSD is positively related to ROA and is highly significant for the whole and the crisis periods. This is because Syria is among the less developed countries, and greater financial system development can enhance efficiency and profitability, which was reflected in my empirical results. The expansion and growth of banking assets during the crisis period were caused mainly by two factors. The first factor was the staggering increase in demand for loans during the years 2016–2018 when security conditions were improving in major cities (i.e., Damascus, Aleppo, and Homs). This surge in demand was attributed not only to improving conditions but also to confidence gained by business owners and industrialists in the short run, which boosted their desire to expand their operating activities and enhance the working capital of their businesses, therefore increasing the demand for loans (which in turns increased the fierce competition and assets among banks). Second, in a period where security conditions were improving in the major cities, some of the industrial zones were able to operate again and many of the clients whose loans were classified as "non-performing" were able to reach rescheduling deals with their banks; therefore, a large proportion of the LLPs that existed had been reduced accordingly and banks were able to enhance their financial positions with an increasing capacity for generating income (and increasing assets on their balance sheets due to the restoration of these non-performing loans (NPLs)). These two reasons reflected positively on the income banks were able to generate during this period relative to banks' assets, which means an increasing ROA.

GGDP does not have a significant impact on bank profitability after the onset of the crisis. However, it has a trivial negative and significant effect on ROA during the pre-crisis period 2007:Q1–2012:Q4. As the banking sector in Syria was a promising market, before the crisis, for prospective newcomers from foreign banks in the region (Lebanon, Jordan, and Gulf countries), the rivalry between Syrian and foreign banks became fiercer; hence, this effect reflected the increased ease of entry into the Syrian market before the crisis.

Table 4.8 reports the results for ROE which is in line with Table 4.7. In general, the results back — to a large extent — the previous findings. CAP has a significant and positive impact on ROE in all periods and its effect is much emphasized during the crisis. CR is negative and highly significant for all different periods and its impact on ROE is larger during the crisis. COSEFF is negative and highly significant for all different periods, indicating that higher efficiency in managing costs would be translated into higher efficiency. NTA is found to have a significant and positive impact during the pre-crisis and crisis periods with the effect being significant at 10% and

Table 4.8. Regression results when ROE is the dependent variable.

	Whole sample (2007:Q1–2018:Q4)				Pre-crisis sub-sample (2007:Q1–2012:Q4)				Crisis sub-sample (2013:Q1–2018:Q4)			
	(1) ROE Bank-specific variables		(2) ROE All variables		(3) ROE Bank-specific variables		(4) ROE All variables		(5) ROE Bank-specific variables		(6) ROE All variables	
Dependent variable	Coeff.	Std.E	Coeff.	Std.E	Coeff.	Std.E	Coeff.	Std.E	Coeff.	Std.E	Coeff.	Std.E
CAP	0.2669*	0.7346	0.2701**	0.6962	0.2574*	0.1225	0.2632**	0.1109	0.3044**	0.9308	0.3148**	0.8378
CR	−0.1125*	0.2228	−0.1262*	0.2271	−0.0736*	0.3016	−0.0832**	0.4278	−0.1811*	0.1995	−0.1951**	0.2110
LIQ	0.5413	0.6593	0.5652	0.6357	0.3343	0.1259	0.2286	0.1358	−0.2144	0.6926	0.3714	0.7324
COSEFF	−0.2377**	0.8142	−0.2487**	1.0307	−0.2111*	0.4621	−0.2271**	0.4571	−0.3247*	1.4601	−0.3301**	1.7213
NTA	0.3109*	0.1848	0.3226*	0.1877	0.1269*	0.1824	0.1478**	0.1116	0.4778**	0.0959	0.4828***	0.0939
BSD			0.2468***	0.0638			0.0900**	0.0388			0.4131**	0.2775
INF			−0.3947	0.4189			−0.3645***	0.1071			−0.8828	1.2938
GGDP			−0.0200	0.0019			−0.0110***	0.0074			−0.0047	0.0022
D09	−0.1443	0.0938	−0.1364**	0.0496	−0.0275***	0.0081	−0.0732**	0.0255				
D10	−0.2181	0.1238	−0.2739**	0.0904	−0.0611**	0.0197	−0.1083***	0.0249				
D11	−0.2525*	0.1349	−0.2925**	0.1104	−0.0991**	0.0332	−0.1483***	0.0264				
D12	−0.2601*	0.1239	−0.2958**	0.1111	−0.0840**	0.0336	−0.1391***	0.0333				
D13	−0.1879*	0.0932	−0.3415***	0.0760					−0.1359*	0.0721	−0.4574***	0.1340
D14	−0.1204**	0.0388	−0.1591***	0.0396					−0.1198**	0.0453	−0.0606*	0.0315
D15	0.0834	0.0623	0.0557	0.0669					0.0907	0.0901	0.1937*	0.1043
D17	−0.3250***	0.0492	−0.2812***	0.0383					−0.3451***	0.0398	−0.0874	0.1079
D18	−0.2791***	0.0410	−0.2645***	0.0345					−0.2783***	0.0331	−0.1007	0.0864
Constant	−0.0546	0.2676	−0.3889	0.2746	−0.0158	0.0395	−0.0210	0.0421	0.0939	0.3432	−1.0990	0.6109
Number of Obs.	233		233		104		104		129		129	
R-squared	0.7573		0.7723		0.6988		0.8276		0.6433		0.6843	
Number of banks	11		11		11		11		11		11	

Notes: Coeff.: Value of the coefficient, Std.E: Robust standard errors. $^{***}p < 0.01$, $^{**}p < 0.05$, $^{*}p < 0.1$.

1%, respectively. NTA increased in the crisis period by approx. 41%. This is because banks were better able to achieve an increasing share of revenues from sources other than loans (domiciliation of salaries, payment for bills, etc.), while the demand for loans (hence income from interests) was decreasing due to the deterioration of economic conditions. On the other hand, equity was decreasing in real terms, which led to a positive impact of this variable on ROE.

BSD is found to have a positive (and significant) impact on ROE in all the periods considered; its impact during the crisis is 3.5 times its effect in the pre-crisis period. As indicated earlier, the expansion and growth of banking assets are considered to be one of the most important indicators of the speed of prosperity and recovery in the banking sector, and despite the crisis, the assets of private banks in Syria increased during the year 2016 (compared to 2015) by 48.8% to reach about SYP 1.789 billion, surpassing the 2010 level by 224%.[9] The expansion in banks' assets indicated a staggering increase in loans during the years 2016–2018, which has reflected positively on the income banks were able to generate during this period relative to equity, which means an increasing ROE. INF was found to have a negative (and significant) impact on ROE during the pre-crisis only. During this period, the Syrian economy was starting to heat up as a natural result of the several steps taken by the government to open up the economy and to implement the many schemes of reform and modernization. The inflation rate in Syria — during the pre-crisis — peaked in the year 2008 approaching 15.15% and this was due to the accelerating developments in the global economy, especially the sharp rise in fuel and food prices since the beginning of 2008, the increasing exposure of the Syrian economy to the outside world, and its increasing dependence on the global economy. As a result, inflation in Syria was gradually linked to the sharp volatility in global prices, as well as the decreasing industrial and agricultural outputs. Hence, banks' managers were not capable of anticipating these inflationary forces, which left a toll on banks' profitability. Finally, GGDP has a negative and significant impact on ROE (although small in magnitude) during the pre-crisis period, which is in line with its impact on ROA before the crisis as well.

[9]https://kassioun.org/economic/item/57466-31267/.

4.5. Concluding Remarks

Identifying the underlying factors that influence banks' profitability is essential, not only for banks' managers but also for numerous stakeholders such as CBS, the government, and monetary authorities in Syria. This chapter examines how bank-specific characteristics, industry-specific and macroeconomic factors affect the profitability of 11 private commercial banks (which represent almost 70% of the banking sector) in Syria over the period 2007:Q1–2018:Q4. To account for the impacts of the Syrian crisis, I divided my sample into a pre-crisis period (2007:Q1–2012:Q4) and a crisis period (2013:Q1–2018:Q4). My econometric model is estimated through fixed effects (FE) estimator taking each bank's ROA and ROE as the dependent variable. The findings (i) give insights on how the behavior of some determinants has changed due to the crisis, (ii) pinpoint the presence of differences in profitability among banks in my sample, and (iii) showcase that a significant amount of this variation is explained by the factors included.

Overall, the results provide some interesting new insights into the mechanisms that determine the profitability of private banks in Syria. They are relevant for two reasons. First, the results confirm findings in the literature obtained from previous studies on bank profitability. Second, I consider a richer dataset due to the inclusion of 48 quarters starting from 2007:Q1 to 2018:Q4. The evidence reported in this study not only relates to a recent period but also covers a sensitive period that was characterized by some important changes in the Syrian banking industry. Also, by considering two sub-samples, additional insights were obtained regarding how the crisis has left its marks on banking in Syria.

The study has certain limitations; hence, further developments comprise some valuable venues for future research. First, it would be feasible to include specific information concerning the management and board members, e.g., education, skill level, experience, gender, and independence, all of which are perceived to be increasingly important determinants in comprehending banks' profitability. Second, this study is also subject to limitations related to the number of observations in my sample (528 observations), because of the relatively small number and a short history of private banks in Syria. Although the size of my sample might be small (compared to samples in other studies), I attempted to include as much data as possible given the information that was available to me. Therefore, future studies might consider the inclusion of state-owned banks in Syria.[10] As time goes on, fortunately, a more exhaustive dataset for Syrian banks is gradually becoming available. Therefore, future research can use this emerging and larger sample to provide a more comprehensive study of the determinants of profitability for the Syrian banking sector.

References

Agustini, M. (2011). Factors influencing the profitability of listed Indonesian commercial banks before and during financial global crisis. *Indonesian Capital Market Review*, *4*(1), 29–40.

Ali, K., Akhtar, M. F., & Ahmed, H. Z. (2011). Bank-specific and macroeconomic indicators of profitability — Empirical evidence from the commercial banks of Pakistan. *International Journal of Business and Social Science*, *2*, 235–242.

Al-Jafari, M. K. & Alchami, M. (2014). Determinants of bank profitability: Evidence from Syria. *Journal of Applied Finance & Banking*, *4*(1), 17.

Almumani, M. A. (2013). Impact of managerial factors on commercial bank profitability: Empirical evidence from Jordan. *International Journal of Academic Research in Accounting, Finance & Management Sciences*, *3*(3), 298–310.

Alper, D. & Anbar, A. (2011). Determinants of commercial bank profitability: Empirical evidence from Turkey. *Business & Economics Research Journal*, *2*, 139–152.

Al-Qudah, A. M. & Jaradat, M. A. (2013). The impact of macroeconomic variables and banks characteristics on Jordanian Islamic banks profitability: Empirical evidence. *International Business Research*. https://doi.org/10.5539/ibr.v6n10p153.

[10] I decided to exclude state-owned banks in my sample for two reasons: First, their financial statements (i.e., balance sheets, income statements, and annual reports) are reported based on the Syrian unified accounting system and need to be readjusted according to the International Financial Reporting Standards (IFRS), a task that was beyond my capabilities given the limited time and personal funds I have for this project. Second, my request for financial statements of some of the state-owned banks was declined based on "security concerns" as per the Syrian officials, hence this will bias my sample since too many values will be missing.

Ameur, I. G. B. & Mhiri, S. M. (2013). Explanatory factors of bank performance evidence from Tunisia. *International Journal of Economics, Finance and Management, 13*(C5), 1–12.

Arellano, M. & Bond, S. (1991). Some tests of specification for panel Carlo application to data: Evidence and an employment equations. *Review Literature and Arts of the Americas, 58*(2), 277–297.

Arellano, M. & Bover, O. (1995). Another look at the instrumental variable estimation of error-components models. *Journal of Econometrics.* https://doi.org/10.1016/0304-4076(94)01642-D.

Athanasoglou, P. P., Brissimis, S. N., & Delis, M. D. (2008). Bank-specific, industry-specific and macroeconomic determinants of bank profitability. *Journal of International Financial Markets, Institutions and Money.* https://doi.org/10.1016/j.intfin.2006.07.001.

Ayadi, N. & Boujelbene, Y. (2012). The determinants of the profitability of the Tunisian deposit banks. *IBIMA Business Review Journal.* https://doi.org/10.5171/2012.165418.

Ayaydin, H. & Karakaya, A. (2014). The effect of bank capital on profitability and risk in Turkish banking. *International Journal of Social Science, 5*(1), 252–271.

Bazzi, S. & Clemens, M. A. (2013). Blunt instruments: Avoiding common pitfalls in identifying the causes of economic growth. *American Economic Journal: Macroeconomics.* https://doi.org/10.1257/mac.5.2.152.

Bessis, J. (2011). Risk management in banking, Section 6. In *Risk Management in Banking*, John Wiley & Sons, Ltd.; The Atrium, Southern Gate, Chichester, West Sussex, PO19 8SQ, United Kingdom.

Bourke, P. (1989). Concentration and other determinants of bank profitability in Europe, North America and Australia. *Journal of Banking and Finance.* https://doi.org/10.1016/0378-4266(89)90020-4.

Chow, G. C. (1960). Tests of equality between sets of coefficients in two linear regressions. *Econometrica.* https://doi.org/10.2307/1910133.

Chronopoulos, D., Liu, H., McMillan, F., & Wilson, J. (2012). The dynamics of US Bank profitability. http://ssrn.com/abstract=1972835.

Dalwai, T., Singh, D., & Ananda, S. (2022). Intellectual capital, bank stability and risk-taking: Evidence from Asian emerging markets. *Competitiveness Review, 32*(6), 995–1024. https://doi.org/10.1108/CR-03-2021-0031.

Demirgüç-Kunt, A. & Huizinga, H. (1999). Determinants of commercial bank interest margins and profitability: Some international evidence. *World Bank Economic Review.* https://doi.org/10.1093/wber/13.2.379.

Dietrich, A. & Wanzenried, G. (2011). Determinants of bank profitability before and during the crisis: Evidence from Switzerland. *Journal of International Financial Markets, Institutions and Money.* https://doi.org/10.1016/j.intfin.2010.11.002.

Dietrich, A. & Wanzenried, G. (2014). The determinants of commercial banking profitability in low-, middle-, and high-income countries. *Quarterly Review of Economics and Finance.* https://doi.org/10.1016/j.qref.2014.03.001.

Diwani, M. & D'Ecclesia, R. L. (2022). International evidence on bank profitability: A survey. *Journal of Rivista Bancaria — Minerva Bancaria,* (1–2), 77–131.

Driscoll, J. C. & Kraay, A. C. (1998). Consistent covariance matrix estimation with spatially dependent panel data. *Review of Economics and Statistics.* https://doi.org/10.1162/003465398557825.

Francis, M. E. (2013). Determinants of commercial bank profitability in Sub-Saharan Africa. *International Journal of Economics & Finance, 5*(9), 134–147.

García-Herrero, A., Gavilá, S., & Santabárbara, D. (2009). What explains the low profitability of Chinese banks? *Journal of Banking and Finance, 33*(11), 2080–2092. https://doi.org/10.1016/j.jbankfin.2009.05.005.

Golin, J. & Delhaise, P. (2013). *The Bank Credit Analysis Handbook: A Guide for Analysts, Bankers and Investors.* John Wiley & Sons, Hoboken, New Jersey, USA.

Guru, B., Staunton, J., & Balashanmugam, B. (2002). Determinants of commercial bank profitability in Malaysia. *Journal of Money, Credit and Banking.* https://doi.org/10.18381/eq.v12i1.4855.

Jabbar, H. (2014). Determinants of banks profitability. *IOSR Journal of Business and Management, 16*(1), 109–113.

Kennedy, P. (2008). *A Guide to Econometrics* (6th edn.). Oxford: Willey Blackwell.

Khrawish, H. A. (2011). Determinants of commercial banks performance: Evidence from Jordan. *International Research Journal of Finance and Economics, 1,* 148–159.

Kraay, A. (2015). Weak instruments in growth regressions: Implications for recent cross-country evidence on inequality and growth. World Bank Policy Research Working Paper, Washington, DC 20433, (7494).

Lee, C. C. & Hsieh, M. F. (2013). Beyond bank competition and profitability: Can moral hazard tell us more? *Journal of Financial Services Research, 44*(1), 87–109.

Maddala, G. S. & Wu, S. (1999). A comparative study of unit root tests with panel data and a new simple test. *Oxford Bulletin of Economics and Statistics.* https://doi.org/10.1111/1468-0084.0610s1631.

Masood, O. & Ashraf, M. (2012). Bank-specific and macroeconomic profitability determinants of Islamic banks: The case of different countries. *Qualitative Research in Financial Markets*. https://doi.org/10.1108/17554171211252565.

Molyneux, P. & Thornton, J. (1992). Determinants of European bank profitability: A note. *Journal of Banking and Finance*. https://doi.org/10.1016/0378-4266(92)90065-8.

Perry, P. (1992). Do banks gain or lose from inflation? *Journal of Retail Banking*, *14*(2), 25–30.

Poposka, K. & Trpkoski, M. (2013). Secondary model for bank profitability management-test on the case of Macedonian banking sector. *Research Journal of Finance and Accounting*, *4*(6), 216–225.

Raza, S. A., Jawaid, S. T., & Shafqat, J. (2013). Profitability of the banking sector of Pakistan: Panel evidence from macroeconomic determinants. Munich Personal RePEc Archive. https://econpapers.repec.org/RePEc:pra:mprapa:48485.

Revell, J. (1979). Inflation and financial institutions. *Financial Times*, London.

Saeed, M. S. (2014). Bank-related, industry-related and macroeconomic factors affecting bank profitability: A case of the United Kingdom. *Research Journal of Finance and Accounting*, *5*(2), 42–50.

Shen, C. H., Chen, Y. K., Kao, L. F., & Yeh, C. Y. (2009). Bank liquidity risk and performance. Working Paper. Department of Finance, National University of Kaohsiung, pp. 1–37.

Staikouras, C. K. & Wood, G. E. (2011). The determinants of European Bank profitability. *International Business & Economics Research Journal (IBER)*. https://doi.org/10.19030/iber.v3i6.3699.

Sufian, F. (2009). Determinants of bank profitability in a developing economy: Empirical evidence from the china banking sector. *Journal of Asia-Pacific Business*. https://doi.org/10.1080/10599230903340205.

Sufian, F. (2010). Does foreign presence foster Islamic banks' performance? Empirical evidence from Malaysia. *Journal of Islamic Accounting and Business Research*. https://doi.org/10.1108/17590811011086723.

Sufian, F. (2011). Profitability of the Korean banking sector: Panel evidence on bank-specific and macroeconomic determinants. *Journal of Economics and Management*, *7*(1), 43–72.

Tan, Y. & Floros, C. (2012). Bank profitability and inflation: The case of China. *Journal of Economic Studies*. https://doi.org/10.1108/01443581211274610.

Trujillo-Ponce, A. (2013). What determines the profitability of banks? Evidence from Spain. *Accounting & Finance*, *53*, 561–586.

Turgutlu, E. (2014). Dynamics of profitability in the Turkish banking industry. *Ege Academic Review, 14*(1), 43–52.

Van Ommeren, S. (2011). *An Examination of the Determinants of Banks' Profitability in the European Banking Sector.* Unpublished master's thesis, Erasmus University Rotterdam, Hoboken, New Jersey, USA.

Vejzagic, M. & Zarafat, H. (2014). An analysis of macroeconomic determinants of commercial banks profitability in Malaysia for the period 1995–2011. *Asian Economic and Financial Review, 4*(1), 41–57.

Williams, R., Allison, P. D., & Moral-Benito, E. (2018). Linear dynamic panel-data estimation using maximum likelihood and structural equation modeling. *Stata Journal.* https://doi.org/10.1177/1536867x1801800201.

https://doi.org/10.1142/9781800614734_0005

Chapter 5

The Impact of COVID-19 News on Financial Market Volatility in MENA Countries

Oumayma Elbach, Abdelkader Mohamed Sghaier Derbali, and Moufida Ben Saada

Abstract

This chapter examines the impact of COVID-19 news in the USA on the volatility of financial markets in the Middle East and North Africa (MENA) zone. We examine the effect of surprises from financial markets announcements relating to new, confirmed, and death cases of COVID-19 in each country in the sample. We use the GARCH (1.1) specification by incorporating the surprise component in the estimated model during the period from January 1, 2019 until December 31, 2020. The empirical findings show that the evolution of the daily returns and volatilities of the stock indexes of the MENA zone used in our research shows very significant peaks in particular in the first three months of 2020 during the most significant spread of the COVID-19 epidemic. We show that the announcements of new cases of COVID-19 in the United States (NCUSA) have a significant impact on the Lebanon stock index and on Tunisia's stock index. Announcements of confirmed cases (CCUSA) of COVID-19 present a relative and insignificant impact on all stock market indices of the MENA zone used in our research. Finally, the announcements of the death cases of COVID-19 in the United States (DCUSA) have a significant impact on the stock market index of Morocco, Saudi Arabia, and United Arab Emirates. This chapter is the first to examine the effect of surprises from financial markets announcements relating to new, confirmed, and death cases of COVID-19 on the volatility of financial markets in the MENA zone.

Keywords: COVID-19, surprise, stock market, crisis, MENA zone

5.1. Introduction

The COVID-19 health pandemic, like all previous crises, has severely disrupted both financial markets via stock indexes and the real economy around the world. This pandemic has consequently given rise to major interventions by states in terms of monetary and budgetary policy. The acuteness of the impact of this health crisis has prompted the university community to seek its causes, its effects on the microeconomic and macroeconomic level, and to build different models. Macro-financial models have been extended to analyze the impact of epidemics and the relevance of public interventions. Recent research has assessed the current financial fragility and its relationship to COVID-19 crisis sequences and regulations since 2019 (Zaremba *et al.*, 2020; Albulescu, 2020; Goodell, 2020; Zhang *et al.*, 2020; Costola *et al.*, 2020; Ahundjanov *et al.*, 2020; Engelhardt *et al.*, 2021; Derbali *et al.*, 2021a, 2021b).

The rapid increase in the number of COVID-19 cases around the world has raised concerns about its long-term influence on the global economy. The volatility of the financial market is an important influence. It is generally characterized by rapid change and unpredictability. In practical conditions, it is a statistical measure of the variance among the potential returns of an assumed stock index. In other words, market volatility is defined by the magnitude of index price fluctuations that a market causes over a period of time. While a market is believed to be extremely volatile, it is frequently very unstable and encounters substantial variations in value. Due to its instability, an extremely volatile market is correlated with elevated risk and should be contacted with concern. Typically, extreme market volatility is frequently correlated with economic suffering, while small market volatility is frequently correlated with economic growth.

The US market appears to be the most affected by the COVID-19 pandemic (Al-Awadhi *et al.*, 2020; Phan & Narayan, 2020). The financial markets of the Middle East and North Africa (MENA) zone, which includes all the countries of the MENA, have not been so immune from the consequences of this crisis. The review of empirical research has been limited to studying the consequences of COVID-19 in a single context on different continents or to making comparisons between different countries. The study of the impact of COVID-19 in the US and its influence on the volatility of stock market indices in the MENA zone is unexplored by researchers. To overcome this gap, the objective of this work has been to study the impact of COVID-19 news in the US, in terms of confirmed cases and cases of death, on the volatility of financial markets in the MENA region, mainly Tunisia, Morocco, Palestine, Oman, Saudi Arabia, Bahrain, Egypt, Qatar, Lebanon, United Arab Emirates, and Jordan.

More explicitly, in our work, we study the impact of COVID-19 news on the volatility of financial markets in the MENA zone during the period from January 1, 2019 until December 31, 2020. We examine the effect of surprises from financial market announcements relating to new, confirmed, and death cases of COVID-19 in each country in the sample as well as the US, which is the most affected country in the world. In addition, we study the volatility of financial markets in MENA countries before and during the recent pandemic.

Based on our empirical results, we show that the evolution of the daily returns of the stock indexes of the 11 countries of the MENA zone used in our research shows very significant peaks in particular in the first three months of 2020 during the most significant spread of the COVID-19 epidemic. We find the coincidence of the peaks with the spread of COVID-19 may justify the impact of this epidemic on international financial markets, mostly in the MENA zone. Also, we remark that the conditional volatilities of stock indices of the MENA zone reach their maximum in the first three months of the year 2020.

The empirical results show that the announcements of the new cases of COVID-19 in the United States (NCUSA) have a positive and significant impact on the Lebanon stock index. Also, NCUSA's COVID-19 announcements generate a negative and significant impact on Tunisia's stock index. Announcements of confirmed cases (CCUSA) of COVID-19 present a relative and insignificant impact on all stock market indices of MENA zone countries used in our research.

Finally, the announcements from the death cases of COVID-19 in the United States (DCUSA) have a negative and significant impact on the stock market index of Morocco. The COVID-19 DCUSA in the US has a positive and significant impact on both the stock index of Saudi Arabia and that of the United Arab Emirates.

The rest of this chapter is organized as follows: In the Section 5.2, we present a literature review. Section 5.3 exposes the methodology. In Section 5.4, we present the data. Section 5.5 summarizes the empirical findings. Section 5.6 presents the robustness test of empirical results. Finally, Section 5.7 concludes.

5.2. Literature Review

Mensi *et al.* (2020) study the effects of the COVID-19 pandemic on the multifractality of gold and oil prices, established on increasing and decreasing movements. They use the Multifractal Asymmetric Dissociated Fluctuation Analysis (A-MF-DFA) methodology for an intraday 15-minute interval dataset. Their empirical results reveal strong evidence for asymmetric multifractality, which increases as the fractal scale increases. In addition, they demonstrate that multifractality is particularly more important in the movement of weakness (profit) of Brent oil (gold), and this excess asymmetry has been further highlighted by the outbreak of COVID-19.

Gharib *et al.* (2021) study the causal link between spot prices of crude oil and gold to evaluate how the economic effect of the COVID-19 pandemic influenced them. They examine the prices of West Texas Light (WTI) crude oil and gold during the study period from January 4, 2010 to May 4, 2020. They notice frequent periods of moderate explosiveness in the WTI markets and gold. In addition, they demonstrate a bilateral contagion impact of bubbles on the oil and gold markets through the current coronavirus outbreak.

He *et al.* (2020) examine the direct effects and transmission of the COVID-19 epidemic on international stock markets, such as China, Italy, South Korea, France, Spain, Germany, Japan, and the US. He *et al.* (2020) use t-standard tests and non-parametric Mann–Whitney tests as the appropriate econometric methodology. In addition, He *et al.* (2020) analyze a dataset of daily performance relative to international stock markets used in China, Italy, South Korea, France, Spain, Germany, Japan, and the US. Then, He *et al.* (2020) conclude that the coronavirus has a negative and crucial but short-term influence on the stock markets of affected countries. Furthermore, they find that the impact of the coronavirus on the international stock markets used has influences of two-way transmission between the Asian stock markets and the European and American stock markets.

Additionally, Sansa (2020) initially examines the influence of the coronavirus pandemic on international stock markets throughout the study period from March 1, 2020 to March 25, 2020 in China and the US. Next, Sansa (2020) validates that there is a positive and significant link between the confirmed cases of COVID-19 and the international stock markets used in his study (Shanghai Stock Exchange and New York Dow Jones) during the period of March 1, 2020 to March 25, 2020 in China and the USA. Also, this empirical result states that the COVID-19 pandemic exerted an essential and considerable influence on the international stock markets during the period from March 1, 2020 to March 25, 2020 in China and the USA.

In addition, the new COVID-19 epidemic has particularly influenced international financial markets around the world. It has generated an extraordinary degree of risk, forcing shareholders to tolerate large deficits on any given day of the week. In March 2020, the stock market in the US hit the four-period price surge process in ten days. The most important stock markets recorded in the US, such as the Dow Jones Industrial Average (DJIA) and the Standard & Poor's 500 Index (S&P 500), have fallen significantly (Wagner, 2020).

Many international stock markets around the world have experienced their fastest index decline in the past. Stock markets in Europe, Africa, and Asia also fell (Ashraf, 2020). Assuming the melodramatic arrangements detected recently in many international financial markets all over the world, various current researchers have used many experimental methods to examine the ultimate impacts of the coronavirus on international stock market returns and the level of risk in various countries and influenced states such as China, US, Japan, Korea, Singapore, Germany, Italy, and United Kingdom (Liu *et al.*, 2020; Sharif *et al.*, 2020; Derbali *et al.*, 2021b).

The reviews of the literature have detected the response of international financial markets to the recent epidemic of COVID-19. Professionals and investigators have pointed out that international financial markets have responded immediately to the COVID-19 pandemic. Ramelli & Wagner (2020) state that the market immediately commenced to respond to interests about the prospective economic and financial impacts of COVID-19.

Baret *et al.* (2020) study the influence of the COVID-19 pandemic on international financial market indices and banks. Baret *et al.* (2020) conclude that the COVID-19 pandemic has enormous influence on international financial market indices by means of the collapse of shares, oil, stocks, and bonds throughout the worldwide. This is a confirmation that the COVID-19 outbreak has certainly caused international financial markets to focus and react differently on asset portfolios. Additionally, Baret *et al.* (2020) find that since February 21, 2020 bond yields and oil and stock prices have dropped considerably, and billions of dollars, in virtually all portfolio classifications, have required safety and security.

Youssef *et al.* (2021) investigate the dynamic correlation between stock market indices and the influence of economic policy uncertainty (EPU) in eight countries where the COVID-19 pandemic was most widespread (i.e., China, Italy, France, Germany, Spain, Russia, US, and United Kingdom) by utilizing the time-varying VAR approach (TVP-VAR) for daily data throughout the period of study from 01/01/2015 to 05/18/2020. Their outcomes reveal that the stock markets have been particularly correlated during the period of study, but the dynamic effect achieved remarkable peaks during the COVID-19 epidemic in the first quarter of 2020. Furthermore, they find that the European stock markets (excluding Italy) have spread the outside effect to all stock markets other than the ones they obtained, principally through the COVID-19 epidemic.

In this literature review, the following hypotheses are tested:

H_1: The announcement of new COVID-19 cases in the US is impacting the volatility of stock indices in the MENA region.

H_2: The announcement of a confirmed COVID-19 case in the US affects the volatility of stock indices in the MENA region.

H_3: The announcement of COVID-19 death cases in the US is impacting the volatility of stock indices in the MENA region.

5.3. Methodology

Volatility is an important dimension for finance and economics principally in portfolio managing and optimization, risk measurement and managing, and the pricing of stock market indices. Leptokurtosis (asymmetry), volatility clustering (kurtosis), and leverage are insufficient to explain many of the common core characteristics that relate the financial dataset to linear and nonlinear models and estimates.

This is because the homoscedasticity assumption is not appropriate when using a financial dataset. To estimate return and volatility, Engle (1982) establishes the ARCH (Conditional Autoregressive Heteroskedastic Model) specification, which is further stretched by Bollerslev (1986) to the GARCH (Generalized Autoregressive Conditional Heteroskedastic) model. This type of modeling is generally performed on chronic series with variable volatility. Indeed, financial series are characterized by a variance that is not stable over time. For this type of data, we see, for example, that for some fairly long periods, the volatility is low. This is followed for long periods by high volatility.

This type of time series is characterized by behavior where volatility is low and which tends to follow one another for a known period, as well as, for other periods, by high volatility which tends to follow one another. We then say that the volatility, or variance, of the process is autoregressive since it depends on its past values. Thus, the ARCH (p) (Engle, 1982) and GARCH (p, q) (Bollerslev, 1986) type processes are better suited to take account of this volatile behavior.

The steps of the heteroskedasticity test (ARCH test) are as follows:

(1) Calculate the residual of the regression model ε_t.
(2) Calculate the square of the residuals ε_t^2.
(3) Perform an autoregressive regression of the residuals on p lags where only significant lags are kept:

$$\varepsilon_t^2 = \alpha_0 + \sum_{i=1}^{p} \alpha_i \varepsilon_{t-i}^2. \tag{5.1}$$

(4) Calculate the Lagrange multiplier statistic (LM):

$$LM = nR^2, \tag{5.2}$$

where n and R^2 are, respectively, the number of observations and the coefficient of determination from the regression of the previous step.

Si $LM = nR^2 > \chi^2(p)$, the most appropriate modeling is considered to be of the ARCH(p) type.

Consider $\{x_t\}_{t\in Z}$ a stochastic process of type ARCH(p) (Conditionally Heteroskedastic Autoregressive of order p):

$$x_t = \mu + \varepsilon_t \tag{5.3}$$

and

$$f_{\varepsilon_t|x_{t-1},x_{t-2}\cdots} \to N(0, h_t), \tag{5.4}$$

where its conditional distribution on past information is

$$f_{x_t|x_{t-1},x_{t-2}\cdots} \to N(\mu, h_t) \tag{5.5}$$

with

$$h_t = \varepsilon_t^2 = \alpha_0 + \sum_{i=1}^{p} \alpha_i \varepsilon_{t-i}^2 \tag{5.6}$$

and where

$$\alpha_i \geq 0, \sum_{i=1}^{p} \alpha_i < 1. \tag{5.7}$$

The conditional distribution of the process $\{x_t\}_{t\in\mathbb{Z}}$, that is to say, conditional on its past values, thus has a variance which depends on the past values of x_t.

The conditional expectation is

$$E(x_t|x_{t-1}, x_{t-2}\cdots) = \mu, \quad \forall t. \tag{5.8}$$

The conditional variance is:

$$\text{var}(x_t|x_{t-1}, x_{t-2}\cdots) = h_t, \quad \forall t. \tag{5.9}$$

However, the unconditional, or marginal, distribution of the process $\{x_t\}_{t\in Z}$ is not normal. Thereby,

$$E(x_t) = \mu, \quad \forall t, \tag{5.10}$$

$$\text{var}(x_t) = \frac{\alpha_0}{1 - \sum_{i=1}^{p} \alpha_i}, \quad \forall t. \tag{5.11}$$

This last relation is only valid when the roots of the polynomial $\sum_{i=1}^{p} \alpha_i L^{p-i}$ are outside the unit circle. After taking into account the volatility, the process $\{x_t\}_{t \in Z}$ can be written:

$$x_t = \mu + \sqrt{h_t} w_t \tag{5.12}$$

and

$$w_t \to N(0, 1). \tag{5.13}$$

For the presentation of the GARCH model, it is a generalization of the ARCH(p) process, with:

$$h_t = \varepsilon_t^2 = \alpha_0 + \sum_{i=1}^{p} \alpha_i \varepsilon_{t-i}^2 + \sum_{j=1}^{q} \beta_j h_{t-j}. \tag{5.14}$$

Under the conditions: $\alpha_i \geq 0$ and $\beta_j \geq 0$ and $\sum_{i=1}^{p} \alpha_i + \sum_{j=1}^{q} \beta_j < 1$.

The class of ARCH and GARCH models represents a tailored reaction to income given the specifics of volatility that cannot be accounted for by "classical" techniques. As well, this form of model is established in a univariate context. The expansion of this class of model to a multivariate context made it likely to alleviate the critiques of univariate models which demonstrated inadequacy in to validating the structure of the guarantees portfolio. Certainly, financial theory suggests that the covariances among assets play a defining role in the decision-making of investors in their investment policies.

In this work, we provide a review of the financial and economic literature by integrating an exogenous factor in the GARCH $(1, 1)$ measurement, which computes the COVID-19 shock in the US and its influence on the volatility of stock market indices in the MENA zone. Therefore, the anticipated equivalent of the GARCH model $(1, 1)$ is suggested as follows:

$$h_t = \varepsilon_t^2 = \alpha_0 + \sum_{i=1}^{p} \alpha_i \varepsilon_{t-i}^2 + \sum_{j=1}^{q} \beta_j h_{t-j} + \mu_t S_t, \tag{5.15}$$

where h_t is the dependent variable (to be explained), which is the conditional volatility of the stock market indices of MENA zone countries on day t, and S_t is the independent (explanatory) variable, which indicates the unexpected surprise reports of COVID-19 in the US at day t.

Based on Kuttner (2001), in this chapter, we measure the component of surprise as the scale version of the variation in confirmed cases and deaths from COVID-19 to one day in a period of occurrence (d known as the US COVID-19 Confirmed Case and Death Report). Evidently, the shock element for every confirmed case and adjustment of death cases in the US are presented by the following corresponding:

$$S = \frac{D}{D-d}(f_d - f_{d-1}) \tag{5.16}$$

with f_d involving the total of new (NCUSA), confirmed (CCUSA), and death (DCUSA) cases of COVID-19 in USA at the end of the statement hour (day) d, f_{d-1} characterizing the total new, confirmed, and death cases COVID-19 in USA at the end of the hour statement (day) $(d-1)$, and D revealing the total days of the month.

5.4. Data

The impact of COVID-19 is testing the fragile resilience of the MENA region. This can further exacerbate regional competition and political instability. The virus outbreak has indeed impacted political developments within MENA economies, and their ability to restore and sustain their social contracts is increasingly being questioned.

Our choice of MENA countries seems relevant since the financial benefits are significant and few studies have analyzed this context. We present the database employed in this thesis, which consists of everyday time series of returns and conditional volatilities of stock market indices of MENA economies. Next, as part of the investigation into the impact of announcements of confirmed COVID-19 cases, we focus on the anticipated and surprise elements in the variation of confirmed cases and deaths of COVID-19 in the US.

Our example consists of 11 countries in the MENA zone studied during the period from January 1, 2019 to January 31, 2020 according to Table 5.1. The database utilized in this chapter is obtained from three data sources listed in the following addresses: https://markets.businessinsider.com/currencies, https://data.europa.eu/euodp/en/home, and https://fr.investing.com. The selection of the variation in new, confirmed, and death cases of COVID-19 in the US is validated

Table 5.1. The unconditional correlation matrix.

No.	Country	Name of stock market index	Code
1	Saudi Arabia	SSE TADAWUL	SSE_TADAWUL
2	Palestine	PSE Al-Quds	PSE_AL_QUDS
3	Bahrain	BSE BAX	BSE_BAX
4	Egypt	ESE EGX	ESE_EGX
5	UEA	UEASE ADX	UEASE_ADX
6	Jordan	JSE AMMAN	JSE_AMMAN
7	Lebanon	LSE BLSI	LSE_BLSI
8	Oman	OSE MSI	OSE_MSI
9	Qatar	QSE QSI	QSE_QSI
10	Morocco	MSE MASI	MSE_MASI
11	Tunisia	TSE TUNINDEX	TSE_TUNINDEX

by the assumption that the US was the country most influenced by the pandemic COVID-19 for the study period.

We assume that all gold and bitcoin stock indices are converted to a logarithmic structure. Then, we apply the logarithmic return such that $r_t = \ln(p_t/p_{t-1})$, with P_t representing the stock market price index at time t and P_{t-1} representing the stock market price index at time $t-1$. The list of countries making up the sample is provided in Table 5.1.

In Table 5.2, we summarize the descriptive statistics relating to the daily returns of stock market indices of MENA countries during the study period from January 1, 2019 to December 31, 2020. Based on the results presented in the table, we observe that the smallest average return is equal to −7.04E-06 for the SSE_TADAWUL index (Saudi Arabia) but the largest average is equal to 9.22E-05 for the BSE_BAX index (Bahrain). For the expected volatility of the estimated daily return of stock market indices of MENA countries, which is determined by the standard deviation statistics, we see that the LSE_BLSI (Lebanon) index has the highest daily volatility while the lowest daily rate is that of the PSE_AL_QUDS index (Palestine).

The estimated statistics from Skewness show a negative sign for all stock market indices of MENA countries except the LSE_BLSI (Lebanon) index, which shows a positive sign. The negative sign associated with the asymmetry statistic shows that the estimated distribution of stock market indices of MENA countries (except the

Table 5.2. Descriptive statistics.

Index	BSE_BAX	ESE_EGX	JSE_AMMAN	LSE_BLSI	MSE_MASI	OSE_MSI	PSE_AL_QUDS	QSE_QSI	SSE_TADAWUL	TSE_TUNINDEX	UEASE_ADX
Country	Bahrain	Egypt	Jordan	Lebanon	Morocco	Oman	Palestine	Qatar	Saudi Arabia	Tunisia	United Arab Emirates
Mean	9.22E-05	−0.000269	−0.000207	−0.000322	1.12E-05	−0.000139	−0.000122	−2.16E-05	−7.04E-06	−3.34E-05	2.79E-05
Median	0.000233	8.61E-05	1.51E-06	−6.14E-05	4.07E-05	−0.000114	−0.000152	1.09E-05	0.000459	8.06E-05	9.30E-05
Maximum	0.010510	0.024983	0.008668	0.068207	0.023041	0.017112	0.011254	0.014664	0.028426	0.008240	0.035074
Minimum	−0.026060	−0.053817	−0.020269	−0.053150	−0.040093	−0.024907	−0.016248	−0.044331	−0.073889	−0.018179	−0.036508
Std. dev.	0.002994	0.006453	0.002458	0.007836	0.004248	0.002719	0.001933	0.004439	0.007375	0.002304	0.006018
Skewness	−2.405922	−2.258924	−1.810608	1.117204	−2.464654	−1.199919	−0.982133	−2.264779	−3.420416	−2.325285	−0.465337
Kurtosis	20.93203	19.22908	15.41588	36.53804	28.56637	20.82952	16.63308	24.58119	30.02868	18.32355	16.09750
Jarque-Bera	7181.488	5912.378	3484.735	23537.35	14123.70	6742.731	3952.486	10130.52	16194.72	5342.479	3591.886
Prob.	0.000000	0.000000	0.000000	0.000000	0.000000	0.000000	0.000000	0.000000	0.000000	0.000000	0.000000
Obs.	500	500	500	500	500	500	500	500	500	500	500

Notes: This table presents a summary of descriptive statistics of the daily returns of the stock indexes of the 11 MENA countries (Bahrain, Egypt, Jordan, Lebanon, Morocco, Oman, Palestine, Qatar, Saudi Arabia, Tunisia, and United Arab Emirates) used in our research during the study period from January 1, 2019 to December 31, 2020.

LSE_BLSI index) is skewed to the left while the estimated distribution of the LSE_BLSI (Lebanon) index is asymmetric to the right. In addition, the estimated kurtosis coefficient statistics are high and greater than unity (1). Finally, based on the estimated values of the statistics of Jarque-Bera, Skewness, and Kurtosis, we confirm the rejection of the null hypothesis compared to the normal dispersion of the stock market indices of the countries of the MENA zone used in our research.

Figure 5.1 shows the evolution of the daily returns of the stock indexes of the 11 countries of the MENA zone used in our research during the study period from January 1, 2019 to December 31, 2020. We see that the daily returns of the stock indexes of the 11 countries in the MENA zone show very significant peaks in their evolutions. These peaks are observed in particular during the first three months of 2020 during the most significant spread of the COVID-19 epidemic. These three months are marked by the high level of confirmed cases of COVID-19 and death cases in all countries of the world, particularly in the US. Also, the coincidence of the peaks and the spread of COVID-19 may justify the impact of this epidemic on international financial markets, mainly in the MENA zone.

Table 5.3 summarizes the most important statistics for the unconditional correlation matrix (Pearson correlation) for stock market indices of MENA countries during the study period from January 1, 2019 to December 31, 2020. From the correlation unconditional shown in this table, we see that there is a positive and negative correlation between the three indicators used to express the effect of the announcements relating to COVID-19 in the US and the stock market indices of the countries of the MENA zone. The first CCUSA indicator (confirmed cases in the USA) shows a positive correlation with the following indices: BSE_BAX, LSE_BLSI, MSE_MASI, PSE_AL_QUDS, SSE_TADAWUL, TSE_TUNINDEX, and UEASE_ADX. It also exhibits a negative correlation with the following indices: ESE_EGX, JSE_AMMAN, OSE_MSI, and QSE_QSI. This result proves that the shocks of COVID-19 can justify the impact of announcements of confirmed cases of COVID-19 in the USA on the stock market indices of countries in the MENA zone during the study period from January 1, 2019 to December 31, 2020.

The second NCUSA indicator (new cases in the USA) shows a positive correlation with the following indices: ESE_EGX,

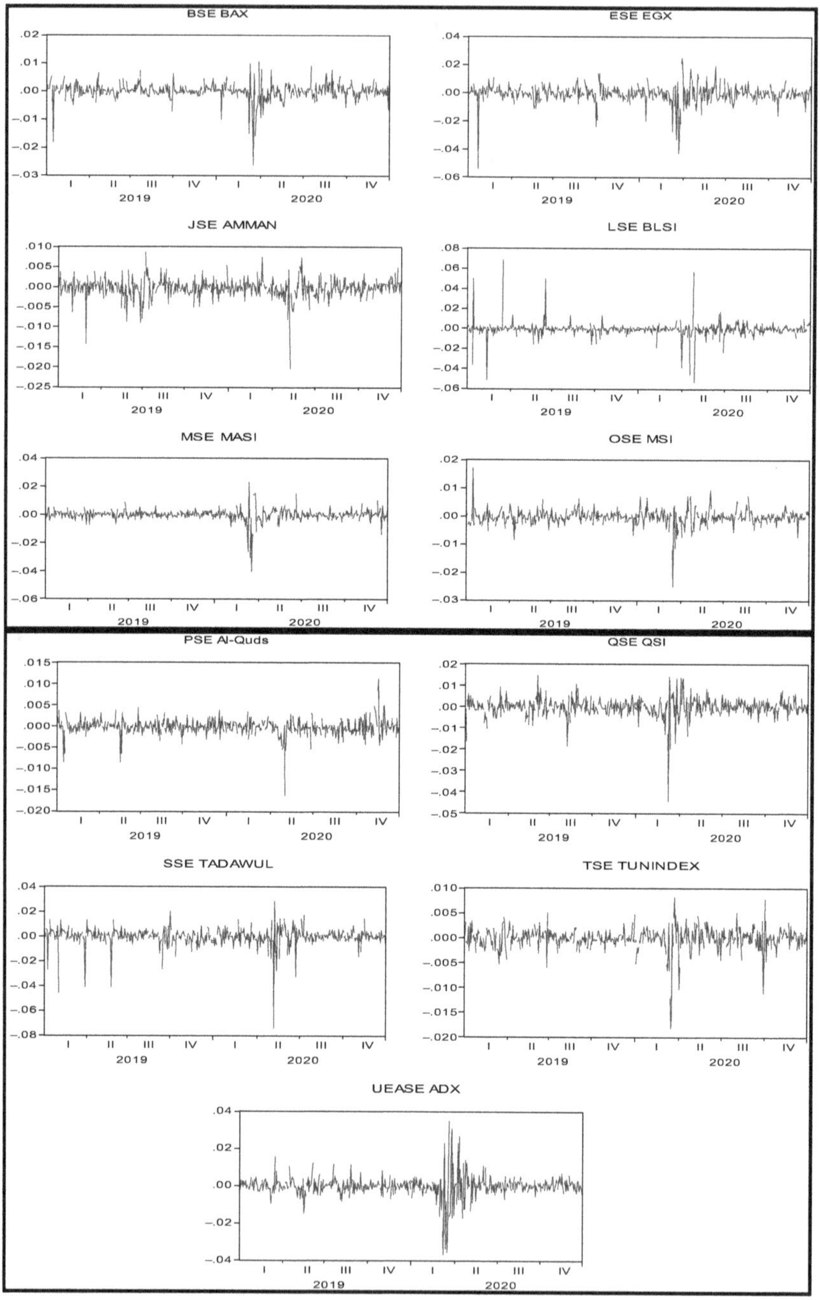

Figure 5.1. The evolution of stock market returns in the MENA zone.

Table 5.3. The unconditional correlation matrix.

	BSE_ BAX	ESE_ EGX	JSE_ AMMAN	LSE_ BLSI	MSE_ MASI	OSE_ MSI	PSE_ AL_QUDS
	Bahrain	Egypt	Jordan	Lebanon	Morocco	Oman	Palestine
BSE_BAX	1	0.070	0.082	0.053	0.112	0.036	0.038
ESE_EGX	0.070	1	0.028	0.010	0.095	0.087	−0.048
JSE_AMMAN	0.082	0.028	1	0.034	−0.022	0.052	0.034
LSE_BLSI	0.053	0.010	0.034	1	−0.005	0.011	0.006
MSE_MASI	0.112	0.095	−0.022	−0.005	1	0.070	−0.059
OSE_MSI	0.036	0.087	0.052	0.011	0.070	1	−0.071
PSE_AL_QUDS	0.038	−0.048	0.034	0.006	−0.059	−0.071	1
QSE_QSI	0.134	0.023	0.060	−0.001	−0.001	0.000	−0.002
SSE_TADAWUL	0.012	−0.053	0.048	−0.018	0.000	0.056	−0.036
TSE_TUNINDEX	0.223	0.035	−0.006	0.043	0.373	0.188	0.011
UEASE_ADX	0.294	−0.056	0.013	0.071	0.128	0.038	0.061
CCUSA	0.006	−0.011	−0.061	0.004	0.022	−0.035	0.072
DCUSA	−0.027	0.004	0.018	−0.101	0.013	0.005	0.015
NCUSA	−0.012	−0.091	−0.020	0.138	−0.017	0.061	−0.051

(Continued)

Table 5.3. (*Continued*)

	QSE_ QSI	SSE_ TADAWUL	TSE_ TUNINDEX	UEASE_ ADX	CCUSA	DCUSA	NCUSA
	Qatar	Saudi Arabia	Tunisia	United Arab Emirates	United States		
BSE_BAX	0.134	0.012	0.223	0.294	0.006	−0.027	−0.012
ESE_EGX	0.023	−0.053	0.035	−0.056	−0.011	0.004	−0.091
JSE_AMMAN	0.060	0.048	−0.006	0.013	−0.061	0.018	−0.020
LSE_BLSI	−0.001	−0.018	0.043	0.071	0.004	−0.101	0.138
MSE_MASI	−0.001	0.000	0.373	0.128	0.022	0.013	−0.017
OSE_MSI	0.000	0.056	0.188	0.038	−0.035	0.005	0.061
PSE_AL_QUDS	−0.002	−0.036	0.011	0.061	0.072	0.015	−0.051
QSE_QSI	1	−0.040	0.033	0.318	−0.108	−0.008	−0.060
SSE_TADAWUL	−0.040	1	0.066	−0.028	0.072	0.091	0.029
TSE_TUNINDEX	0.033	0.066	1	0.232	0.021	0.021	−0.029
UEASE_ADX	0.318	−0.028	0.232	1	0.016	−0.055	−0.036
CCUSA	−0.108	0.072	0.021	0.016	1	0.016	0.045
DCUSA	−0.008	0.091	0.021	−0.055	0.016	1	0.056
NCUSA	−0.060	0.029	−0.029	−0.036	0.045	0.056	1

Notes: This table presents the unconditional correlation matrix between the daily returns of the stock indices of the 11 countries of the MENA zone (Bahrain, Egypt, Jordan, Lebanon, Morocco, Oman, Palestine, Qatar, Saudi Arabia, Tunisia, and The United Arab Emirates) used in our research and the three indicators used to measure the component of surprise resulting from announcements of new, confirmed, and death cases from COVID-19 during the study period from January 1, 2019 to December 31, 2020.

JSE_AMMAN, MSE_MASI, OSE_MSI, PSE_AL_QUDS, SSE_TADAWUL, and TSE_TUNINDEX. It also exhibits a negative correlation with the following indices: BSE_BAX, LSE_BLSI, QSE_QSI, and UEASE_ADX. This result shows that the shocks resulting from the announcements of new cases of COVID-19 in the USA impact the stock market indices of countries in the MENA zone during the study period from January 1, 2019 to December 31, 2020.

Finally, the third DCUSA indicator (death cases in the USA) shows a positive correlation with the following indices: LSE_BLSI, OSE_MSI, and SSE_TADAWUL. It also exhibits a negative correlation with the following indices: BSE_BAX, ESE_EGX, JSE_AMMAN, MSE_MASI, PSE_AL_QUDS, QSE_QSI, TSE_TUNINDEX, and UEASE_ADX. This result shows that the shocks resulting from the announcements of new cases of COVID-19 in the USA affect the stock market indices of countries in the MENA zone during the study period from January 1, 2019 to December 31, 2020.

We use the augmented Dickey–Fuller test and the Phillips Perron test to study the stationarity of the stock market indices of MENA countries used in our research during the study period from January 1, 2019 to December 31, 2020. From Table 5.3, we conclude that all the stock market indices used in our chapter are stationary in level based on the values of the statistics "*t*-statistic" and the level of probability "Prob. *<5%" relating to the tests of Dickey–Fuller increased and in the test of Phillips Perron. Subsequently, the absence of unit roots at the level of the indices used justifies the absence of the problems during the estimation of the models used.

5.5. Empirical Results

Figure 5.2 shows the evolution of conditional volatilities of stock market indices of MENA countries used in our research during the study period from January 1, 2019 to December 31, 2020. We can see that the conditional volatilities of stock indices of the MENA zone reach their maximum in the first three months of the year 2020. This period evidences a high intensity of confirmed cases of COVID-19 and cases of death in most Western countries, mainly in the USA. Additionally, Figure 5.2 can confirm the impact of COVID-19 announcements on MENA financial markets.

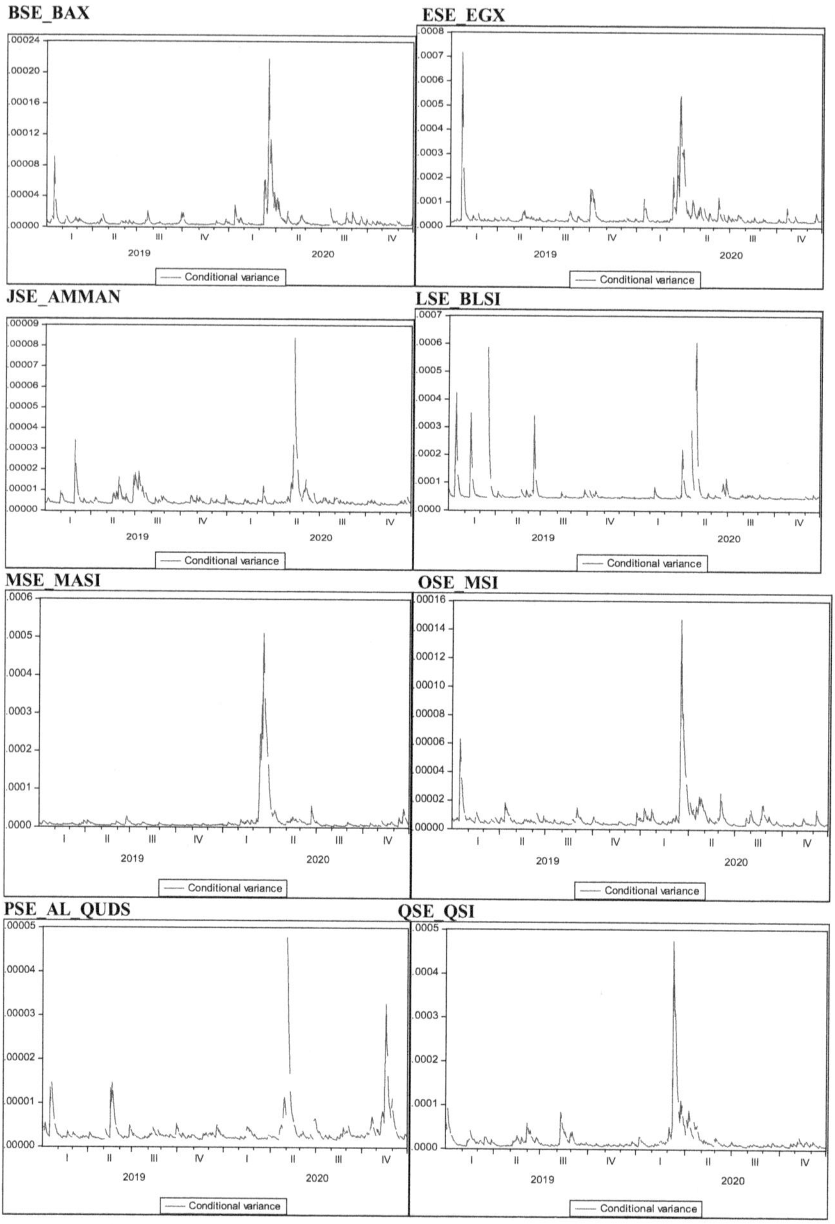

Figure 5.2. The conditional volatilities of stock market indices in the MENA zone.

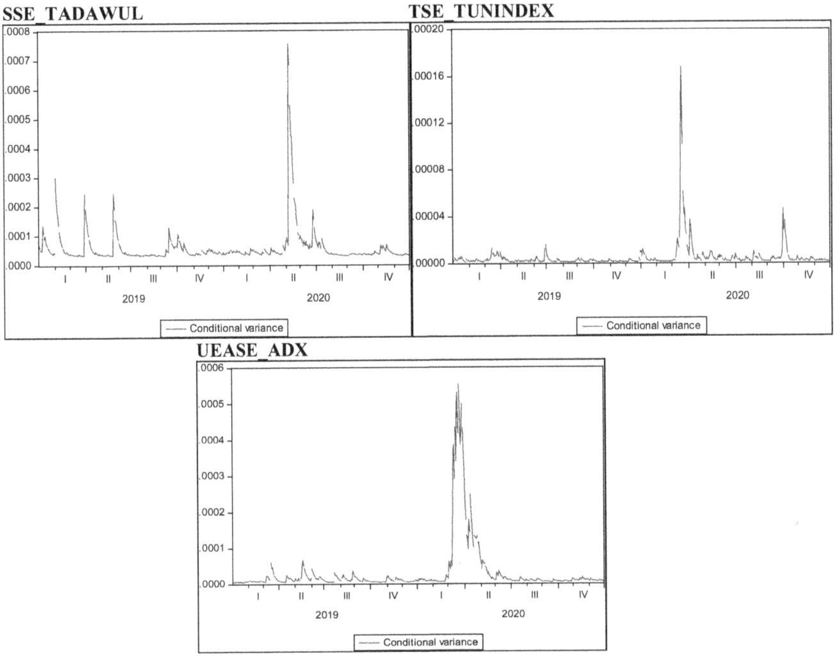

Figure 5.2. (*Continued*)

Table 5.4 summarizes the descriptive statistics relating to the three indicators used to measure the surprise component resulting from the announcements of confirmed, new, and death cases from COVID-19 during the study period from January 1, 2019 to December 31, 2020. Based on the results presented in this table, we observe that the smallest mean is equal to 0.000532 for the variable CCUSA (the cases confirmed in the USA), but the largest mean is equal to 0.015775 for the variable DCUSA (cases of death in the USA). For the estimated expected volatility of the three indicators used to measure the surprise component from COVID-19 announcements in the US, which is determined by the standard deviation statistic, we see that the DCUSA variable has the highest daily volatility while that the lowest daily volatility is that of the variable CCUSA.

Skewness's estimated statistics show a positive sign for all three metrics used to measure the surprise component from COVID-19 announcements. The positive sign associated with the asymmetry statistic shows that the estimated distribution of the three indicators

Table 5.4. The unit root test

Test	Country	Augmented Dickey–Fuller test statistic			Phillips Perron test statistic		
		t-stat	Prob.*	Stationarity	Adj. t-stat	Prob.*	Stationarity
BSE_BAX	Bahrain	−9.952795	0.0000	Yes	−19.95854	0.0000	Yes
ESE_EGX	Egypt	−18.09491	0.0000	Yes	−18.03359	0.0000	Yes
JSE_AMMAN	Jordan	−8.041487	0.0000	Yes	−19.75581	0.0000	Yes
LSE_BLSI	Lebanon	−26.08405	0.0000	Yes	−26.19445	0.0000	Yes
MSE_MASI	Morocco	−18.72617	0.0000	Yes	−18.74209	0.0000	Yes
OSE_MSI	Oman	−17.36152	0.0000	Yes	−17.49819	0.0000	Yes
PSE_AL_QUDS	Palestine	−19.95114	0.0000	Yes	−20.63348	0.0000	Yes
QSE_QSI	Qatar	−21.25371	0.0000	Yes	−21.29700	0.0000	Yes
SSE_TADAWUL	Saudi Arabia	−9.684188	0.0000	Yes	−23.10742	0.0000	Yes
TSE_TUNINDEX	Tunisia	−15.09679	0.0000	Yes	−15.15934	0.0000	Yes
UEASE_ADX	United Arab Emirates	−10.89707	0.0000	Yes	−21.47859	0.0000	Yes

Notes: This table summarizes the unit root test of the daily returns of the stock indexes of the 11 MENA countries (Bahrain, Egypt, Jordan, Lebanon, Morocco, Oman, Palestine, Qatar, Saudi Arabia, Tunisia and The United Arab Emirates) used in our research work and during the study period from January 1, 2019 to December 31, 2020. We use the augmented Dickey–Fuller test and the Phillips Perron test to study the stationarity of the different stock market indices used in our this chapter. The statistical significance at the threshold of 1% is noted by *.

Table 5.5. Descriptive statistics of surprise components.

	NCUSA	CCUSA	DCUSA
Mean	0.004526	0.000532	0.015775
Median	0.000000	0.000000	0.000000
Maximum	1.783979	1.250725	1.975281
Minimum	−2.077267	−0.824727	−1.950323
Std. dev.	0.271697	0.101437	0.346238
Skewness	0.331656	4.504925	0.011424
Kurtosis	21.10045	71.68887	16.73402
Jarque-Bera	6834.712	99986.22	3929.661
Prob.	0.000000	0.000000	0.000000
Obs.	500	500	500

Notes: This table summarizes the descriptive statistics of the surprise from the announcements of new, confirmed, and death cases of COVID-19 and the surprises in the reporting of death cases in the US during the study period from January 1, 2019 to December 31, 2020. New, confirmed, and death cases of COVID-19 are collected from https://data.europa.eu/euodp/en/ho me. Then, we follow the approach of Kuttner (2001) and specify the surprises discovered using the change in new, confirmed, and death cases of COVID-19 for each day.

is skewed to the right. In addition, the estimated kurtosis coefficient statistics are high and greater than unity (1). Finally, based on the estimated values of the statistics of Jarque-Bera, Skewness, and Kurtosis, we confirm the rejection of the null hypothesis compared to the normal dispersion of the three indicators used in our research.

Then, we use the augmented Dickey–Fuller test and the Phillips Perron test to study the stationarity of the three indicators used to measure the surprise component resulting from the COVID-19 announcements in the US during the study period from January 1, 2019 to December 31, 2020. From Table 5.5, we conclude that the three indicators used in our chapter are stationary in level based on the values of "t-statistic" and on the "Prob. $* < 5\%$" relating to the augmented Dickey–Fuller tests and the Phillips Perron test. Subsequently, the absence of unit roots at the level of the three indicators justifies the inexistence of the problems during the estimation of the models used.

Figure 5.3 shows the evolution of the conditional volatilities of the three indicators used to measure the surprise component resulting

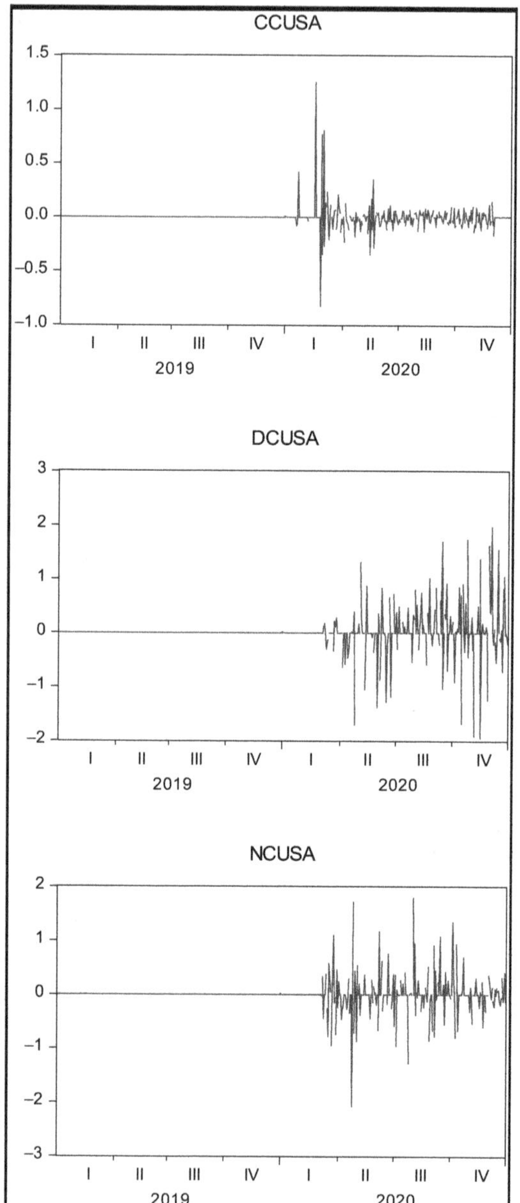

Figure 5.3. The unit root test of surprise components.

from the COVID-19 announcements in the US during the study period from January 1, 2019 to December 31, 2020. We see that the conditional volatilities of the three indicators (NCUSA, CCUSA, and DCUSA) reach their maximum in the first three months of the year 2020.

In econometrics, the autoregressive conditional heteroskedasticity (ARCH) model is a statistical model for time series data that describes the variance of the current error term or innovation as a function of the actual sizes of the error terms of the periods previous; frequently, the variance is associated with the squares of preceding inventions. The ARCH model is suitable when the error variance in a time series observes an autoregressive (AR) model; if an autoregressive moving average (ARMA) model is understood for the error variance, the model is a generalized autoregressive conditional heteroskedasticity (GARCH) model.

Then, ARCH specification are frequently employed to model financial time series that show time-varying volatility and volatility grouping, that is, phases of instabilities punctuated with times of relative composure. ARCH-type models are occasionally believed to be components of the family of stochastic volatility specifications, though this is precisely inaccurate since at time t the volatility is absolutely predetermined (deterministic), taking into account the preceding values.

The results of the GARCH model estimation of the stock market indices of MENA zone countries used in our research throughout the study period from January 1, 2019 to December 31, 2020 are presented in Table 5.6. Thus, we have used two types of estimates: an estimate without integration of surprise and an estimate with integration of surprise measured by the three indicators, NCUSA, CCUSA, and DCUSA.

In the first estimate, we estimate the GARCH model (1.1) for the stock market indices of 11 MENA countries. On the basis of the estimation results, there is a significant and a positive effect for the two parameters of the GARCH model (1.1) at a significance level of 1%. This effect is observed in the three estimates with integration of surprise measured by the three variables, NCUSA, CCUSA, and DCUSA.

Table 5.6. The unit root test of surprise components.

	Augmented Dickey–Fuller test statistic			Phillips Perron test statistic		
Test	t-stat	Prob.*	Stationarity	Adj. t-stat	Prob.*	Stationarity
NCUSA	−31.07856	0.0000	Yes	−31.41265	0.0000	Yes
CCUSA	−3.770931	0.0035	Yes	−31.90741	0.0000	Yes
DCUSA	−7.621472	0.0000	Yes	−25.80942	0.0000	Yes

Notes: This table summarizes the unit root test of the three indicators used to measure the component of surprise from COVID-19 announcements in the US used in our research during the study period from January 1, 2019 to December 31, 2020. We use the augmented Dickey–Fuller test and the Phillips Perron test to study the stationarity of the three indicators used in this chapter.

Then, we use the GARCH model (1.1) for the stock market indices of MENA zone countries used in our research by integrating the first component of the surprise, namely, the NCUSA. According to the results presented in Table 5.6, we note that the announcements of the NCUSA have a positive and significant influence on the LSE_BLSI (Lebanon) index at a threshold of 1%. This means that if the variable NCUSA increases by one unit, then the return of the Lebanon stock index increases by 0.004611 units. So, we can explain this by the sensitivity of the financial market of Lebanon to external effects such as the announcements of the NCUSA. It appears from this relationship that the Lebanese market is so fragile that it is largely dependent on the American market due to its dire economic conditions (over-indebtedness, inflation, flagrant drop in the value of the currency, etc.).

According to the same results presented in Table 5.7, we also note that the announcements of the NCUSA have a negative and significant impact on the TSE_TUNINDEX index (Tunisia) at a threshold of 1%. This means that if the NCUSA variable increases by one unit, then the return on the Tunisian stock market index decreases by 0.00040 units. This can be explained by the sensitivity of the Tunisian financial market to external effects such as the announcements of the NCUSA. Also, one can justify the presence of dependence between

Table 5.7. The empirical results of GARCH estimation.

Stock market indices	Country	Estimation without integration of surprise			Estimation with integration of surprise NCUSA			
		The estimated parameters						
		α_0	α_i	β_j	α_0	α_i	β_j	μ_t
BSE_BAX	Bahrain	1.36E−06	0.258181	0.587006	1.38E−06	0.269501	0.576582	0.000286
		(6.4101)*	(5.5552)*	(10.071)*	(6.6084)*	(5.2818)*	(9.5893)*	(0.8413)
ESE_EGX	Egypt	8.92E−06	0.239556	0.558154	8.94E−06	0.239199	0.557628	−0.00027
		(5.6632)*	(4.2301)*	(7.3593)*	(5.6094)*	(4.1638)*	(7.2588)*	(−0.297)
JSE_AMMAN	Jordan	1.21E−06	0.151981	0.628047	1.24E−06	0.156528	0.618319	−0.00041
		(4.6582)*	(5.5847)*	(8.8285)*	(4.6436)*	(5.5118)*	(8.4252)*	(−1.074)
LSE_BLSI	Lebanon	1.85E−05	0.116136	0.594044	5.26E−05	0.185237	−0.05801	0.004611
		(12.427)*	(6.1090)*	(18.810)*	(39.336)*	(4.1199)*	(−3.203)*	(10.480)*
MSE_MASI	Morocco	8.79E−07	0.213456	0.717708	7.99E−07	0.207038	0.731708	−0.00036
		(3.6500)*	(6.9404)*	(16.272)*	(3.4442)*	(7.0012)*	(17.469)*	(−1.001)
OSE_MSI	Oman	8.14E−07	0.198439	0.704870	8.02E−07	0.197800	0.707197	0.000245
		(4.7829)*	(8.5223)*	(20.960)*	(4.7956)*	(8.4717)*	(21.213)*	(0.5162)
PSE_AL_QUDS	Palestine	4.14E−07	0.158956	0.727314	4.12E−07	0.158539	0.728143	−0.00016
		(4.36137)*	(5.9775)*	(17.066)*	(4.3640)*	(5.9759)*	(17.165)*	(−0.543)
QSE_QSI	Qatar	1.23E−06	0.220418	0.727767	1.21E−06	0.221131	0.728479	0.000304
		(4.4255)*	(10.9501)*	(22.961)*	(4.4092)*	(9.8338)*	(22.751)*	(0.4496)
SSE_TADAWUL	Saudi Arabia	7.39E−06	0.127438	0.759228	7.81E−06	0.144247	0.740799	−0.00116
		(3.3373)*	(3.5419)*	(11.245)*	(3.2233)*	(3.2446)*	(9.7113)*	(−1.243)
TSE_TUNINDEX	Tunisia	4.47E−07	0.315094	0.589078	4.56E−07	0.331362	0.572891	(−0.00040)
		(6.5044)*	(6.2834)*	(18.576)*	(6.2137)*	(6.4067)*	(17.037)*	(−2.580)
UEASE_ADX	United Arab Emirates	1.16E−06	0.193567	0.749914	1.15E−06	0.193206	0.750675	−0.00081
		(4.6787)*	(6.1446)*	(20.266)*	(4.6700)*	(6.1959)*	(20.397)*	(−1.017)

(*Continued*)

Table 5.7. (*Continued*)

Stock market indices	Country	Estimation with integration of surprise							
		CCUSA				DCUSA			
		The estimated parameters							
		$\boldsymbol{\alpha}_0$	$\boldsymbol{\alpha}_i$	$\boldsymbol{\beta}_j$	$\boldsymbol{\mu}_t$	$\boldsymbol{\alpha}_0$	$\boldsymbol{\alpha}_i$	$\boldsymbol{\beta}_j$	$\boldsymbol{\mu}_t$
BSE_BAX	Bahrain	1.39E−06	0.266186	0.577287	0.000655	0.256402	0.256402	0.588634	−0.00020
		(6.6453)*	(5.4321)*	(9.7304)*	(0.4614)	(5.5699)*	(5.5699)*	(10.118)*	(−0.554)
ESE_EGX	Egypt	8.91E−06	0.238442	0.558905	0.000674	8.92E−06	0.239482	0.558119	2.97E−05
		(5.5965)*	(4.0906)*	(7.2651)*	(0.2456)	(5.5413)*	(4.1039)*	(7.1746)*	(0.0362)
JSE_AMMAN	Jordan	1.14E−06	0.149714	0.642295	−0.00183	1.22E−06	0.152024	0.627160	0.000204
		(4.5833)*	(5.5917)*	(9.2577)*	(−1.416)	(4.5621)*	(5.4493)*	(8.5742)*	(0.8427)
LSE_BLSI	Lebanon	1.85E−05	0.116242	0.594175	0.000338	1.99E−05	0.113178	0.569224	−0.00153
		(12.320)*	(6.0886)*	(18.706)*	(0.0525)	(7.1276)*	(5.8197)*	(9.7964)*	(−0.946)
MSE_MASI	Morocco	8.75E−07	0.212513	0.718846	0.000326	8.26E−07	0.220734	0.718179	(−0.00056)
		(3.6350)*	(6.8857)*	(16.323)*	(0.2226)	(3.6010)*	(6.7900)*	(16.505)*	(−−2.28)**
OSE_MSI	Oman	8.32E−07	0.198614	0.701806	−0.00033	8.14E−07	0.198418	0.704827	6.49E−06
		(4.7546)*	(8.5551)*	(20.264)*	(−0.388)	(4.7824)*	(8.5015)*	(20.951)*	(0.0184)
PSE_AL_QUDS	Palestine	4.14E−07	0.158138	0.727723	0.000713	4.15E−07	0.158855	0.727228	5.04E−05
		(4.3658)*	(5.9657)*	(17.074)*	(0.6647)	(4.3438)*	(5.8575)*	(16.944)*	(0.2528)
QSE_QSI	Qatar	1.22E−06	0.218921	0.729413	0.000358	1.20E−06	0.225747	0.725922	0.000385
		(4.4203)*	(8.3228)*	(21.957)*	(0.2825)	(4.3296)*	(10.913)*	(23.018)*	(1.1086)
SSE_TADAWUL	Saudi Arabia	7.58E−06	0.134600	0.750405	0.004962	8.43E−06	0.148625	0.724043	0.001906
		(3.2541)*	(3.3716)*	(10.379)*	(0.8876)	(3.0233)*	(3.0315)*	(8.2846)*	(2.1465)**
TSE_TUNINDEX	Tunisia	4.53E−07	0.320785	0.583334	0.000527	4.71E−07	0.336228	0.566243	0.000232
		(6.4786)*	(6.2893)*	(18.133)*	(0.6300)	(6.6272)*	(6.0851)*	(16.833)*	(1.6136)
UEASE_ADX	United Arab Emirates	1.19E−06	0.198664	0.743111	−0.00180	1.22E−06	0.203034	0.737266	(−0.00073)
		(4.8877)*	(5.9873)*	(20.086)*	(−1.126)	(4.7219)*	(5.9558)*	(18.569)*	(−1.78)***

Notes: This table summarizes the coefficients estimated from GARCH models (1,1). To empirically test this model, we used the daily returns of stock market indices of MENA countries used in our research during the study period from January 1, 2019 to December 31, 2020. The dependent variable is defined by volatility conditional ($\boldsymbol{h}_t$) of each stock market index used. $\boldsymbol{\alpha}_0$, $\boldsymbol{\alpha}_i$, $\boldsymbol{\beta}_j$, and $\boldsymbol{\mu}_t$ are the coefficients of the explanatory variables estimated in our research. The statistical significance at the threshold of 1%, 5%, and 10% is noted as *, **, and ***. Values in parentheses show the t-students for each variable.

the financial markets in the US and Tunisia due in large part to the closeness of trade between the two countries and the significant indebtedness of Tunisia, which seeks sources of financing. In addition, it appears that the announcements of the NCUSA have a relative and insignificant impact on the other stock market indices of the countries of the MENA zone used in our research during the period of study from January 1, 2019 to December 31, 2020.

In the third estimate, we integrate the variable CCUSA, which measures the announcements of the CCUSA during the study period from January 1, 2019 to December 31, 2020. Thus, we notice that this variable presents a relative and insignificant impact on all stock market indices of MENA countries used in our research. This is because investors are already aware of confirmed cases, and it is the announcements of new cases that are more relevant.

Finally, in the fourth estimate, we integrate the variable DCUSA, which measures the announcements of the DCUSA during the study period from January 1, 2019 to December 31, 2020.

5.6. Robustness Test of Empirical Results

The purpose of our research is to investigate the influence of COVID-19 on financial markets in the MENA zone during the study period from January 1, 2019 to December 31, 2020. Consequently, the experimental outcomes in our chapter show that announcements from COVID-19 in the US have an impact on stock market indices of countries in the MENA zone, mainly on stock market indices in Lebanon, Tunisia, Morocco, Saudi Arabia, and the United Arab Emirates.

To confirm these results, we present the Robustness test of the empirical results. This test is presented in Figure 5.4, in which we test the conditional volatility of stock market indices in Lebanon, Tunisia, Morocco, Saudi Arabia, and the United Arab Emirates without integration and with integration of the COVID-19 component. This figure proves the existence of the impact of COVID-19 on financial markets in the MENA zone during the study period from January 1, 2019 to December 31, 2020.

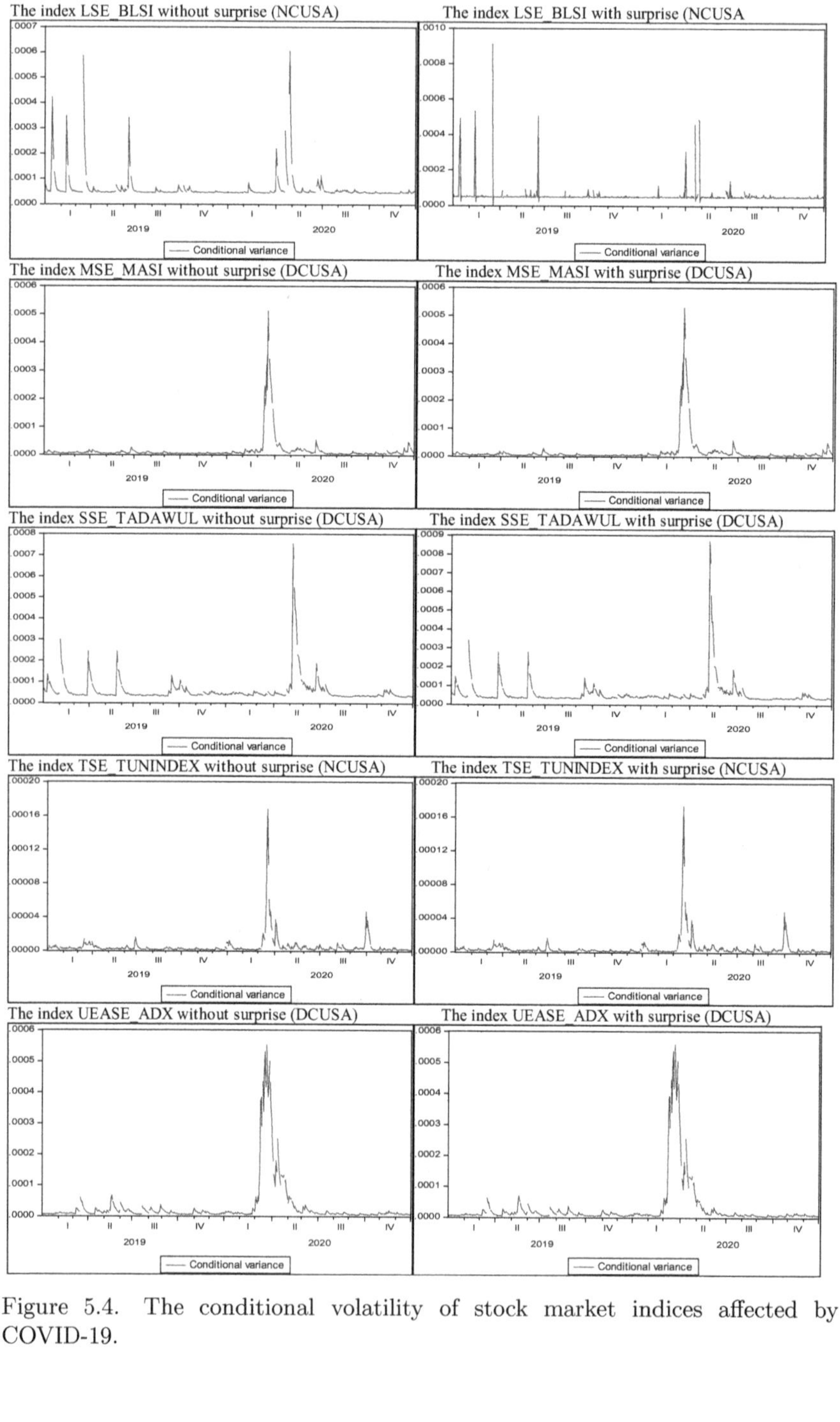

Figure 5.4. The conditional volatility of stock market indices affected by COVID-19.

5.7. Conclusion

To achieve the objective of this chapter, we present an extensive literature review of the effect of COVID-19 case announcements on stock market indices in several contexts. This literature review showed different results. It is for this reason that we formulate three hypotheses to be tested at the methodological level. The use of the GARCH estimation model is the most appropriate for this chapter. The empirical results show that the announcements of the NCUSA have a positive and significant influence on the Lebanon stock index. NCUSA-19 announcements also generate a negative and significant impact on Tunisia's stock index. On the other hand, NCUSA's announcements of COVID-19 generate a relative and insignificant impact on the other stock market indices of countries in the MENA zone.

Announcements of confirmed cases (CCUSA) present a relative and insignificant influence on all stock market indices of MENA zone countries used in our research.

The announcements from the DCUSA have a negative and significant influence on the stock market index of Morocco. The DCUSA announcements in the US have a positive and significant impact on the stock index of both Saudi Arabia and the United Arab Emirates. However, the announcements of DCUSA have a relative and insignificant impact on the other stock market indices of the countries of the MENA zone.

To conclude, we can say that the announcements from COVID-19 in the US have an impact on the stock market indices of countries in the MENA zone, mainly on the stock indexes of Lebanon, Tunisia, Morocco, Saudi Arabia, and the United Arab Emirates. Thus, we responded to our objective by affirming that there is an effect of COVID-19 on the financial markets of the MENA zone throughout the study period from January 1, 2019 to December 31, 2020.

Our results present an advantage for the analysis of the financial and economic consequences of the epidemic by offering a confirmation that the surprises of the COVID-19 virus have two-way ripple effects on the international financial stock markets mainly the markets of the MENA zone. This paper is a very important motivation for investors, policy makers, portfolio risk managers and administrators.

This chapter provides important motivation for investors, policymakers, portfolio risk managers, and administrators.

From a policymaking perspective, discovering accurate and helpful justifications of the volatility spillovers through the international financial stock markets, especially in the MENA zone, is essential in establishing useful monetary policy strategies and healthy approaches. From the perspective of portfolio risk managers and administrators, our experimental outcomes are reliable with the recommendation of cross-market hedging. Our experimental outcomes have useful consequences. They are beneficial for policymakers who have to make judgments and preferences on financial solidity processes.

Finally, our chapter presents an essential limitation for the incorporation on other control variables in the estimated model. In this case, to improve upon our chapter, one can use other indicators, such as monetary policy surprises, war surprises, political surprises, and economic and social indicators. These indicators can explain the volatility of the financial stock market indices in the MENA zone.

Acknowledgments

The authors are grateful to the editors of this book and the anonymous referees for their extremely helpful recommendations to enhance the quality of the chapter.

References

Ahundjanov, B. B., Akhundjanov, S. B., & Okhunjanov, B. B. (2020). Information search and financial markets under COVID-19. *Entropy*, *22*(7), 791. https://doi.org/10.3390/e22070791.

Al-Awadhi, A. M., Alsaifi, K., Al-Awadhi, A., & Alhammadi, S. (2020). Death and contagious infectious diseases: Impact of the COVID-19 virus on stock market returns. *Journal of Behavioral and Experimental Finance*, *27*(3), 100326. https://doi.org/10.1016/j.jbef.2020.100326.

Albulescu, C. T. (2020). COVID-19 and the United States financial markets' volatility. *Finance Research Letters, 38*(1), 101699. https://doi.org/10.1016/j.frl.2020.101699.

Ashraf, B. N. (2020). Stock markets' reaction to COVID-19: Cases or fatalities? *Research in International Business and Finance, 54*(4), 101249. https://doi.org/10.1016/j.ribaf.2020.101249.

Baret, S., Celner, A., Reilly, M. O., & Shilling, M. (2020). COVID-19 potential implications for the banking and capital markets sector. *Maintaining Business And operational resilience, 10*, 1–20. https://www2.deloitte.com/us/en/insights/economy/covid-19/banking-and-capital-markets-impact-covid-19.html?id=us:2em:3pa:financial-services:eng:di:031720.

Bollerslev, T. (1986). Generalized autoregressive conditional heteroskedasticity. *Journal of Econometrics, 31*(3), 307–327. https://doi.org/10.1016/0304-4076(86)90063-1.

Costola, M., Nofer, M., Hinz, O., & Pelizzon, L. (2020). *Machine Learning Sentiment Analysis, COVID-19 News and Stock Market Reactions.* SAFE Working Paper, No. 288. http://hdl.handle.net/10419/224131.

Derbali, A., Naoui, K., & Jamel, L. (2021a). COVID-19 news in USA and in China: Which is suitable in explaining the nexus among Bitcoin and Gold? P*acific Accounting Review, 33*(5), 578–595. https://doi.org/10.1108/PAR-09-2020-0170.

Derbali, A., Naoui, K. Ben Sassi, M., & Amiri, M. M. (2021b). Do COVID-19 epidemic explains the dynamic conditional correlation between China's stock market index and international stock market indices? *The Chinese Economy, 55*(3), 227–242. https://doi.org/10.1080/10971475.2021.1958453.

Engle, R. F. (1982). Autoregressive conditional heteroskedasticity with estimates of the variance of united kingdom inflation. *Econometrica, 50*(4), 987–1007. https://doi.org/10.2307/1912773.

Engelhardt, N., Krause, M., & Neukirchen, D. (2021). Trust and stock market volatility during the COVID-19 crisis. *Finance Research Letters, 38*(1), 101873. https://doi.org/10.1016/j.frl.2020.101873.

Gharib, C., Mefteh-Wali, S., & Ben Jabeur, S. (2021). The bubble contagion effect of COVID-19 outbreak: Evidence from crude oil and gold markets. *Finance research letters, 38*(1), 101703. https://doi.org/10.1016/j.frl.2020.101703.

Goodell, J. W. (2020). COVID-19 and finance: Agendas for future research. Finance Research Letters, *35*(7), 101512. https://doi.org/10.1016/j.frl.2020.101512.

He, P., Sun, Y., Zhang, Y., & Li, T. (2020). COVID-19's impact on stock prices across different sectors: An event study based on the Chinese stock. *Emerging Markets Finance and Trade*, *56*(10), 2198–2212. https://doi.org/10.1080/1540496X.2020.1785865.

Kuttner, K. N. (2001). Monetary policy surprises and interest rates: Evidence from the fed funds futures market, *Journal of Monetary Economics*, *47*(3), 523–544. https://doi.org/10.1016/S0304-3932(01)00055-1.

Liu, L., Wang, E. Z., & Lee, C. C. (2020). Impact of the COVID-19 pandemic on the crude oil and stock markets in the US: A time-varying analysis. *Energy Research Letters*, *1*(1), 1–5. https://doi.org/10.46557/001c.13154.

Mensi, W., Sensoy, A., Vo, X. V., & Kang, S. H. (2020). Impact of COVID-19 outbreak on asymmetric multifractality of gold and oil prices, *Resources Policy*, *9*(1), 101829. https://doi.org/10.1016/j.resourpol.2020.101829.

Phan, D. H. B. & Narayan, P. K. (2020). Country responses and the reaction of the stock market to COVID-19: A preliminary exposition. *Emerging Markets Finance and Trade*, *56*(10), 2138–2150. https://doi.org/10.1080/1540496X.2020.1784719.

Sansa, N. A. (2020). The impact of the COVID-19 on the financial markets: Evidence from China and USA. *Electronic Research Journal of Social Sciences and Humanities*, *2*(20), 29–39. https://dx.doi.org/10.2139/ssrn.3567901.

Sharif, A., Aloui, C., & Yarovaya, L. (2020). COVID-19 pandemic, oil prices, stock market, geopolitical risk and policy uncertainty nexus in the US economy: Fresh evidence from the wavelet-based approach. *International Review of Financial Analysis*, *70*(6), 101496. https://doi.org/10.1016/j.irfa.2020.101496.

Zhang, D., Hu, M., & Jibc, Q. (2020). Financial markets under the global pandemic of COVID-19. *Finance Research Letters*, *36*(10), 101528. https://doi.org/10.1016/j.frl.2020.101528.

Zaremba, A., Kizys, R., Aharon, D. Y., & Demir, E. (2020). Infected markets: Novel coronavirus, government interventions, and stock return volatility around the globe. *Finance Research Letters*, *35*(7), 101597. https://doi.org/10.1016/j.frl.2020.101597.

Youssef, M., Mokni, K., & Ajmi, A. N. (2021). Dynamic connectedness between stock markets in the presence of the COVID-19 pandemic: Does economic policy uncertainty matter? *Financial Innovation*, *7*(13), 1–27. https://doi.org/10.1186/s40854-021-00227-3.

Wagner, A. F. (2020). What the stock market tells us about the post-COVID-19 world. *Nature Human Behaviour*, *4*(1), 440. https://doi.org/10.1038/s41562-020-0869-y.

https://doi.org/10.1142/9781800614734_0006

Chapter 6

Financial Development and Corporate Governance Efficiency: An Overview of MENA

Ahmed Mohamed Habib

Abstract

This section discusses financial development and corporate governance efficiency in the Middle East and North Africa (MENA) region. Macroeconomic soundness is essential for developing financial sector services, and corporate governance is a substantial factor in determining firm performance. Insufficient corporate governance can harm shareholders' interests and lead to undesirable results such as business insolvency. In addition, firms face many business risks and challenges related to regulation, competition, market and customer trends, technology shifts, supply chains, cost management, financing, performance monitoring, business rescue from insolvency, and total value optimization. Therefore, we discuss the nature and level of financial development and corporate governance in the MENA region, the problems faced by institutions in the MENA region that hinder financial development, the adoption of best practices in terms of corporate governance, and the role of efficient corporate governance as a key to overcoming some of these challenges and achieving continuous improvement using the data envelopment analysis (DEA) approach.

Keywords: Financial development, corporate governance, MENA, business risks, data envelopment analysis

6.1. Introduction

Macroeconomic soundness is essential for the development of services in the financial sector. The theoretical rationale for linking economic growth and financial development is that a well-developed financial system improves intermediation efficiency by reducing information, transaction, and monitoring costs. Additionally, a well-developed financial system encourages investment by identifying and supporting profitable business possibilities, enabling trading, mobilizing funds, facilitating goods and service interchanges, managing risks, and monitoring managerial performance (Alhares *et al.*, 2019; Dewri, 2021; Farah *et al.*, 2021). Accordingly, these procedures efficiently allocate resources, enhance intellectual and working capital management, and improve technical advancement rates, contributing to economic growth. In addition, the legal and political conditions within which the financial system functions are major factors in the variety and quality of services provided by financial institutions (Alhares *et al.*, 2019; Dewri, 2021; Farah *et al.*, 2021). Banks hesitate to offer credit when an incompetent court system, corrupt bureaucracy, or political institution impedes the recovery of non-performing loans (NPLs) in developing nations. In underdeveloped financial systems, rules on lending or deposit rates and credit orientations are common forms of repression (Farah *et al.*, 2021). Pushing banks to provide subsidized or directed loans to particular industries or to limit the credit amount that can be assigned can distort the credit market and reduce efficiency. In a capitalist economy, one of the most important responsibilities of financial intermediaries is to specify the most favorable enterprises and investment schemes and assign resources accordingly (Dewri, 2021; Farah *et al.*, 2021). Therefore, nations should employ suitable macroeconomic procedures and policies, promote contests in the sector, and build robust, transparent legal and institutional frameworks for their actions. Specifically, prudential regulation, oversight, robust creditor rights, and contract enforcement are required. Government-imposed limitations and price distortions can impede the development of the financial sector. In developing nations, these procedures can lead to financial repression, including directed credit, interest rate caps for deposits and loans, reserve ratios, inflation taxes, contracts, and agreements between firms and banks. In addition, a substantial body of research demonstrates that these procedures can impede economic development, as a high level of financial repression influences an annual decrease of over one percentage point in per capita GDP growth.

Additionally, firms that desire to shine in a business environment seek to employ effective and stringent controls to avoid business failures and prejudice shareholders' interests. The UK Cadbury Committee describes corporate governance as a system in which firms are directed and controlled, in other words, how firms run. Ineffective oversight by directors typically leads to mismanagement, fraud, and excessive rewards. Many governments institute legal control over directors and firm management to avert such disasters. Therefore, governance is necessary for all firms, public, private, commercial, and non-profit, to direct and control their business activities. In the US, corporate governance rules were developed after the Sarbanes–Oxley Act of 2002. The main function of the Sarbanes–Oxley Act is to protect investors by implementing many measures to improve disclosure accuracy and firm control (Parkinson, 2018). The Sarbanes–Oxley Act, subsequent laws issued by the Securities and Exchange Commission (SEC), and regulatory bodies' guidelines improved corporate governance practices in the US and other industrialized nations (Parkinson, 2018). In Europe, the European Commission develops and updates a series of corporate governance directives and guides as a foundation for all states to follow, and leaves each state to employ these directives according to its systems and laws. These efforts aim to improve transparency rules, make businesses more efficient and sustainable, and protect shareholders and other parties, such as employees and creditors, with a particular interest in firms (Parkinson, 2018).

Corporate governance is based on many mechanisms that can be classified into internal and external mechanisms. A firm's stakeholders establish internal mechanisms to observe management operations and mitigate agency costs. Internal tools or mechanisms can include an effective board of directors (BoD), managerial or executive compensation, and ownership structures (Di Vito & Trottier, 2022; Refakar & Ravaonorohanta, 2020; Salehi *et al.*, 2018). The responsibilities of the BoD include monitoring management performance, endorsing decisions, and choosing a chief executive officer (CEO). Additionally, the BoD is responsible for shareholders and stakeholders, directing the firm to achieve its mission, protecting the invested capital, and maximizing firm value. Therefore, board effectiveness is key to firm success. For the BoD to perform its duties regarding direction and oversight, a set of committees from among its non-executive members, such as audit, remuneration, and nomination committees, should be formed. In general, this chapter discusses some important issues regarding the efficacy of boards and their characteristics, such as the size of the BoD, independence, CEO–chairman duality, board meetings, directors' busyness, and board committees.

Regarding the size of the BoD, its impact on corporate performance remains indistinct. However, both small and large sizes can result in undesirable outcomes. Therefore, BoD size should be in equilibrium and harmonious regarding the requirements of a member's knowledge and skills, as well as the challenges faced by the firm (Di Vito & Trottier, 2022; Refakar & Ravaonorohanta, 2020; Salehi *et al.*, 2018). One of the most common measures is board diversity, which includes diverse thoughts and competencies. Furthermore, the proportion of women on boards has been considered a modern trend in recent years, indicating board diversity. In addition, independent directors are efficacious monitors, as they do not have an economic interest in management or the firm. Thus, the percentage of independent directors indicates a BoD's independence. Independent directors in a BoD may improve the directors' decision quality, improve supervision and monitoring, and enhance a firm's overall performance and value (Dewri, 2021; Tulcanaza-Prieto & Lee, 2022). However, independent directors may negatively affect performance, as the CEO may be reluctant to expose confidential information, and exposing what underlies some proposed policies may encourage the BoD to interfere with protecting shareholders' rights. In brief, there is a need for an optimal or appropriate ratio of independent directors to make a BoD more effective.

A CEO's dual position as chairperson jeopardies the capability of the BoD to sustain independent judgment. This duality can increase agency costs. Additionally, CEO duality affects board performance because merging both positions harms corporate performance and weakens the efficiency of BoD control (Di Vito & Trottier, 2022; Refakar & Ravaonorohanta, 2020; Salehi *et al.*, 2018). Thus, separating the CEO and chairman is essential for enhancing BoD efficiency. Regarding board meetings, the BoD should continually gather to examine and discover solutions to a firm's issues and challenges.

In addition, a BoD that meets frequently will benefit stakeholders and enhance overall firm performance. Infrequent meetings can threaten effective BoD monitoring, as directors do not pay reasonable attention to firms. Moreover, directors' busyness is another issue, as the BoD executes the monitoring process on behalf of stakeholders. Therefore, it may be unlikely that directors who operate multiple boards achieve their functions efficiently, as some argue that directors with multiple exterior board seats may become so engaged that they do not perform their monitoring roles efficiently, which may reduce their corporate performance and value (Di Vito & Trottier, 2022; Refakar & Ravaonorohanta, 2020; Salehi *et al.*, 2018). However, some argue that the number of exterior directorships may reveal director quality, as directors on multiple exterior boards may be better experienced, have better commercial contact, deliver sounder recommendations, and provide better monitoring (Di Vito & Trottier, 2022; Refakar & Ravaonorohanta, 2020; Salehi *et al.*, 2018). Additionally, if employed appropriately, BoD committees enhance the board's effectiveness and corporate performance, which may reduce agency problems. In addition, setting up three committees for the BoD is advised: audit, remuneration, and nomination committees. The audit committee concentrates on matters pertinent to a firm's economic reporting integrity and enhances the interaction between management, exterior auditors, and directors. The committee consists of independent directors who continually meet each other. Frequent audit committee meetings reduce economic reporting hypocrisy. The remuneration committee concentrates on matters pertinent to reasonable remuneration policies of a corporation associated with performance. Appropriate compensation packages encourage top management to operate efficiently and boost corporate performance. Some confirm that a committee must consist of independent directors and meet continually (Di Vito & Trottier, 2022; Refakar & Ravaonorohanta, 2020; Salehi *et al.*, 2018). Furthermore, the board nomination committee focuses on assessing a firm's BoD performance and examines the skills and characteristics required of board candidates and other employees of a firm. Others argue that CEO compensation is an essential segment of governance that may influence the stock market's economic performance and returns. However, others contend that compensation cannot be regarded as a tool for aligning interests because increased compensation may not always be associated with improved governance or performance (Di Vito & Trottier, 2022; Refakar & Ravaonorohanta, 2020; Salehi *et al.*, 2018).

Furthermore, a company's ownership structure is considered a corporate governance mechanism that aligns the interests of stakeholders and managers (Di Vito & Trottier, 2022; Refakar & Ravaonorohanta, 2020; Salehi *et al.*, 2018). Concentrated ownership is related to fewer agency problems, as large blockholders and stakeholders have a greater impact on the BoD and the power and motivation to observe management closely. Regardless, concentrated ownership may be accompanied by confiscation of minority shareholders. However, stakeholders hesitate to closely observe management in dispersed ownership because of costs and free-rider problems. Some argue that CEO equity ownership may mitigate agency costs (Di Vito & Trottier, 2022; Refakar & Ravaonorohanta, 2020; Salehi *et al.*, 2018). They claim that directors operate most effectively in improving a corporation's performance if they have an ownership stake. However, directors usually hold only a small portion of the corporation's equity. Thus, CEO equity ownership is insufficient to mitigate agency costs. Additionally, some argue that BoD equity ownership (directors' equity ownership) motivates directors to act as owners and mitigate agency problems (Di Vito & Trottier, 2022; Refakar & Ravaonorohanta, 2020; Salehi *et al.*, 2018). They contended that elevated equity ownership reduces agency costs and enhances a corporation's overall performance. On the other hand, regarding institutional ownership, some argue that, based on the free-rider issue, small stakeholders are expensive to operate as management monitors (Di Vito & Trottier, 2022; Refakar & Ravaonorohanta, 2020; Salehi *et al.*, 2018). By contrast, larger institutional owners are motivated to observe management because of the size and extent of their holdings. Institutional owners have outstanding resources and expertise that can assist them in observing management performance efficiently. Thus, they can mitigate or reduce agency problems. However, some argue that institutional owners may have neither expertise nor time to operate as influential monitors (Di Vito & Trottier, 2022; Refakar & Ravaonorohanta, 2020; Salehi *et al.*, 2018). In the real world, institutional owners hold considerable shares, and their representatives on the BoD operate well to enhance a corporation's overall performance. In addition, representatives of the BoD preclude management from operating for their interests and alleviate the agency's problem.

External mechanisms are measures enforced outside the organization and beyond the firm's authority. They serve a corrective function for all corporations within a jurisdiction, prohibiting opportunistic management behavior. These tools can help reduce the demand for interior tools while providing safety measures if interior mechanisms are defective. Exterior mechanisms safeguard stakeholders through lawful systems, corporate control markets, managerial labor markets, institutional investor monitoring, and disciplinary procedures resulting from financial debt (Di Vito & Trottier, 2022; Refakar & Ravaonorohanta, 2020; Salehi *et al.*, 2018). External mechanisms include laws and regulations, debt holders' rights, takeover threats, capital markets, managerial labor, and product market competition. For example, debt holders provide funds and loans to firms and observe managers or control BoD composition. In addition, they can exert privileges determined by covenants to safeguard their interests by employing the firm's assets as collateral to protect against bankruptcy or insolvency. In addition, debt holders monitor corporations with higher debt levels more closely to ensure that managers operate efficiently to maximize corporate value. Additionally, takeovers can be an effective exterior mechanism when interior governance mechanisms are inefficient. A takeover force is a sufficient alarm for opportunistic managers to maintain elevated management quality. Takeover offers may be wake-up calls for inefficient firms. Some claim that takeover endeavors are signs of weak internal governance. The takeover offer allows the BoD to check the manager's performance and modify the compensation policy.

Financial development in the MENA region lags significantly behind that of developed nations. They also differ considerably among MENA countries, as some nations have developed their sectors, whereas others have made modest headways in this regard. Additionally, regarding the corporate governance situation in the MENA region, MENA economies have implemented changes to promote corporate governance by addressing this dilemma. However, this process is time consuming because of many challenges. Based on previous literature, the following research gap was incorporated as the objective of this study:

(a) Investigate the nature and level of financial development and corporate governance in the MENA region.
(b) Recognize the limitations and challenges faced by institutions in the MENA region that hinder financial development and corporate governance efficiency.
(c) Recognize the DEA's role as a benchmark technique for enhancing corporate governance efficiency.

The remainder of this chapter is organized as follows. Section 6.2 presents the background information. Section 6.3 discusses the financial development in the MENA region. Section 6.4 discusses corporate governance in the MENA region as an emerging market. Section 6.5 considers corporate governance efficiency using the DEA approach. Section 6.6 presents the literature review. Section 6.7 clarifies the research design of the study. Section 6.8 presents the discussion. Finally, Section 6.9 presents the conclusions of this study.

6.2. Background

Considering the MENA region's financial development, it outperforms most other emerging countries in financial growth but lag significantly behind developed nations. MENA countries also differ considerably among themselves, as some nations have enhanced their sectors while others have made modest headways. Additionally, MENA economies have implemented changes to promote corporate governance by addressing the corporate governance dilemma (Alhares *et al.*, 2019). However, this process is time consuming because of many challenges. These challenges include the presence of few women on business boards. Other issues include beneficial ownership structures, related-party transactions, protection of minority investors, board information reporting, and disclosures such as remuneration and qualifications. Furthermore, access to corporate finance remains constrained in some economies, and the governance of state-owned enterprises (SOEs) must be improved. Targeted changes can enhance firm performance while increasing the region's capacity for competitiveness and inclusive growth.

6.3. Financial Development in the MENA Region

In the MENA nations, the Gulf Cooperation Council (GCC) countries are examples of nations with well-developed financial sectors, particularly in the banking industry. Overall, the MENA nations fare well in terms of financial openness, regulation, and supervision. However, other countries, especially those outside the GCC, must strengthen their institutional settings and foster the evolution of the non-banking sector as more work remains to be done to reach the level of development of the GCC countries. Therefore, contemporary banking and financial capabilities need to be developed. Regarding monetary policy, the inflexible setting or non-existence of secondary markets for government assets prevents central banks from extensively utilizing open market activities. Moreover, some nations lack a coherent framework for planning and implementing monetary policy. Regarding the institutional environment, in a large portion of the MENA region, institutional conditions such as bureaucracy, laws and order, court systems, and property rights are of insufficient quality. This may inhibit investment growth and, consequently, impair development. More work remains to be done to achieve best practices. Regarding financial openness, the MENA nations have progressively extended their capital accounts. Half of the world's nations have unrestricted financial sectors; however, more work remains to be done to reach the level of development in the GCC countries. Regarding supervision and governance, numerous MENA nations, such as the GCC states, Tunisia, Morocco, Lebanon, and Jordan, have bolstered banking regulations and supervision, built up-to-date systems to manage regular prudential data, and inspected and audited banks. Furthermore, they increased their capital adequacy ratios (CARs) and decreased their loans to adapt to the international Basel requirements. Regarding the non-banking financial industry, most regions need further growth in the non-banking financial sector, including stock and bond markets, pension funds, insurance companies, and mutual funds.

As a result of the integration of global capital markets and globalization trends, the challenge for MENA decision-makers is to adopt intelligent macroeconomic policies along with structural reforms to move away from financially restrictive policies. Macro-stabilization measures should be supplemented by providing a structured environment conducive to financial growth, including less government intervention in economic activities and credit distribution, to improve the competitiveness and quality of the private sector. Endeavors should be targeted at regions where economic growth seems to be weakest. Additionally, for some nations, this entails a reduction in government involvement in the financial system, including a reduction in the monetary financing of budget deficits and a decline in the public ownership of financial institutions. This leads to an improvement in the quality and competitiveness of the financial sector, an increase in competition, investments in intellectual capital, and the enhancement of legal conditions, which favor economic and investment development and intellectual capital over time.

6.4. Corporate Governance in the MENA Region as an Emerging Market

Market crises in developing countries have attracted attention due to the lack of governance in emerging economies. Furthermore, globalization and international investment have expanded the demand for practical monitoring tools for management and improved the market structure. Many techniques have been developed to resolve corporate governance issues in the US, UK, and European countries, giving rise to several best governance practices. Internal mechanisms include influential directors' boards, managerial or executive compensation, ownership structures, and monitoring by significant shareholders. In contrast, external mechanisms include laws and regulations, debt holders' rights, takeover threats, capital markets, managerial labor markets, and product market competition. In addition, regulatory agencies in industrialized countries respond to the governance difficulties faced by these countries. This is why these procedures have proven successful in industrialized nations. Nevertheless, the suggested strategies may not be adequate because emerging countries have political, legislative, and social backdrops that differ from those in developed markets. Indeed, because emerging economies have lower transparency, weaker regulatory frameworks, higher ownership structures, and less-evolved economic markets, techniques that work in evolved economies may not work as well in emerging economies. Consequently, the soundest corporate governance practices should be used differently in these economies. Furthermore, the advocated procedures are intended to tackle the primary agency problem and are inapplicable in emerging economies where ownership concentration causes agency problems between minority shareholders and owners. Therefore, these economies' corporate governance practices and norms are lower than those of the developed economies.

Considering the MENA situation, countries have implemented changes to promote corporate governance. However, this process is time consuming because of its many challenges. These challenges include the presence of a few women on business boards. Other issues include beneficial ownership structures, related party transactions, minority investor protection, board information reporting, and disclosure, such as remuneration and qualifications. Furthermore, access to corporate finance remains constrained in some economies, and the governance of state-owned enterprises (SOEs) must be improved. Targeted changes can enhance firm performance while increasing a region's capacity for competitiveness and inclusive growth. In 2016, the MENA government launched the MENA-OECD Competitiveness Program. The program aimed to develop the private sector, attract investment, and encourage entrepreneurship to boost economic growth and deliver job opportunities in the MENA region. To accomplish this, the program adopts horizontal visions through interaction, experiences, and ability enhancement necessary to identify, implement, and monitor business environment improvements. Overall, this is considered a platform or forum for discussing strategic solutions to familiar challenges or issues in the MENA region, investigating pathways for promoting inclusive growth, delivering job opportunities, and encouraging regional and international integration in the MENA region. The working group in the competitiveness program supports the development of the best corporate governance frameworks and policies, which are essential building blocks for attracting capital and promoting private sector growth and competitiveness. In addition, it supports MENA reform efforts by employing the G20/OECD principles and directions of corporate governance as measures to improve corporate governance practices in the region. Furthermore, the economic initiatives of MENA economies can be reinforced by continuous improvements in corporate governance practices and policies and the importance of alignment with international corporate governance standards.

In general, when comparing the states of developed and emerging economies, it can be said that governance norms in developed economies rely on a particular institutional context that contains dispersed ownership, increased attention from institutional investors, and an efficient equity market. Boards have an elevated ratio of independent directors to align the interests of stakeholders and managers. Audit firms permit information to flow from directors to the capital markets to ensure transparency, and the takeover market operates in weak corporations. The efficacy of governance mechanisms may differ significantly between developed and emerging economies. The characteristics of emerging and less developed economies frequently lead to deficient governance. Firms in these economies are often closely controlled by their founding families. Subordinate regulations do not shield investors and exhibit lower levels of transparency. In addition, stakeholders' lawful rights, legal systems, and enforcement are spineless. Policymakers should promote and enable corporations to employ the soundest governance criteria. Therefore, there is a need to enhance the economic, political, social, and legal environments to adopt optimal governance mechanisms and guidelines. This is the main challenge for decision-makers in these economies to advance and achieve the best global practices. Improvements should be gradual, with continuous evaluation to rectify deviations. Accordingly, the author suggests using the DEA methodology, as it can be an essential means to assist policymakers in continuously improving governance performance. The DEA methodology is robust for benchmarking and comparing overall performance with the best regional and international practices. In addition, the DEA methodology plays a vital role in helping policymakers correct deviations in concert to achieve the best practices.

6.5. Corporate Governance Efficiency: DEA Approach

Measuring efficiency is a considerable matter for decision-making units (DMUs), which can be countries, segments, organizations, branches, interior departments, or anything that can include sub-elements. As DMUs seek to develop their businesses and continue to overcome challenges, measuring their performance and practices is necessary to objectively correct deviations. This is the basis for accounting and administrative accountability and a challenge for decision-makers to achieve continuous improvement.

Efficiency can be evaluated through one of two paths: the first is parametric, requiring specific conditions and pre-description at the beginning to estimate the efficiency function; the second is non-parametric because it does not require data to have specific statistical distributions. The DEA approach is an essential non-parametric technique for measuring efficiency, as it does not require an explicit specification of the form of the underlying production technology and is formed by piecewise linear segments that connect the set of frontier observations (Habib & Kayani, 2022; Habib & Shahwan, 2020; Shahwan & Habib, 2023). Beyond the advantages of not requiring a priori specification of the functional form for the frontier and enabling more flexibility and ease of use, the DEA method decomposes the efficiency measure into several components. This aids management in searching for sources of inefficiency by applying mathematical programming techniques (Habib & Kayani, 2022; Habib & Mourad, 2023; Habib & Shahwan, 2020).

DEA was initially proposed as a method for evaluating relative efficiency in 1978 by Charnes, Cooper, and Rhodes (CCR). When considering efficiency, it was assumed that constant returns to scale (CRS) existed between inputs and outputs. In 1984, Banker, Chames, and Cooper (BCC) developed the CCR model to account for variable returns to scale (VRS) and to evaluate both pure and scale efficiencies (Habib & Mourad, 2022; Mourad, 2022; Mourad *et al.*, 2021). Since then, many researchers and business institutions have employed this methodology in various fields, and some scholars have attempted to develop more flexible basic models.

DEA is based on mathematical programming to determine the optimal mix of inputs and outputs for the DMUs. This can be defined as a tool or means to evaluate and improve performance through guidelines that can help policymakers (if employed well) enhance the performance of DMUs. Owing to the model's simplicity, DEA has gained popularity as a technique for evaluating the relative efficiency of DMUs using best-observed practices. DEA is an effective technique for determining the relative efficiency of a group of DMUs because it provides valuable information for continuous improvement and best practices. Moreover, DEA stands out as a benchmark methodology because it focuses on the best practices of DMUs rather than on assessments of central tendencies, as other methods do, such as ratios and regression methods. Furthermore, this technique is becoming increasingly popular in various sectors and contributes significantly to operational research and management (Cooper *et al.*, 2007; Dalwai *et al.*, 2023; Habib, 2022; Habib & Dalwai, 2023; Habib & Mourad, 2022; Mourad *et al.*, 2022; Ozcan, 2014).

6.6. Literature Review

Owing to inherent information asymmetries in transactions in the banking sector, proper banking regulations and controls are a crucial part of the financial sector's evolution. In addition, regulatory organizations must ensure that depositors' equity is safeguarded, bolster confidence in the banking industry, and facilitate financial intermediation. The issue of regulation and supervision evaluates bank performance in terms of capital adequacy criteria and management of NPLs. These regulations and controls should be efficient because government constraints on the banking sector and excessive regulation and supervision may inhibit financial growth. As a result of the integration of global capital markets and globalization trends, the extent of financial institutions' openness has become an increasingly important factor in total development, as the openness of the financial sector reflects whether there are government limitations in the financial industry, which may hinder economic development (Alhares *et al.*, 2019; Dewri, 2021; Farah *et al.*, 2021).

Considering the financial development in the MENA region, MENA countries outperform the majority of other emerging countries in terms of the degree of financial growth but lag significantly behind developed nations. In addition, financial development levels differ considerably in MENA countries, as some nations have enhanced their sectors while others have made modest headways (Alhares *et al.*, 2019; Dewri, 2021; Farah *et al.*, 2021). For financial development, the MENA region should reform its financial sector systems and policies to achieve significant progress and sustain economic growth. Theoretically and empirically, policies strengthening the financial sector's performance result in more robust economic growth. However, a lagging financial sector can hinder economic opportunities. To generate and sustain economic growth, decision-makers in the MENA region should encourage and enhance financial development and eradicate financial repression as part of their development strategy.

Corporate governance has also captured the attention of researchers and organizations. In both developed and developing countries, the importance of corporate governance for joint stock companies is emphasized, especially for those whose shares are traded on the stock exchange, to tighten control over their programs and activities (Appuhami & Bhuyan, 2015; Dalwai & Mohammadi, 2020; Dalwai *et al.*, 2015; Demise, 2006; Dittmar & Mahrt-Smith, 2007; Elloumi & Gueyié, 2001; Li *et al.*, 2021; Manzaneque *et al.*, 2016; Shahwan & Habib, 2020; von Koch *et al.*, 2020; Younas *et al.*, 2021). The need for corporate governance stems from the separation between ownership and management of publicly owned companies. The emergence of agency theory and the associated shedding of light on the problems that arise as a result of conflicts of interest between members of corporate boards and shareholders has led to a reflection on the necessity of having a set of laws and regulations that work to protect the interests of shareholders and limit the financial and administrative manipulation carried out by members of the boards of directors to maximize their benefits, as they are the bodies that hold the reins of matters within companies. Lack of shareholder activity and agency problems may hurt corporate governance. Insufficient control over directors and senior management typically leads to governance concerns. This lack of control may hinder a company's plans and lead to fraud by directors (Habib & Mourad, 2023; Shahwan & Habib, 2020). A lack of shareholder activity and agency issues might contribute to the poor oversight of directors. Most private firm directors are stockholders, reducing the agency problem. Owing to the development of the business environment and the evolution of the size, activities, and expertise needed to run firms, there is a need to separate the power between shareholders and management. Governance concerns are generally attributed to the separation of power between the shareholders and management. The directors are shareholder agents tasked with forming contracts with third parties. This allows shareholders to focus on their principal objectives — share price appreciation and dividend income — rather than on corporate management.

In addition, the profit distribution dilemma is considered one of the most critical issues in financial management because of its direct relationship with shareholders and its repercussions for share prices in the financial market. This issue is still subject to much controversy in the fields of financial management and financial investments. Dividend policy is related to dividing a company's net income into dividends to shareholders and retained earnings. The agency model of dividend distribution shows that shareholders with more significant privileges can use their ability to affect dividend policies and obtain greater rights through legal protection or governance applications. Agency theory assumes that shareholders prefer dividend distribution options over retained earnings, which may be more robust in emerging markets. Therefore, a dividend policy that considers the organization's objective of maximizing shareholder wealth should be implemented. Furthermore, interest in corporate governance has increased to raise confidence in national economies, deepen the role of capital markets, and encourage investment by preserving the rights and interests of all parties, as investors desire to participate in successful revenue-generating institutions and companies (Habib, 2023). Therefore, corporate governance has become an urgent topic in the agenda of international institutions and organizations, such as the World Bank, the United Nations Development Project, the Organization for Economic Cooperation and Development (OECD), and other international, regional, and local organizations (Demise, 2006).

6.7. Research Design

Based on secondary sources, this conceptual study discusses financial development and corporate governance efficiency in the MENA region. The research methodology of the present work includes investigating the nature and level of financial development and corporate governance in the MENA region. Next, we discuss the limitations and challenges faced by institutions in the region that hinder their progress toward financial growth and corporate governance efficiency. Finally, we discuss the role of the DEA in enhancing corporate governance efficiency.

6.8. Discussion

Considering financial development in the MENA region, countries outperform the majority of other emerging countries in terms of the degree of financial growth but lag significantly behind developed nations. Additionally, significant variations exist in the levels of financial development among countries in the MENA region, with certain nations experiencing substantial advancements in their financial sectors. By contrast, others have made modest progress. In addition, MENA economies have implemented changes to promote corporate governance by addressing the corporate governance dilemma (Alhares *et al.*, 2019). However, this process is time consuming because of its many challenges. These challenges include the presence of few women on business boards. Other issues include effective ownership structures, related party transactions, minority investor protection, board information reporting, and disclosure, such as remuneration and qualifications. Furthermore, access to corporate finance remains constrained in some economies, and the governance of state-owned enterprises (SOEs) must be improved. Targeted changes can enhance firm performance while increasing a region's capacity for competitiveness and inclusive growth.

As a methodology for evaluating performance from a comprehensive perspective, the DEA application requires the determination of the following elements: analysis goals, DMUs and the period for assessment, input and output variables, an appropriate DEA model and its orientation, implementation, evaluation of efficiency, and conveying results to decision-makers to recognize the efficiency level and therapy for deficiencies in performance. Figure 6.1 shows the DEA framework and describes the steps required for sound analysis.

Considering corporate governance, efficiency can be assessed from several perspectives. For example, if we need to evaluate the efficiency of DMUs (several countries) in terms of governance practices, the evaluation process can be visualized as follows:

(a) *Setting goals for the analysis*: For example, assessing corporate governance efficiency in several countries.
(b) *Selecting the DMUs and analysis period*: The decision-making units and period under investigation.
(c) *Selecting the inputs and outputs used*: Determine the appropriate inputs and outputs that reflect the objectives of the analysis, as each goal has relevant variables. The inputs can be set in light of the internal and external mechanisms, such as the BoD size, number of annual board meetings, number of BoD committees,

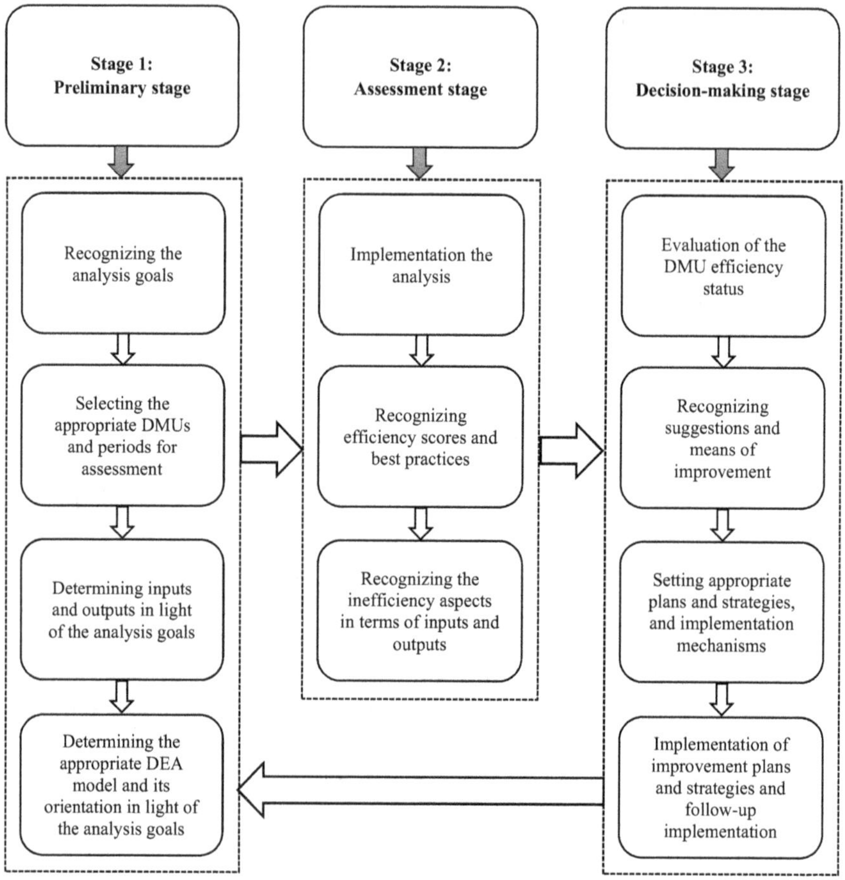

Figure 6.1. The DEA framework.

number of yearly committee meetings, proportion of independent directors, existence of CEO–chairman duality, board meetings, existence of directors' busyness, availability of BoD knowledge and skills, presence of women on BoD, ownership structure type, institutional ownership, nature of laws and regulations, debt holders' rights, likelihood of a takeover threat, nature of capital markets, nature of the managerial labor market, and nature of product market competition. Additionally, outputs can be set based on the corporate governance score obtained from environmental, social, and governance (ESG) criteria or through official reports and disclosures from relevant international institutions.

(d) *Selecting the appropriate DEA model and its orientation in light of the analysis objectives*: For example, there are many models such as radial, additive, and slack-based measures (SBM).
(e) *Implementation and assessment of efficiency*: The selected efficiency model is used to analyze the results of relative efficiency and obtain procedures for possible improvements in inputs and outputs.
(f) *Conveying results to policymakers*: Delivering the efficiency report and possible improvements to policymakers to check inefficiency aspects, thus taking appropriate actions in light of cost–benefit considerations to overcome inefficiency and achieve best practices.
(g) *Follow-up implementation and feedback*: Verify the efficiency improvement process and effectiveness of the selected actions.

6.9. Conclusion

Macroeconomic soundness is essential for the development of services in the financial sector. As a result of the integration of global capital markets and globalization trends, the challenge for MENA policymakers is to adopt intelligent macroeconomic policies along with structural reforms to move away from financially restrictive policies. Macro-stabilization measures should be supplemented by providing a structured environment conducive to financial growth, including less government intervention in economic activities and credit distribution, to improve the competitiveness of the private sector and the quality of the financial industry. Endeavors should be targeted at regions where economic growth seems weakest. Additionally, for some nations, this entails a reduction in government involvement in the financial system, including a reduction in the monetary financing of budget deficits and a reduction in the public ownership of financial institutions. This leads to an improvement in the quality and competitiveness of the financial sector, as well as an increase in competition, investments in intellectual capital, and the enhancement of legal conditions, which have a favorable effect on economic and investment development and intellectual capital over time. In addition, when comparing the states of developed and emerging economies, it can be said that the characteristics of emerging and less-developed economies frequently lead to deficient governance.

In these economies, firms are often closely controlled by their founding families and are less transparent. Subordinate regulations do not shield stakeholders' legal rights, and the legal system and its enforcement are spineless. Policymakers should try to promote and enable corporations to employ the soundest governance criteria. In addition, there is a need to enhance the economic, political, social, and legal environments to adopt optimal governance mechanisms and guidelines. The main challenge for policymakers in these economies is to advance and achieve the best global practices. Improvements should be gradual, with continuous evaluation to rectify any deviations. Therefore, the author suggests using the DEA methodology, as it can be an essential means to assist policymakers in continuously improving governance performance. The DEA methodology is robust for benchmarking and comparing overall performance with the best regional and international practices. In addition, the DEA methodology plays a vital role in helping policymakers discover deviations in performance to achieve best practices.

References

Alhares, A., Dominic, G., & Al Abed, R. (2019). The corporate governance practices: Evidence from MENA countries. *Theoretical Economics Letters*, *9*(4), 999–1019. https://doi.org/10.4236/tel.2019.94065.

Appuhami, R. & Bhuyan, M. (2015). Examining the influence of corporate governance on intellectual capital efficiency. *Managerial Auditing Journal*, *30*(4/5), 347–372. https://doi.org/10.1108/maj-04-2014-1022.

Cooper, W. W., Seiford, L. M., & Tone, K. (2007). *Data Envelopment Analysis* (2nd edn.). USA: Springer. https://doi.org/10.1007/978-0-387-45283-8.

Dalwai, T. & Mohammadi, S. S. (2020). Intellectual capital and corporate governance: An evaluation of Oman's financial sector companies. *Journal of Intellectual Capital*, *21*(6), 1125–1152. https://doi.org/10.1108/JIC-09-2018-0151.

Dalwai, T. A. R., Basiruddin, R., & Abdul Rasid, S. Z. (2015). A critical review of relationship between corporate governance and firm performance: GCC banking sector perspective. *Corporate Governance*, *15*(1), 18–30. https://doi.org/10.1108/CG-04-2013-0048.

Dalwai, T., Habib, A. M., Mohammadi, S. S., & Hussainey, K. (2023). Does managerial ability and auditor report readability affect corporate liquidity and cost of debt? *Asian Review of Accounting*, (ahead-of-print), 1–23. https://doi.org/10.1108/ARA-06-2022-0151.

Demise, N. (2006). OECD Principles of Corporate Governance. In *Corporate Governance in Japan* (pp. 109–117). Japan: Springer. https://doi.org/10.1007/978-4-431-30920-8_10.

Dewri, L. V. (2021). A critical assessment of interrelationship among corporate governance, financial performance, refined economic value added to measure firm value and return on stock. *Journal of the Knowledge Economy.* https://doi.org/10.1007/s13132-021-00808-8.

Di Vito, J. & Trottier, K. (2022). A literature review on corporate governance mechanisms: Past, present, and future*. *Accounting Perspectives, 21*(2), 207–235. https://doi.org/10.1111/1911-3838.12279.

Dittmar, A. & Mahrt-Smith, J. (2007). Corporate governance and the value of cash holdings. *Journal of Financial Economics, 83*(3), 599–634. https://doi.org/10.1016/j.jfineco.2005.12.006.

Elloumi, F. & Gueyié, J. P. (2001). Financial distress and corporate governance: An empirical analysis. *Corporate Governance: The International Journal of Business in Society, 1*(1), 15–23. https://doi.org/10.1108/14720700110389548.

Farah, B., Elias, R., Aguilera, R., & Abi Saad, E. (2021). Corporate governance in the Middle East and North Africa: A systematic review of current trends and opportunities for future research. *Corporate Governance: An International Review, 29*(6), 630–660. https://doi.org/10.1111/corg.12377.

Habib, A. M. (2022). Does the efficiency of working capital management and environmental, social, and governance performance affect a firm's value? Evidence from the United States. *Financial Markets, Institutions and Risks, 6*(3), 18–25. https://doi.org/10.21272/fmir.6(3).18-25.2022.

Habib, A. M. (2023). Do business strategies and environmental, social, and governance (ESG) performance mitigate the likelihood of financial distress? *A Multiple Mediation Model, Heliyon, 9*(7), e17847. https://doi.org/10.1016/j.heliyon.2023.e17847.

Habib, A. M. & Dalwai, T. (2023). Does the efficiency of a firm's intellectual capital and working capital management affect its performance? *Journal of the Knowledge Economy*, (ahead-of-print), 1–28. https://doi.org/10.1007/s13132-023-01138-7.

Habib, A. M. & Kayani, U. N. (2022). Does the efficiency of working capital management affect a firm's financial distress? Evidence from UAE. *Corporate Governance: The International Journal of Business in Society, 22*(7), 1567–1586. https://doi.org/10.1108/cg-12-2021-0440.

Habib, A. M. & Kayani, U. N. (2023). Evaluating the super-efficiency of working capital management using data envelopment analysis: Does

COVID-19 matter? *Operational Research Forum*, (ahead-of-print), 1–20. https://doi.org/10.1007/s43069-023-00217-4.

Habib, A. M. & Mourad, N. (2022). Analyzing the efficiency of working capital management: A new approach based on DEA-Malmquist technology. *Operations Research Forum*, *3*(3), 32. https://doi.org/10.1007/s43069-022-00155-7.

Habib, A. M. & Mourad, N. (2023). The influence of environmental, social, and governance (ESG) practices on US firms' performance: Evidence from the coronavirus crisis. *Journal of the Knowledge Economy*, (ahead-of-print), 1–20. https://doi.org/10.1007/s13132-023-01278-w.

Habib, A. M. & Shahwan, T. M. (2020). Measuring the operational and financial efficiency using a Malmquist data envelopment analysis: A case of Egyptian hospitals. *Benchmarking: An International Journal*, *27*(9), 2521–2536. https://doi.org/10.1108/bij-01-2020-0041.

Li, Z., Crook, J., Andreeva, G., & Tang, Y. (2021). Predicting the risk of financial distress using corporate governance measures. *Pacific-Basin Finance Journal*, *68*, 101334. https://doi.org/10.1016/j.pacfin.2020.101334.

Manzaneque, M., Priego, A. M., & Merino, E. (2016). Corporate governance effect on financial distress likelihood: Evidence from Spain. *Revista de Contabilidad*, *19*(1), 111–121. https://doi.org/10.1016/j.rcsar.2015.04.001.

Mourad, N. (2022). Second-order conic programming for data envelopment analysis models. *Periodicals of Engineering and Natural Sciences*, *10*(2), 487–499. https://doi.org/10.21533/pen.v10i2.2992.

Mourad, N., Habib, A. M., & Tharwat, A. (2021). Appraising healthcare systems' efficiency in facing COVID-19 through data envelopment analysis. *Decision Science Letters*, *10*(3), 301–310. https://doi.org/10.5267/j.dsl.2021.2.007.

Mourad, N., Tharwat, A., Habib, A. M., Wafik, D., & Hamed, M. A. (2022). Appraising the economic efficiency of european football teams: Evidence from COVID-19 crisis using data envelop analysis. *Journal of Positive School Psychology*, *6*(8), 4383–4403. https://journalppw.com/index.php/jpsp/article/view/10611.

Ozcan, Y. A. (2014). *Health Care Benchmarking and Performance Evaluation* (2nd edn., Vol. 210). USA: Springer. https://doi.org/10.1007/978-1-4899-7472-3.

Parkinson, M. M. (2018). Financial distress, insolvency and business rescue. In (pp. 43–64). Springer International Publishing. https://doi.org/10.1007/978-3-319-77110-6_3.

Refakar, M. & Ravaonorohanta, N. (2020). The effectiveness of governance mechanisms in emerging markets: A review. *Corporate Ownership & Control*, *17*(3), 8–26. https://doi.org/10.22495/cocv17i3art1.

Salehi, M., Tarighi, H., & Safdari, S. (2018). The relation between corporate governance mechanisms, executive compensation and audit fees. *Management Research Review, 41*(8), 939–967. https://doi.org/10.1108/mrr-12-2016-0277.

Shahwan, T. M. & Habib, A. M. (2020). Does the efficiency of corporate governance and intellectual capital affect a firm's financial distress? Evidence from Egypt. *Journal of Intellectual Capital, 21*(3), 403–430. https://doi.org/10.1108/jic-06-2019-0143.

Shahwan, T. M. & Habib, A. M. (2023). Do corporate social responsibility practices affect the relative efficiency of Egyptian conventional and Islamic banks? *International Journal of Emerging Markets, 18*(2), 439–462. https://doi.org/10.1108/IJOEM-05-2020-0518.

Tulcanaza-Prieto, A. B. & Lee, Y. (2022). Real earnings management, firm value, and corporate governance: Evidence from the Korean market. *International Journal of Financial Studies, 10*(19), 1–23. https://doi.org/10.3390/ijfs10010019.

von Koch, C., Ludvigsson-Wallette, M., & Nilsson, O. (2020). In search of corporate governance in franchising. *Journal of Marketing Channels, 26*(3), 178–193. https://doi.org/10.1080/1046669X.2020.1763536.

Younas, N., Uddin, S., Awan, T., & Khan, M. Y. (2021). Corporate governance and financial distress: Asian emerging market perspective. *Corporate Governance: The International Journal of Business in Society, 21*(4), 702–715. https://doi.org/10.1108/cg-04-2020-0119.

https://doi.org/10.1142/9781800614734_0007

Chapter 7

Banking System in Oman

Husam Basiddiq and Seemab Rana

Abstract

This chapter provides an understanding of the banking system development and structure in the Sultanate of Oman. It reviews existing literature and reports on the banking system in Oman between 1970 and 2020, and it provides a brief history of the Omani banking system before 1970. It also highlights the recent banking sector performance and the important role played by technology and the Central Bank of Oman (CBO) during the COVID-19 pandemic. This review demonstrates that the Omani banking system and sector experienced substantial developments in the regulatory and institutional framework due to which the performance of the banking sector remained stable in recent years. However, like other countries, the COVID-19 pandemic and the economic downturn affected the performance of banks, reducing banks' profitability and increasing non-performing loans and assets. Despite this, the Omani banking system remained resilient, and the measures and policy initiatives taken by the CBO and the application of technology helped mitigate the adverse influence of the COVID-19 pandemic.

Keywords: Banking system, CBO, banking sector, banks performance, Oman

7.1. Introduction

The efficiency of a banking sector indicates the state of well-being of an economy as banks drive the economy by the provision of funds and financial support for the economic sectors in the country. Thus, banks stimulate liquidity creation and capital accumulation, and ease access to financial products and services, enabling economic growth. They also help governments formulate the monetary policy, which is essential to attain economic growth devoid of inflation (Bilal *et al.*, 2016). In Oman, the banking system is regarded as the backbone of socio-economic development. Since the evolution of the banking system, Oman's day-to-day transactions have depended substantially on banks. It is the primary supplier of credit to the citizens as well as the focal point for everyday transactions for the business and economic sectors (CBO, 2016).

This chapter provides insight into the development of the entire Omani banking system. It takes into account the banking system before 1970 and discusses the gradual developments in the Omani banking regulatory and institutional framework since 1970. It also highlights the recent performance of banks, the adverse effect of COVID-19 on the Omani banking sector, how this effect was mitigated by the Central Bank of Oman (CBO), and the implementation of technology in banks' operations. The review suggests the existence of a weak financial system and a considerably small financial sector before 1970, where gradual and noticeable development took place after the production and export oil and the establishment of the CBO. However, the banking market is still dominated mainly by a few banks, and the expansion of the banking sector and operations often takes place through mergers and acquisitions. Finally, the review demonstrates that the recent performance of banks witnessed a steady improvement in terms of the aggregate assets, credits, and deposits of the banking sector. However, influenced by the COVID-19 pandemic and the economic downturn, the profits of the banking sector decreased and the non-performing loans (NPLs) and assets increased.

This chapter might be helpful for postgraduate students and researchers who are aiming to pursue research on the Omani banking sector as it provides a more holistic understanding of the Omani banking system. The insights of this review might also help individuals and investors make more informed decisions when aiming at investing in the Omani banking sector. It is divided into five sections. Section 7.2 reviews the literature on the developments of the Omani banking system. Section 7.3 highlights the recent performance of the banks before and during the COVID-19 pandemic, whereas

Section 7.4 discusses the role of technology and CBO in alleviating the effects of COVID-19. Finally, Section 7.5 concludes this chapter.

7.2. Literature Review

This section reviews the literature on the development of the Omani banking system. It is divided into 3 sub-headings. Section 7.2.1 discusses Oman's banking system before 1970, Section 7.2.2 reviews the development of the banking regulatory framework sector, and Section 7.2.3 reviews the development of the banking institutional framework.

7.2.1. *The banking system before 1970*

Oman has a long and independent history dating back to the 3rd millennium BC. For a long time, it was the most developed country in the Gulf region, with large and prosperous agricultural and fishing industries. However, in terms of a banking system, Oman was the least developed in the region. Until 1969, there were no local banks in Oman. The Omani banking sector comprised a small number of foreign banks, with no national authority regulating and supervising the banking market. Further, some foreign currencies were used and circulated in the country, including the Indian rupee, the Maria Theresa dollar, Gulf Indian rupees, and the Pound Sterling (Al-lawati, 2022). Banking activities were carried out by three foreign banks, namely, the British Bank of the Middle East (BBME), otherwise called HSBC,[1] the Chartered Bank (the Orient),[2] and Grindlays Bank (the Ottoman Bank). BBME was the first foreign commercial bank to operate in Oman, having been established in 1948; it assisted the government in currency management and was the sole commercial bank for a period of 20 years until the Chartered Bank started its banking operations in 1968. This was followed by Grindlays Bank in 1969 (see Table 7.1).

[1]It was called HSBC Middle East and is now called HSBC Oman Bank after merging with a local commercial bank.

[2]Its name has now changed to Standard Chartered Bank.

Table 7.1. Banks that operated in Oman before 1970.

Bank name	Bank type	Year of establishment
British Bank of the Middle East	Foreign	1948
Chartered Bank (the Orient)	Foreign	1968
Grindlays Bank (the Ottoman Bank)	Foreign	1969

Source: CBO (2009).

The small and undeveloped Omani banking system existed alongside weak infrastructure, public services, and economy. As Skeet (1992), Peterson (2004), and Looney (2009) noted, Oman had no roads, modern ports, electricity, or office space for the government outside of the capital. There were only 3 schools. The economy was dominated by agriculture, which accounted for 75% of the country's gross domestic product (GDP), whereas industries, including oil production, only accounted for 8% of the GDP (Sangeetha, 2012; Wippel, 2012; BTI, 2012[3]). This suggests that Oman had to make great effort to develop the country in general and the economy and the financial system in particular. However, in 1962, oil was discovered and Oman started exporting nearly half a million barrels per year between 1967 and 1969 (Oxford Business Group, 2015). The exploration of oil was a turning point in the Omani economy that led to a decisive change in the financial system in Oman.

7.2.2. *The regulatory framework*

Allen and Rigsbee II (2014) suggest that Oman's production of oil has increased substantially since 1970. This growth in oil production was in line with the increase in the global market's oil price, enabling steady development of the Omani economy that ultimately led to the existence of a resilient financial system in Oman. The banking system witnessed gradual development in the regulatory framework. In 1970, Oman established the Muscat Monetary Authority (MMA) to control national and foreign currency reserves, which issued the

[3]BTI is a Bertelsmann Stiftung's Transformation Index. It evaluates and analyzes transformation processes towards democracy and inclusive market economy worldwide.

first national banknote, the Saidi Rial, replacing the foreign currencies used in the country before 1970 (Kothaneth, 2022, Central Bank of Oman). In 1972, the Currency Law was issued, replacing the MMA with the Oman Currency Board (OCB) (Kothaneth, 2022; Central Bank of Oman; Azad *et al.*, 2011), and the Omani Rial became the official currency of the country, replacing the Saidi Rial (Kothaneth, 2022, Central Bank of Oman). The Currency Law permitted the OCB to act as a central bank and monetary authority, and accept demand deposits from commercial banks and international organizations. However, it was not permitted to be involved in direct trade activities, with the only exception of buying and selling foreign currencies and gold.

The banking system developed somewhat between 1970 and 1974, wherein all commercial banks had to submit an annual financial report to the OCB's financial controller. In addition, all applications for new banking licenses or the removal of existing ones had to go through a Royal Decree process and consultation period with the OCB before the issuance of a decree. However, the supervisory functions of the OCB were unable to accommodate the institutional expansion in the sector. Accordingly, Oman introduced a Banking Law in 1974 to set the legal foundations for the banking sector and to enhance the power of the OCB. This ultimately resulted in the establishment of the CBO in 1974 (Elghuweel, 2015; Al-Kalbani, 2008; Al-lawati, 2022). These provisions were modified in 2002 in keeping with local and global economic changes (Elghuweel, 2015).

The most significant change in relation to the Omani regulatory framework was the establishment of the CBO. As suggested by Al Hasni (2021), this enabled a substantial improvement in the Omani financial system and financial and monetary stability in the country. The CBO started its supervisory operations in 1975. It is entirely state owned and is directed and controlled by the Board of Governors, which drafts the monetary policy and the necessary measures to ensure effective functioning of the CBO and the banking system as a whole. Like other central banks all over the world, the CBO assumes certain conventional roles, including acting as a national depository agency, releasing and managing national currency, and issuing authorizations to emerging banks and financial institutions (Elghuweel, 2015; Al-Kalbani, 2008; Peterson, 2004). Al Hasni (2021) also noted other roles that are performed by the CBO, including the provision of funds to the government in case of fiscal deficit, management of foreign exchange reserves and debts, and sale and purchase of banks' financial instruments. The CBO has acted as a fiscal agent in managing the government's debt instruments, such as treasury bills (with maturity periods of 28, 91, and 182 days), since 1987 and development bonds (with maturity period often between 2 and 10 years and semi-annually paid interest) since 1991 (Martey, 1999). Both instruments are issued through a competitive auction process where the former is regarded as the main liquidity instrument for the local commercial banks (Martey, 1999), and the latter is open to both residents and non-residents (CBO).[4] In terms of monetary role, as Al-Lawati (2022) suggests, the CBO helps the government to manage economic instabilities by modifying monetary policies conducive to sustained economic progression. The CBO uses monetary policies to affect aggregate demand, interest rate, circulation of money, bank service charges, and reserve ratio to deal with economic fluctuations caused by volatile oil prices and global circumstances.

The primary responsibility of the CBO is to lay down regulations to discipline and regulate the banking sector and all the transactions between the banks and their stakeholders. In 1991, it was granted the power to remove and suspend banks' licenses and activities, which was applied to take over the branches of the Luxembourg-based Bank of Credit and Commerce International when it was liquidated in 1991 (Oxford Business Group, 2017). Other important regulations include those concerning banks' capital requirements and lending limitations. It stipulates a minimum capital requirement for local and foreign banks, which has increased gradually over the years. Table 7.2 shows the main changes in minimum capital requirements in the past 30 years.

In terms of lending limitations, all banking institutions must adhere to a range of lending limitations. They are permitted to enhance their lending limitation to 25% of their net worth on a standalone basis, provided the government's share in the bank's

[4]Information obtained from the CBO. https://cbo.gov.om/Pages/AgencyFunction.aspx#:~:text=Government%20Treasury%20Bills%3A%20Treasury%20Bills,%2Dto%2Dday%20recurrent%20expenditures.

Table 7.2. Main changes in minimum capital requirements.

Year	Local banks	Foreign banks
1983	1,000,000	1,000,000
1992	10,000,000	3,000,000
1996	20,000,000	3,000,000
2003	20,000,000	5,000,000
2006	50,000,000	10,000,000
2007	100,000,000	20,000,000

Source: Report by the banking control department of the CBO.

ownership is no less than 25% or if lending is provided for an infrastructure project. A report by the banking control department, information available in the CBO, and articles of banking law all indicate lending types and limitations stipulated by the CBO as shown in Table 7.3.

In Oman, the interest rates on deposits have been liberalized since 1993 and all lending rates have been deregulated and determined by the market forces and the movement of LIBOR since 1994, with the exception of consumer loan rates which may change occasionally according to the developments in the economy (Martey, 1999; Al-Muharrami, 2016). According to the CBO, all banking institutions that operate in Oman should also assess credit risk through a five-tiered risk classification system, while providing retail and commercial loans parallel to their internal risk management policies. Table 7.4 summarizes the five-tiered risk classification system for retail and commercial loans.

In regard to the operations of Islamic banks in Oman, the CBO issued some rules and guidance on the permitted operations of Islamic banks and branches. They offer virtually all the products and services offered by Islamic banks elsewhere. They enter into or make arrangements for others to enter into Islamic financial contracts, including *Murabaha* (deferred payment sale), *Ijarah* (Islamic leasing), *Musharakah* (joint ventures), Diminishing *Musharaka*,[5]

[5]A bank enters into ownership with the consumer in a property or enterprise where the ownership share of the bank gradually diminishes and the ownership of the consumer increases.

Table 7.3. Main lending types and limitations imposed by the CBO.

Lending type	Category	Lending limitation
Single obligor	• Resident • Companies with more than 25% government ownership (subject to CBO approval) • Large national joint venture project (subject to CBO approval) • SAOG companies	15% of the bank's net worth 25% of the bank's net worth (on a standalone basis) 15% of the bank's net worth (on a standalone basis)
Senior member in bank's management and related parties	• Senior individual member • Aggregate exposure to all senior members	10% of the bank's net worth 35% of the bank's net worth or any limit specified by the Board of Governors
Non-resident	• Non-resident • Aggregate non-resident exposure	2.5% of the bank's net worth 20% of the bank's net worth
Personal loans		35% of the bank's total credit
Housing loans		15% of the bank's total credit
Loans secured by real estate		60% of the bank's net worth or 60% of all time and saving deposits, other than inter-bank deposits or government deposits, whichever is higher

Source: CBO reports.

Mudaraba (profit-sharing), *Bai' Salam* (forward sale), *Musawama*,[6] and *Istina'a* (contract manufacturing). However, they are not allowed to perform *Tawarruq* or Commodity *Murabaha*[7] in the market, which is an instrument that is used by Islamic banks in some countries

[6]The sale transaction takes place between the seller and the buyer without any reference to the commodity price and costs incurred by the seller.

[7]"Tawarruq is a sale contract whereby a buyer buys an asset from a seller with deferred payment and subsequently sells the asset to the third party on cash with a price lesser than the deferred price, for the purpose of obtaining cash" (Dusuki, 2007, p. 16).

Table 7.4. The five-tiered risk classification system for retail and commercial loans.

Type of risk classification system	Retail loan	Commercial loan
Standard	Meeting all payment obligations or payments that have been overdue for less than 60 days	Payment of interest or the principle is current and no financial weaknesses have been observed
Special mention	Payment is overdue by more than 60 days or less than 90 days	Potential weak loans resulted from early liquidity problems or inadequate financial information
Substandard	Remained overdue for more than 60 days but less than 180 days	Remained overdue for 90 days or more but less than 270 days
Doubtful	Remained overdue for 180 days or more, but less than 360 days	Remained overdue for 270 days or more, but less than 630 days
Loss	Remained unpaid for 360 days or more	Remained overdue for 630 days or more

Source: CBO reports (CBO, 2009).

such as Saudi Arabia, United Arab Emirates, and Malaysia to manage short-term liquidity (Dusuki, 2007). However, Islamic banks in Oman are permitted to use Commodity Murabaha only in the case of a genuine threat to the survival of the bank or if the conversion process of a certain conventional bank into an Islamic bank cannot be accomplished without using Commodity Murabaha transactions. In this case, the CBO allows the use of Commodity Murabaha transactions for a maximum period of three months.[8] Like all Islamic banks elsewhere, banks that operate on the basis of Islamic principles in Oman are also obliged to establish an independent Shariah supervisory board alongside the board of directors, the role of which is to ensure that the bank's financial activities and operations comply with these principles. This means that any product and service proposals

[8]Information obtained from CBO's Islamic banking regulation framework. https://cbo.gov.om/sites/assets/Documents/English/LawRegulations/IBRF.pdf.

brought before the bank's board and the CBO must also be reviewed and approved by the Shariah supervisory board before a final decision can be made.

In addition to the regulation and supervision of the Omani financial market by the CBO, the Capital Market Authority (CMA) regulates and supervises a number of financial institutions. The launch of the CMA in 1998 was seen as a significant event — an independent regulatory and supervisory government body (Dalwai and Mohammadi, 2020; Elghuweel, 2015; Al-Kalbani, 2008). It supervises the banks listed on the Muscat Stock Exchange (MSE). It aims to promote the effectiveness of the capital market, standardize its processes, and ensure adherence to the professional code of conduct, discipline, and regulations among all securities dealers and companies falling under its supervision and jurisdiction. It also regulates and supervises insurance companies, brokerage firms, investment firms, and the Muscat Stock Exchange (MSX) (CBO, 2013; Financial Action Task Force, 2011).

7.2.3. *The institutional framework*

According to Elghuweel (2015), the institutional framework of the financial sector in Oman can be classified as banking and non-banking financial sectors. The banking sector comprises conventional banks, Islamic banks, and specialized banks, while the non-banking financial sector includes foreign exchange financial establishments (some of which engage in remittance transactions), insurance companies, financing companies (including financial leasing and hire purchase activities), brokerage firms, investment firms, private and public sector pension funds, and the MSX (CBO, 2013; Financial Action Task Force, 2011). However, the banking sector is the key component of the Omani financing system, as it allows lenders and borrowers to carry out fund exchanges (Elghuweel, 2015; Rath *et al.*, 2014; Sangeetha, 2012), and possesses the most financial sector assets. As Kasturi (2018) suggests, the total assets of the banking sector accounted for 94% of the overall assets of the financial sector.

Oman witnessed substantial development with respect to its banking institutional framework. Between 1970 and 1974, three new foreign banks entered the Omani banking sector: Arab Bank,[9] Habib Bank,[10] and Bank Melli Iran.[11] Further, a local commercial bank was established in 1973, the National Bank of Oman (NBO), which was the first local commercial bank offering banking services in Oman. After the establishment of the CBO in 1974, the Omani banking sector witnessed the emergence of additional and different types of banks. The second local commercial bank, namely, the Commercial Bank of Oman, was established in 1976, and First Abu Dhabi Bank, Bank Saderat Iran,[12] and Bank of Baroda[13] were established in 1976 as foreign banks, followed by the emergence of three government-owned specialized banks — Oman Bank for Development in 1977, Oman Housing Bank in 1977, and the Oman Bank for Agriculture and Fisheries in 1981.

As noted by the International Monetary Fund (IMF) and the CBO, the Oman Bank for Development provided micro loans to entrepreneurs and small and medium business owners for small projects through 20 branches as of 2021. It also started offering loans to small fishermen and farmers after its merger with the Oman Bank for Agriculture and Fisheries in 1997. Oman Housing Bank provided long-term soft housing loans for Omanis through nine branches operating in Oman as of 2021. More recently, the number of local and foreign commercial banks has increased significantly. According to the CBO (2021a), by the end of 2020, there were 16 conventional banks, of which seven were local (six were listed on the Muscat Stock Exchange in 2020) and nine were branches of foreign banks. There were 453 branches of conventional banks operating overall

[9]It was a foreign bank called the Arab Bank and it converted into a local bank in 1984, with the name Oman Arab Bank.

[10]It was the first Pakistani commercial bank established in Pakistan in 1947. It has 8 branches currently operating in Oman.

[11]It was the first Iranian commercial bank established in Iran in 1928.

[12]It has an established international banking network in several countries, such as Germany, the United Kingdom, France, Greece, Lebanon, Bahrain, Qatar, UAE, Oman, Uzbekistan, Afghanistan, and Turkmenistan.

[13]It has established four branches in Oman.

in the sultanate in 2020 (a decrease of 17 branches in comparison to 2016).

Generally, there are a number of notable differences between the Omani banking system and systems in developed countries, all of which are likely to have significant impacts on financial options of and financing for businesses. First, as Sbeiti (2010) suggests, since neither bond markets nor mutual funds markets are well developed in Oman, commercial banks play a significant role in Omani business and finance. Second, the banking market is dominated mainly by Bank Muscat,[14] Bank Dhofar,[15] and NBO, with Bank Muscat regarded as the largest bank in Oman, occupying around 36% market share in 2020 (Financial Stability Report, 2021). The total assets of Bank Muscat, Bank Dhofar, and NBO reached approximately OMR 12.454 ($32.387), 4.258 ($11.074), and 3.633 ($9.448) million in 2020, respectively, suggesting that Bank Muscat's total assets are larger than the assets of Bank Dhofar and NBO together.

However, the Omani banking industry became a dual banking system where two different banking systems exist after the inception of the Islamic banking system in 2012. Conventional banks are now competing against Islamic banks, which offer virtually all the products and services that conventional banks do but in the compliance with the Islamic approach to financing. This means that Omani and Muslim resident consumers in Oman can meet their financial needs in a way that satisfies their religious tenets and beliefs. The Omani banking sector saw the establishment of full-fledged Islamic banks and the setting up of Islamic banking branches by local banks (Sangeetha, 2012). As the CBO (2021a) report indicates, there were 2 full-fledged Islamic banks and 5 Islamic windows of local banks in 2020. According to the Financial Stability Report (2021), the total assets of Islamic banks reached OMR 5.2 ($13.524) billion with a market share of 14.3% in 2020, and the amount of deposits and financing stood at OMR 4.3 ($11.183) billion in 2020, accounting for 15.7% of the total deposits of the banking sector. As suggested by

[14]It was called the Oman Overseas Trust Bank from 1981 to 1985. Then, its name changed to Bank Muscat in 1986.

[15]It was a foreign bank called the Banque Paribas. The bank then converted into a local bank called the Bank Dhofar Al-Omani Al-Fransi in 1990, before changing its name to Bank Dhofar in 2003.

Al-Muharrami (2016) and Sangeetha (2012), these commercial banks are privately owned, with minority stakes in some banks being owned by the government.

The institutional framework of the Omani banking sector also experienced several banks' mergers and acquisitions, the introduction of some new banks, and the withdrawal of a few. The most recent major development in the institutional framework was the acquisition of Oman Arab Bank (a conventional bank) by Alizz Islamic Bank (an Islamic bank). Oman Arab bank became a public joint stock company, while its Islamic banking window was merged with Alizz Islamic Bank. Another notable merger was between HSBC Middle East Bank Limited and the Oman International Bank in 2012. In 1998, a merger between the Commercial Bank of Oman and the Bank of Oman, Bahrain, and Kuwait also took place. Further, Bank Muscat's special supplement report (2020)[16] shows a number of acquisitions and mergers. It acquired the Oman Banking Corporation in 1989 and the Industrial Bank of Oman, and merged with Al Bank Al Ahli Al Omani in 1993 and the Commercial Bank of Oman in 2000, making it the largest bank in Oman. However, as Al-Muharrami's (2016) study indicates, the size of the largest bank in Oman, Bank Muscat, was ranked 19 in comparison to the GCC banks in 2015 and 721 world-wise in terms of total assets.

Like Bank Muscat, the expansion of Bank Dhofar was stimulated mainly through acquisitions and mergers. It acquired the assets and liabilities of the Banque Paribas in 1990 (Bank Dhofar Annual Report, 1992),[17] the Luxembourg-based Bank of Credit and Commerce International from the CBO in 1992, and 16 branches of Commercial Bank of Oman in 2000. A merger also existed between Bank Dhofar and Majan International Bank in 2002 (Oxford Business Group, 2017). Oman Arab Bank emerged as a result of the acquisition of the branches of the Arab Bank in 1984. It then expanded its operation through the acquisition of the retail branches of the Omani European Bank in 1992.

As shown in Table 7.5, two new local banks, Sohar International Bank and Al Ahli Bank, were established in 2007 and a few foreign

[16]https://www.bankmuscat.com/en/Documents/pdf/BankMuscat_En.pdf.

[17]https://www.bankdhofar.com/UploadedFiles/UserMedia/file/InvestorRelations/A_Reports/1993.pdf.

Table 7.5. Licensed banks operating in the Sultanate of Oman.

Name of the bank	Date of establishment	No. of branches
Bank Muscat (domestic bank)	1981	Local 174, Int. 2
NBO (domestic bank)	1973	Local 60, Int. 2
HSBC Bank Oman (domestic bank)	1975	85
Oman Arab Bank (domestic bank)	1973	50
Bank Dhofar (domestic bank)	1990	56
Sohar International Bank (domestic bank)	2007	30
Al Ahli Bank (domestic bank)	2007	21
Standard Chartered Bank (foreign bank)	1968	1
Habib Bank (foreign bank)	1972	8
Bank Melli Iran (foreign bank)	1974	1
Bank Saderat Iran (foreign bank)	1976	2
Bank of Baroda (foreign bank)	1976	4
State Bank of India (foreign bank)	2004	1
First Bank of Abu Dhabi (foreign bank)	1976	7
Bank of Beirut (foreign Bank)	2006	5
Qatar National Bank (foreign bank)	2007	6
Bank Nizwa (domestic Islamic bank)	2012	17
Alizz Islamic Bank (subsidy of Oman Arab Bank)	2013	17
Meethaq (Islamic Window of Bank Muscat)	2013	24
Sohar Islamic (Window of Sohar Int. Bank)	2013	8
Maisarah (Islamic Window of Bank Dhofar)	2013	10
Muzun (Islamic Window of NBO)	2013	6
Al Hilal (Islamic Window of Al Ahli Bank)	2013	15
Oman Bank for Development (specialized bank)	1977	20
Oman Housing Bank (specialized bank)	1977	9

Source: CBO's annual reports.

banks entered the Omani banking sector (CBO, 2009). There were also two attempts by Bank Dhofar to occupy a larger market share by merging with Sohar International Bank and the NBO. Despite all the work and effort to achieve this, no consensus was reached in both mergers and they were ultimately called off by the shareholders. However, there is potential for additional mergers between banks in Oman as a merger proposal was announced recently between Bank Nizwa (Islamic) and Sohar International Bank (Muscat Daily, 2022). Despite this development in the Omani banking sector, it is still regarded as a small banking sector. However, given the relatively small population, Oman had a higher banking density in 2016 (16.4 branches per 100,000 inhabitants) than the other bigger banking sectors in the gulf countries such as Saudi Arabia (8.8) and United Arab Emirates (12.4) (Oxford Business Group, 2019).

7.3. Recent Performance of the Banking Sector

The COVID-19 pandemic is perceived as an appalling global monetary catastrophe. The pandemic period was a period of challenges and the realization of the true potential of the world economy including the banking industry. The adverse effects were also supplemented by the decline in oil prices. Despite this, the CBO's annual reports indicate steady improvement in the Omani banking sector in recent years. The total assets and the aggregate deposits (see Figure 7.1) of banking sector increased by 19.8% (from OMR 29,885.9 ($77,726.65) billion in 2016 to OMR 35,814.1 ($93,144.6) billion in 2020) and 18.3% (from 20,423.5 ($53,117.035) billion in 2016 to 24,156.5 ($62,825.747) billion in 2020), respectively. The private sector credit and deposits constitute the largest proportion of the total credit and deposits of commercial banks during this period.

However, the profits of commercial banks (see Figure 7.2) decreased by 35.5% in 2020, from OMR 374.7 ($974.5) million in 2016 to OMR 241.4 ($627.8) million in 2020, affected by the COVID-19 pandemic and the economic downturn (CBO, 2021a, 2021b).

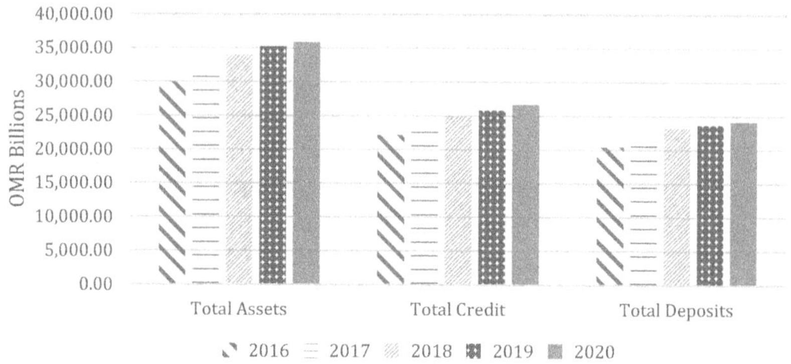

Figure 7.1. Commercial banks total assets, credits and deposits from 2016 to 2020.

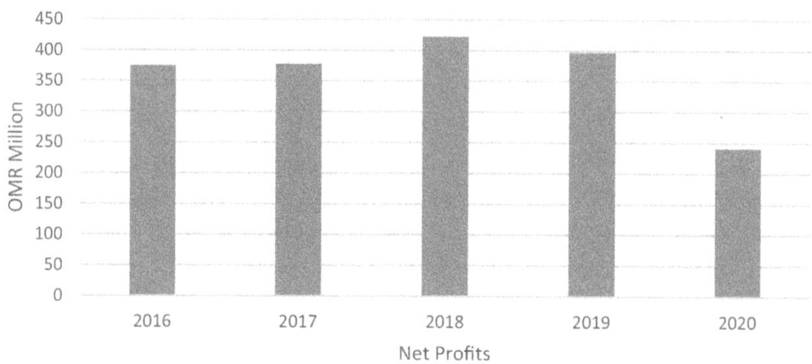

Figure 7.2. Commercial banks profits from 2016 to 2020.

The adverse impacts of the economy and the pandemic also led to an increase in provisions and write-offs, wherein the net interest margin remained intact (*The Financial Stability Report*, 2021). The increase in the provision for non-performing assets (see Figure 7.3) in 2019 (33.3%) and 2020 (49.5%) resulted in a rise in NPLs. In 2019 and 2020, the stock of gross NPLs of the banking sector amounted to OMR 890,000 ($2.314 million) and OMR 1.111 ($2.889) million, constituting 3.5% and 4.2% of the banks' gross loans, respectively (2016: 1.8%), while the net NPLs amounted to OMR 406,000 ($1.056 million) in 2020, constituting 1.6% of the net loans (2019:1.4%). The restructured NPLs also increased. In 2018, the restructured NPLs were OMR 564,000 ($1.466 million) and then increased to OMR

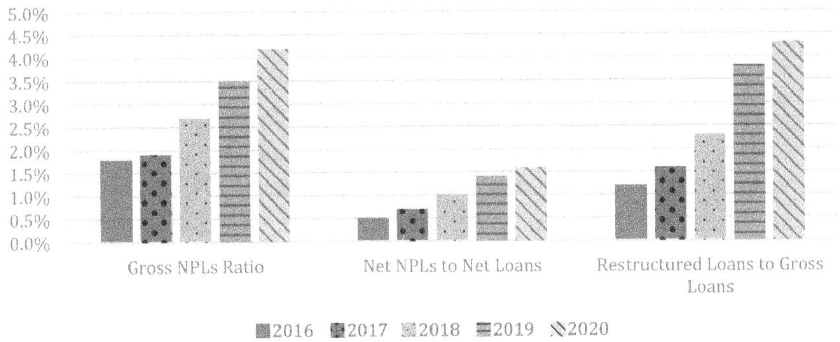

Figure 7.3. NPLs and restructured loans trends and increase from 2016 to 2020.

970,000 ($2.522 million) and OMR 1.144 ($2.975) million in 2019 and 2020, respectively (CBO, 2021a, 2021b).

It is worth mentioning that the contribution of Islamic banking to the country's economy was nominal in the early years of its inception. As Mohammed & Alam (2020) stated, both major Islamic banks in Oman (Alizz and Nizwa) encountered losses in the first years of their operations. Alizz Islamic bank's loss was estimated at around OMR 1684320, whereas Bank Nizwa was unable to make a profit until 2015. However, Islamic banks witnessed a considerable improvement after 2015, attributed to the higher level of consumer awareness of the Islamic banks' products (Mihajat, 2019). According to Bilal *et al.* (2016), the total assets held by the Islamic banks (IB) and the IB windows of conventional banks in March 2016 reached OMR 2.5 billion ($6.5 billion), compared to OMR 1.5 billion ($3.9 billion) in 2015. This made the Islamic banks' market share increase from 5.1% to 7.8% by 2016. However, as Mihajat (2021) suggests, the outbreak of COVID-19 hinders the growth of Islamic banks due to a lack of *sukuk* issuance, insufficient liquidity instruments, and limited capital in Islamic finance.

7.4. The Role of Technology and CBO in Mitigating COVID-19 Effects

Exceptional measures were taken by the banking industry to reduce the spread of the COVID-19 pandemic in Oman. It ensured the implementation of hygiene protocols and social distancing as per the instructions of concerned authorities, i.e., the Ministry of Health, Supreme Committee, and regulators for the safety of stakeholders (Fitch Solutions, 2021). Physical branches were closed, banknotes were disinfected, and appointment systems were disabled to combat the spread of the virus. Due to the lockdown and restrictions, the banking sector's operations and services were disrupted. Oman's banking industry risk indicator (BIRI) showed the highest score, representing a risk level that was 3.63 out of 100 in 2020 (Fitch Solutions, 2021). The COVID-19 period was the hardest for the banking sector, first, due to devastating energy demand and decline in petroleum-related products and, second, because of a lack technological advancement to carry on operational activities. This was when the banking sector realized the significance of technological development for its survival.

Hidayat (2020) stated that, on the one hand, the customer's swift adoption of e-banking globally forced entire financial institutions to change services and product provision modes from conventional to advanced. On the other hand, the slow spread of COVID-19 at the beginning of the pandemic in Oman gave the opportunity for the banking industry to make significant technological shift, enabling them to alleviate the adverse impacts of the pandemic on the Omani banking sector. Banks carried out a continuous stream of technological advancement through artificial intelligence in mobile and internet banking to provide a varied range of services and transactions to their customers from the comfort of their homes (KPMG, 2020).[18] Online mortgage apps were introduced via smart devices, voice-assisted devices, and touchpoints. These measures helped in the creation of the safest possible environment along with the enhancement of financial skills of the customers using technology, while adopting blockchain-based customer transactions methods and keeping cybersecurity in mind. These actions proved fruitful for the banks and caused a 1000% increase in the usage of touchpoints. During this challenging period of the pandemic, technological enhancement improved the banking sector's performance, and consequently, the banking sector not only maintained its current growth rate but also coped with

[18]https://assets.kpmg/content/dam/kpmg/om/pdf-2020/06/oman-banking-perspectives.pdf.

global strategic shifts (e.g., closing banks' branches and developing new policies) (CBO, 2021b).[19]

Moreover, the CBO announced a range of measures and policy initiatives. The CBO offered liquidity management solutions and played the role of a lender of last resort to the bank entities. The CBO backed financial institutions by accommodating the financing installments for customers who were affected by COVID-19 (KPMG, 2020). Subsequently, the banking sector was able to offer finance programs, reduce services charges, reschedule installment repayments, distribute charity funds, and support those who were laid off within the sultanate amid the pandemic (Fitch Solutions, 2021).[20] Taken together, although Oman's economy was affected adversely during the COVID-19 pandemic due to the contraction of economic activities and a decline in global oil prices, the overall growth in the banking sector was marginally positive due to the robust banking regulatory framework. The banking sector also remained successful in minimizing losses.

7.5. Summary and Conclusion

This chapter aimed to enhance the understanding of the Omani banking system. To achieve this, it reviewed the existing literature and reports on the banking regulatory and institutional frameworks over the last 50 years. It also discussed the recent banking sector performance and the role of technology and the CBO in counterbalancing the negative effects caused by the COVID-19 pandemic. On the whole, the review suggests the non-existence of local banks and a national authority regulating and supervising the Omani banking market before 1970s, with only 3 foreign banks being operated in Oman during that period. However, the Omani banking system developed substantially afterward, attributed mainly to the expansion of the oil sector and the supervisory and regulatory authority of the CBO on the banking sector. This led to a gradual increase in the

[19]https://www.cnb.cz/export/sites/cnb/en/financial-stability/.galleries/fs_reports/fsr_2020-2021/fsr_2020-2021.pdf.

[20]https://www.fitchsolutions.com/sites/default/files/2021-04/Oman-Banking-Financial-Services-Report.pdf.

number of banks and the existence of a dual banking system comprising both conventional and Islamic banks. However, the Omani banking sector is the main constituent of the Omani financing system, dominated by a few banks. Further, bond and mutual funds markets are not well developed in Oman. Accordingly, limited commercial banks are regarded as the main sources of funds for individuals' and companies' businesses and investments. These banks expand their operations mainly through mergers and acquisitions and have experienced steady performance in recent years. They were marginally affected by the COVID-19 pandemic due to the higher adoption of technology and the measures taken by the CBO.

References

Al-Kalbani, M. (2008). The quality of annual corporate reports in an emerging economy: The case of Oman. Doctoral dissertation, Cardiff University, UK.

Al-lawati, H. (2022). Evolution of Omani's banking sector. *Oman Daily Observer.* https://www.omanobserver.om/article/1115845/opinion/business/evolution-of-omans-banking-sector.

Allen, C. H. & Rigsbee II, W. L. (2014). *Oman under Qaboos: From Coup to Constitution, 1970–1996.* London: Routledge.

Al-Muharrami, S. (2016). Evaluation of banks in Oman: Assessment to GCC's benchmark. In Al Ghassani, A, Al Lawati, A, and Ananda, S (Eds.), *Banking Sector in Oman: Strategic Issues, Challenges and Future Scenario, College of Banking and Financial Studies. Muscat.* pp. 47–60. https://scholar.google.com/scholar?hl=en&as_sdt=0%2C5&q=Banking+Sector+in+Oman%3A+Strategic+Issues%2C+Challenges+and+Future+Scenario&btnG=.

Azad, I. Sadi, S., & Faiyaz, M. (2011). Growth of banking sector in the sultanate of Oman: An analysis. *International Journal of Finance & Policy Analysis, 3*(1), 91–107.

Bertelsmann Stiftung (2012). *BTI 2012 — Oman Country Report.* Gütersloh: Bertelsmann Stiftung.

Bilal, Z. O., Durrah, O. M., & Atiya, T. M. (2016). Comparative study on performance of Islamic Banks and Conventional Banks: Evidence from Oman. *International Journal of Economics and Financial Issues, 6*(4), 1835–1841.

BTI. (2012). Oman Country Report. Gütersloh: Bertelsmann Stiftung. https://bti-project.org/fileadmin/api/content/en/downloads/reports/country_report_2012_OMN.pdf.

CBO. (2009). Report of Banking Control Departments 2009. Central Bank of Oman.

CBO. (2013). Annual Report 2012. Central Bank of Oman.

CBO. (2016). Annual Report 2015. Central Bank of Oman.

CBO. (2021a). Annual Report 2020. Central Bank of Oman. https://cbo.gov.om/Pages/AnnualReport.aspx.

CBO. (2021b). Financial Stability Report 2021. Central Bank of Oman.

Dalwai, T. & Mohammadi, S. S. (2020). Intellectual capital and corporate governance: an evaluation of Oman's financial sector companies. *Journal of Intellectual Capital*, *21*(6), 1125–1152.

Dusuki, A. (2007). Commodity Murabahah programme (CMP): An innovative approach to liquidity management. *Journal of Islamic Economics, Banking and Finance*, *3*(1), 1–23.

Elghuweel, M. (2015). Empirical essays on corporate governance and corporate decisions in emerging economies: The case of Oman. Doctoral dissertation, University of Glasgow, UK.

Financial Action Task Force. (2011). Anti-Money Laundering and Combating the Financing of Terrorism. Middle East and North Africa Financial Action Task Force. https://www.menafatf.org/sites/default/files/Mutual_Evaluation _Report_of_the_Sultanate_of_Oman.pdf.

Fitch Solutions. (2021). Oman's Banking and Financial Services Report 2021. Fitch Solutions Country Risk and Industry Research. https://www.fitchsolutions.com/sites/default/files/2021-04/Oman-Banking-Financial-Services-Report.pdf.

Hasni, A. (2021). Constraints of non-oil-related SMEs' access to bank funding: Credit discouragement incidents in oil-based economy. Doctoral dissertation, University of Glasgow, UK.

Hidayat, S. E. (2020). Islamic Economy in ASEAN Countries during the COVID-19 Era. Retrieved at November 2020 from kneks.go.id.

Kasturi, R. (2018). Performance analysis of Oman's banking sector using select financial indicators. *Journal of Commerce and Accounting Research*, *7*(4), 31–39.

KPMG. (2020). Oman banking perspectives 2020: Adapting for new technologies, regulations and culture. Publication number: 2901, KPMG Lower Gulf Creative team, UAE and Oman. https://assets.kpmg.com/content/dam/kpmg/om/pdf-2020/06/oman-banking-perspectives.pdf.

Kothaneth, L. (2022). What's on a Banknote? *Oman Daily Observer*. https://www.omanobserver.om/article/1116448/oman/community/whats-on-a-banknote.

Looney, R. (2009). The Omani and Bahraini Paths to Development. https://www.wider.unu.edu/sites/default/files/RP2009-38.pdf.

Martey, E. (1999). Financial intermediation and the evolving role of the Central Bank. In Treichel, V, and Mansur, A. (Eds.), Oman beyond the Oil Horizon: Policies toward sustainable growth. International Monetary Fund, pp. 31–39. https://www.elibrary.imf.org/view/books/084/30 05013-9781557758330-en/ch05.xml.

Mihajat, M. (2021). Oman's Islamic banking performance amidst COVID-19 outbreak: Prospects and challenges. *Journal of Economics and Business*, *6*(1), 38–51. p-ISSN: 2503-4235 e-ISSN: 2503-4243.

Mihajat, M. I. S. (2019). Shari'ah governance framework in IFIs in Oman: Issues and challenges. In T. Azid, A. Alnodel, & M. Qureshi (Eds.). *Research in Corporate and Shari'ah Governance in the Muslim World: Theory and Practice*. Emerald. DOI: 10.1108/9781789730074.

Mohammed, S. & Alam, N. M. (2020). Financial perspectives of Islamic banks in Oman. *Financial Studies*, *24*(2(88)), 50–63.

Oxford Business Group. (2015). *The Economy is Well Positioned for Long-term Expansion*. Oxford Business Group. https://oxfordbusinessgroup.com/reports/oman/2015-report/economy/the-economy-is-well-positioned-for-long-term-expansion.

Oxford Business Group. (2017). *Oman's Banking Sector Records Rises in Assets, Lending and Deposits*. Oxford Business Group. https://oxfordbusinessgroup.com/overview/solid-performance-sector-records-rises-assets-lending-and-deposits-central-bank-keeps-tabs-liquidity.

Oxford Business Group. (2019). *Oman's Economic Rebound Set to Spur Growth Among Banking Sector's Lenders*. Oxford Business Group. https://oxfordbusinessgroup.com/reports/oman/2019-report/economy/brighter-prospects-despite-challenging-regulatory-changes-the-broader-economic-rebound-is-set-to-spur-growth-among-lenders.

Peterson, J. E. (2004). Oman: Three and a half decades of change and development. *Middle East Policy*, *XI*(2), 125–137.

Rath, D., Mishra, D., & Al Yahai, Q. (2014). Concentration and competition in Oman's banking sector: Implications for financial stability. Working Paper. https://papers.ssrn.com/sol3/papers.cfm?abstract_id=2427601.

Sangeetha, J. (2012). Financial crisis and Omani commercial banks: A performance review. *European Journal of Business and Management*, *4*(8), 171–176.

Skeet, I. (1992). *Oman: Politics and Development*. Basingstoke: Macmillan.

Wippel, S. (2012). Economic integration from a country perspective: Oman in the Gulf cooperation council. In *Proceedings of the BRISMES Annual Conference — Revolution and Revolt: Understanding the Forms and Causes of Change*, March 26–28, 2012, London, pp. 1–11.

https://doi.org/10.1142/9781800614734_0008

Chapter 8

Proposed Framework for Measuring a Bank's Progress in Implementing Financial Inclusion: An Exploratory Study in Egypt

Hamada Elsaid Elmaasrawy Elsayed Ghazi and Omar Ikbal Tawfik

Abstract

This study presents a proposed multidimensional framework for measuring the level of application of financial inclusion (FI) at the individual bank level based on international expertise and experience in the field of FI application by relying on a balanced scorecard, clarifying the advantages and disadvantages of FI for banks, and reviewing previous attempts to build an indicator to measure FI. After reviewing the literature and conducting a series of interviews with bank managers in Egypt, this study concludes that bank application of FI has many benefits, such as diversifying banking assets, attracting new customers, stabilizing deposits, and reducing liquidity risks as well as providing a large database to banks, which can contribute to the possibility of introducing new products that can satisfy customer needs and building credit evaluation models to facilitate access to financing. However, the application of FI may have negative effects on banks, as providing basic financial services at zero cost (or costs lower than actual bank costs) may lead to a low level of welfare for financial service users and providers. At the same time, service providers may refrain from providing financial services when they have little incentive to do so. In addition, this study finds that all the indicators for measuring FI are used at the state level, and no indicator exists for measuring FI at the individual bank level. Therefore, this study proposes a multidimensional framework for measuring the level of application of FI at the bank level based on four perspectives of a balanced scorecard to contribute to the development of bank performance by providing appropriate and accurate information that can help the bank management in identifying shortcomings and weaknesses as well as opportunities for improvement and strengths, which can be exploited to improve future performance.

Keywords: Financial inclusion, balanced scorecard, availability of banking services, usage of banking services

8.1. Introduction

Recently, as financial inclusion (FI) emerged as an important issue in the global development policy agenda, widespread interest in inclusive financial systems was observed. This phenomenon made FI an important issue and a political priority in many countries, given its positive impact on the economy by reducing the poverty level, increasing savings and consumption levels, and improving income distribution.

Banks play a key role in initiating the application of FI as the main provider of most financial services and intermediaries between savers and investors. The concept of FI revolves mainly around the possibility of accessing the financial services provided by financial institutions to the largest segment of society.

Several definitions of FI were presented by scholars. For instance, Allen *et al.* (2016) defined FI as a course of action that can ensure access, availability, and use of formal financial services by all individuals and businesses in the economy. The G20 defined FI as the measures taken by regulatory bodies to enhance the access and use of all segments of society (marginalized and affluent groups) of financial services and products that are commensurate with their needs, provided in a fair and transparent manner at a reasonable cost. The Organization for Economic Cooperation and Development defined FI as the process through which access to a wide range of formal and controlled financial services and products is achieved at a reasonable cost in a manner that can ensure the use of financial services and products by all segments of society (Ibrahim & Al-Saeedi, 2019).

From the previous definitions, we derive the most important components of FI as follows:

- Providing official and audited financial services to all members of society.

- Diversifying financial services and products to suit the needs of different segments of society.
- Providing financial services in a fair and transparent manner at a reasonable cost.
- Expanding the range of segments of society that can use financial services, especially the marginalized and low-income segments.

Thus, we define FI as the process through which all financial transactions of individuals and community institutions are linked with official financial institutions, subject to supervision, through their provision of diverse financial services that are transparent, fair, affordable, and appropriate for all members of society.

Given the importance of FI at the national level from economic and social perspectives, banks must expand activities that meet the requirements of FI. Although banks are a tool for society to achieve progress, growth, and prosperity, the expansion of activities meeting the requirements of FI should not affect their main and strategic goals, as institutions for achieving profit, survival, and continuity in the future.

Currently, FI is considered as a key factor for achieving seven of the 17 Sustainable Development Goals. The G20 committed to promoting FI worldwide and reaffirmed its commitment to implementing the G20 High Principles on Digital FI. A number of banks introduced various initiatives to promote FI in their country, in addition to the initiatives of central banks. Moreover, several organizations play an active role at the international level in setting standards to improve FI, such as the International Finance Corporation, International Monetary Fund, Alliance for FI (AFI), and Consultative Group to Assist the Poor, which are among the major international players involved in promoting FI activities (Bose *et al.*, 2016). The Global Partnership for FI was established in 2010, and the World Bank established the Global Findex Database[1] in 2011, which is the most comprehensive dataset on how adults save, borrow, make payments, and manage risks. Launched with funding from the Bill & Melinda Gates Foundation, the database has published reports every three years since 2011.

In 2016, the Central Bank of Egypt established the Central Administration for FI to play a pivotal role in coordinating with

[1]https://globalfindex.worldbank.org/.

different agencies, whether internally or externally, with the aim of supporting and enhancing FI (Zaghloul, 2003, 2010). Internal coordination occurs between the various departments of the bank to launch initiatives and programs supporting FI, and external coordination involves various bodies for planning different activities (Telecommunication Union, 2014). The Central Bank of Egypt works in accordance with the best international practices, thereby qualifying it to join global initiatives and international institutions concerned with FI to exchange experiences and learn from peers. The most important entities and initiatives include the AFI and Regional Initiative to Strengthen FI in Arab Countries. In another framework, the Central Bank of Egypt is an active member of the regional work team to enhance FI in the Arab region (i.e., FI Task Force). FI is one of the main pillars for achieving Egypt's 2030 strategy. Indicators showed a significant increase in FI rates in the past 6 years. The total number of people with accounts that can enable them to conduct financial transactions, including accounts in banks or the Egyptian Post, mobile phone wallets, or prepaid cards, is 36.8 million or 56.2% of the total number of people 16 years of age or older out of a total of 65.4 million (www.cbe.org.eg).

Despite the efforts exerted to measure the level of application of FI in various countries, all attempts were made at the state level or global level in general. The main objective of this chapter is to present a proposed multidimensional framework to measure the level of application of FI at the individual bank level based on international expertise and experience in the field of FI application. The proposed framework will contribute to the development of banks' performance by providing appropriate and accurate information that can help the bank management in identifying shortcomings and weaknesses as well as opportunities for improvement and strengths, which can be exploited to improve future performance, through a set of indicators to measure the different dimensions of FI. The proposed framework is integrated and comprehensive to measure the level of application of FI and will contribute to striking a balance between measures that meet current needs and those that can ensure the sustainable development of individual banks.

The rest of this chapter is divided as follows: Section 8.2 reviews the literature, Section 8.3 describes the research methodology, Section 8.4 presents the proposed framework for measuring bank progress in implementing FI, and Section 8.5 concludes the study and provides several recommendations.

8.2. Literature Review

Previous studies addressed FI from three dimensions. The studies that addressed the dimensions of FI are summarized in Table 8.1.

By reviewing the literature, we believe that previous studies attempted to measure FI at the bank level as a whole in a specific country or at the level of several countries around the world. However,

Table 8.1. Previous studies on FI.

Authors	Dimension of FI	Contents of the dimensions of FI
Kumar & Mishra (2010)	Banking outreach	Number of deposit accounts per person • Number of credit accounts per person • Number of bank offices per person • Average saving amount per deposit account • Average credit amount per credit account
	The demand for financial services at household level	The number of people with access to savings from both formal and informal sources • The number of people with access to credit from both formal and informal sources • The number of people with access to savings from formal sources only
Kunt & Klapper (2013)	Formal account	Percent of adults who have an account in a formal financial institution
	Formal saving	Percent of adults reported having savings (in a formal financial institution)
	The usage of bank credit (formal credit)	Percent of adults having borrowed from a formal financial institution
Cámara & Tuesta (2014, 2017)	Usage	Percent of people holding at least one financial product such as a banking account, mobile banking, credit, or debit card • Percent of people keeping savings • Percent of people having a loan in a formal financial institution
	Barriers	Distance from a formal financial institution or access points • Affordability or lack of money to open an account • The lack of trust in the financial system
	Access	The physical point of services offered by the number of commercial bank branches (per 100,000 adults) and Number of ATMs (per 100,000 adults)

(*Continued*)

Table 8.1. (*Continued*)

Authors	Dimension of FI	Contents of the dimensions of FI
Lenka & Barik (2018)	Banking penetration	The proportion of people having bank accounts
	Availability of banking services	The number of bank outlets (per 1,000 populations)
		• The number of ATM per 1,000 people • The number of bank employees per customer
	Usage of banking services	The volume of credit and deposits as the proportion of the country's GDP
Al-Adwey (2019)	Access	The number of bank branches
		The bundle of digital services that involves high levels of process automation and web-based services
	Usage	The number of bank accounts opened by adults
		The volume of outstanding deposit for adults
		The volume of outstanding loans for adults
Hanivan & Nasrudin (2019)	Access	Account
		Debit card
		Credit card
		E-money card
	Availability	Branches
		ATMS
	Usage	Debit transactions
		Credit transactions
		Credit-to-GDP
Ezzahid & Elouaourti (2021)	Access	Number of ATMs per 100,000 adults
		Number of branches of commercial banks (per 100,000 adults)
	Usage	Ratio of domestic credit provided by the banking sector to the GDP (% of GDP)
		Deposits as % of GDP

no previous study has attempted to measure FI at the individual bank level.

8.3. Research Methodology

8.3.1. *Research approach*

FI was examined extensively at the country level around the world, but measurement of progress in implementing FI at the individual bank level and the extent to which individual banks contribute effectively to FI implementation were not addressed in previous studies, which can explain our adoption of a qualitative approach in this study to capture the complexity of the phenomenon and richness of the data. Our decision to adopt a non-quantitative approach stems from the need to understand the specificity of the application of FI in the context of the Arab Republic of Egypt, as the Central Bank of Egypt established the Central Department of FI in 2016 and has since been taking gradual and accelerated steps to implement FI in the Egyptian state. For this study, we conducted 14 interviews with CEOs of Egyptian banks from July 20, 2022 to September 25, 2022. We conducted six interviews face to face and eight interviews over the phone. We encountered some challenges while preparing for the interviews and identifying the individuals to be interviewed, such as the refusal of many managers to be interviewed, citing lack of time or intention to not disclose any information about their bank. The average duration of each interview was 60 minutes, with the longest interview lasting two hours and the shortest interview lasting only 20 minutes. Table 8.2 presents a descriptive summary of the interviewees.

8.3.2. *Data collection and analytical method*

We collected the data through interviews. Our objective in using personal interviews as our data collection strategy was to record the perceptions of the bank executives of how they responded to and interacted with the FI initiatives and plans carried out by the Central Bank of Egypt. In addition, we assessed the extent of each bank's commitment to FI and the executive managers' position on the expansion of FI and the main reasons behind it, which may constitute an obstacle to FI expansion from the perspective of the executive directors. At the same time, to explore the point of view of the executive directors on the best way to measure the bank's progress in implementing FI, we conducted thematic analysis, as it fits our objective and the nature of the collected data (from the interviews). Topic analysis is one of the methods used in analyzing qualitative data, in which researchers organize and place the data under specific topics or categories and then explain and interpret them analytically to find answers to their research questions. Objective analysis

Table 8.2. Descriptive summary of interviews.

	Positions	Field of study	Formal education background	Gender	Years of experience	Ownership structure the bank
1	Vice President of the bank branch	Accounting	Master of Professional Accounting (MPA)	Male	21	State ownership
2	Bank manager	Accounting	Master's Degree	Male	17	Joint ownership
3	President of the bank branch	Management	PH.D.	Male	22	Private sector ownership
4	President of the bank branch	Finance	Bachelor's Degree	Female	18	State ownership
5	Credit manager	Economic	Master's Degree	Male	18	Joint ownership
6	Vice President of the bank branch	Accounting	Master of Professional Accounting (MPA)	Female	23	State ownership
7	Bank manager	Management	Doctor of Business Administration (DBA)	Male	31	Joint ownership
8	Credit manager	Accounting	Master of Professional Accounting (MPA)	Female	19	State ownership
9	President of the bank branch	Finance	Master of Business Administration (MBA)	Male	27	Private sector ownership
10	Credit risk manager	Accounting	Master of Professional Accounting (MPA)	Male	31	State ownership
11	Credit manager	Accounting	PH.D.	Female	21	Joint ownership
12	President of the bank branch	Economic	Master's Degree	Male	24	State ownership
13	Bank manager	Accounting	Bachelor's Degree	Male	29	State ownership
14	Credit manager	Management	Master's Degree	Male		State ownership

may be conducted by focusing on the commonalities of the data, but a common or recurring topic may not necessarily be significant or meaningful (Miles & Huberman, 1994; Abdennadher *et al.*, 2022).

8.3.3. *Findings*

Our findings showed that the banks operating in the Egyptian state were committed to implementing the plans and initiatives of the Central Bank to expand FI, including public sector banks, private sector banks, and banks owned jointly by the public and private sectors. However, the extent of the effective participation of each bank in FI depends on many factors, and problems exist on the appropriate evaluation of each bank's participation in FI. We present several findings:

(1) Four major procedures are employed to coincide with international celebrations and occasions, during which the banking sector targets all segments of society by being outside branches and offering the opening of accounts without fees or a minimum deposit, and sponsors financial education activities for citizens. The four annual events approved by the Central Bank of Egypt occur in three separate months throughout the year, starting with celebrations for women in March, coinciding with International Women's Day, through Arab Day for FI in April, and then celebrations for the youth in August in conjunction with International Youth Day, and finally the savings celebrations in October. We used indicators for each of the four procedures to measure the extent of the expansion of each bank and each branch of the same bank. All the interviewees agreed that metrics were used in each of the four procedures. We employed scales to measure the extent of the expansion of each bank and each branch of the same bank. For example, for March, we used the following FI measures: "How many accounts were opened by the new bank for women during the celebrations in March?" "How many credit cards were issued to women during the celebrations in March?" "How many new clients were women during the celebrations in March?" "How many female clients applied for a loan for the first time?" We also used measures for August: "How many new bank accounts were opened in the name of a young individual during the period of celebration in August?" "How many new

credit cards were issued for young people during the celebrations in August?" "How many new clients were young people during the celebration period in August?" "How many young clients applied for a loan for the first time?"

(2) The Central Bank of Egypt adopted several steps within the framework to disseminate financial culture, including intensive media awareness campaigns about the concept of FI and deployment of awareness convoys to rural and remote areas to spread awareness of various financial services and their benefits, especially during the four annual events approved by the Central Bank. For the question "What is the extent of the participation of your bank or branch of your bank in spreading awareness of various financial services and their benefits during the four annual events approved by the Central Bank of Egypt?", most of the interviewees agreed that their bank should contribute to disseminating financial culture and spreading awareness of various types of financial services, which may vary from one bank to another. For example, one of the branch managers shared that he/she allowed the participation of a large number of employees in spreading financial culture (president of a government bank branch; interviewee #12). Meanwhile, several managers stated that they adhered to the minimum number of employees required to disseminate financial culture and allocated the rest of the bank employees' time to normal tasks (interviewee #1, #4, #6, and #13). Furthermore, the managers of privately owned banks shared that the dissemination of financial culture must be accompanied by the achievement of the bank's goals. Therefore, the banks complied with the Central Bank's decision to spread financial culture by offering and providing financial services that helped the banks achieve their goals, provided that the dissemination was performed by ordinary employees instead of additional employees allocated for the activity (interviewee #3 and #9). Thus, the government banks participated more than the private banks in spreading financial culture. For example, in the annual procedures for the four events approved by the Central Bank of Egypt, the private banks adhered to the minimum number of required employees, according to their decision to assign one employee, such as one from each branch, to participate in spreading financial culture, whereas the number of employees

assigned by the government banks for such an activity varied. Some of the bank and branch managers adhered to the minimum number of employees required to spread financial culture and allocated the rest of their employees' time to regular tasks. Meanwhile, some of the bank and branch managers of government banks allowed a large number of employees to participate in spreading financial culture.

(3) The Central Bank of Egypt launched initiatives to provide financing to micro, small, and medium-sized companies. The most important initiative was obligating banks to increase the volume of credit for such companies to 20% of the total portfolio of the credit facilities of each bank, with a maximum amount of GBP 500,000 for each project of small and micro enterprises. For the question "Did your bank expand the granting of credit to new categories of customers to expand its FI base?", most of the interviewees agreed that obligating banks to increase the volume of credit for such companies to 20% of the total portfolio of the credit facilities of each bank, with a maximum amount of GBP 500,000, helped expand FI. The bank managers' answers to this question were clear, as some banks relied on horizontal expansion in lending to small projects. In other words, they did not give the minimum amount of GBP 500 to any small project. Small projects were lent GBP 50,000–GBP 100,000, especially those applying to the bank for the first time, to expand the FI base. Some of the banks gave loans to a large number of small projects and customers (interviewee #7, #10, #11, and #14), whereas the other banks relied on lending to medium-sized and small projects, with the maximum allowed amount of GBP 500,000. Most of the customers who obtained such loans were existing bank clients, whereas only a small percentage of the clients who obtained such loans were new clients (interviewee #3, #5, and #9).

(4) For the question "From your point of view, is the system for assessing the extent of your bank's expansion appropriate, and does it encourage the bank management to further expand FI? In other words, why are some bank administrations enthusiastic about their effective contribution to FI?", most of the interviewees agreed that the bank management was not motivated to implement the FI procedures, as financial outcomes in terms of

> revenues appear in the long term, whereas the cost of expanding FI is deducted in the current period, because many of the incentives, returns, and rewards received by the managers in the current period depend on the net profit. A manager of a government bank stated that without the bank's commitment to achieving the national goals of the country, it would not need to spend all its funds on FI, which can reduce the bank's profitability (interviewee #14).

The findings clearly show that a majority of the managers of the Egyptian banks were forced to implement FI, in the best case, whereas some adhered to the minimum requirement only because their incentives and rewards depend on the net profit in the current period, which was negatively affected by the cost of FI in the current period. In the succeeding section, we present the proposed multidimensional framework for measuring the level of application of FI at the individual bank level, which may contribute to developing banks' performance by providing appropriate and accurate information that can help the bank management in identifying shortcomings and weaknesses as well as opportunities for improvement and strengths. The framework employs a set of indicators to measure the different dimensions of FI; thus, it may be used to evaluate the performance of the bank management in light of FI.

8.4. Proposed Framework for Measuring Bank Progress in Implementing FI

The application of FI by banks can lead to an increase in their costs and consequently, a decrease in their profitability in the short term. Therefore, the bank management must assume the role of a coordinator between stakeholders (i.e., owners, creditors, customers, and employees). Conflict may exist between the owners' goals and those of the other stakeholders, which can be resolved by abandoning the goal of maximizing the owners' wealth in the short term and achieving only a satisfactory increase in such wealth, thereby giving the other stakeholders an opportunity to participate in the wealth accumulation in the short term (Dalwai *et al.*, 2014; Hindi, 2009). Therefore, banks must examine various FI activities before expanding them. In light of the previous discussion, the proposed framework is a multidimensional framework that considers the effects of employing FI at all levels of a bank to make improvements and corrections and sound decisions to enhance its performance in the short and long terms.

Several approaches can be used to measure bank progress in implementing FI, such as a balanced score card (BSC), the successful performance dimension model (SDM), the reference frame metrics, and the performance table. We relied on a BSC to measure the level of application of FI at the individual bank level. The application of a BSC can achieve two main objectives:

(1) Administrative control by helping managers monitor and tighten control over activities by defining a set of major objectives and measures related to the four dimensions to achieve improved performance.
(2) Operational control by helping managers monitor the company's performance when implementing activities in accordance with the strategic foundation and extent required to complete the work (Al-Shaabani, 2017).

In a BSC, three approaches can be used to integrate and include aspects related to FI:

(1) *Subsumption method*: This method requires defining the FI elements and aspects to be included in the four dimensions of a BSC.
(2) *Addition of a fifth dimension to a BSC*: This method involves adding a fifth perspective to the BSC, including FI elements and aspects. The addition of a new perspective to the BSC requires the FI elements and aspects to be related to the strategic aspects.
(3) *Extraction of a BSC for performance*: A BSC can be used for the clear and in-depth management of various FI aspects.

A BSC links the objectives of the four perspectives as well as the key performance indicators necessary to measure progress in achieving the strategic objectives. Thus, a score card can contribute to measuring banks' level of application of FI through its four perspectives.

To implement the proposed model, first, banks must define their performance standards and develop strategic objectives for each perspective. Second, the banks must determine whether they successfully achieved their preset goals. Third, the banks must develop a unique BSC appropriate for their situation. Table 8.3 outlines

Table 8.3. Strategic objectives and key performance measures.

Perspective	Strategic activity	Objectives	Key Performance Indicators — KPI
Financial perspective	Increasing revenue opportunities	Increase profits through interest income and commissions	The percentage of revenue generated from new services and products designed to enhance FI.
			Percentage of revenue generated from new clients that were attracted by FI products.
			Return on Assets (ROA).
	Improving the cost structure	Reducing the costs of financial intermediation of the bank and increasing efficiency	The cost of each new customer individually or in groups who were attracted by FI products.
			The ratio of bad loans from small customers to total bad loans.
			The ratio of operating cost to total assets.
			Net interest margin (NIM).
	Increasing the utilization of funds	Efficient use of funds	Economic value added EVA. Residual Income RI. Return on invested capital ROI. Return on Equity (ROE).
Customer perspective (individuals and institutions targeted by FI)	Availability	Increasing market share	Market rate coverage.
			The ratio of small savings accounts (for individuals and institutions) to the total savings accounts compared to the previous year or compared to competing banks or compared to the target plan.
	Selection/Service	Attracting new customers and continuous customer retention	New customers' growth rate.
			Ratio of new small savers (individuals and institutions) who own bank accounts to total savers to last year or compared to competing banks or compared to the target plan.
			Ratio of new savings accounts for small new savers (individuals and institutions) who own bank accounts to total savers compared to last year or compared to competing banks or compared to the target plan.
			Ratio of individuals who receive loans from the bank compared to the previous year.

	Functionality	Increase per customer profit	The profitability of each client individually or in groups of new clients attracted by FI products.
	Quality	Increase customer satisfaction	Degree of customer satisfaction ratio of individuals who receive financial services (at least one service such as bank accounts, mobile phone services, and credit cards).
			Ratio of total mortgage loans to total loans granted to individuals.
			The ratio of total credit cards to total loans granted to individuals. Personal Loans Ratio to the total loans.
			The percentage of the increase in funding for NGOs, the percentage of the increase in support for women and families with special needs, the percentage of the increase in environmental financing.
			The percentage of increase in small and medium-sized enterprises financed by the bank.
Internal operations perspective	Operational process management	Increased transaction efficiency	Reducing the waiting time within the bank compared to previous periods or compared to competitors.
		Increase the effectiveness, efficiency, and quality of each of the goals and routine tasks	Speed in the credit study of the customer compared to previous periods or compared to competitors.
			Accuracy in measuring the credit risk of the customer.
			The number of documents to open a current account.
			The number of documents to open a deposit account.
			The number of days required to grant a consumer loan.
			The number of days required for the granting of the mortgage loan.
	Innovative processes	Innovation of products and services	The number of new services and products.
			Introducing new services that are compatible with Islamic law.
			The success ratio of new banking services to the number of new services and products.
			The number of services and products that have been accepted and that have achieved the goals to the number of new services and products.

(Continued)

Table 8.3. (*Continued*)

Perspective	Strategic activity	Objectives	Key Performance Indicators — KPI
	Customer management	Enhance customer value	The number of customer complaints. Minimum amount to open a current account. Minimum amount to open a deposit account. Minimum amount of consumer loans. Minimum amount of real estate loans. Consumer loan fees (% of minimum loan amount). Mortgage fees (% of minimum loan amount). Annual fee for deposit account. Annual fee for current account. Amount of fees for using ATM cards (% per \$100). International and local money transfer cost (% per \$250).
	Organizational and social processes	Increased availability of banking services	Geographical expansion of bank branches (counting bank branches per 1000 km^2). Population expansion of bank branches (number of bank branches per 100,000 adults). Geographical spread of ATMs (the number of ATMs per 1,000 km^2). ATM population spread (number of ATMs per 100,000 adults). Percentage of funds allocated to finance small and micro enterprises.
Learning and growth perspective	Human capital	Continuous professional development of employees	The number of employees who received training (the number of training hours for each worker) on the strategy adopted by the bank to implement FI.
		Increasing employee satisfaction and motivation	The number of training hours for each worker on the strategy adopted by the bank to implement FI. Error rate for employees during the application of FI. Average rate of incentives and rewards for 2 years for success in implementing the strategy adopted by the bank to implement FI. The percentage of increase in health, cultural, and sports services provided to the bank's employees.

Organizational capital	Developing the bank's organizational capital	The percentage of employees' participation in the decision (the number of managers with decision-making authority/ total number of employees).
		The number of employees in leadership positions by calculating the number of managers in all branches of the bank.
		The level of supremacy of the FI application culture in the bank.
Information capital	Development and improvement of information technology	The number of employees participating in the development and maintenance of programs (IT).
		The extent of turnout and interaction from customers with the bank's website and the bank's pages on social media.
		The rate of development in building comprehensive databases that include historical credit data records for individuals and small and medium-sized businesses.
		The extent of benefiting from the huge databases provided by the FI of banks in the analysis and exploration, in a way that affects the possibility of offering new products that satisfy the needs of these segments.

Source: Stojkovski & Nenovski (2021), Arora (2010), Sarma (2008), Kumar & Mishra (2010), Kunt & Klapper (2013), Lenka & Barik (2018), and Al-Adwey (2019).

the strategic objectives and key performance measures according to the proposed framework for measuring FI implementation.

8.5. Conclusion and Recommendations

FI has many benefits for banks, including diversifying banking assets, attracting new clients, stabilizing deposits, and reducing liquidity risks, in addition to providing a large database. Such a database is useful for analysis and exploration, which can affect the possibility of launching new products that can satisfy the needs of different customer segments and building credit evaluation models to facilitate access to financing. In addition, FI can lead to the diversification of asset and liability portfolios, which can enhance the distribution of risks and avoid their concentration (Mohan, 2006; Ozen and Grima, 2020; Mehrotra and Yetman, 2015). However, the application of FI may have a negative effect on banks. The provision of basic financial services at zero cost (or costs lower than actual costs) may lead to a reduced level of welfare for financial service users and providers, and discourage service providers from offering such services when they have little incentive to do so. In addition, banks will require a considerable amount of information about new customers and the market, including conducting historical and credit data analyses and market assessments, to make sound decisions when dealing with customers.

Various indicators were used to measure FI; however, all the indicators for measuring FI were used at the state level, and no indicator exists for measuring FI at the individual bank level. Therefore, the main contribution of our study is to provide a multidimensional framework for measuring the level of application of FI at the individual bank level using a BSC. The proposed framework is integrated and comprehensive enough to measure the level of FI implementation and works by striking a balance between measures that meet the current requirements and those that can ensure the sustainable development of individual banks. In other words, the proposed framework for measuring bank progress in implementing FI is a multidimensional framework that considers the effects of the application of FI at all bank levels, which is useful for making improvements, corrections, and sound decisions to enhance a bank's performance in the short and long terms. We propose a multidimensional framework for measuring the level of application of FI at the individual bank level based on the four perspectives of a BSC (i.e., financial perspective, customer perspective, internal operations perspective, and learning and growth perspective). The framework targets the best performance practices at the business organization level and can strike a balance between the external performance measures (i.e., linked with external parties, such as return on investment and customer satisfaction) and internal performance measures related to processes that create value for customers and shareholders (e.g., process efficiency and employee satisfaction), in addition to the correlation between the performance measures that represent performance drivers and measures representing outcome measures.

A BSC can clarify the different effects of the application of FI on the development of a bank's performance by showing them at all levels of the bank and not focusing only on the bank's final products, that is, financial services provided to customers. The proposed framework aims to contribute to the development of banks' performance by providing appropriate and accurate information that can help the bank management in identifying shortcomings and weaknesses as well as opportunities for improvement and strengths, which can be exploited to improve future performance. Therefore, banks must calculate their steps effectively in terms of profitability, costs, and expected impact for each decision to expand the application of FI to improve their performance in the short and long terms.

The limitation of this study is its exploratory nature; that is to say, this study identifies indicators for measuring FI through four perspectives of a BSC through a review of the literature and indicators for measuring global FI issued by various agencies. Given this limitation, future research can examine the determinants of banks' expansion in the application of FI, impact of the disclosure of the application of FI on banks' financial performance, and impact of the expansion of the application of FI on credit risks. Furthermore, future studies can build other indicators (e.g., the SDM, BK reference framework metrics, and TDB performance table) to measure FI at the individual bank level.

References

Abdennadher, S., Grassa, R., Abdulla, H., & Alfalasi, A. (2021). The effects of blockchain technology on the accounting and assurance profession in the UAE: An exploratory study. *Journal of Financial Reporting and Accounting*, *20*(1), 53–71.

Al-Adwey, L. (2019). Does FI improve the financial performance of commercial banks in Egypt? Pooled OL Approach. *Journal of Accounting Research*, *6*(1), 1–28.

Allen, F., Demirguc-Kunt, A., Klapper, L., & Peria, M. S. M. (2016). The foundations of financial inclusion: Understanding ownership and use of formal accounts. *Journal of Financial Intermediation*, *27*, 1–30.

Al-Shaabani, S. I. (2017). A proposal to develop the balanced scorecard as a tool for evaluating the tool in light of sustainable development — An applied study on the Hammam Al-Alil Cement Factory in Nineveh, Iraq. *Anbar University Journal for Economic and Administrative Sciences*, *17*, 342–376.

Bansal, A. (2012 October–December). Profitable models for FI. *Global Journal of Management and Research*, 1–9.

BCBS (2016). Guidance on applying the core principles for effective banking supervision to the regulation and supervision of institutions relevant to FI. *Consultative Document*, 31 March.

Bose, S., Bhattacharyya, A., & Islam, S. (2016). Dynamics of firm-level FI: Empirical evidence from an emerging economy. *Journal of Banking and Finance Law and Practice*, *27*(1), 47–68.

Camara, N., Pena, X., & Tuesta, D. (2014). Factors that matter for financial inclusion: Evidence from Peru. *The International Journal of Finance*, *14*(9).

Dalwai, T., Chugh, G., Prasad, S., & Mohammadi, S. S. (2014). Can effective corporate governance of Islamic banks enhance financial inclusion in the Sultanate of Oman? *International Journal of Humanities and Social Sciences (IJHSS)*, Conference Edition, Apr 2014, pp. 61–74. https://www.researchgate.net/publication/322790818_Can_Effective_Corporate_Governance_Of_Islamic_Banks_Enhance_Financial_Inclusion_In_The_Sultanate_Of_Oman.

Demirgüç-Kunt, A. & Klapper, L. (2013). Measuring financial inclusion: Explaining variation in use of financial services across and within countries. *Brookings Papers on Economic Activity*, *2013*(1), 279–340.

Ezzahid, E. & Elouaourti, Z. (2021). Financial inclusion, mobile banking, informal finance and financial exclusion: Micro-level evidence from Morocco. *International Journal of Social Economics*, *48*(7), 1060–1086.

Global Partnership for FI (GPFI). (2011). The First G20 Global Partnership for FI (GPFI) Forum. Forum Report Published on October 1st, 2011. Retrieved on 18 September 2018. https://www.gpfi.org/sites/default/files/documents/GPFI%20Forum%20Report.pdf.

Hanivan, H. & Nasrudin, N. (2019). A financial inclusion index for Indonesia. *Bulletin of Monetary Economics and Banking*, *22*(3), 351–366.

Hindi, M. I. (2009). *Modern Thought in Financial Analysis and Performance Evaluation: An Introduction to Corporate Governance* (1st edn.). Alexandria, Egypt, University Knowledge House.

Ibrahim, M. Z. & Al-Saedy, S. S. (2019). The role of FI in activating the stock market: An applied study on banks listed on the Egyptian stock exchange. *Scientific Journal of Commerce and Finance*, Special Issue of the Third Scientific Conference of the Faculty of Commerce, Tanta University, *39*(1), 305–360. https://journals.ekb.eg/issue_18831_36368.html.

Kumar, C. & Mishra, S. (2010). Banking outreach and household level access: Analyzing FI in India. In *13th Annual Conference on Money and Finance in the Indian Economy*. http://www.igidr.ac.in/conf/oldmoney/Banking%20Outreach%20and%20Household%20level%20Access.pdf.

Lenka, S. K. & Barik, R. (2018). A discourse analysis of FI: Post-liberalization mapping in rural and urban India. *Journal of Financial Economic Policy*, *10*(3), 406–425. DOI: 10.1108/jfep-11-2015-0065.

Mehrotra, A. N. & Yetman, J. (2015). Financial inclusion-issues for central banks. *BIS Quarterly Review* (2015), *83*(96). https://www.bis.org/publ/qtrpdf/.

Miles, M. B. & Huberman, A. M. (1994). *Qualitative Data Analysis: An Expanded Sourcebook*. Sage.

Mohan, R. (2006). Economic growth, financial deepening, and FI. In *Dynamics of Indian Banking*, BIS Review 113, pp. 92–120. https://www.bis.org/review/r061121e.pdf.

Ozili, P. K. (2018). Impact of digital finance on FI and stability. *Borsa Istanbul Review*, *18*(4), 329–340.

Ozen, E. & Grima, S. (Eds.). (2020). *Uncertainty and Challenges in Contemporary Economic Behaviour*. Emerald Studies in Finance, Insurance, And Risk Management, 1st edn.

Sarma, M. (2008). Index of financial inclusion (No. 215). Working Paper. Indian Council for Research on International Economic Relations (ICRIER), New Delhi.

Stojkovski, V. & Nenovski, B. (2021). Balanced scorecard model in the banking sector. *International Journal of Science and Research*, *10*(3), 1627–1630.

Telecommunication Union (ITU). 2016 Issue Brief Series, Inter-Agency Task Force on Financing for Development, July. United Nations. http://www.un.org/esa/ffd/wpcontent/uploads/2016/01/Digital-Financial_Inclusion_ITU_IATFIssue-Brief.pdf.

United Nations (2016). Digital FI. International World Bank policy Research Working Paper, No. 6577.

Zaghloul, G. A. (2003). Using the balanced performance scale in building a system for measuring strategic performance in the Egyptian business environment. *The Scientific Journal of Commerce and Finance, 23*(1), 317–380.

Zaghloul, J. A.-R. (2010). Using the balanced performance scale in building a four-way measurement model for strategic and operational performance management of intellectual assets. *Twelfth Symposium on Ways to Develop Accountancy in the Kingdom of Saudi Arabia, Entitled: The Accounting Profession in Saudi Arabia and the Challenges of the Twenty-first Century*. http://iefpedia.com.

https://doi.org/10.1142/9781800614734_0009

Chapter 9

Independence of Central Bank of Egypt and Exchange Rate Regimes

Mustafa Kasim and Khaled Hussainey

Abstract

In this chapter, we assess macroeconomic independence using the prices of goods and services and short-term interest rates throughout a range of time periods categorized by alternative exchange rate regimes. To assess how well-floating exchange rates have increased Egypt's macroeconomic independence from the European Union (EU) and the United States (US), the ARDL model (autoregressive distributed lag) or Bounds Test has been devised. We examine a number of hypotheses concerning global transmission, interest rate and price movement, and international trade using this empirical methodology. According to the findings, Egypt's products market and monetary policy are, over the long term, completely independent from those of base regions like the European Union and the United States. Because of this, the Central Bank of Egypt (CBE) may decide its plan of action (policy direction) and define its goals without being impacted by shocks from the EU and the US.

Keywords: Macroeconomics independence, goods market, monetary policy, Central Bank of Egypt, and exchange rate regimes

9.1. Introduction

Interdependence of macroeconomics is considered to be a widespread and critical issue in the literature of open economy, especially as the system of exchange rate regimes across the countries has developed from pegged (fixed) exchange rates to a more flexible (floating) exchange rate system. It is well acknowledged that monetary policy affects how economic decisions are made. The New Keynesian theoretical framework assumes that prices are fully flexible in the short run. If this is not the case, the central bank might temporarily affect real interest rates, which will affect real output in addition to nominal prices. It is a frequent misconception that central banks have specific goals for controlling the independence of the products market. In order for monetary policy to best achieve these goals, the central bank needs keep an eye on both interest rates and prices (Tng and Kwek, 2015). Thus, by maintaining its independence from foreign central bank policies that it may attach its currency to, the central bank can achieve its aims for trade and monetary policy.

In light of this, the issue of adopting a more flexible exchange rate can help the economy accomplish its objectives, such as a stable and independent interest rate, and price, which is viewed as a vital concern by both the banking and financial industries. One benefit of flexible exchange rates, according to conventional open economy macroeconomics models, such as those based on Mundell–Fleming, is that countries are not constrained by the "trilemma", which holds that it is impossible to have fixed exchange rates, capital mobility, and an independent monetary policy at the same time. But at the end of the day, monetary policy independence is a matter of empirical evidence. The degree of monetary policy autonomy is significantly decreased if, for whatever reason, a particular central bank thinks that it must emulate the policies of other nations (Edwards, 2015).

The independence of the products market and the independence of monetary policy are two main categories of macroeconomic independence. The term "goods market independence" refers to the ability of market prices in two countries to fluctuate independently. The ability of interest rates in two countries to fluctuate (or be managed) independently of one another is referred to as monetary independence. The interdependence of national economics was described by Tollison & Willett (1973) as the sensitivity of economic behavior in one country (a developing country) to the growth of another (developed country). The ability of market prices to fluctuate independently within two countries is referred to as "goods market independence". The ability of interest rates in two countries to change (or be managed) independently of one another is referred to as monetary independence.

Objectively, this chapter examines the independence of the goods market and monetary policy in Egypt. To do so, this study investigates the long-run relationship between Egyptian (domestic) consumer price index and short-term interest rate to the European Union (EU), and United States (US) (foreigner base regions) consumer price index, and interest rate, regarding purchasing power parity (PPP) and uncovered interest parity (UIP). More specifically, does adopting a flexible exchange rate by the Egyptian central bank promote an independent consumer price index and interest rate to the foreign (EU) and (US) consumer price index and interest rate? For this research question, we look at the two variables separately; first, we are going to test for the independence of goods market and, second, look for the independence of monetary policy between Egypt and the EU, and US as the base countries.

The usual argument is that the autonomy of monetary policy is enhanced under floating rates because the central bank is relieved of the obligation to maintain the fixed exchange rate. A convenient explanation is offered by the two parity requirements, UIP and PPP. In a world where goods and assets are completely interchangeable, domestic inflation and the interest rate might not differ from their international counterparts under fixed exchange rates, which would result in a total loss of monetary control in a tiny economy. Contrarily, exchange rate flexibility allows for variations in interest and inflation rates between the US and other countries. The Trilemma policy, which states that a government cannot simultaneously opt for open financial markets, fixed exchange rates, and monetary autonomy, is another argument that strengthens PPP and UIP arguments. Instead, it is limited to choosing no more than two of these three, which is another argument. As a result, the central bank must decide whether to use a fixed exchange rate system to stabilize its exchange rate regime or a free floating exchange rate system to be independent of its monetary policy.

The purpose of this study is to fill in gaps in the body of knowledge about these issues, starting with the classification of Egypt's exchange rate regimes. A closer look at the exchange rate regimes that Egypt has used from 1980 to 2016 shows that even though the central bank of Egypt (CBE) announced the adoption of a freely floating exchange rate regime between 2003 and 2004; however, in practice, the CBE intervened judiciously to effectively maintain the stability of the Egyptian pound exchange rate against the dollar (Selim, 2012; Massoud & Willett, 2014). In addition, according to Calvo & Reinhart (2002), developing nations that have a nominally floating exchange rate regime frequently forbid their exchange rates from floating in practice and utilize the interest rate as a tool to stabilize exchange rate fluctuations and minimize the danger of devaluation. As a result, a floating regime's primary advantage is not realized, and nations lose the capacity to employ monetary policy to further domestic goals. In addition, according to Reinhart & Rogoff (2004), 50% of developing countries classify their exchange rate in an unfair manner (i.e., despite the central bank's announcement of adopting a freely floating exchange rate, there is still intervention to keep the exchange rate stable). Due to the fear of floating, it is uncertain if flexible exchange rates are effective in enabling emerging countries to run their own independent monetary policy. Since the Central Bank of Egypt intervened during this time, it is not appropriate to describe the years 2003 to 2004 as a period of freely floating currency rates. Instead, we will treat this time as a period of managed floating exchange rates.

The existing literature emphasizes that a previous study, conducted by An *et al.*, 2016, specifically addressed goods market independence and monetary policy. This was accomplished by employing a co-integration and Error Correction Model (ECM) to investigate the relationship. Because the ECM cannot be applied unless all variables are integrated in the same sequence, this methodology has a number of drawbacks (Sargan, 1964). Another drawback of adopting the ECM is that the delays are constrained, making it impossible to accurately represent the long-term relationships between the variables, whereas the long-term relationship variables are completely stated and unconstrained (Nkoro & Uko, 2016). Because of this, the research in this chapter uses Autoregressive Distributed Lag (ARDL), also known as the Unrestricted Error Correction Model (UECM), established by Pesaran *et al.* (1999). Even when the data have a mixed level of integration (level I(0) and I(1)), using such techniques makes it possible to investigate long-term relationships.

Consequently, the current chapter seeks to make the following contributions to the existing literature: First, it delves into an examination of the independence relationship between the goods market and monetary policy in Egypt. Second, it involves the reclassification of Egypt's exchange rate regime spanning 1980 to 2016, with a specific focus on the intervention strategies employed by the Central Bank of Egypt to stabilize the exchange rate. The study also analyzes how such interventions impact the independence of both the goods market and monetary policy. Lastly, the research employs the Autoregressive Distributed Lag (ARDL) co-integration technique, or the bound test of co-integration, as an analytical tool. This tool is used to identify and establish the long-term correlation between Egypt's goods market and monetary policy, and corresponding variables within the American and European base regions, to which Egypt's currency is linked.

9.2. Theoretical Literature Review

The following ideas can theoretically express the framework of the interdependence of pricing and interest rate between two countries.

9.2.1. *Law of one price (LOOP)*

The law of one price (also known as LOOP) is a theory of economics that holds that, in competitive markets devoid of transportation costs and governmental trade restrictions, the price of identical goods in various markets must be the same when taking into account currency exchange rates and when their prices are expressed in terms of the same currency.

The law of one price is a restatement of the axiom that identical goods must trade at the same relative prices regardless of where they are sold when trade is open and costless. The law of one price establishes a single connection between domestic prices of goods and exchange rates and is formally stated as follows:

Let P^i_{US} be the dollar price of good i, when sold in the US, corresponding to the Egyptian Pound price in Egypt. Then, the law of one price implies that the dollar price of good i is the same wherever it is sold:

$$P^i_{\mathrm{US}} = \mathrm{EX}_{\mathrm{EGP/Dollar}} * P^i_{\mathrm{EGP}}.$$

Equivalently, the Egyptian pound (EGP)/US Dollar exchange rate is the ratio of good i's Egypt and US money prices, $\mathrm{EX}_{\mathrm{EGP/Dollar}} = P^i_{\mathrm{EGP}}/P^i_{\mathrm{Dollar}}$.

9.2.2. *Purchasing power parity (PPP)*

According to the principle of purchasing power parity, the ratio between the price levels of two countries' currencies determines the exchange rate between their currencies. The price level of a nation's reference basket of commodities and services reflects the currency's domestic buying power. Accordingly, the purchasing power parity hypothesis predicts that a rise in domestic prices that results in a decline in the purchasing power of domestic currency will be accompanied by a commensurate decline in the value of that currency on the foreign exchange market. According to PPP, a rise in the currency's domestic buying power will be correlated with a commensurate increase in the value of the currency. Let P EGP be the price of a reference commodity basket sold in Egypt and P (US) be the price of the same basket in the US in order to represent the PPP theory in symbols. According to PPP, the exchange rate between Egyptian pounds and US dollars will be as follows, assuming that a single basket accurately depicts the purchasing power of money in both nations:

$$\mathrm{EX}_{\mathrm{EGP}/\$} = \frac{P_{\mathrm{EGP}}}{P_{\mathrm{US}}}. \tag{9.1}$$

By rearranging Eq. (9.1) to read

$$P_{\mathrm{EGP}} = \mathrm{EX}_{\mathrm{EGP}}/\$ * P_{\mathrm{US}},$$

an alternative interpretation of PPP results. The left side of this equation is the Egyptian pound price of the reference commodity basket in Egypt, while the right side is the Egyptian pound price of the reference basket when purchased in the US, that is, its dollar price multiplied by the Egyptian pound price of a dollar. These two prices are the same if PPP holds. PPP thus asserts that all countries' price levels are equal when measured in terms of the same currency. In other words, the right side of the final equation calculates how much an Egyptian pound is worth in dollars when used in the US. Therefore, PPP is valid if, at the current exchange rates, the domestic purchasing power of each currency is always equal to its foreign purchasing power.

9.2.3. *Uncovered interest parity (UIP)*

As a result of foreign exchange trading, the idea of interest rate parity was created, which connects the difference between spot and future exchange rates with the difference between foreign and domestic interest rates. According to this parity requirement, the domestic interest rate must be equal to the international interest rate plus the anticipated change in exchange rates. Given the current interest rate disparity, the future exchange rate should properly adapt, provided investors are risk neutral and have reasonable expectations.

If interest rate parity holds true, investors will be indifferent to interest rates in two countries whether the position is covered or uncovered as the exchange rate adjusted return will be the same. The future exchange rate should depreciate by exactly the interest rate differential. If covered and uncovered interest rate parities both hold, this implies the forward rate is an unbiased predictor of the future spot rate. In the case of covered interest rate parity, the domestic interest rate, r_t, is represented as

$$r_t = r_t^* + f_t - s_t,$$

where r_t^* is the foreign interest rate, f_t is the forward rate, and s_t is the current spot rate. Unlike covered interest parity with an available forward rate, UIP is more difficult to test as expectations of future exchange rates are not directly observable. Accordingly, UIP operates under the assumption that the current forward rate will equal the expected exchange rate plus a forecast error defined as

$$f_t = E(s_{t+1}) + E_{t+1}. \tag{9.2}$$

Hence, Eq. (9.2) can be rewritten as

$$r_t = r_t^* + s_{t+1} - s_t + E_{t+1}$$

or rearranged as

$$s_{t+1} - s_t = r_t - r_t^* + E_{t+1}.$$

9.3. Empirical Literature Reviews

It has been the subject of numerous studies to determine whether flexible exchange rate regimes promote the independence of the goods market and monetary policy. The standard defense is that because the central bank is freed from the responsibility of upholding a fixed exchange rate, monetary policy has greater autonomy when interest rates are floating.

In a review of the literature related to the **goods market**, by reexamining the connection between exchange rates and relative pricing for Japan and the US, Cheng (1999) expanded and enhanced the knowledge. In the long run, the study discovered a causal relationship between the price ratio and the flexible exchange rate in the US and Japan via interest rates. This result confirms the PPP theory, according to which currency exchange rates move in response to shifts in the price ratio between two nations. Furthermore, Goldberg & Campa (2010) assessed the relative weight of the various pathways that support the consumer price index's (CPI) receptivity to import prices and exchange rates across 21 industrialized economies. They discovered that locally produced items, traded goods, and non-traded goods are all affected by changes in exchange rates and import prices.

However, An *et al.* (2016) conducted more research on the question of whether a floating exchange rate for Japan will strengthen the independence of the products market while taking capital control into account. They discovered that although a floating exchange rate increases the independence of the goods market, it is capital controls — not exchange rates — that support the independence of the goods market.

In a review of the independence of **monetary policy**, the first group of studies supports the argument that an independent monetary policy increases under a floating exchange rate regime. Frankel *et al.* (2004) experimentally evaluated the degree to which the choice of exchange rate regime affects the sensitivity of domestic (national) interest rates to foreign (international) interest rates. Between 1970 and 1999, they used data from a large sample of both emerging and developed nations worldwide. The findings demonstrated that, in contrast to nations where exchange rates are pegged, those with floating exchange rates tend to have autonomous monetary policies. Similarly, as part of his examination into how a fixed exchange rate affects monetary policy, Shambaugh (2004) classed nations as pegged or unpegged in order to ascertain whether or not those with fixed exchange rates are required to adhere to the base economy's interest rate. Shambaugh (2004) asserts that the trilemma is still present and that it supports the policy of an open economy. He added that countries cannot simultaneously have fixed exchange rates, domestic monetary autonomy, and free capital markets, and that fixed exchange rate countries, either voluntarily or inadvertently, restrict the autonomy of their monetary policy to the base region. He came to the conclusion that nations with fixed exchange rates do, in fact, track the interest rate of the base region more closely than nations with flexible exchange rates, and that nations with floating exchange rates do, too, though not to the same degree as nations with fixed exchange rates. In an empirical analysis of the choice of exchange rate regimes in the context of East Asian economies, Kim & Lee (2008) revealed that after adopting floating exchange rate systems, local interest rates in Korea and Thailand became less sensitive to global interest rates. However, they discovered that Japan's floating exchange arrangement had stronger monetary policy independence than a pegged country like Hong Kong. According to Li & Tsai's (2013) analysis of the effects of China's flexible exchange rate regime and monetary policy between 2005 and 2008, loosening the exchange rate regime can increase the independence of China's monetary police, resulting in more independent and efficient open market operations. Grossmann *et al.* (2014) looked into the dynamics of exchange rate volatility and its high frequency in the interaction between monetary policy and macroeconomic variables on the destabilization component of exchange rate volatility. According to the findings, nations that implement a floating exchange rate have the chance to break free from the "impossible trinity", which leads to monetary independence, capital mobility, and increased exchange rate stability. Additionally, their study implies that while developing nations can achieve the same goal by pursuing policies that result in greater terms of trade, rich countries may be able to stabilize their exchange rates by aiming for lower inflation rates. In their study, An *et al.* (2016) examine the degree of capital mobility and various exchange rate systems used during various time periods to categorize macroeconomic independence. To assess how well floating exchange rates have increased Japan's macroeconomic independence from the US, a co-integration VAR methodology has been devised. Their findings indicate that although Japan's monetary independence has decreased over time, it retains some degree of monetary autonomy due to the floating exchange rate system. In a similar study focused on Central and Eastern European Countries (CEECs), in all CEE nations with the exception of Hungary, Dąbrowski *et al.* (2019) identified a level relationship between the domestic and international interest rate. They also concurred that "trilemma policy arrangements, including exchange rate flexibility", continue to influence how sensitive Central and Eastern European nations' interest rates are to changes in policy and shocks. Other studies conducted in various contexts, including advanced and emerging market economies (Georgiadis & Zhu, 2019), have observed consistent findings with the trilemma's predictions from the 2000s. These findings are evident across different situations, such as advanced and developing market economies. This means that the sensitivity of local rates to the policy rates of the base region is decreased by both exchange rate flexibility and capital constraints. The idea that the financial channel of exchange rates decreases the extent to which local policymakers choose to make use of the monetary autonomy provided by flexible exchange rates in particular circumstances is supported by data discovered by Georgiadis & Zhu (2019). An economy with a flexible exchange rate is more sensitive to base-country policy rates when it has negative foreign-currency exposures from bank and portfolio debt on its external balance sheet and when the base-country monetary policy is tightened.

However, some of finding comes against the argument that highlight monetary policy could be promoted under a flexible exchange rate. Clarida *et al.* (1998) found evidence indicating that the central banks of E3 countries were significantly influenced by German monetary policy in their examination of monetary policy in two groups of countries, G3 (Germany, Japan, and the US) and E3 (the United Kingdom, France, and Italy). Even though it was discovered that monetary policy in industrialized nations responds to the exchange rate, the size of the reaction was found to be modest. With similar findings, exchange rate flexibility, monetary independence, and capital account openness were quantified by Aizenman *et al.* (2013) while accounting for recent significant international reserve buildup. Their results showed that the weighted sum of the three trilemma variables adds up to a constant, with an increase in one variable causing a decrease in the weighted sum of the other two variables. It was discovered in Dąbrowski *et al.*'s (2019) study of the relationship between the domestic and foreign interest rates in CEE countries that only in Hungary were they further not in agreement that "trilemma policy arrangements, including exchange rate flexibility", continue to affect the sensitivity of interest rates to policy changes and shocks in the Central and Eastern European economies. Other studies found evidence to support the idea that nations with more flexible regimes react to changes in US interest rates considerably more strongly, with the best exchange rate regimes depending on the specific country's circumstances and time horizons (Frankel, 1999). Schmukler *et al.* (2000) suggested that flexible regimes do not allow much monetary independence and that the speed of adjustment supports the conventional view that countries with fixed regimes can adjust much more quickly than countries with more flexible arrangements in a more in-depth study that included a large sample of developing and industrialized economies between 1970 and 1999. The Global Financial Cycle, according to Rey (2015), poses a threat to the trilemma policy's viability since US monetary policy shocks are transmitted internationally and have an impact on financial conditions even in inflation-targeting countries with significant financial markets. Therefore, in a world of significant capital flows, flexible exchange rates are insufficient to provide monetary independence. Similarly, the Czech Republic and Poland were able to maintain their monetary independence when the European Central Bank (ECB) tightened its monetary policy, according to Dąbrowski *et al.*'s (2019) analysis of the macroeconomic trilemma in the context of Central and Eastern European Countries (CEECs). In the same year, Goczek & Partyka (2019) examined the genuine independence of E.U.A. non-euro members and discovered that domestic interest rates mirror those of the single currency. Despite the protection provided by floating exchange rate systems and inflation-targeting frameworks, this suggests low monetary independence.

The second group of studies represents the argument that the autonomy of monetary policy increases under a pegged exchange rate. The impact of changes in the money supply on production, interest rates, and exchange rates was studied by Stockman & Ohanian (1993). They discovered that even in the presence of pegged exchange rates, countries nevertheless exhibit some short-term monetary policy independence. Recently, Edwards (2015) discovered that these developing markets are impacted by changes in the US interest rate in order to address the question of whether or not an increase in the US interest rate affects emerging markets with flexible exchange rates, specifically Chile, Colombia, and Mexico. The idea of "fear to float" may help to explain the findings of this study. According to models in the Mundell–Fleming tradition, if capital mobility is less than ideal, a rise in the international interest rate, which is produced by the Federal Reserve, will cause an "incipient external deficit" and a depreciation of the domestic currency. Indeed, restoring equilibrium requires a currency adjustment. However, if there is "fear to float", the local government may be tempted to tighten its own monetary policy in an effort to prevent the depreciation of the local currency.

However, some studies have found that independence of monetary policy would not be possible to increase under a pegged exchange rate regime. In a study of Saudi Arabia, Akikina & Al-Hoshan (2003) used annual data from 1960 to 1994 with open capital flow and constant exchange rates to examine the independence of the central bank's monetary policy. The findings showed that Saudi Arabia's monetary authority, at best, had a tenuous grip on the country's money supply. The findings also indicated that capital flight in Saudi Arabia is positively and significantly impacted by the anticipated shift in exchange rate depreciation. Consistent with this, the empirical research of Frankel *et al.* (2004) examined the degree to which the choice of exchange rate regime affects the sensitivity of domestic interest rates to foreign interest rates. The findings demonstrated that nations with pegged exchange rates are less monetary policy independent than those with floating exchange rates. In a study of whether or not capital control keeps the countries away from US monetary policy shocks, Miniane & Rogers (2007) demonstrated that nations with fixed exchange rates and open financial markets respond to base shocks more closely. Furthermore, in their study, which examined the potential channels through which major industrial country interest rates affect other economies, Di Giovanni & Shambaugh (2008) discovered that pegged countries only react to the rate of the country to which they are linked; they do not respond to any global interest rates. They came to the conclusion that pegging results in a loss of monetary autonomy, which affects the economy. Furthermore, Bluedorn & Bowdler (2010) estimated international interest rate linkage under different currency rate regimes using base region interest rates, reassessing the "difficult trinity". According to their findings, the interest rate responds more strongly to changes in foreign interest rates than it does to exogenous shocks in a fixed exchange rate system with an open financial market. In a study of monetary authorities of twelve new EU members, Vašíček (2010) discovered that central banks in nations with fixed exchange rates appeared to react to an interest rate peg with the Euro area, given that the central bank sets the short-term interest rate exogenously. In his study of whether the globalization of the early 1990s caused the loss of monetary policy independence in India, Paul (2012) observed that even in the 1960s, when the country kept a fixed exchange rate and there was no globalization, due to foreign exchange restrictions, India had lost its independence in monetary policy. The fact that a country can still exercise monetary policy independence even in the presence of unrestricted capital flows so long as it does not maintain a stable exchange rate suggests that this independence is significantly rooted in the regime of exchange rates as well as the presence of foreign exchange constraints, rather than necessarily in globalization. An Asian nation might have managed to evade the clutches of the impossible trinity. A case in point is their examination of Malaysia's journey, where they unearthed a consistent relationship between US and Malaysian interest rates during the period when Malaysia upheld a fixed exchange rate coupled with an open capital account system. This led them to the deduction that Malaysia is not impervious to the challenges posed by the impossible trinity.

9.4. Hypothesis Development and Research Design

9.4.1. *Hypothesis development*

Does the presence of flexible exchange rate regimes lead to an increase in the independence of the goods market and monetary policy? Does the Egyptian central bank's use of a flexible exchange rate encourage the use of a consumer price index and interest rate that are distinct from those of the US and the EU? In order to answer this research question, we will examine the two variables separately. First, we will check the independence of the goods market, and then we will examine the independence of the monetary policy between Egypt and the base regions of the EU and the US.

The following hypothesis (Ha) will investigate the assessment of goods market independence:

EU H_0: EGPCPI = EUCPI $\neq 0$ [Egyptian and European price are cointegrated]

H_1: EGPCPI = EUCPI =0 [Egyptian and European price are NOT co-integrated]

US H_0: EGPCPI= USCPI $\neq 0$ [Egyptian and F American interest rate are co-integrated]

H_1: EGPCPI = USCPI = 0 [Egyptian and American interest rate are NOT co-integrated]

The following hypothesis (Hb) is used to assess monetary independence:

EU H_0: EGPIN = EUIN $\neq 0$ [Egyptian and European interest rate are co-integrated]

H_0: EGPIN = EUIN = 0 [Egyptian and European interest rate are NOT co-integrated]

US H_0: EGPIN = USIN $\neq 0$ [Egyptian and American interest rate are co-integrated]

H_1: EGPIN = USIN = 0 [Egyptian and American interest rate are NOT co-integrated]

Where, the interest rate within the country is represented by EGPIN, which stands for the Egyptian interest rate. The external interest rate, related to Europe, is abbreviated as EUIN, representing the European interest rate. The foreign interest rate, specifically associated with the US, is denoted by USIN, signifying the American interest rate. The domestic consumer price index is referred to as EGPCPI, standing for the Egyptian consumer price index. EUCPI signifies the international consumer price index, focusing on Europe, and USCPI refers to the international consumer price indexcentered around the US.

9.4.2. *Research design*

The range of data used for this study is on a monthly basis from January 1980 to December 2016 for seven variables in the case of Egypt, the EU, and the US. The data were collected from various government and economics websites, including those run by the Federal Reserve Economic Data[1] (FRED), World Bank Data,[2] the Global Economy,[3] and Central Bank of Egypt[4] (CBE). These variables are defined as follows: (i) The Egyptian Pound, often known as Exchange Rate (EX), is the Arab Republic of Egypt's official currency. It has been figured as EGP/US. (ii) The Domestic Price (DCPI) indicator, which serves as Egypt's consumer price index, looks at the weighted average of the costs of a variety of consumer products and services. (iii) Nominal domestic interest rate is denoted by the abbreviation DIN, which stands for Egypt's short-term interest rate and measures the effects of monetary policy without taking inflation into account. (iv) Foreign Price (FCPI) is used as a proxy for the US consumer price index and calculates the weighted average of prices for a range of goods and services. (v) The Foreign Interest Rate, or FIN, represents the US short-term interest rate and measures the effects of monetary policy

The analysis used in this study is built on the Applying Autoregressive Distributed Lag (ARDL) Co-integration technique, often known as the Bound Test of Co-integration or Unrestricted Error Correction Model (UECM). The UECM was created by Pesaran *et al.* (1999, 2001) utilizing methodologies to explore both the short- and long-term relationships even if the data contain a mixed level of integration — level I(0) and I(1). Therefore, in order to apply the Autoregressive Distributed Lag (ARDL), the following steps need to perfectly apply unit root test (ADF and P.P), determination of optimum lag length, Autoregressive Distributed Lag (ARDL) model, Wald test, and lastly the diagnostic test (serial correlation and CUSUM test).

The five-dimensional auto-regressive distributed lag (ARDL) model can be written as

$$\Delta Y_t = \beta_0 + \sum \beta_i \Delta Y_{t-i} + \sum \delta_i \Delta X_{t-1} + \varphi_1 Y_{t-1} + \varphi_2 X_{t-1} + \varepsilon_t, \tag{9.3}$$

here, β_i and δ_i pertain to the short-term indicators, while φ_1 and φ_2 represent the long-term indexes. Additionally, ε_t describes an

[1]https://fred.stlouisfed.org/.
[2]http://microdata.worldbank.org/index.php/home.
[3]https://www.theglobaleconomy.com/.
[4]https://www.cbe.org.eg/en/Pages/default.aspx.

intended "disturbance" term. Y_t has a "distributed lag" component in the form of successive lags of the explanatory variable and is clarified by lagged values of itself (X). Sometimes, the distributed lag portion of the model's structure is not applied to the current value of X_t.

Therefore, regarding the term and condition of the Autoregressive Distributed Lag (ARDL) model, this study designs the investigation of the independence of the commodity market and monetary policy, respectively, as shown in Eqs. (9.4a) and (9.4b):

$$\begin{aligned}\Delta\mathrm{DCPI}_t = \beta_0 &+ \sum \beta_1 \Delta\mathrm{DCPI}_{t-i} + \sum \delta_2 \Delta\mathrm{EX}_{t-1} \\ &+ \sum \delta_3 \Delta\mathrm{FCPI}_{t-1} + \varphi_1 \mathrm{DCPI}_{t-1} + \varphi_2 \mathrm{EX}_{t-1} \\ &+ \varphi_3 \mathrm{FCPI}_{t-1} + \varepsilon_t, \end{aligned} \tag{9.4a}$$

$$\begin{aligned}\Delta\mathrm{DIN}_t = \beta_0 &+ \sum \beta_1 \Delta\mathrm{DIN}_{t-i} + \sum \delta_2 \Delta\mathrm{EX}_{t-1} \\ &+ \Delta\mathrm{FIN}_{t-1} + \varphi_1 \mathrm{DIN}_{t-1} \\ &+ \varphi_2 \mathrm{EX}_{t-1} + \varphi_3 \mathrm{FIN}_{t-1} + \varepsilon_t, \end{aligned} \tag{9.4b}$$

here, β_1, δ_2, and δ_3 correspond to short-run coefficients, while φ_1, φ_2, and φ_3 represent the long-term coefficients. Additionally, ε_t denotes the term "error" or "disturbance" (white noise).

When applying the ARDL model, the first step involves verifying stationarity since one of the conditions of the ARDL model is that mixed orders of integration should be stationary at I(1) rather than I(2). To assess stationarity, the Phillips Perron (PP) test and the Augmented Dickey–Fuller (ADF) test are employed for all variables.

Subsequently, the selection of the optimal lag time is examined. Finally, the Wald test is utilized to determine the long-term relationship between the variables under investigation.

9.5. Empirical Result and Discussion

9.5.1. *Unit root tests*

Tables 9.1, 9.2, and 9.3 present the findings of the ADF and PP tests for the periods of fixed exchange rates (1980–1990), managed floating exchange rates (1991–2004), and inflation-targeting policy (2005–2016), respectively.

Table 9.1. Augmented Dickey–Fuller and Phillips Perron tests (Fixed exchange rates).

	Fixed exchange rate regime (1980–1990)			
	In levels		1st differences	
Variables	t-statistic ADF	t-statistic PP	t-statistic ADF	t-statistic PP
EX	−2.899	−4.584	−3.675**	−4.653***
DCPI	−3.298	−3.904	−4.524***	−8.052***
DIN	−3.249	−2.954	−4.123***	−8.409***
EUCPI	−0.832	−0.281	−4.058***	−7.002***
EUIN	−1.588	−2.221	−5.752***	−8.458***
USCPI	−2.173	−1.869	−4.676***	−8.123***
USIN	−3.621	−2.461	−4.185***	−7.615***

Notes: Kinnon (1996) critical value at 1% = −4.030, at 5% = −3.445, and at 10% = −3.147. *** and ** represent significance at the 99% and 95% level of confidence, respectively.

Table 9.2. Augmented Dickey–Fuller and Phillips Perron tests (Managed floating exchange rate).

	Managed floating exchange rate regime (1991–2004)			
	In levels		1st differences	
Variables	t-statistic ADF	t-statistic PP	t-statistic ADF	t-statistic PP
EX	−1.494	−0.296	−3.173**	−8.295***
DCPI	−0.266	−1.316	−5.417***	−10.148***
DIN	−1.004	−0.984	−5.758***	−10.114***
EUCPI	−2.004	−1.645	−5.114***	−9.675***
EUIN	−3.209	−2.676	−5.770***	−9.704***
USCPI	−2.931	−2.583	−4.987***	−8.881***
USIN	−2.045	−1.722	−4.267***	−8.399***

Notes: Kinnon (1996) critical value at 1% = −4.014, at 5% = −3.437, and at 10% = −3.142. *** and ** represent significance at the 99% and 95% level of confidence, respectively.

Table 9.3. Augmented Dickey–Fuller and Phillips Perron tests (Inflation-targeting policy).

	Inflation-targeting policy (2005–2016)			
	In levels		1st differences	
Variables	t-statistic ADF	t-statistic PP	t-statistic ADF	t-statistic PP
EX	3.482	6.003	−1.021	−4.328***
DCPI	−1.293	−1.791	−2.870	−9.101***
DIN	0.972	0.521	−2.945	−8.044***
EUCPI	−2.179	−2.380	−5.960***	−9.106***
EUIN	−1.724	−1.232	−4.614***	−8.018***
USCPI	−2.189	−2.402	−6.244***	−9.069***
USIN	−1.089	−1.327	−7.404***	−7.477***

Notes: Kinnon (1996) critical value at 1% = −4.024, at 5% = −3.442, and at 10% = −3.145. *** represents significance at the 99% level of confidence, respectively.

According to Tables 9.1, 9.2, and 9.3, the ADF and PP tests' findings confirm that all variables, including EX, DCPI, DIN, EUCPI, EUIN, USCPI, and USIN, have unit roots (Phillips, 1988). As a result, all of these variables are combined, suggesting that the Autoregressive Distributed Lag (ARDL) model can be used to examine the association between the variables across the three regimes all over the time period (1980–2016).

9.5.2. *The long-run relationship*

Examine the long-term relationships between the variables in each of the following modules using the bound test (Wald test): first, the DCPI module, which looks at the long-term association between the domestic goods market (DCPI) and the global market for goods in the US and the European Union; second, the DIN module, which looks at the long-term relationships between the domestic interest rate (DIN) and the foreign interest rate (FIN).

9.5.3. *Pegged regime — PEXR (1980–1990)*

Tables 9.4 and 9.5 summarize the DCPI model's conclusions for the EU, utilizing the data to demonstrate that there is no co-integration between the EU and the Egyptian consumer price index. At all significance levels, the F-statistic is smaller than the lower value. As the F-statistic is smaller than the lower value at all levels of significance, the DCPI model does not demonstrate co-integration between the domestic and overseas consumer price index, in this instance of the US.

The results of the DIN model, in this example for the EU, are shown in Tables 9.6 and 9.7. The F-statistic indicates that there is no association between the foreign and domestic interest rates at any

Table 9.4. Wald test for DCPI model (EU) — PEXR (1980–1990).

Wald test for DCPI model Null hypothesis: DCPI = EUCPI = 0			
Test statistic	Value	df	Prob.
F-statistic	2.9195	(3,123)	0.0368***
Chi-square	8.7586	3	0.0327

Notes: The lower and upper values are, respectively, represented as follows in Pesaran's table at ($K = 1$), [(5.59–6.26), (6.59–7.30), (7.46–8.27), and (8.74–9.63)] for unconstrained intercept and unrestricted trend at (0.01, 0.025, 0.05, and 0.10). *** represents significance at the 99% level of confidence.

Table 9.5. Wald test for DCPI model (US) — PEXR (1980–1990).

Wald test for DCPI model Null hypothesis: DCPI = FCPI = 0			
Test statistic	Value	df	Prob.
F-statistic	3.0182	(6,115)	0.0089***
Chi-square	18.1095	6	0.0060

Notes: The lower and upper values are, respectively, represented as follows in Pesaran's table at ($K = 3$), [(5.17–6.36), (4.52–5.62), (4.01–5.07), and (3.47–4.45)] for unconstrained intercept and unrestricted trend at (0.01, 0.025, 0.05, and 0.10). *** represents significance at the 99% level of confidence.

Table 9.6. Wald test for DIN model (EU) — PEXR (1980–1990).

Wald test for DIN model Null hypothesis: DIN = EUIN = 0			
Test statistic	Value	df	Prob.
F-statistic	1.975292	(3,119)	0.1214***
Chi-square	5.925875	3	0.1153

Notes: The lower and upper values are, respectively, represented as follows in Pesaran's table at ($K = 2$), [(4.19–5.06), (4.87–5.85), (5.49–6.59), and (6.34–7.52)] for unconstrained intercept and unrestricted trend at (0.01, 0.025, 0.05, and 0.10). *** represents significance at the 99% level of confidence.

Table 9.7. Wald test for DIN model (US) — PEXR (1980-1990).

Wald test for DIN model Null hypothesis: DIN = FIN = 0			
Test statistic	Value	df	Prob.
F-statistic	2.890339	(2,115)	0.0596***
Chi-square	5.780679	2	0.0556

Notes: The lower and upper values are, respectively, represented as follows in Pesaran's table at ($K = 3$), [(5.17–6.36), (4.52–5.62), (4.01–5.07), and (3.47–4.45)] for unconstrained intercept and unrestricted trend at (0.01, 0.025, 0.05, and 0.10). *** represents significance at the 99% level of confidence.

levels of significance. The F-statistic for the DIN model in this US scenario is smaller than the lower value at all levels of significance, indicating that there is no correlation between the domestic and international interest rates.

9.5.4. *Managed floating regime — MFEXR (1991–2004)*

The results of the DCPI model in this instance, which are shown in Tables 9.8 and 9.9, indicate that the F-stat in both the US and the EU, where the data are based, is less than the lowest value at all levels of significance, indicating that there is no long-term association between the foreign and domestic CPI. Moreover, due to the F-statistic being less than the lowest value in all degrees of

Table 9.8. Wald test for DCPI model (EU) — MFEXR (1991-2004).

Wald test for DCPI model Null hypothesis: DCPI = EUCPI = 0			
Test statistic	Value	df	Prob.
F-statistic	3.970	(3,155)	0.0093***
Chi-square	11.91194	3	0.0077

Notes: The lower and upper values are, respectively, represented as follows in Pesaran's table at ($K = 2$), [(4.19–5.06), (4.87–5.85), (5.49–6.59), and (6.34–7.52)] for unconstrained intercept and unrestricted trend at (0.01, 0.025, 0.05, and 0.10). *** represents significance at the 99% level of confidence.

Table 9.9. Wald test for DCPI model (US) — MFEXR (1991–2004).

Wald test for DCPI model Null hypothesis: DCPI = FCPI = 0			
Test statistic	Value	df	Prob.
F-statistic	2.339889	(2,151)	0.0998***
Chi-square	4.679778	2	0.0963

Notes: The lower and upper values are, respectively, represented as follows in Pesaran's table at ($K = 3$), [(5.17–6.36), (4.52–5.62), (4.01–5.07), and (3.47–4.45)] for unconstrained intercept and unrestricted trend at (0.01, 0.025, 0.05, and 0.10). *** represents significance at the 99% level of confidence.

Table 9.10. Wald test for DIN model (EU) — MFEXR (1991–2004).

Wald test for DIN model Null hypothesis: DIN = EUIN = 0			
Test statistic	Value	df	Prob.
F-statistic	1.995	(3,155)	0.1170***
Chi-square	5.986	3	0.1123

Notes: The lower and upper values are, respectively, represented as follows in Pesaran's table at ($K = 2$), [(4.19–5.06), (4.87–5.85), (5.49–6.59), and (6.34–7.52)] for unconstrained intercept and unrestricted trend at (0.01, 0.025, 0.05, and 0.10). *** represents significance at the 99% level of confidence.

Table 9.11. Wald test for DIN model (US) — MFEXR (1991–2004).

Wald test for DIN model Null hypothesis: DIN = FIN = 0			
Test statistic	Value	df	Prob.
F-statistic	2.961190	(2,151)	0.0548***
Chi-square	5.922380	2	0.0518

Notes: The lower and upper values are, respectively, represented as follows in Pesaran's table at ($K = 3$), [(5.17–6.36), (4.52–5.62), (4.01–5.07), and (3.47–4.45)] for unconstrained intercept and unrestricted trend at (0.01, 0.025, 0.05, and 0.10). *** represents significance at the 99% level of confidence.

significance, the DIN model result shown in Tables 9.10 and 9.11 illustrates that there is no co-integration between domestic and foreign interest rates.

9.5.5. *Inflation-targeting policy — ITP (2005–2016)*

In the context of the scenario involving the EU and the US, it is evident from Tables 9.12 and 9.13 that the F-statistic consistently falls below the lower critical value across all significant levels. This outcome signifies the absence of along-run relationship between the domestic and international consumer price indexes. Turning attention to the findings presented in Tables 9.14 and 9.15 for the EU and the US, as demonstrated by the DIN model's output, a similar conclusion emerges. The F-statistic remains consistently below the

Table 9.12. Wald test for DCPI model (EU) — ITP (2005–2016).

Wald test for DCPI model Null hypothesis: DCPI = EUCPI = 0			
Test statistic	Value	df	Prob.
F-statistic	1.3274	(3,135)	0.268***
Chi-square	3.9822	3	0.2634

Notes: The lower and upper values are, respectively, represented as follows in Pesaran's table at ($K = 1$), [(5.59–6.26), (6.59–7.30), (7.46–8.27), and (8.74–9.63)] for unconstrained intercept and unrestricted trend at (0.01, 0.025, 0.05, and 0.10). *** represents significance at the 99% level of confidence.

Table 9.13. Wald test for DCPI model (US) — ITP (2005–2016).

Wald test for DCPI model Null hypothesis: DCPI = FCPI = 0			
Test statistic	Value	df	Prob.
F-statistic	3.080594	(2,127)	0.0494***
Chi-square	6.161187	2	0.0459

Notes: The lower and upper values are, respectively, represented as follows in Pesaran's table at (K = 3), [(5.17–6.36), (4.52–5.62), (4.01–5.07), and (3.47–4.45)] for unconstrained intercept and unrestricted trend at (0.01, 0.025, 0.05, and 0.10). *** represents significance at the 99% level of confidence.

Table 9.14. Wald test for DIN model (EU) — ITP (2005–2016)

Wald test for DIN model Null hypothesis: DIN = EUIN = 0			
Test statistic	Value	df	Prob.
F-statistic	1.1602	(3,131)	0.3275***
Chi-square	3.4808	3	0.3233

Notes: The lower and upper values are, respectively, represented as follows in Pesaran's table at (K = 2), [(4.19–5.06), (4.87–5.85), (5.49–6.59), and (6.34–7.52)] for unconstrained intercept and unrestricted trend at (0.01, 0.025, 0.05, and 0.10). *** represents significance at the 99% level of confidence.

Table 9.15. Wald test for DIN model (US) — ITP (2005–2016).

Wald test for DIN model Null hypothesis: DIN = FIN = 0			
Test statistic	Value	df	Prob.
F-statistic	2.135653	(2,123)	0.1225***
Chi-square	4.271305	2	0.1182

Notes: The lower and upper values are, respectively, represented as follows in Pesaran's table at (K = 4), [(5.17–6.36), (4.52–5.62), (4.01–5.07), and (3.47–4.45)] for unconstrained intercept and unrestricted trend at (0.01, 0.025, 0.05, and 0.10). *** represents significance at the 99% level of confidence.

Table 9.16. LM test for DCPI and DIN model — PEXR (1980–1990).

		DCPI model		
EU	F-statistic	0.597	Prob. F(1,122)	0.441
	Obs. $*$ R-squared	0.633	Prob. Chi-square (1)	0.426
US	F-statistic	2.219	Prob. F(3,112)	0.089
	Obs. $*$ R-squared	7.183	Prob. Chi-square (3)	0.066
		DIN model		
EU	F-statistic	1.040	Prob. F(2,117)	0.356
	Obs. $*$ R-squared	2.290	Prob. Chi-square (2)	0.324
US	F-statistic	0.680	Prob. F(3,12)	0.565
	Obs. $*$ R-squared	2.290	Prob. Chi-square (3)	0.514

Table 9.17. LM test for DCPI and DIN model — MFEXR (1991–2004).

		DCPI model		
EU	F-statistic	0.456	Prob. F(2,153)	0.634
	Obs. $*$ R-squared	0.978	Prob. Chi-square (2)	0.613
US	F-statistic	0.432	Prob. F(3,148)	0.729
	Obs. $*$ R-squared	1.426	Prob. Chi-square (3)	0.699
		DIN model		
EU	F-statistic	2.628	Prob. F(2,153)	0.075
	Obs. $*$ R-squared	5.48	Prob. Chi-square (2)	0.064
US	F-statistic	0.637	Prob. F(3,148)	0.592
	Obs. $*$ R-squared	2.090	Prob. Chi-square (3)	0.553

lower critical value for all relevant levels, indicating the absence of a long-term association between domestic and foreign interest rates.

For more robustness, Tables 9.16, 9.17, and 9.18, and the residual and stability diagnostics using the Breusch–Godfrey Serial Correlation (LM test) and CUSUM test, respectively, ensure the reliability of the results of all DCPI and DIN models. For brevity, these results are not shown. The results indicate that both models are totally free of serial correlation, and they are also stable to explain the relationships between the variables.

Table 9.18. LM test for DCPI and DIN model — ITP (2005–2016).

		DCPI model		
EU	F-statistic	1.815	Prob. $F(1,134)$	0.180
	Obs. $*$ R-squared	1.898	Prob. Chi-square (1)	0.168
US	F-statistic	1.479	Prob. $F(3,124)$	0.223
	Obs. $*$ R-squared	4.837	Prob. Chi-square (3)	0.184
		DIN model		
EU	F-statistic	2.462	Prob. $F(2,129)$	0.089
	Obs. $*$ R-squared	5.185	Prob. Chi-square (2)	0.074
US	F-statistic	0.891	Prob. $F(4,119)$	0.471
	Obs. $*$ R-squared	4.042	Prob. Chi-square (4)	0.400

9.6. Discussion

Upon critical examination, the findings within the context of a pegged exchange rate regime highlight the absence of correlation between both prices and interest rates during the period of pegged exchange rates from 1980 to 1990 in Egypt, when compared to the corresponding conditions in the EU and the US. This outcome of goods market and monetary policy independence contradicts the predictions made by PPP and UIP theories. These theories suggest that in a small open economy operating under a pegged exchange rate regime, domestic inflation and interest rates should align with their foreign counterparts, potentially resulting in a loss of economic independence. It's worth noting that this finding is in line with the conclusions drawn and supported by Stockman & Ohanian (1993) and Edwards (2015). So, regarding this outcome, the Egyptian central bank achieves its local goal, which is maintaining the stability of the economy without being affected by external shock. Additionally, this finding shows a unique result in term of goods market independence: The Central Bank of Egypt can have autonomy to determine local price without being affected by external shocks.

In contrast to the other flexible system, which was managed under a floating exchange rate regime and an inflation-targeting policy between 1991 and 2004 and 2005 and 2016, respectively, the outcome demonstrates that there is no correlation between the price and short-term interest rate in Egypt and its foreign counterparts in the EU and the US. This outcome of independence of good market and monetary policy is not consistent with what the PPP and UIP theories have announced, which says that in a small open economy and a flexible exchange rate regime, domestic inflation and the interest rate may not deviate from foreign counterparts and lead to complete loss of independence. This finding is consistent and supported by Frankel *et al.* (2004), Shambaugh (2004), Kim & Lee (2008), Li & Tsai (2013), Grossmann *et al.* (2014), An *et al.* (2016), Dąbrowski *et al.* (2019), and Georgiadis & Zhu (2019). Therefore, this analysis suggests that Egypt may be able to stabilize the exchange rates by targeting any flexible system, either by targeting lower inflation rates or by managing a floating rate of exchange.

9.7. Summary and Conclusion

The investigation of whether or not flexible exchange rate regimes promote the independence of the goods market and monetary policy revealed that Egyptian short-term interest rates and prices have not followed those of the EU and the US. This shows that in the long run, Egypt's price and rate of interest are completely independent of those of Egypt's main trading partners, the US and EU. Thus, in this situation, the Egyptian Central Bank (CBE) can set its policy and target its objectives without being affected by the EU and/or the US shocks, namely, price of goods and services and short-term interest rates.

Interestingly, this result does not entirely support the Trilemma policy's claim that "countries with flexible exchange rate regimes and an open financial sector can be independent of monetary policy". In accordance with uncovered interest parity (UIP) and purchasing power parity (PPP), "domestic inflation and the interest rate may not deviate from their foreign counterparts under fixed exchange rates, leading to a complete loss of monetary control in a small economy". Additionally, "in a small open economy with perfect capital mobility, the domestic interest rate is determined by world interest rate".

Hence, the conclusions drawn from this study suggest that, alongside flexible exchange rate regimes, the pegged exchange rate regime in Egypt can also achieve autonomy in both its goods market and monetary policy. This finding is supported by a number of scholars, including Stockman & Ohanian (1993), Frankel (1999), Schmukler *et al.* (2000), Paul (2012), Rey (2015), Dąbrowski *et al.* (2019), and Goczek & Partyka (2019). The results of this study also imply that capital control and the condition of foreign exchange reserves[5] are related to other indicators of monetary policy and goods market independence in addition to exchange rate regimes. In addition, consistent with Mora *et al.* (2013), by selling the foreign exchange reserve, the Central Bank of Egypt can maintain its exchange rate stability, as well as covering the current account deficit. On the other hand, by controlling the inflow of capital in and out, the government can maintain the domestic commodity market and monetary policies independent of any external shocks (An *et al.*, 2016).

So, for further research regarding the war between Russia and Ukraine, we note that the Central Bank of Egypt raised the interest rate in response to the change in the Federal Reserve's interest rate. It is clear that this response or change in the Egyptian interest rate is not related to changes in the exchange rate policy and is not related to the policy adopted by the Central Bank of Egypt to maintain the stability of its currency against the US dollar. Instead of representing government intervention, which could be one of the factors contributing to the potential loss of monetary policy independence for the sake of stability (Calvo & Reinhart, 2002), it's worth noting that the sensitivity of local policy rates to base region policy rates tend to be more pronounced for an economy with a flexible exchange rate. This is particularly true when the economy exhibits negative foreign currency exposures arising from portfolio debt and bank liabilities on its external balance sheet, and when the monetary policy of the base country is tightened (Georgiadis & Zhu, 2019).

[5]Paul (2012) highlighted that a country can exercise monetary policy independence even under free capital flows as long as it does not maintain a stable exchange rate. Thus, monetary policy independence is substantially anchored in the exchange rate regime along with the state of foreign exchange constraint, and not necessarily in globalization.

References

Aizenman, J., Chinn, M. D., & Ito, H. (2013). The "impossible trinity" hypothesis in an era of global imbalances: Measurement and testing. *Review of International Economics, 21*(3), 447–458.

Akikina, K. R. & Al-Hoshan, H. (2003). Independence of monetary policy under fixed exchange rates: The case of Saudi Arabia. *Applied Economics, 35*(4), 437–448.

An, L., Kim, Y., & You, Y. J. (2016). Floating exchange rates and macroeconomic independence. *International Review of Economics & Finance, 42*, 23–35.

Bluedorn, J. C. & Bowdler, C. (2010). The empirics of international monetary transmission: Identification and the impossible trinity. *Journal of Money, Credit and Banking, 42*(4), 679–713.

Calvo, G. A. & Reinhart, C. M. (2002). Fear of floating. *The Quarterly Journal of Economics, 117*(2), 379–408.

Cheng, B. S. (1999). Beyond the purchasing power parity: Testing for cointegration and causality between exchange rates, prices, and interest rates. *Journal of International Money and Finance, 18*(6), 911–924.

Clarida, R., Gali , J., & Gertler, M. (1998). Monetary policy rules in practice: Some international evidence. *European Economic Review, 42*(6), 1033–1067.

Dąbrowski, M. A., Papież, M., & Śmiech, S. (2019). Monetary independence of Central and Eastern European economies with flexible exchange rate regimes. *Eastern European Economics, 57*(4), 295–316.

Di Giovanni, J. & Shambaugh, J. C. (2008). The impact of foreign interest rates on the economy: The role of the exchange rate regime. *Journal of International Economics, 74*(2), 341–361.

Edwards, S. (2015). Monetary policy independence under flexible exchange rates: An illusion? *The World Economy, 38*(5), 773–787.

Frankel, J. (1999). No single currency regime is right for all countries or at all times. *International Finance and Macroeconomics.* Working Paper Series (No. 7338). National Bureau of Economic Research.

Frankel, J., Schmukler, S. L., & Serven, L. (2004). Global transmission of interest rates: Monetary independence and currency regime. *Journal of International Money and Finance, 23*(5), 701–733.

Georgiadis, G. & Zhu, F. (2019). Monetary policy spillovers, capital controls and exchange rate flexibility, and the financial channel of exchange rates. European Central Bank Working Paper Series (No. 2256).

Goczek, Ł. & Partyka, K. J. (2019). Too small to be independent? On the influence of ECB monetary policy on interest rates of the EEA countries. *Economic Modelling, 78*, 180–191.

Goh, S. K. & Mcnown, R. (2015). Examining the exchange rate regime–monetary policy autonomy nexus: Evidence from Malaysia. *International Review of Economics & Finance, 35*, 292–303.

Goldberg, L. S. & Campa, J. M. (2010). The sensitivity of the CPI to exchange rates: Distribution margins, imported inputs, and trade exposure. *The Review of Economics and Statistics, 92*(2), 392–407.

Grossmann, A. & Orlov, A. G. (2014). A panel-regressions investigation of exchange rate volatility. *International Journal of Finance & Economics, 19*(4), 303–326.

Kim, C. J. & Lee, J. W. (2008). Exchange rate regime and monetary policy independence in East Asia. *Pacific Economic Review, 13*(2), 155–170.

Li, S. & Tsai, L. C. (2013). Would a relaxation of the exchange rate regime increase the independence of Chinese monetary policy? Evidence from China. *Emerging Markets Finance and Trade, 49*(3), 103–123.

Massoud, A. & Willett, T. D. (2014). Egypt's exchange rate regime policy after the float. *Journal of Economic Perspectives, 28*(2), 209–226.

Miniane, J. & Rogers, J. H. (2007). Capital controls and the international transmission of US money shocks. *Journal of Money, Credit and Banking, 39*(5), 1003–1035.

Nkoro, E. & Uko, A. K. (2016). Autoregressive Distributed Lag (ARDL) cointegration technique: Application and interpretation. *Journal of Statistical and Econometric Methods, 5*(4), 63–91.

Paul, B. P. (2012). Globalization and monetary-policy independence in India. *The Journal of Developing Areas, 46*(2), 205–211.

Pesaran, M. H., Shin, Y., & Smith, R. J. (2001). Bounds testing approaches to the analysis of level relationships. *Journal of Applied Econometrics, 16*(3), 289–326.

Pesaran, M. H., Shin, Y., & Smith, R. P. (1999). Pooled mean group estimation of dynamic heterogeneous panels. *Journal of the American Statistical Association, 94*(446), 621–634.

Phillips, P. C. & Perron, P. J. B. (1988). Testing for a unit root in time series regression. *Biometrika, 75*(2), 335–346.

Reinhart, C. M. & Rogoff, K. S. (2004). The modern history of exchange rate arrangements: A reinterpretation. *The Quarterly Journal of Economics, 119*(1), 1–48.

Rey, H. (2015). International channels of transmission of monetary policy and the Mundellian Trilemma. *IMF Economic Review, 64*(1), 6–35.

Sargan, J. D. (1964). Wages and prices in the United Kingdom: A study in econometric methodology. In P. E. Hart, G. Mills, & J. K. Whitaker (Eds.). *Econometric Analysis for National Economic Planning, 16*, 25–54.

Schmukler, S., Servén, L., & Frankel, J. (2000). *Global Transmission of Interest Rates: Monetary Independence and the Currency Regime.* The World Bank.

Selim, H. (2012). Exploring the role of the exchange rate in monetary policy in Egypt. In A Paper Presented in the ERF 18th Annual Conference.

Shambaugh, J. C. (2004). The effect of fixed exchange rates on monetary policy. *The Quarterly Journal of Economics, 119*(1), 301–352.

Stockman, A. C. & Ohanian, L. E. (1993). *Short-run Independence of Monetary Policy Under Pegged Exchange Rates and Effects of Money on Exchange Rates And Interest Rates.* National Bureau of Economic Research. Working Paper Series (No. 4585).

Tng, B. H. & Kwek, K. T. (2015). Financial stress, economic activity and monetary policy in the ASEAN-5 economies. *Applied Economics, 47*(48), 5169–5185.

Tollison, R. D. & Willett, T. D. (1973). International integration and the interdependence of economic variables. *International Organization, 27*(2), 255–271.

Vašíček, B. (2010). Monetary policy rules and inflation processes in open emerging economies: Evidence from twelve new EU members. *Eastern European Economics, 48*(4), 36–58.

https://doi.org/10.1142/9781800614734_0010

Chapter 10

The Impact of Capital Adequacy and Non-Performing Loans on Loan Loss Provisions for Gulf Cooperation Council (GCC) Banks: Econometric Study Using Panel Data

Hala Fadheel Elfergani, Asma S. Abdelhamid Alzwi and Ali Zagoub

Abstract

This chapter examines the impact of capital adequacy ratios (CARs) and non-performing loans (NPLs) and the application of IFRS 9 on loan loss provisions (LLPs). It also analyzes the impact of LLPs and NPLs and the application of IFRS 9 on CARs for a sample of Gulf banks during the period 2012–2021. Panel data analysis was adopted to reach an appropriate model to study the effect of independent variables on dependent variables. The results of the study showed that most Gulf banks did not find statistically significant differences in the performance of the CAR and NPL indicators before and after applying IFRS 9. However, there were statistically significant differences in the performance of the LLP indicator before and after applying IFRS 9 in favor of applying IFRS 9 (after 2018). The study also found that there was a difference in the performance of the indicators. The study also found that there is a negative impact of CAR on LLP, and vice versa. On the other hand, the effect of NPL was positive on both CAR and LLP, while there was no effect of IFRS 9 adoption on both CAR and LLP. The importance of studying CAR and LLP is highlighted by the importance of financial solvency that may be affected after obligating banks to apply IFRS 9 in January 2018; therefore, the results of this experimental study can add to the limited knowledge about the behavior of CAR, LLP, and NPL before and after IFRS 9 adoption in developing countries. This chapter contributes to the limited literature on CAR, LLP, and NPL before and after IFRS 9 adoption in developing countries in general and GCC countries in particular. Reviewing previous literature, there was a scarcity of studies that examined the effect of CAR on LLP or the effect of LLP on CAR, as well as the effect of adopting IFRS 9 on both CAR and LLP in GCC banks. Very limited research has been conducted in developing countries in general. This is important taking into consideration the environmental factors in developing countries, which can give a different view on the issue of CAR, LLP, and the extent to which they are affected by the application of the IFRS 9 standard.

Keywords: Capital adequacy ratio (CAR), non-performing loan (NPL), loan loss provision (LLP), International Financial Reporting Standards (IFRS 9)

10.1. Introduction

Banks are a financial intermediary whose main role is to collect money from the community and redirect it back through the credit process, which in turn involves risks that banks must manage effectively to ensure the continuity of their business, reduce the possibility of facing losses, and maintain the quality of their assets and the formation of sufficient loan loss provisions (LLPs) to meet the possibility of the counterparty (the borrower) failing to meet their obligations (Fitriaro & Arfianto, 2016; Heningtyas *et al.*, 2021).

Banks paid great attention to LLP by following the IFRS 9 guide issued by the International Accounting Standards Board (IASB) (2021) (Arif *et al.*, 2020). The International Financial Reporting Standards (IFRS 9) is the latest of these standards and replaces the international standard IFRS 39. In agreement with the international standard IFRS 39, LLPs are calculated based on the Incurred Losses Approach (Cafferman, 2015), i.e., recognizing losses after they have actually occurred. As for IFRS 9, which adopts the Expected Losses Approach, losses can be recognized even if they have not yet occurred, which may result in larger LLPs.

The Basel Committee on Banking Supervision (BCBS) stated that the new model for calculating credit losses will cause a quantitative and qualitative change in the impairment provisions.

The Committee indicated that it is possible that the LLPs may be much higher due to the introduction of the concept of calculating losses for the life of loans and the introduction of forward-looking information in assessing losses that affect regulatory capital ratios (BCSB, 2017), which may pose a risk to capital adequacy. This is due to the expected increase in the volume of the LLPs, due to the reliance of banks on expected losses rather than actual losses, which may result in restrictions on bank lending and affect the financial stability of banks, according to Karadima & Louri (2020).

It can be said that the increase in provisions results in a reduction of the profitability of banks and could have a negative impact on regulatory capital and liquidity ratios, which reduce the ability of banks to lend (Ibrahim, 2018). However, on the other hand, others studies (Mechraoui, 2019; Al-Shabasi, 2021) have indicated that the IFRS 9 contributes to maintaining the capital, due to a shift to the formation of provisions according to the expected losses approach, which raises conservatism and results in an increase in solvency, given the formation of the appropriate provision that maintains the capital adequacy ratio (CAR), by forcing banks to increase capital to face potential expected losses and meet regulatory requirements, which enhances the confidence of depositors in banks due to the provision of more guarantees and protection in a way that enables liquidity and fulfillment of the obligations when they are due. This is because of the standard links, through the use of accurate objective models, between the accounting value losses provisions and the components of the capital adequacy standard (Yang, 2017).

Non-performing loans (NPLs) play a major role in influencing loan loss provisions (LLPs). Studies (Beatty & Liao, 2020; Tao, 2020; Kim *et al.*, 2019) have shown that an increase in problematic loans indicates NPLs. This leads to an increase in the size of provisions estimated to face potential losses; therefore, it is expected that the IFRS 9 will result in a reconsideration of the definition and a difference in the frameworks that govern NPLs in line with the concept of expected losses (Bholat *et al.*, 2018).

Although many studies have shown that the IFRS 9 will lead to an increase in LLP, certain studies (Deloitte, 2019) in English banks have shown that the levels of LLP after the adoption of the standard in 2018 were the same as previous levels or slightly less than those formed under IAS 39, and therefore the implementation of IFRS 9 did not entail fundamental changes as expected, either in terms of financial results or sources of regulatory capital, which was further confirmed by the study of Magdalena & Martani (2020). In contrast, in another study (KPMG, 2018) of Gulf Cooperation Council banks, the application of IFRS 9 in the first year led to an increase in provisions of loan losses compared to provisions prepared under the IAS 39 standard.

In another direction, it can be said that a decrease in CARs can affect the assessment of LLPs, as the capital management hypothesis states that a decrease in CARs from the required regulatory levels will motivate managers to estimate LLPs in order to avoid violation of the minimum requirements of Regulatory Capital Ratio (RCR), thus avoiding a decrease in capital adequacy. This was shown by (Ozili & Outa, 2017b; Ozili, 2019a), where, the decrease in the regulatory capital ratios under the minimum ratios that regulatory required, may lead banks to use LLPs as a form of bank capital. They argue that when bank equity capital is low, banks will overstate LLPs to compensate for their lower level of capital, and will reduce LLPs when they have sufficient capital, reflecting the use of LLPs for capital management purposes.

From the above, it can be concluded that the studies were conflicting with regard to the size of LLPs; some of them confirmed the increase of LLPs, while others proved that there was no effect or decrease in LLPs after adopting the IFRS 9 standard. Some literature further showed the effect of LLP on the CAR through its impact on the regulatory capital (RC), and to the contrary, studies have shown that the level of the CAR may affect the estimation of LLP, in particular given the tendency of most banks to apply IFRS 9 and their attempt to comply with the directions of the Basel Committee for banking supervision. The problem of the our study was to identify the to which extent LLPs and NPL impact CAR after adoption of IFRS 9, as well as testing the extent of the impact of CAR and NPL on LLP in the banking sector of the Gulf Cooperation Council countries.

In view of the importance that professional and regulatory organizations attach to CAR, LLP, and the ratio of NPL compared to total assets, especially after adopting IFRS 9, it is crucial to shine a spotlight on the behavior of these variables before and after IFRS 9 adoption, and find out whether concerns about IFRS 9 adoption are truly warranted. Against this background, this study aims to test whether there are statistically significant differences in the indicators of CAR, LLP, and NPL before and after applying IFRS 9. Additionally, this study further aims to measuring the effect of CAR on LLP and vice versa during the study period. To achieve this, the study is organized as follows: Section 10.2 provides a background on the LLP in light of the IFRS 9 along with a review of the NPL literature and its relationship with LLP and CAR. Section 10.3 describes the data used in this study, while Section 10.4 describes the study methodology. Section 10.5 tests the various hypotheses and reports the descriptive analyses as well as the main results. Finally, Section 10.6 concludes the chapter and suggests ideas for further research.

10.2. Literature Review and Developing Hypotheses

10.2.1. *Loan loss provisions (LLPs) under the International Financial Reporting Standards (IFRS 9)*

LLPs are amounts set aside by lending institutions to cover expected losses in the loan portfolio in order to offset credit risk when lenders are unable to repay due to economic conditions (Ozili & Outa, 2017b); therefore, banks reserve an amount to captivate expected losses in the finance portfolio to face any possible default, which helps to protect the financial positions of the banks (Beatty & Lioa, 2009).

LLPs played a major role in the global financial crisis that afflicted global financial institutions since 2007, when users of reports became suspicious of the usefulness of the proactive information that reports contained to helped effectively in future aspirations to reduce such crises. LLPs prepared in accordance with IAS 39 played a pivotal role in this crisis, as LLPs were calculated when impartial indication of impairment was obtained as a result of one or more loss affecting the expected cash flows that can be measured objectively. In the case of existing physical evidence, the amount of loss is measured as the difference between the book value of the financial asset and the present value of the estimated cash flows discounted at the effective interest rate, excluding expected losses after the date the of balance sheet (Gebhardet, 2016), which caused a delay in recognizing losses and thus exacerbated the crisis that afflicted the banks during the global financial crisis. Therefore, the International Financial Reporting Board (IASB) and the US Financial Accounting Standards Board (FASB) sought to find a model that would enable expected credit losses to be taken into account and more precautionary provisions could be booked. Therefore, discussions and studies between professional organizations and stakeholders led to the final form of the draft of Global Financial Reporting Standard (GFRS 9), which has been mandatorily implemented starting from January 2018, with early applications being allowed before that.

It can be said that all banks in the international and Arab environment have switched to estimating LLP under the IFRS 9 by using the Expected Loan Loss Model (ELLM) which consists of three credit stages. The first stage relates to short-term assets and assets with good credit quality since initial recognition and impairment loss are recognized for the next 12 months. The second stage is applied when a significant increase in credit risk has taken place, but the quality of assets has not decreased since initial recognition. A losses in this phase is recognized over the lifetime of the financial asset. The third stage is related to assets whose credit quality deteriorated to a level at which credit loss is actually incurred and the probability of default reaches 100%. Therefore, the provisions under IFRS 9 are estimated and measured according to expected losses, not actual losses, as is the case in IAS 39. This may lead to an increase in the size of provisions for credit losses charged to income, and thus lower levels of income during the first periods of the acquisition of the financial asset under IFRS 9, compared to the levels of income that were calculated according to the IAS 39 (Restoy & Zamil, 2017).

Despite the expected increase in the amount of provisions when applying the IFRS 9 compared to those prepared in accordance with the IAS 39, previous studies had conflicting results in this regard. The study by Magdalena and Martani (2020) stated that there are no fundamental differences between the total and estimated provisions under the IAS 39 and IFRS 9; the study by Seitz *et al.* (2018) notes that although LLPs made under IFRS 9 are not higher than provisions resulting from IAS 39, they exceed them in times of crisis, and these provisions are highly volatile due to changes in the market environment. In contrast, the study by Al-Nsour & Abuaddous (2022) on Gulf banks found that there are fundamental differences in the percentage of LLP after adopting the IFRS 9.

Shahin & Al-Baghdadi (2019) also showed that Egyptian banks reduced the loan loss allowance (LLA) ratios for 2018 compared to 2017, due to their commitment to creating the IFRS 9 risk reserves, This may indicate the concern of the banks' officials to the impact of the expected significant increase in the LLP for coming years, and thus reduce the annual bank's profits. On the other hand, according to the Al-Mashrawi (2019), the application of the IFRS 9 in Dubai Islamic Bank led to an increase in provision that was met with a capital increase, with the aim of fulfilling the IFRS 9 requirements and increasing solvency. Also, banks may reduce the size of LLA during the first years of applying the IFRS 9 and create a risk reserve for the standard added to the numerator of the capital adequacy equation, in order to reduce the future impact resulting from the increase in the provisions and to support CAR.

Through the controversy between the previous studies, it can be deduced that the size of provisions may increase during the first years of the application of the IFRS 9, in order to guard against expected losses resulting from the application of the standard. This will force banks to increase and improve the capital quality, which will be reflected positively in the long run. Kund & Rugilo (2019) found that the application of the IFRS 9 negatively affects financial solvency due to the increase in loan provisions, but this negative impact turns positive on financial solvency. This was evident during the COVID-19 period, as the banks that successfully applied the standard were able to adapt to rapid economic changes through the recognition of provisions and impairment of value, which strengthened their financial solvency (Al-Nsour & Abuaddous, 2022).

10.2.2. *Non-performing loans (NPLs), loan loss provisions (LLPs), and capital adequacy ratio (CAR) in the banking sector*

NPLs refer to a situation in which a customer is unable to pay all or part of his obligations to the bank, i.e., failure to pay the installments that were pledged when contracting with the bank to obtain the loan. The Arab Monetary Fund clarified that the IFRS 9 did not give a specific definition of default, and banks must adopt a definition commensurate with that approved internally in credit risk management, but banks can use the definition specified by the Basel Board on Banking Supervision approved for supervisory resolutions, which includes the following:

(1) *Forward-looking dimension*: If it becomes clear that the borrower has become unable to fulfill his obligations toward the bank even if the latter has not resorted to pursuing the customer by using his legal right to own, liquidate, and enforce the guarantees or pledges made by the debtor when granting him the loan.
(2) *Objective dimension*: If the debtor is more than 90 days late from the date of payment of his obligations toward the bank (Safa & Abu Mouris, 2020).

Moreover, not all loans granted are risk free; some of them may involve significant risks, threatening the safety of the bank (Elnahass *et al.*, 2018). A high percentage of NPLs indicates a low credit quality. The study by Basu *et al.* (2020) showed that LLPs are inversely related to the quality of the loan portfolio, and LLPs move in the same direction as the change in NPLs, meaning that LLPs are more sensitive to the increase in NPLs. Therefore, banks review guarantees to reduce credit risk, and some banks may require a specific percentage of NPLs, such as Bank Indonesia, which stipulates that the safe limit for NPLs of the bank does not exceed 5% (Heningtyas *et al.*, 2021).

It can be said (Ozili, 2017) that credit risk factors (bad loans) significantly affect the level of banks' provisions during the study period, which means that the rise in the NPL ratio is reflected in an increase in the LLP size. This was shown by several studies (Heningtyas *et al.*, 2021; Beatty & Liao, 2020; Tao, 2020; Kim *et al.*, 2019), which found that a higher percentage of NPL meant a higher credit risk level and thus an increase in the proportion of LLP retained to meet the expected non-payment losses.

In addition, it can be said that NPLs affect CAR, as high non-performing loan rates affect a bank's performance in the short term through two main channels. First, NPLs generate less income for banks, which reduces their profitability and increase the negative impact on capital. It can also reduce the capital of banks when

NPLs are written off. In severe cases, high NPLs can make the bank bankrupt. Second, high NPLs tie up a great deal of banks' human and financial incomes, which makes it difficult for banks to extend new credit to companies and individuals (European Commission, 2018), which means that NPLs have a negative impact on capital adequacy. Another study (Ozili, 2020), which aimed to study NPLs in regular and irregular European banks before and after the global financial crisis showed that there was a significant negative relationship between NPL and CAR in irregular banks after the financial crisis. A study by Rahadian & Permana (2021) confirmed those results, NPLs may cause the cost of the provision for loan losses to exceed the interest generated on the loans, reducing the Bank's income and negatively impacting capital adequacy. This is fully consistent with the results obtained by Ozili (2019b) and Khan *et al.* (2020), which concluded that NPL negatively affects regulatory capital; one of the explanations is that banks with relatively low capital have incentives to engage in risky lending behavior which increases NPLs.

As for the regular banks, a study (Ozili, 2020) showed that banks maintain higher regulatory capital ratios when they expect an increase in NPL, and irregular banks that exceed the regulatory capital requirements suffer from a rise in NPL. This means a positive outcome of investment adequacy on NPL. This is consistent with results obtained by others (Yulianti *et al.*, 2018; Ismauland, 2014; Achir, 2014; Wood and Skinner, 2018), which found the positive effect of capital adequacy on NPL; one of the explanations is that CAR works to absorb the risks of losses faced by banks, i.e., the higher the interest rate on the credit granted, the greater the ability of banks to reduce risks and cover them through reserves formed by comparing capital and risk-weighted assets. According to Demirguc-Kunt & Huizinga (1999), banks with high stages of CAR may seek more risk, which leads to riskier credit portfolios. It is interesting that the study by Barus & Erick (2016) showed that there is no relationship between NPL and capital adequacy, which is consistent with some of the partial findings from another study (Ozili, 2020). It showed that CAR does not have a significant effect on NPL in regular banks. This means that regulatory capital risks may be insensitive to risks in regular banks, or it may be because the first level of regulatory capital (Tier 1), that may be used to lessen other risks such as market and interest rate risks instead of mitigating credit risk, according to Ozili (2020).

10.2.3. *Capital adequacy ratio (CAR) and loan loss provisions (LLPs) in the banking division*

CAR is defined as the percentage of capital that shows the ability of the bank to provide funds for the purposes of business development and absorb the risks of losing funds resulting from banking operations (Fitriana & Arfianto, 2015). It was defined by the Bank for International Settlements as a measure of the amount of capital that must be held in proportion to the risk-weighted assets (BCBS, 2005).

Several studies have addressed the impact of LLP on CAR, as well as the impact of CAR on LLP, either directly or indirectly. With regard to the impact of LLP on capital adequacy, the study by Nugroho *et al.* (2021) tested the partial or crossover effects of the independent variables represented by LLP, NPL, and the amount of third-part fund (TPF) in CAR. The study found that LLP, NPL, and TPF together had a significant impact on capital adequacy, meaning that provisions with supporting variables affected banks' capital adequacy.

It is worth noting that the transition to the IFRS 9 may affect the LLP and CAR. The study of Sultanoğlu (2018) explained and analyzed the expected qualitative and quantitative effects of the transition to the IFRS 9 in European banks, and compared it with the Turkish banking industry. The study found that the application of the IFRS 9 in European banks is expected to increase by 13%, with a decrease in Common Equity Capital Tier 1 (CET1) by 18%, and then a decrease in the CAR. As for Turkish banks, the total amount of provisions will decrease by 4.1% and this will have a positive impact on the regulatory Common Equity Tier 1/Tier 1 (CET1) and CAR. This indicates that the application of the IFRS 9 has adverse effects on capital adequacy through a negative impact on regulatory capital.

In the same context, the study by Krüger *et al.* (2018) aimed to analyze the impact of expected loan loss provisions (ELLPs) under both the IFRS 9 and Generally Accepted Accounting Principles (GAAPs) on fluctuations in qualified regulatory capital and net income. One of the most important results is that the IFRS 9 leads to a reduction in the first level of regulatory capital and this decline is sharp during periods of economic downturn and in low-quality credit portfolios, as well as in banks that do not stress capital standards during economic recession and are lenient with the significant increase in credit risk.

As for the study by Groff & Mörec (2021), it focused on the effect the IFRS 9 on equity, which was very weak and almost limited, and these results were consistent with the study by Khan & Damyanova (2018). But the results were contrary to those by Loew *et al.* (2019), which showed that there is an impact of IFRS 9 on the regulatory capital by 20 basis points, with higher standard deviation of 145 basis points, due to an increase in impairment and provisions, and then a decrease in equity by 1.8%. This means that the obligation of applying IFRS 9 may have an impact on capital adequacy through provisions that may increase in times of crisis, where the capital represents a main channel through which the accounting rules can affect the bank's behavior and thus the financial stability, as the recognition of losses and provisions and the rules of impairment determine the banks' profits and equity and can have a direct impact on the regulatory capital that is determined by the regulations (Lee *et al.*, 2020).

It can be said that LLPs may affect regulatory capital through the incentives of capital management using loan LLPs. Elnahass *et al.* (2018) found important evidence that conventional banks engage in capital and profit management practices through LLP, and this result was more evident in conventional banks compared to Islamic ones. It can also be noted that capital management occurs when bank managers use discretionary additions to achieve regulatory capital goals; the regulatory capital ratio is an important indicator, reflecting the bank's risks, showing its ability to support the current capital structure, and indicating the risk of default.

Bonin & Kosak (2013) proposed an alternative theory of capital management, whereby in the absence of minimum capital ratios — capital ratios that are lower than desired by regulators — banks will view LLP as a form of capital; therefore, banks overestimate LLPs to compensate for the reduction in the level of principal. This theory is consistent with the results of the Le Quang (2019), which showed that banks with lower capitalization rates increase the level of LLPs in order to use them as a capital in response to market discipline, it is also consistent with the results of the study by Ozili & Outa (2017b),

Abu-Serdaneh (2018), and Elnahass *et al.* (2018), which showed that LLP can be used for capital purposes. Banks with low capital can build a higher LLP in order to increase the CAR, which means that the positive relationship between LLP and CAR means shows the provisions of capital management. Another study (Heningtyas *et al.*, 2021) showed a negative relationship between LLP and CAR for a sample of conventional Indonesian banks, meaning that no provisions are used in capital management.

By reviewing previous studies regarding the impact of LLP on CAR, it can be said that an increase in LLP after the adoption of the IFRS 9 may reduce capital adequacy, since there is a direct link between LLP and the regulatory capital Tier 1; the LLPs express the current period expenses that reduce equity (Common Equity Tier 1) through retained earnings, and the increase in the LLP reduces the accounting profit, which is reflected in the retained earnings and thus a decrease in the first level of regulatory capital. In addition, this increase in LLP affects the cumulative LLA and thus reduces the book value of the bank's total assets, hence the poor position of shareholders' equity.

BCBS sought to reduce the negative impact of provisions through the possibility of adding back a part of the provisions to the regulatory capital, which means the possibility of overcoming the negative impact on the regulatory capital (Tier 1) resulting from the increase in LLPs. Basel I adds the general provisions in the first level of the regulatory capital up to a maximum of 1.25% of the risk-weighted assets (RWAs), and excludes the specific provisions, and the Basel II maintains the same treatment for banks that follow the standardized approach (SA). But in the event that the bank follows the internal rating-based approach (IRB), a comparison is made between the expected losses (ELs) calculated under the regulatory requirements and the accounting credit losses (CLs). If there is a shortfall in accounting losses, it is deducted equally from the capital Tier 1 and the capital Tier 2, but in the case of exceeding the accounting credit losses (CL), the difference is added to the capital Tier 2 with a maximum of 0.6% of the risk-weighted assets (RWA) (BCBS, 2004, 2006). Basel III is consistent with the treatments in Basel II, except that the shortfall in accounting losses compared to regulatory losses (ELs) is deducted entirely from the regulatory capital Tier 1 in an attempt to reduce the opportunistic incentives for management, which are made by exploiting the allocations via the retained earnings channel to raise capital (Krüger *et al.*, 2018).

In the opposite direction, capital adequacy can affect LLP when capital adequacy in banks is low; managers book more provisions to meet regulatory requirements (Dong *et al.*, 2012), where the capital hypothesis states that including LLP in calculating RCR will motivate bank managers to estimate higher LLP, with a view to increasing regulatory capital. Therefore, bank managers' awareness of the costs associated with violating minimum regulatory capital requirements creates strong incentives to use provisions to increase the CAR to the desired level (Ahmed *et al.*, 1998).

By reviewing the previous literature, it can be said that the relationship between LLP and NPL is a positive relationship. When the percentage of NPL increases, banks will pay for their efforts to support their funds in order to cover credit losses. It can also be noted that an increase in the size of LLP could negatively affect capital adequacy, due to the negative impact on the numerator of the capital adequacy equation, and this may cause banks to worry about the application of the IFRS 9. On the other hand, the application of the IFRS 9 may force banks to improve the quality of capital and become more prudent against expected losses. In addition, banks may have the IFRS 9-related reserves added to the capital equation numerator, which reduces the impact of the decline in capital adequacy.

Nevertheless, the decrease in the size of LLP reflects positively on the profitability of banks and retained earnings, which positively reflect on capital adequacy. However, banks' exploitation of provisions to increase CARs can be reduced through regulatory treatment of the difference between provisions for loan losses in accordance with Basel requirements and accounting provisions. On the other hand, capital adequacy may affect the size of the LLP expense, and banks with low levels of capital may seek to form more provisions in order to increase capital. Among the hypotheses for this behavior is looking at the provisions as a capital, that banks can use it to expand the lending. Accordingly and based on the literature related to the relationships between the study variables represented in NPL, LLP, and CAR, the following study hypotheses are derived:

$\mathbf{H_1}$: There are no statistically significant differences at the level of significance (0.05) for CAR, NPLs, and LLPs before and after the adoption of the IFRS 9 in the banking sector of the GCC countries.

H_2: There is no effect of capital adequacy, the percentage of non-performing loans, and the dummy variable that expresses the application of the IFRS 9 on provisions for loan losses in the banking sector of the GCC countries.

H_3: There is no effect on LLPs, NPLs ratio, and the dummy variable that expresses the application of the IFRS 9 on capital adequacy in the banking sector of the GCC countries.

10.3. Data

10.3.1. *Study variables*

Due to the limitations imposed by the quality of the data obtained, the current study requires adjustments in how to measure some of the explanatory variables (independent) and the dependent variable. This is because the study contains four variables that stand in for the most significant variables that are expected to have an impact on the dependent variable. The most important variables that were selected and included in the current study are shown in the Table 10.1.

10.3.2. *Population study and sampling*

The population study consists of banks operating in the countries of the Gulf Cooperation Council (GCC). The banks operating in these countries were counted through websites in order to obtain the largest possible number of banks. Five large banks from each country were selected from which data could be obtained for the period from 2012 to 2022; this period was targeted by the study

Table 10.1. Study variables.

Sr. No.	Variables	Code	Type	Data
1.	Provision for loan losses	LLP/TL	Dependent/Independent	Financial reporting
2.	Enough money	CAR	Dependent/Independent	
3.	Non-performing loans	NPL/TL	Dependent/Independent	
4.	Dummy variable	Dummy/V	Independent	

with the aim of measuring the impact of adopting the International Financial Reporting Standards on the relationship between CAR and LLPs in the presence of NPLs. This effect is measured through a dummy variable that takes the value zero for the period from 2012 to 2017, and the value 1 for the period from 2018 to 2021.

The focus is on the banks of these countries and not others, for the following reasons:

(1) These countries have applied the International Financial Reporting Standards IFRS 9 since the beginning of 2018, enabling them to obtain data for the longest possible time series, which is the maximum application period that can be obtained — a period of 4 years.
(2) Published data is available from banks operating in these countries, either in Arabic or English, which is not available in banks in the Maghreb countries, for example.
(3) The strength and convergence of the economies of these countries ensure data homogeneity as much as possible.
(4) There is stability in these countries due to the absence of conflicts and wars that affect economic activity.

Table 10.2 shows a sample of the banks that were targeted for this study.

Table 10.2. Country name with the bank name.

Country	Bank name
Kingdom of Saudi Arabia	Riyadh Bank, Saudi British Bank (SABB), French Saudi Bank.
State of Qatar	National Bank, Commercial Bank, Doha Bank, Qatar National Bank.
Bahrain	United Arab Bank, Arab Banking Corporation, Bank of Bahrain and Kuwait, National Bank of Bahrain.
Sultanate of Oman	Bank Sohar, Bank Dhofar, Bank Muscat, National Bank of Oman, Oman Arab Bank.
United Arab Emirates	United Arab Bank, Ras Al Khaimah Bank, Fujairah Bank, First Abu Dhabi Bank, Umm Al Quw Bank.
Kuwait	National Bank of Kuwait, Burgan Bank, ABK, Commercial Bank of Kuwait, Gulf Bank.

10.4. Methodology

10.4.1. *Descriptive analysis of the study indicators*

The descriptive statistics of the study indicators were calculated for years 2012–2021 as follows.

10.4.2. *Test of normality*

Although the data have to be analyzed (see Table 10.3), one needs to know whether the data follow a normal distribution or not. There are two broad classifications of statistical tests used in data analysis, namely, parametric and non-parametric.

Table 10.3. The lowest and highest value, mean and standard deviations of the indicators.

State	Indicator	Minimum	Maximum	Mean	Std. dev.
Saudi Arabia	CAR	0.14800	0.22000	0.18474	0.01907
	NPL	0.00770	0.03460	0.01660	0.00721
	LLP	0.00132	0.02082	0.00669	0.00324
State of Qatar	CAR	0.13510	0.21000	0.17126	0.01828
	NPL	0.00000	0.16850	0.00954	0.03091
	LLP	0.00016	0.04518	0.00730	0.00839
Bahrain	CAR	0.13000	0.40000	0.21953	0.07957
	NPL	0.01840	0.10450	0.05432	0.02716
	LLP	0.00192	0.07479	0.01010	0.01277
Oman	CAR	0.13000	0.21000	0.16525	0.02124
	NPL	0.00430	0.20220	0.02842	0.03153
	LLP	0.00068	0.01465	0.00622	0.00345
United Arab Emirates	CAR	0.13100	0.45000	0.21292	0.08221
	NPL	0.01580	0.15720	0.05499	0.03172
	LLP	0.00207	0.07574	0.02117	0.01881
Kuwait	CAR	0.14000	0.38000	0.19548	0.05551
	NPL	0.00000	0.11930	0.03554	0.02621
	LLP	0.00222	0.04378	0.01715	0.00834
Total	CAR	0.13000	0.45000	0.19196	0.05669
	NPL	0.00000	0.20220	0.03364	0.03119
	LLP	0.00016	0.07574	0.01209	0.01228

Notes: Includes the study indicators for the Arab Gulf countries for the years 2012–2021, where it is shown in general that the mean of the CAR indicator for the period studied was 0.19196 with a standard deviation of 0.05669, the mean of the NPL indicator was 0.03364 with a standard deviation of 0.031187, and the mean for the LLP indicator was 0.012085, with a standard deviation of (0.01228).

Table 10.4. Kolmogorov–Smirnov test of normality.

Sr. No.	Variables	Kolmogorov–Smirnov	N	p-value
1.	Capital adequacy	0.878	250	0.057
2.	NPL/TL	0.889	250	0.061
3.	LLP/TL	0.853	250	0.052

10.4.3. *Kolmogorov–Smirnov test*

To achieve the objectives of the study and analyze the collected data, the Kolmogorov–Smirnov test was used for each study variable individually to determine whether the data follow a normal distribution or not. It is clear that the use of the parametric techniques is more appropriate in this study, as shown in Table 10.4. The statistical significance of all variables is greater than $\alpha = 0.05$, so we accept the hypothesis that the data are no different from the normal distribution. Therefore, the hypotheses can be tested on the parametric approach.

10.5. Testing of the Hypotheses

The study hypotheses will be tested as given in the following.

10.5.1. *The first main hypothesis*

There are no statistically significant differences ($\alpha = 0.05$) for the study indicators (CAR, NPLs, and LLPs) before and after adopting the international standard IFRS 9 for the studied period (2012–2021) in the banking sector of the Gulf Cooperation Council Countries.

The first main hypothesis can be tested more accurately through the sub-hypotheses that emerge from it as follows:

10.5.1.1. *The first sub-hypothesis*

The first sub-hypothesis was formulated in the form of a null hypothesis that "there are no statistically significant differences ($\alpha = 0.05$) for the studied indicators (CAR, NPLs, and LLPs) before and after adopting the international standard IFRS 9 for the studied period (2012–2021) in the banking sector of the Gulf Cooperation Council countries (for all countries)".

Table 10.5. Test for IFRS 9 adoption before/after 2018 for study indicators of GCC Countries.

Indicator	Period	*N*	Mean	Std. dev.	df	*t*-value	*p*-value
CAR	Before	6	0.18731	0.05343	248	−1.595	0.112
	After	4	0.19895	0.06086			
NPL	Before	6	0.03065	0.02846	248	−1.862	0.064
	After	4	0.03811	0.03455			
LLP	Before	6	0.01127	0.01174	248	−2.199	0.025*
	After	4	0.01331	0.01301			

Note: * significance level at 5% level.

To determine the degree of differences in the study variables before and after the adoption of the international standard IFRS 9 (before and after 2018) for all countries during the years (2012–2021), the t-test was used for two independent samples.

It can be seen from Table 10.5 that the value of the t-test for the CAR indicator was −1.595, and the p-value was 0.112, which is greater than the significance level ($\alpha = 0.05$), so the null hypothesis was accepted. This means that there are no statistically significant differences in the CAR indicator before and after adopting the international standard IFRS 9 for GCC Countries.

As for the NPL indicator, it is noted from Table 10.5 that the value of the t-test was −1.862, and the p-value was 0.064, which is greater than the significance level ($\alpha = 0.05$), so the null hypothesis was accepted. This means that there are no statistically significant differences in the NPL indicator before and after 2018.

Regarding the LLP indicator, it is noted from Table 10.5 that the value of the t-test was about −2.199, and the p-value was (0.025), which is less than the significance level ($\alpha = 0.05$), so the null hypothesis was rejected. This means that there are statistically significant differences in the LLP indicator after 2018.

10.5.1.2. *The second sub-hypothesis*

The second sub-hypothesis was formulated in the form of a null hypothesis as "there are no statistically significant differences ($\alpha = 0.05$) for the studied indicators (CAR, NPLs, and LLPs) before and after adopting the international standard IFRS 9 for the studied

Table 10.6. Test for adopting of IFRS 9 before/after 2018 for study indicators of Saudi Arabia.

Indicator	Period	N	Mean	Std. dev.	df	t-value	p-value
CAR	Before	6	0.17463	0.01496	48	−6.018	0.000**
	After	4	0.19990	0.01389			
NPL	Before	6	0.03065	0.02846	48	−4.730	0.000**
	After	4	0.03811	0.03455			
LLP	Before	6	0.01127	0.01174	48	−2.167	0.035*
	After	4	0.01331	0.01301			

Note: * significance level at 5% level, ** significant at 1% level.

period (2012–2021) in the banking sector of the Gulf Cooperation Council countries (for each country)".

To determine the degree of differences in the study variables before and after the adoption of the international standard IFRS 9 (before and after 2018) for each country during the years 2012–2021, t-test was used for two independent samples.

Table 10.6 shows that the value of t-test for the CAR indicator was −6.018, and the p-value was 0.000, which is less than the significance level ($\alpha = 0.01$), so the null hypothesis was rejected. This means that there is a significant difference in the CAR indicator before and after 2018. The adoption of IFRS 9 after 2018 has been estimated to have caused an important effect from the CAR indicator.

It is interesting to note that, at a 1% level, there is a significant difference in the NPL indicator. It is noted from Table 10.4 that the value of t-test was −4.730, and the p-value was 0.000, so the null hypothesis was rejected. This means there is a highly significant difference in the NPL indicator before and after adopting the IFRS 9 after 2018.

Regarding the LLP indicator, it is noted that the value of t-test was about −2.167, and the p-value was 0.035, which is less than the significance level ($\alpha = 0.05$), so the null hypothesis was rejected. This means that there are statistically significant differences in the LLP indicator before and after adopting the IFRS 9.

Table 10.7 shows that the value of t-test for the CAR indicator was 2.335, and the associated p-value of the t-test (i.e., 0.027) signals that it is very unlikely to find such a value if the null hypothesis is true.

Table 10.7. Test for adopting IFRS 9 before/after 2018 for study indicators of Qatar.

Indicator	Period	*N*	Mean	Std. dev.	df	*t*-value	*p*-value
CAR	Before	6	0.16533	0.01960	28	−2.335	0.027*
	After	4	0.18014	0.01198			
NPL	Before	6	0.00498	0.00808	28	−0.989	0.331
	After	4	0.01638	0.04830			
LLP	Before	6	0.00508	0.00524	28	−1.895	0.048*
	After	4	0.01063	0.01110			

Note: * significance level at 5% level.

At a 5% level of significance, the null hypothesis is therefore rejected. The adoption of IFRS 9 after 2018 may have improved the CAR indicator more than before 2018, which is how the *t*-test found a significant difference.

It can be seen that, at a 5% level, there is no significant difference in the NPL indicator in banking in Qatar (p-value > 0.05). The associated p-value of the t-test (i.e., 0.331) indicates that the null hypothesis is likely to be true and it is accepted at a 5% significance level. Therefore, it can be inferred from the test results that the differences observed in the NPL indicator before and after 2018 are not statistically significant (see Table 10.6).

Table 10.7 also presents that, at a 5% level, there is significant difference in the LLP indicator of adoption of IFRS 9 before and after 2018 (p-value < 0.05). The associated p-value of the t-test (p-value $=$ 0.048) indicates that it is almost unlikely to find such a value if null hypothesis is true and, therefore, the null hypothesis is rejected at a 5% significance level. These results indicate that adoption of IFRS 9 after 2018 in the LLP indicates more improvement than before 2018.

It can be seen from Table 10.8 that the value of t-test for the CAR indicator was −0.367, and the p-value was 0.716, which is greater than the significance level ($\alpha = 0.05$), so the null hypothesis was accepted. This means that there are no statistically significant differences in the CAR indicator before and after 2018 (before and after adopting the international standard IFRS 9 for GCC Countries).

It can be seen that, at a 5% level, there is no significant difference in the NPL indicator in banking in Bahrain (p-value > 0.05). The associated p-value of the t-test (i.e., 0.301) indicates that the null hypothesis is likely to be true and it is accepted at a 5% significance level. Therefore, it can be inferred from the test results that the differences observed in the NPL indicator before and after 2018 are not statistically significant (see Table 10.7).

Table 10.8 also demonstrates that, at a 5% level, there is no significant difference in the LLP indicator in adoption of IFRS 9 before and after 2018 (p-value > 0.05). The associated p-value of the t-test (p-value = 0.350) indicates that it is likely to be true and it is accepted at a 5% significance level. Therefore, the null hypothesis is accepted at a 5% significance level. These results indicate that adoption of IFRS 9 after 2018 with regard to the LLP indicator is the same as before 2018.

Table 10.9 shows that the value of t-test for the CAR indicator was −2.529, and the associated p-value of the t-test (i.e., 0.016) signals that it is very unlikely to find such a value if the null hypothesis is

Table 10.8. Test for adopting IFRS 9 before/after 2018 for study indicators of Bahrain.

Indicator	Period	N	Mean	Std. dev.	df	t-value	p-value
CAR	Before	6	0.21511	0.08195	28	−0.367	0.716
	After	4	0.22617	0.07895			
NPL	Before	6	0.05858	0.02946	28	1.054	0.301
	After	4	0.04793	0.02301			
LLP	Before	6	0.01191	0.01601	28	0.951	0.350
	After	4	0.00738	0.00456			

Table 10.9. Test for adopting of IFRS 9 before/after 2018 for study indicators of Muscat.

Indicator	Period	N	Mean	Std. dev.	df	t-value	p-value
CAR	Before	6	0.15875	0.01777	38	−2.529	0.016*
	After	4	0.17500	0.02280			
NPL	Before	6	0.02635	0.03815	38	−0.502	0.618
	After	4	0.03152	0.01832			
LLP	Before	6	0.00556	0.00286	38	−1.507	0.140
	After	4	0.00721	0.00409			

Note: * significance level at 5% level.

true. Therefore, the null hypothesis is rejected at a 5% significance level. The reason that the t-test found a significant difference might be because of adoption of IFRS 9 after 2018 in the CAR indicator more improvement than before 2018.

It can be seen that, at a 5% level, there is no significant difference in the NPL indicator in banking in Muscat (p-value > 0.05). The associated p-value of the t-test (i.e., 0.618) indicates that the null hypothesis is likely to be true and it is accepted at a 5% significance level. Therefore, it can be inferred from the test results that the differences observed in the NPL indicator before and after 2018 are not statistically significant (see Table 10.9). The results suggest that there were similar observations before and after adoption of IFRS 9 in 2018.

Table 10.9 also demonstrates that, at a 5% level, there is no significant difference in the LLP indicator of adoption of IFRS 9 before and after 2018 (p-value > 0.05). The associated p-value of the t-test (p-value $= 0.140$) indicates that it is likely to be true and it is accepted at a 5% significance level. Therefore, the null hypothesis is accepted at a 5% significance level. According to these results, the LLP index did not change significantly after the adoption of the international standard IFRS 9.

It can be seen from Table 10.10 that the value of the t-test for the CAR indicator was 0.029, and the p-value was (0.977), which is greater than the significance level ($\alpha = 0.05$) so the null hypothesis was accepted. This means that there are no statistically significant differences in the CAR indicator before and after 2018

Table 10.10. Test for adopting IFRS 9 before/after 2018 for study indicators of Emirates.

Indicator	Period	N	Mean	Std. dev.	df	t-value	p-value
CAR	Before	6	0.21320	0.07003	48	0.029	0.977
	After	4	0.21250	0.09973			
NPL	Before	6	0.04525	0.02189	48	−1.753	0.048*
	After	4	0.06959	0.03859			
LLP	Before	6	0.01867	0.01741	48	−1.746	0.049*
	After	4	0.02491	0.02061			

Note: * significance level at 5% level.

(before and after adopting the international standard IFRS 9 for GCC Countries).

It is interesting to note (Table 10.10) that, at a 5% level, there is a significant difference in the NPL indicator. It is noted (Table 10.8) that the value of the t-test was -1.753, and the p-value was 0.048, so the null hypothesis was rejected, which means there is a significant difference in the NPL indicator before and after adoption of IFRS 9 in 2018. As a result, the results indicate that the NPL indicator after the adoption of IFRS 9 has changed compared to what it was before the adoption.

Table 10.10 also presents that, at a 5% level, there is a significant difference in the LLP indicator of adoption of IFRS 9 before and after 2018 (p-value < 0.05). The associated p-value of the t-test (p-value $=$ 0.049) indicates that it is almost unlikely to find such a value if null hypothesis is true and, therefore, the null hypothesis is rejected at a 5% significance level (see Table 10.10). These results indicate that the adoption of IFRS 9 after 2018 in the LLP has indicated greater improvement than before 2018.

It can be seen from Table 10.11 that the value of t-test for the CAR indicator was -0.316, and the p-value was 0.753, which is greater than the significance level ($\alpha = 0.05$), so the null hypothesis was accepted. This means that there are no statistically significant differences in the CAR indicator before and after 2018 (before and after adopting the international standard IFRS 9 for GCC Countries).

It can be seen that, at a 5% level, there is no significant difference in the NPL indicator in banking in Kuwait (p-value > 0.05). The associated p-value of the t-test (i.e., 0.981) indicates that the null

Table 10.11. Test for adopting of IFRS 9 before/after 2018 for study indicators of Kuwait.

Indicator	Period	N	Mean	Std. dev.	df	t-value	p-value
CAR	Before	6	0.19343	0.05271	48	−0.316	0.753
	After	4	0.19855	0.06075			
NPL	Before	6	0.03546	0.02219	48	−0.024	0.981
	After	4	0.03565	0.03194			
LLP	Before	6	0.01712	0.00744	48	−0.024	0.980
	After	4					

hypothesis is likely to be true and it is accepted at a 5% significance level. Therefore, it can be inferred from the test results that the differences observed in the NPL indicator before and after 2018 are not statistically significant (see Table 10.11). The results suggest similar observations before the 2018 IFRS 9 adoption.

Table 10.11 also demonstrates that, at a 5% level, there is no significant difference in the LLP indicator of adoption of IFRS 9 before and after 2018 (p-value > 0.05). The associated p-value of the t-test (p-value $= 0.980$) indicates that it is likely to be true and it is accepted at a 5% significance level. Therefore, the null hypothesis is accepted at a 5% significance level. These results indicate that adoption of IFRS 9 after 2018 with regard to the LLP indicator is the same as before 2018.

10.5.2. *The second hypothesis*

10.5.2.1. *Panel data modeling of the study indicators*

In this study, the model used is based on the panel data time series, because of its increased prediction accuracy, which ensures the accuracy of inference and improves the research results by optimizing the use of data in finding causal relationships between the phenomena in question. It takes into account the effect of time change (years) and the effect of the difference between items (banks). Sectional time series models are built according to the following steps:

(1) Use the Hsiao homogenization test,
(2) Estimate of cross-sectional time series models,
(3) Choose the appropriate model,
(4) Check the suitability of the model,
(5) Analyze the results of the appropriate model.

Data obtained from financial reporting need to be analyzed and interpreted to be of use in meeting research objectives and answering the research questions. Therefore, the current study employs analytical statistics for two purposes: to examine the significant differences in two time periods (before/after) and to make inferences about the population parameters from the sample statistics through hypothesis testing of panel data modeling, using the Eviews software.

This study is conducted on six commercial banks in the Gulf Cooperation Council Countries of Saudi Arabia, Qatar, Bahrain, Oman, United Arab Emirates, and Kuwait. The period from 2012 to 2021 was chosen due to the availability of data on the study variables for all selected banks.

10.5.2.2. *How to apply the model*

It is important to find a mathematical equation that expresses the relationship between variables and is used to estimate previous values to predict future values. Therefore, the equation is used to predict changes in the dependent variable that is affected by several independent variables. So, regression analysis is applied to explain the relationship between a dependent variable and one or more independent variables as follows:

(1) The Pooled model is applied to arrive at the extent and relevance of the association between both independent variables and dependent variables, using the association matrix as follows:

$$y_{it} = \beta_0 + \sum_{i=1}^{3} \beta_{pi} x_{pit} + \varepsilon_{it},$$

where
y_{it}: $(i = 1, 2, \ldots, 6)$ and $(t = 1, 2, \ldots, 10)$ represent the variable of the study as shown in Table 10.1 and the provisions for loss of loans charged to income in the annual reports of the banks in question, respectively;
x_{pit}: $(p = 1, 2, 3)$,$(i = 1, 2, \ldots, 6)$, and $(t = 1, 2, \ldots, 10)$ represent the explanatory variables (independent) of the study as shown in Table 10.1, namely, capital adequacy, dummy variability, and non-working loans to the studying banks, respectively;
β_0: constant;
β_{pi}: $(p = 1, 2, 3)$ and $(i = 1, 2, \ldots, 6)$ are the linear regression coefficients;
ε_{ij} : random error.

(2) The fixed effect model is applied.
(3) The random effect model is applied.
(4) The three models are compared to find the best estimate method.

10.5.2.3. *Statistical treatments for outliers*

The topic of extreme values in data, the impact of their existence, and their implications on the results and accuracy of statistical analyses are of interest to many researchers, as there are a number of statistical methods used to detect and identify extreme values in the dataset and address them in the data. The 5% trimmed mean method was used for the amputee average (5% Trimmed Mean), and all extreme values are replaced by the amputee average for each variable separately.

10.5.2.4. *Homogenization test (Hsiao test)*

The use of sectional time series models requires verifying the homogeneity of the data under study and the applicability of these models through the Hsiao test (as presented in 1986), according to following three stages:

- *Total homogeneity testing stage*: By making sure that the constants (β_0) and regression coefficients (β_{ki}) are identical between banks.
- *The stage of testing homogeneity of coefficients*: By making sure that coefficients (β_{pi}) and regression coefficients are identical between banks.
- *The stage of testing the consistency*: By making sure that the individual constants (β_0) are equal, under the assumption that the regression coefficients (β_{pi}) are common to all items.

Based on previous test results, an appropriate model for the study can be identified as follows.

In accordance with Table 10.12 and at a significance level of 0.05, rejecting (H_{01}) means rejecting that the optimal model is the model of total homogeneity, rejecting (H_{02}) means that the coefficient (β_i) is not homogeneous, i.e., not identical for all the banks in this study, and accepting (H_{03}) means that the constants (β_0) is not

Table 10.12. Hsiao (1986) specification tests.

Sr. No.	Hypotheses	F-value	p-value	Decision
1.	1st hypothesis (H_{01})	7.737	0.000	Reject
2.	2nd hypothesis (H_{02})	3.642	0.000	Reject
3.	3rd hypothesis (H_{03})	1.090	0.374	Accept

Source: Prepared by researchers using Eviews.

homogeneous for all banks. Therefore, the model used in the study could be the single effects model.

10.5.2.5. *Resulting of estimating the appropriate model*

It can be inferred from the results of the Hsiao test that the data are not homogeneous according to the banks, and the relationship between the dependent variable and the independent variables can take the form of a fixed or random effects model. Accordingly, in the next stage, we will deal with the estimation of different (panel) data models that take the results as shown in Table 10.13.

Although the results of Table 10.13 indicate that the effects of the pooled model and random effects are appropriate for the cross-sectional data across the banks due to the higher coefficient of determination adjusted for more than the fixed model, it is preferable to continue the analysis and use the Hausman test to compare between the pooled effects model and the random effects model. Table 10.14 shows the Hausman test according to the following test hypotheses:

Table 10.13. Results of model estimation of LLP/LT indicator.

Model \ Coefficient	β_0	β_1	β_2	β_3
Pooled effect model	0.014 (0.000)	−0.047 (0.000)	0.001 (0.407)	0.186 (0.000)
	$R^2 = 0.495$ Adjusted $(R^2) = 0.485$ SE of regression $= 0.030$ F-statistic $= 19.849$ (0.000)			
Fixed effect model	—	−0.051 (0.007)	0.002 (0.178)	0.146 (0.000)
	$R^2 = 0.355$ Adjusted $(R^2) = 0.352$ SE of regression $= 0.016$ F-statistic $= 19.849$ (0.000)			
Random effect model	0.016 (0.000)	−0.048 (0.004)	0.002 (0.200)	0.154 (0.000)
	$R^2 = 0.562$ Adjusted $(R^2) = 0.551$ SE of regression $= 0.018$ F-statistic $= 47.406$ (0.000)			

Source: Prepared by the researchers using Eviews.

Table 10.14. Hausman tests.

Hypotheses	Chi-square	df	p-value	Decision
Hypothesis (H_0)	18.294	3	0.001	Reject

Source: Prepared by the researcher using Eviews.

H_0: The pooled effects model is the appropriate model, versus the alternative hypothesis.

H_1: The random effects model is the appropriate model.

Table 10.14 indicates that it is almost unlikely to find such a value if the null hypothesis is true and, therefore, the null hypothesis is rejected at a significance level, meaning that the random effects model is the appropriate model (p-value < 0.05). Accordingly, the proposed model can be formulated as follows:

$$\begin{aligned}\widehat{LLP/TL}_{\mathrm{it}} &= 0.016 - 0.048\,\mathrm{CAR}_{1\mathrm{it}} + 0.002\,\mathrm{DUMMY}_{\mathrm{V}2\mathrm{it}} \\ &\quad + 0.154\,\mathrm{NPL}_{\mathrm{TL}3\mathrm{it}}.\end{aligned}$$

10.5.2.6. *Overview of lest significant differences (LSDs)*

The least significant difference (LSD) test is used in the context of the analysis of variance, when the F-ratio suggests rejection of the null hypothesis H_0, that is, when the difference between the indicator means is significant. This seems to be important in understanding the procedure of financial reporting and indicators issues. A brief overview of the difference between the indicator means is provided in Table 10.15.

The reason for the negative impact of capital adequacy on loan loss allocations is as follows:

For Saudi banks, the average capital of Bahraini and UAE banks was greater than the average capital of Saudi banks.

For Qatari banks, the average capital of Bahrain and UAE banks was greater than the average capital of Qatar banks.

For Bahraini banks, the average adequacy of capital for Muscat banks was less than the average adequacy of capital for Bahraini banks.

Table 10.15. Multiple comparisons of CAR for GCC banks.

(I) Country	(J) Country	Mean difference (I–J)	Std. error	Sig.
Saudi Arabia	Qatar	0.0134833333	0.0124651099	0.280
	Bahrain	−0.0347933333*	0.0124651099	0.006
	Muscat	0.0194900000	0.0114499345	0.090
	UAE	−0.0281800000*	0.0107951018	0.010
	Kuwait	−0.0107400000	0.0107951018	0.321
Qatar	Bahrain	−0.0482766667*	0.0139364165	0.001
	Muscat	0.0060066667	0.0130363239	0.645
	UAE	−0.0416633333*	0.0124651099	0.001
	Kuwait	−0.0242233333	0.0124651099	0.053
Bahrain	Muscat	0.0542833333*	0.0130363239	0.000
	UAE	0.0066133333	0.0124651099	0.596
	Kuwait	0.0240533333	0.0124651099	0.055
Muscat	UAE	−0.0476700000*	0.0114499345	0.000
	Kuwait	−0.0302300000*	0.0114499345	0.009
UAE	Kuwait	0.0174400000	0.0107951018	0.107

Note: * the mean difference is significant at the 0.05 level.

For Muscat banks, the average adequacy of capital for Emirati and Kuwaiti banks was greater than the average adequacy of capital for Muscat banks.

Table 10.16 shows the results of multiple comparisons of the dedicated loan loss index (LLP/TL) for GCC Banks.

The reason for the negative impact of LLP on capital adequacy is that: the average of LLP of UAE and Kuwaiti banks was greater than the average of LLP of Saudi, Qatar, Bahraini, and Oman banks.

Table 10.17 shows the results of multiple comparisons of the NPL/TL for GCC Banks. Table 10.17 illustrates that for the NPLs have a favorable effect and the reason is that:

The average NPL index for banks in Bahrain, Muscat, Emirates, and Kuwait was greater than the average non-working loans for Saudi banks.

The average NPL index for banks in Bahrain, Muscat, Emirates, and Kuwait was greater than the average non-working loans for Qatari banks.

The average NPL index for banks in Kuwait was lower than the average NPLs for Bahraini banks, while for UAE banks, the average index was greater than the average for Bahraini banks.

Table 10.16. Multiple comparisons of LLP/LT for GCC bank.

(I) Country	(J) Country	Mean difference (I–J)	Std. error	Sig.
Saudi Arabia	Qatar	−0.0006145170	0.002495287	0.806
	Bahrain	−0.0034117242	0.002495287	0.173
	Muscat	0.0004678309	0.002292068	0.838
	UAE	−0.0144778953*	0.002160982	0.000
	Kuwait	−0.0104595769*	0.002160982	0.000
Qatar	Bahrain	−0.0027972073	0.002789816	0.317
	Muscat	0.0010823479	0.002609634	0.679
	UAE	−0.0138633783*	0.002495287	0.000
	Kuwait	−0.0098450600*	0.002495287	0.000
Bahrain	Muscat	0.0038795552	0.002609633	0.138
	UAE	−0.0110661710*	0.002495287	0.000
	Kuwait	−0.0070478527*	0.002495287	0.005
Muscat	UAE	−0.0149457262*	0.002292067	0.000
	Kuwait	−0.0109274078*	0.002292067	0.000
UAE	Kuwait	0.0040183184	0.002160982	0.064

Note: * the mean difference is significant at the 0.05 level.

Table 10.17. Multiple comparisons of NPL/LT for GCC bank.

(I) Country	(J) Country	Mean difference (I–J)	Std. error	Sig.
Saudi Arabia	Qatar	0.0070595275	0.0061558369	0.253
	Bahrain	−0.0377185017*	0.0061558369	0.000
	Muscat	−0.0118122767*	0.0056544973	0.038
	UAE	−0.0383831581*	0.0053311112	0.000
	Kuwait	−0.0189370130*	0.0053311112	0.000
Qatar	Bahrain	−0.0447780292*	0.0068824349	0.000
	Muscat	−0.0188718042*	0.0064379284	0.004
	UAE	−0.0454426855*	0.0061558369	0.000
	Kuwait	−0.0259965405*	0.0061558369	0.000
Bahrain	Muscat	0.0259062250*	0.0064379284	0.000
	UAE	−0.0006646564	0.0061558369	0.914
	Kuwait	0.0187814887*	0.0061558369	0.003
Muscat	UAE	−0.0265708814*	0.0056544973	0.000
	Kuwait	−0.0071247363	0.0056544973	0.209
UAE	Kuwait	0.0194461450*	0.0053311112	0.000

Note: * the mean difference is significant at the 0.05 level.

The average NPLs for UAE and Kuwaiti banks were greater than the average NPLs for Muscat banks.

The average NPLs for Kuwaiti banks were lower than the average NPLs for UAE banks.

10.5.2.7. *Results analysis of the effect of independent variables on LLPs*

It was found that the appropriate model is the random effects model (REM). To ensure the appropriateness of the model, one can refer to Table 10.5 for the regression analysis of the random effects of LLPs for the banks during the period from 2012 to 2021; the value of the correlation coefficient (R) is equal to (0.749), which is a high value, and the determination coefficient (R^2) and the adjusted coefficient of determination (R^2) are equal to (0.562) and (0.551), respectively, which means that 56.2% of the change in LLPs is explained by the change in capital adequacy. The ratio of NPLs to total loans, with the dummy variable before and after 2018, has no effect on the proposed model, and also indicates that the proposed model for the relationship between the independent variables and the dependent variable in this study is somewhat appropriate.

Based on this model, it was found that the independent variables have an impact on the dependent variable (LLPs), with statistical significance (F-statistic $=$ 47.402 (0.000)) at the level of statistical significance ($\alpha = 0.05$). The results of this model indicates also the negative effect of capital adequacy on LLPs, where the Beat value was (0.048). This may be due to the desire of banks with high adequacy ratios (CAR) to keep LLPs low, since LLPs are taken as losses during periods in which they are recognized, and then reduce the retained earnings and thus Common Equity Tier 1 (CET1). This result is consistent with the studies' results of (Ozili & Outa, 2017b; Abuserdaneh, 2018; Elnahass *et al.*, 2018), while it is different with study's result of (Ozili, 2020). This may be due to the desire of banks with high adequacy ratios (CAR) to keep low LLPs, since LLPs are taken as losses during periods in which they are recognized, and then reduce the retained earnings and thus Common Equity Tier 1 (CET1). Despite the fact that the banks of the Gulf Cooperation

Council countries featured in the study achieved high rates of capital adequacy, especially the Kuwaiti, Emirati, and Bahraini banks (Table 10.15), the results of the analysis showed that there were no statistically significant differences in the performance of the capital adequacy index before and after the adoption of IFRS 9 during the study period (Table 10.5). This may be due to the fact that the growth rates of the capital adequacy index were low or that they had sharp fluctuations during the study period. On the other hand, the results of the study showed that there were statistically significant differences in the LLP index for banks before and after the adoption of the IFRS 9 in favor of the period after the adoption of the standard (after 2018) (Table 10.5). This may be due to the banks of the Emirates and Kuwait, which were characterized by high LLPs during the study period (Table 10.15) to form prudential provisions to face any possible deterioration in their credit portfolios due to the banks' shift towards applying the International Financial Reporting Standards IFRS 9.

Table 10.13 indicates that there is no effect of adopting the IFRS 9 on LLP, and this is consistent with some studies (Seitz *et al.*, 2018; Magdalena & Martani, 2020), but differs from some other studies (Deloitte, 2019; Cohen & Edwards, 2017; Novotny-Farkas (2017); Sultanoğlo 2018; KPMG, 2018, Giner & Mora, 2019). The lack of effect of IFRS 9 adoption can be explained by the lack of a fundamental increase in LLP under IFRS 9 compared to the provisions prepared by IAS 39. Therefore, there are no fundamental differences in the provisions prepared under the two standards, meaning that the application of IFRS 9 did not result in significant changes. This can be explained by the fact that LLP formed by IFRS 9 changes greatly according to changes in the market and varies between banks that have more problems than those that do not have problems; the expected losses also differ according to the model used to estimate the probability of default. Therefore, the LLP formed according to IFRS 9 is unlikely to result in an increase in LLP.

Table 10.13 indicates that there is a positive effect of NPL on LLP, as shown by a positive beta value (0.154). This result is consistent with the results of Kim *et al.* (2019); Basu *et al.* (2019); Beatty & Liao (2020); Tao (2020); and Heningtyas *et al.* (2021). This means that LLPs are more sensitive to the increase in NPL. This may be due to the fact that the banks of the study sample suffer from an increase in NPL, in particular banks of Bahrain, Emirates, Kuwait, and Muscat during the study period (Table 10.8), which resulted in reserving of more prudential provisions.

10.5.3. *Third hypothesis*

There is no impact on the capital adequacy in the GCC banking sector of the provision for loan losses and the dummy variable, reflecting the application of the IFRS 9 and the proportion of loans not operating.

10.5.3.1. *Results of estimating the appropriate model*

Based on the results of the Hsiao test in Table 10.4, it can be inferred that the data are not homogeneous according to the banks, and the relationship between the dependent variable and the independent variables can take the form of a fixed or random effect model; accordingly, in the next stage, we will deal with the estimation of different (panel) data models that take the results as shown in Table 10.18.

Table 10.18. Results of model estimation of the CAR indicator.

Model \ Coefficient	β_0	β_1	β_2	β_3
Pooled effect model	0.172 (0.000)	−0.997 (0.000)	0.007 (0.274)	0.855 (0.000)
	$R^2 = 0.197$ Adjusted $(R^2) = 0.187$ SE of regression = 0.050 F-statistic = 20.102 (0.000)			
Fixed effect model	—	−0.671 (0.000)	0.011 (0.005)	0.091 (0.000)
	$R^2 = 0.091$ Adjusted $(R^2) = 0.020$ SE of regression = 0.216 F-statistic = 7.369 (0.007)			
Random effect model	0.186 (0.000)	−0.647 (0.000)	0.010 (0.004)	0.345 (0.000)
	$R^2 = 0.109$ Adjusted $(R^2) = 0.085$ SE of regression = 0.108 F-statistic = 26.127 (0.000)			

Source: Prepared by the researchers using Eviews.

Table 10.19. Hausman tests.

Hypotheses	Chi-square	df	p-value	Decision
Hypothesis (H_0)	15.982	3	0.001	Reject

Source: Prepared by the researchers using Eviews.

Although the results of Table 10.18 indicate that the effects of the pooled model and random effects are appropriate for the cross-sectional data across the banks due to the higher coefficient of determination adjusted for more than the fixed model, it is preferable to continue the analysis and use the Hausman test to compare the pooled effects model and the random effects model. Table 10.19 shows the Hausman test according to the following test hypotheses:

H_0: The pooled effects model is the appropriate model.
H_1: The random effects model is the appropriate model.

Table 10.19 indicates that it is almost unlikely to find such a value if the null hypothesis is true and, therefore, the null hypothesis is rejected at a 5% significance level. This means that the random effects model is the appropriate model (p-value < 0.05). Accordingly, the proposed model can be formulated as follows:

$$\widehat{\text{CAR}}_{\text{it}} = 0.186 - 0.684\frac{\text{LLP}}{\text{TL}}_{\text{1it}} + 0.010\,\text{DUMMY}_{V2it} + 0.345\,\text{NPL}_{\text{TL3it}}.$$

10.5.3.2. *Results of the analysis of the effect of independent variables on adequacy of the capital*

In addition, the results shown in Table 10.18 for the regression analysis of the random effects of the capital adequacy indicate that the value of the correlation coefficient (R^2) is equal to (0.330), which is a value below the average, and that the determination coefficient (R^2) and the adjusted coefficient of determination (R^2) are equal to 0.109 and 0.085, respectively, which means that 10.9% of the change in capital adequacy is explained by the change in provisions LLP-TL, NPL-TL, while the dummy variable before and after 2018 had no effect on the proposed model, the results also indicates that the proposed model for the relationship between the independent variables and the dependent variable in this study is not appropriate. The significance of the model (F-statistic = 26.127 (0.000)) at the level of statistical significance ($\alpha = 0.05$) is noted, along with the significance of the constant (Constant), which confirms that the model is not interpreted by independent variables from a statistical point of view.

Table 10.18 indicates that there is a negative impact of LLP on CAR, which is expressed by the Beta value (−0.647). This result is consistent with certain studies (Kund & Rugilo, 2019; Karadima & Louri, 2020; Nugroho *et al.*, 2021), but differs from others (Al-Shabrawy, 2019; Al-Shabasi, 2021). This negative impact of LLP on CAR may be explained by the fact that the application of IFRS 9 negatively affects financial solvency due to the increase in LLP, i.e., the inverse relationship between LLP and regulatory capital and then CAR, which may indicate that the application of IFRS 9 has adverse effects on CAR through the negative impact on regulatory capital. The negative relationship may also mean the use of LLP in capital management. The sample of the study increased the LLP size, in particular in UAE and Kuwaiti banks, which had a high LLP compared to the rest of the GCC banks during the study period (Table 10.18), which negatively affected CAR. Increasing the size of LLP expense after adopting IFRS 9 may reduce capital adequacy due to the direct link between LLP and the first level of regulatory capital.

Table 10.18 indicates that there is no effect of adopting IFRS 9 on CAR, and this is consistent with some studies (Khan & Damyanova, 2018; Groff & Mörec, 2020) and contradicts others (Sultanoğlu, 2018; Krüger *et al.*, 2018; Loew *et al.*, 2019). This can be explained by the fact that compliance with the application of IFRS 9 in GCC banks in this study had no effect on CAR.

Finally, Table 10.18 indicates that there is a positive effect of NPL on CAR, which is shown by the value of beta (0.345), and this result is consistent with some studies (Ismailand, 2014; Asher *et al.*, 2014; Wood & Skinner, 2018; Yuliante *et al.*, 2018; Ozili, 2020) and disagrees with others (Ozili, 2019b; Khan *et al.*, 2020; Ozili, 2020, Rahadian & Permana, 2021). This can be explained by the fact that Gulf banks maintain higher regulatory capital ratios in anticipation of an increase in NPL and banks that exceed the regulatory capital requirements face higher rates of NPL. This behavior may due to the CAR of the Gulf banks that absorb the risks of losses that they face.

10.6. Conclusion

This study made a contribution to the literature related to LLPs and CAR by presenting empirical evidence on the effect of the CAR, NPL, and the application of IFRS 9 on LLP, as well as the effect of LLP, NPL, and IFRS 9 adoption on CAR for a sample of 28 banks from the Gulf Cooperation Council countries. The study period included the years from 2012–2021 using the panel data method. The results showed that there is a difference in the performance of the study indicators of CAR, LLP, and NPL before and after the adoption of the IFRS 9 (before and after 2018). There is also no effect of IFRS 9 adoption on both CAR and LLP, while the impact of NPL was positive and significant on both LLP and CAR. Furthermore, there is a negative impact of CAR on LLP and vice versa. This negative impact may be due to banks forming high prudential provisions to meet the requirements of the IFRS 9 standard, which may have an impact on the capital adequacy index ratio declining.

The reason for the lack of effect of applying the IFRS 9 standard on both CAR and LLP may be the short period of application of the standard. Future studies should seek to use a diverse sample of Middle Eastern banks in North Africa or European banks. Studies should also seek to reexamine the impact of implementing IFRS 9 over a longer period of time, which may show different results. The study included CAR, LLP, and NPL variables and the effect of the IFRS 9 standard. It would be interesting to examine the impact of LLPs on capital adequacy in light of the presence of other variables such as bank size, total income, total loans, Common Equity Tier 1 (CET1), and taxes, which could obtain different results.

References

Abu-Serdaneh, J. A. (2018). Bank loan-loss accounts, income smoothing, capital management, signaling, and procyclicality: Evidence from Jordan. *Journal of Financial Reporting and Accounting*, *16*(4), 677–693. DOI: 10.1108/JFRA-06-2016-0041.

Achir, R. (2014). Influencing Factors Analysis of Banking Loan Channeling. *Journal Tepak Manajemen Bisnis*, *6*(3), 105–117. https://jtmb.ejournal.unri.ac.id/index.php/JTMB/article/view/2490/2449.

Ahmed, A. S., Takeda, C., & Thomas, S. (1998). Bank loan loss provisions: A reexamination of capital management earnings management and signaling effects. *Journal of Accounting and Economics*, *28*(1), 1–25.

Al-Nsour, R. & Abuaddous, M. (2022). A comparison study between IFRS 9 and IAS 39 in GCC countries. *European Journal of Business and Management Research*, http://dx.doi.org/10.24018/ejbmr.2022.7.6.1687.

Al-Shabasi, M. S. (2021). A proposed model for the accounting measurement of financial risks from the perspective of the international standard IFRS9 for financial reporting and the capital adequacy standard for application to the banking sector (applied study). *The Scientific Journal of Accounting Studies*, *3*(1), 601–671.

Arif, D., Yucha, N., Setiawan, S., Oktarina, D., Martah, V., & Muttaqiin, N. (2020). Applications of goods mutation control form in accounting information system: A Case study in Sumber Indah Perkasa manufacturing, Indonesia. *Journal of Asian Finance, Economics and Business*, *7*, 419–424.

Barus, A. C. & Erick. (2016). Analisis Faktor-Faktor yang Mempengaruhi Non Per-forming Loan Pada Bank Umum di Indonesia. *Journal Wira Ekonomi Mikrosil*, *6*(2), 1–10.

Basel Committee on Banking Supervisions (BCBS) (2004). International convergence of capital standards: A revised framework, bank for international settlements. https://www.bis.org/publ/bcbs107.pdf.

Basel Committee on Banking Supervision (BCBS) (2005). Basel II: International Convergence of Capital Measurement and Capital Standards: A Revised Framework. https://www.bis.org/publ/bcbs118.pdf.

Basel Committee on Banking Supervision (BCBS) (2006). International convergence of capital measurement and capital standards. A Revised framework comprehensive version. https://www.bis.org/publ/bcbs128.pdf.

Basel Committee on Banking Supervision (BCBS) (2017). Regulatory Treatment of Accounting Provisions — Interim Approach and Transitional Arrangements. https://www.bis.org/bcbs/publ/d401.htm.

Basu, S., Vitanza, J., & Wang, W. (2020). Asymmetric loan loss provisioning. *Journal of Accounting and Economics*, *70*(2–3). Article No. 101359.

Beatty, A. & Liao, S. (2009). Regulatory capital ratios loan loss provisioning and procyclicality. *SSRN Electron Journal*, 52. DOI: 10.2139/ssrn.1463374.

Beatty, A. & Liao, S. (2020). Alternative evidence and views on asymmetric loan loss provisioning. *Journal of Accounting and Economics*, *70*(2–3), 101362. DOI: 10.1016/j.jacceco.2020.101362.

Bholat, D., Lastra, R., Markose, H., Miglionico, A., & Sen, K. (2018 January). Non-performing loans: Regulatory and accounting treatments of assets. *Journal of Banking Regulation.* DOI: 10.1057/s41261-017-0058-8.

Bonin, J. & Kosak, M. (2013). Loan loss provisioning in emerging Europe: Precautionary or pro-cyclical. Wesleyan Economics Working Papers No. 010, Wesleyan University Department of Economics. https://ideas.repec.org/p/wes/weswpa/2013-010.html.

Camfferman, K. (2015). The Emergence of the "incurred-loss" model for credit losses in IAS 39. *Accounting in Europe, Taylor & Francis Journals, 12*(1), 1–35. https://doi.org/10.1080/17449480.2015.1012526.

Deloitte (2019). After the first year of IFRS 9 analysis of the initial impact.

Demirguc-Kunt, A. & Huizinga, H. (1999). Determinants of commercial bank interest margins and profitability: Some international evidence. *The World Bank Economic Review, 13*(2), 379–408.

Dong, X., Liu, J., & Hu, H. (2012). Research on the relationship of commercial bank's loan loss provision, earning management and capital management. *Journal of Service and Management, 5*(2), 171–179.

Dugan, J. (2009). Loan loss provisioning and pro-cyclicality remarks by John Dugan controller of the currency before the institute of international bankers, 2 March, Washington DC. http://www.occ.treas.gov/.../speeches/2009/pub-speech (The date of visiting this website is 4-2-2019).

Elnahass, M., Izzeldin, M., & Steele, G. (2018). Capital and earnings management: Evidence from alternative banking business models. *The International Journal of Accounting, 53*, 20–32.

European Commission (EC) (2018). Proposal for a regulation of the European parliament and of the council amending regulation (EU) No. 575/2013 as regards minimum loss coverage for nonperforming exposure: Impact assessment. Accessed on: 5th June, 2018. Available at: European Commission, 2013, Regulation No. 575/2013 on prudential requirements for credit institutions and investment firms (CRR). http://eurlex.europa.eu/legalcontent/EN/TXT/?uri=celex:32013R0575.

Fitriana, M. E. & Arfianto, E. D. (2015). Analisis Pengaruh NPL, CAR, ROA, LDR dan SIZE terhadap CKPN (Studi Kasus pada Bank Konvensional yang Tercatat di Bursa Efek Indonesia 2010–2014). *Diponegoro Journal of Management, 4*, 245–252.

Fitriana, M. E. & Arfianto, E. D. (2016). Analisis Pengaruh NPL, CAR, ROA, LDR dan SIZE Terhadap CKPN (Studi Kasus pada Bank Konvensional yang Tercatat di Bursa Efek Indonesia 2010–2014).

Diponegoro Journal of Management, 245–252. https://ejournal3.undip.ac.id/index.php/djom/article/view/13332.

Gebhardt, G. (2016). Impairments of Greek government bonds under IAS39 and IFES9: A case study. *Accounting in Europe, Taylor & Francis Journals*, *13*(1), 169–196. doi.org/10.1080/17449480.2016.1208833.

Groff, M. & Mörec, B. (2020). IFRS 9 transition effect on equity in a post bank recovery environment: The case of Slovenia. *Economic Research-Ekonomska Istraživanja*, *34*, 1–17. DOI: 10.1080/1331677X.2020.1804425.

Heningtyas, O. S., Isniawati, A., Veronica, A. I., & Astuti, T. (2021). The effect of non performing loan, capital adequacy ratio and income smoothing on loan loss provision with restructuring policy as moderate variables. *Financial: Journal Akuntansi*, *7*(2), 207–223.

Heningtyas, S., Isniawati, A., & Astuti, V. T. (2021). The effect of non performing loan, capital adequacy ratio and income smoothing on loan loss provision with restructuring policy as moderate variables. *Financial: Journal Akuntansi*, *7*(2), 207–223.

Ibrahim, N. A. (2018). Accounting measurement of liquidity risk in commercial banks in light of the banking supervision standards of basel 3 and IFRS 9 Standard: An applied study. *The Egyptian Journal of Business Studies*, *42*(2), 1–40.

International Accounting Standards Board IASB (2021). IAS39 Financial Instruments: Recognition and Measurement, pp. 39–58. https://www.iasplus.com/en/standards/ias/ias39.

Ismaulandy, W. (2014). Analisis variabel DPK, CAR, NPL, LDR, ROA, GWM, danInflasi terhadap Penyaluran Kredit Investasi pada Bank Umum (Periode 2005–2013). *Journal of Ilmiah Ilmu Ekonomi UB*, *2*(2), 1–11.

Jeefrey, N. & Roychowdhury, S. (2014). Do loan loss reserve be have life capital? Evidence from recent bank failures. *Review of Accounting Studies*, *19*(3), 1234–1279.

Karadima, M. & Louri, H. (2020). Economic policy uncertainty and non-performing loans: The moderating role of bank concentration. *Finance Research Letters*, 101458. https://doi.org/10.1016/j.frl.2020.101458.

Khan, E. & Damyanova, V. (2018). European banks capital survives new IFRS 9 accounting impact, but concerns remain. S&P Global Market Intelligence. https://www.spglobal.com/marketintelligence/en/newsinsights/research/european-banks-capital-survives-new-ifrs-9-accountingimpact-but-concerns-remain.

Khan, M. A., Siddique, A., & Sarwar, Z. (2020), Determinants of non-performing loans in the banking sector in developing state. *Asian Journal of Accounting Research*, *5*(1), 135–145. https://doi.org/10.1108/AJAR-10-2019-0080.

Kim, J., Kim, M., & Hwan, J. (2019). The effect of TARP on loan loss provisions and bank transparency. *Journal of Banking and Finance*, *102*, 79–99. https://doi.org/10.1016/j.jbankfin.2019.03.006.

KPMG International Financial Reporting Group (2018). IFRS 9: Transition impact on banks in the Gulf Cooperation Council. *Insights into IFRS: KPMG's*, https://assets.kpmg.com/content/dam/kpmg/qa/pdf/10/ifrs9-transitionimpact-on-banks-in-the-gulf-cooperation-council.pdf.

Krüger, S., Rösch, D., & Scheule, H. (2018). The impact of loan loss provisioning on bank capital requirements. *Journal of Financial Stability*, *36*, 114–129. doi.org/10.1016/j.jfs.2018.02.009.

Kund, A. G. & Rugilo, D. (2019). Assessing the implications of IFRS 9 on financial stability using bank stress tests. Working Paper, University of Cologne.

Le Quang, G. (2019). Discretionary loan loss provisions and market discipline. *Economic Bulletin*, *39*(4), 2931–2941.

Lee, C. M., Wang, Y., & Zhong, Q. (2020). ELPR: A new approach to measuring the capital adequacy of commercial banks. *Letters*, *196*, 109505. https://doi.org/10.1016/j.econlet.2020.1.

Loew, E., Schmidt, L. E., & Thiel, L. F. (2019). Accounting for financial instruments under IFRS 9 — First-time application effects on European banks' balance sheets. *SSRN Electronic Journal*, https://doi.org/10.2139/ssrn.3462299.

Magdalena, F. & Martani, D. (2020). The Effect of IFRS 9 adoption on loan loss provisions. In *International Conference on Rural Development and Entrepreneurship 2019: Enhancing Small Business and Rural Development toward Industrial Revolution*, 4.1, Vol. 5, No. 1, SBN: 978-623-7144-28-1. http://www.jp.feb.unsoed.ac.id/index.php/Icore/article/view/1549.

Mechraoui, S. (2019). The impact of expected credit losses in accordance with international standard IFRS9 regulatory capital. Case of Dubai Islamic Bank. *Journal of Economics, Management and Commercial Sciences*, *12*(2), 742–755.

Nugroho, M. N., Arif, D., & Halik, A. (2021). The effect of loan-loss provision, non performing loans and third-party fund on capital adequacy ratio, *Accounting*, *7*(4), 943–950.

Ozili, P. K. (2017). Discretionary provisioning practices among Western European Banks. *Journal of Financial Economic Policy*, *9*(1), 109–118. https://ssrn.com/abstract=3025139.

Ozili, P. K. (2019a). Loan loss provisioning, income smoothing, signaling, capital management and procyclicality: Does IFRS 9 matter? Empirical evidence from Nigeria. *Mediterranean Journal of Social Sciences*, *6*(2), 224–232. http://dx.doi.org/10.2139/ssrn.2541076.

Ozili, P. K. (2019b). Non-performing loans and financial development. *The Journal of Risk Finance, 20*(1), 59–81.

Ozili, P. K. (2020). Non-performing loans in European systemic and non-systemic banks. *Journal of Financial Economic Policy, 12*(3). 409–424. https://doi.org/10.1108/JFEP-02-2019-0033.

Ozili, P. K. & Outa, E. (2017a). Borsa — Istanbul Review Bank loan loss provisions research: A review. *Borsa Istanbul Review*, https://doi.org/10.1016/j.bir.2017.05.00.1.

Ozili, P. K. & Outa, E. R. (2017b). Bank loan loss provisions research: A review. *Borsa Istanbul Review, 17*(3), 144–163. http://dx.doi.org/10.2139/ssrn.2905874.

Rahadian, R. & Permana, D. (2021). The impact of non-performing loans, return on assets, return on equity, and loan to deposit ratios on minimum capital adequacy requirement based on commercial banks for business activities (BUKU) I 2015–2020. *European Journal of Business and Management Research, 6*, 42–46. DOI: 10.24018/ejbmr.2021.6.6.108.

Restoy, F. & Zamil, R. (2017). Prudential policy considerations under expected loss provisioning: lessons from Asia, FSI Insights, No. 5, October. https://www.bis.org/fsi/publ/insights5.pdf.

Safa, A. & Abu Mouris, G. (2020). Challenges of applying the International Financial Reporting Standards (IFRS9) to Arab banks. *Arab Monetary Fund*, https://www.amf.org.ae/sites/default/files/publications/2022-01/the-challenges-of-implementing-the-international-financial-reporting-standard-ifrs9-for-arab-banks.pdf.

Seitz, B., Dinh, T., & Rathgeber, A. (2018). Understanding loan loss reserves under IFRS 9: A simulation-based approach. *Advances in Quantitative Analysis of Finance and Accounting, 16*, 311–357. https://doi.org/10.2139/ssrn.3462299.

Shaheen, A. A. & Al-Baghdadi, R. M. (2019). Accounting measurement of credit risk in light of Basel 3 banking supervision standards and IFRS9 standard: A field study in Egyptian commercial banks. *The Scientific Journal of Financial and Administrative Studies and Research, 3*(1), 109–156.

Sultanoğlu, B. (2018). Expected credit loss model by Ifrs 9 and its possible early impacts on European and Turkish Banking Sector. *Muhasebe Bilim DünyasıDergisi, 20*(3), 476–506. DOI: 10.31460/mbdd.422581.

Tao, Y. (2020). China's anti-corruption campaign and bank loan loss. *Economics Letters, 196*, 109505. doi.org/10.1016/j.econlet.2020.109505.

Wood, A. & Skinner, N. (2018). Determinants of non-performing loans: Evidence from commercial banks in Barbados.

Yang, B. H. (2017). Point-in-time PD Term Structure Models for Methodologies and Implementations for IFRS 9 ECL and CCAR Stress Testing. *Journal of Risk Model Validation*, *11*(3). https://mpra.ub.uni-muenchen.de/76271/1/MPRA_paper_76271.pdf.

Yulianti, E ., Aliamin, A., & Ibrahim, R. (2018). The effect of capital adequacy and bank size on non-performing loans in Indonesian public banks. *Journal of Accounting Research, Organization and Economics*, *1*, 205–214. DOI: 10.24815/jaroe.v1i2.1170.

https://doi.org/10.1142/9781800614734_0011

Chapter 11

Should We Trust the New Basel III Liquidity Ratio? Evidence from the MENA Banking Systems

Wassim Ben Ayed and Amira Houaneb

Abstract

The purpose of this chapter is to examine the role of bank liquidity in ensuring financial stability. Based on the Basel III liquidity framework guidelines, the authors calculated the NSFR for 124 banks operating in the Middle East and North Africa (MENA) region during the period 2014–2021. The findings of this study show the following: first, the NSFR has a positive impact on financial stability; second, the results highlight that non-performing loans, diversification, bank size, and the business cycle have a negative impact on stability, while the ROE and business cycle have a positive impact; and third, these results support the efforts of the Basel Committee on Banking Supervision (BCBS) in developing guidelines for the NSFR to enhance the liquidity risk management. These results will be useful for authorities and policymakers seeking to clarify the implications of adopting the liquidity requirement for banking behavior.

Keywords: Basel, liquidity ratio, MENA, financial stability

11.1. Introduction

The global financial crisis of 2007 had dramatic effects on the international financial system. Several financial institutions have incurred losses because of poor liquidity management. Thus, the intervention of public and regulatory authorities was essential to restore their solvency and avoid a bank run (Diamond & Dybvig, 1983). In 2008, the BCBS intervened to increase the resilience of the banking sector. The BCBS has published a report titled "Liquidity Risk: Management and Supervisory Challenges". It has since been found that many financial institutions did not follow the liquidity management principles. These challenges prompted the BCBS to issue a new document in September 2008 that outlines the principles for prudential liquidity risk management (BCBS, 2009) on a set of recommendations on management and supervision that should be applied by banks and the regulatory authorities. The main objective is to support better liquidity risk management.

During the period from July 2009 to December 2010, the Committee has strengthened the liquidity framework by proposing two new guidelines. These have two main objectives: (i) to monitor the level of high-quality liquid assets of institutions to enable them to be resistant to liquidity risk and (ii) to help institutions to support the intermediation activity by using more stable sources of funding. To this end, the Committee has required the application of two new liquidity ratios: a first short-term liquidity ratio (LCR) and a second long-term liquidity ratio (NSFR). In December 2010, to address the shortcomings of the liquidity ratio, the Committee reviewed the adoption of the second NSFR based on a study that included 263 banks operating in 23 member jurisdictions. The results of the quantitative impact studies indicated an improvement in several operational areas. The NSFR became a minimum requirement adopted according to a schedule presented in 2010.

Although the liquidity requirements' impact on the banking sector is still unknown, several studies have been conducted to assess the potential impact of these requirements on bank stability (King, 2013; Chalermchatvichien *et al.*, 2014; Ashraf *et al.*, 2016; Abdo *et al.*, 2022; Sidhu *et al.*, 2022). This study has used historical data to conduct retrospective analysis. Most of these studies have focused on the relationship between regulatory requirement, risk, and stability and the potential impact in the context of developed countries (Dietrich *et al.*, 2014; Elliot & Lindblom, 2016; Wei *et al.*, 2017). In contrast, the impact of the structural ratio of Basel III on financial stability of less developed banking sectors has been neglected in the empirical studies.

The implementation of liquidity ratios is a challenge for all economies since most banks have very limited access to risk management instruments. Due to a lack of liquid fixed-income markets, banks and financial institutions in the MENA area have challenges in gaining access to sophisticated risk management instruments. Furthermore, many countries, particularly those in the GCC, do not dispose of high-quality assets since the authorities are hesitant to commit to budget assistance, restricting the issue of longer-term liabilities. Despite the efforts to improve banking supervision through privatization, banking regulation, market orientation, and the integration of private banks, the shortage of risk-based supervision remains a challenge for regulators. With the implementation of these ratios, banks can use techniques that allow for more efficient management of the funding.

Since the 1990s, the banking industry in the MENA region has been concerned with liquidity management (IFSB, 2017). A challenge that regulators will face is the monitoring and management of liquidity risk. The MENA economies, like any other small open economy, are classified as having high levels of banking, with Islamic and conventional banking institutions dominating the entire system (Naceur & Omran, 2011). As a result, they are vulnerable to a growing maturity gap between assets and liabilities of financing operations (Cheng *et al.*, 2012). Consequently, several countries have been involved in the preparation of regulatory proposals to improve supervisory processes. However, several gaps persist, and the regulatory structure does not address the levels of sophistication of the MENA financial institutions.

Currently, the Basel III standard has put the issue of liquidity at the forefront of the banks' concerns. In this chapter, we try analyzing the impact of the adoption of the structural ratio (NSFR) on the stability of MENA banks. In other words, we examine how regulatory liquidity requirements will ensure a stable funding structure. This study makes several contributions to the existing literature. First, this is the first study to extend the literature on the impact of Basel III liquidity regulation to the case of MENA banks. Second, our study bridges the gap in the literature, as most studies focus on developed countries, whereas we investigate the case of emerging economies based on countries in the MENA region. Third, we compare the ratios obtained following the 2014 specification to those obtained following the initial 2010 specification. This allows us to validate the usefulness of the new rules proposed by the Basel Committee on Banking Supervision (BCBS) and, as a result, provide evidence to support the regulatory effort. The remainder of this chapter includes a review of the literature in Section 11.2. In Section 11.3, we outline our research methodology. In Section 11.4, we present the main results. Section 11.5 will be devoted to the conclusion.

11.2. Literature Review

The earliest studies that addressed the issue of the new liquidity requirement were developed by the Basel Committee following the publication of the first version of the ratio in 2010. The regulatory authorities have launched a series of studies to measure the true impact of the Basel III standard. In total, 263 banks operating in 23 jurisdictions, as members of the committee, participated in these quantitative impact studies (QIS). Several QIS procedures were concluded during the period between January 2010 (first version of the NSFR) and December 2014 (last revision). The results have showed that the ratio calculated for Group 1 of banks evolved over the analysis period from 94% in 2012 to 100% in 2014. For Group 2, the ratio deteriorated on average by 1–99% in 2014. The committee highlighted that bank not meeting the regulatory requirement (NSFR < 100%) can change their funding structure.

The issue of financial stability has received attention in the literature. Hong *et al.* (2014) evaluated the relationship between new liquidity risk measures and bank failures, using quarterly data of American commercial bank from 2001 to 2011. They found that the probability of default is negatively correlated with the NSFR ratio and positively correlated with the LCR. The probability of default may be affected by systemic liquidity risk. The authors highlighted that the accumulation of liquidity may have led to market illiquidity at the aggregate level. Thus, they recommended the implementation of a regulatory framework that addresses the liquidity problem from a microprudential and macroprudential perspective. Finally, they concluded that funding liquidity risk was an important driver of bank failure between 2009 and 2010.

Vazquez & Federico (2015) have analyzed the evolution of funding structures of banks and the impact on financial stability for a sample of 11,000 US banks during the period 2001–2009. The results show that banks that faced liquidity problems, with a high leverage ratio, had a high probability of failure. This probability increases with high-risk behaviors. Additionally, small regional banks are more sensitive to liquidity risk than large banks. These results are consistent with the approach proposed by Basel III and emphasize the effectiveness of monetary policy in managing systemic risk.

In an international context, Ashraf *et al.* (2015) have assessed the effectiveness of the Basel III liquidity framework using a dataset of 948 banks operating in 85 countries. The results suggest that the NSFR has a positive and statistically significant impact on the financial stability of banks. However, the NSFR has a negative effect on NPLs, but it is insignificant. As a result, banks with sufficient available funding relative to their required level of funding appreciate stable financial operations.

Lallour & Mio (2016) examined the impact of structural funding ratios on the banking sector's resilience during a time of crisis. The authors investigated the predictive power of various structural funding measures. They demonstrated that structural funding ratios, including the NSFR, could have helped predict the 2006 financial crisis. The authors underline that the deposit to total assets ratio and the NSFR ratio are the most reliable indicators in predicting the crisis.

Chiaramonte & Casu (2017) investigated the impact of Basel III liquidity and capital requirements on bank stability. The study focused on a sample of European banks (EU-28) over the period 2004–2013. The findings highlighted the positive impact of the two-requirement ratio on bank stability. Furthermore, they demonstrated that the NSFR is a key determinant of financial stability. This finding is consistent with the previous studies suggesting that during the global financial crisis, the main source of banking instability was an excessive maturity transformation (Gobat *et al.*, 2014).

Ly *et al.* (2017) examined the impact of the NSFR structural liquidity ratio on systemic risk for American banks from 1991 to 2012 using a partial adjustment model. They reveal that banks with an immediate-trading equilibrium tend to quickly adjust the NSFR in response to the Basel III liquidity requirement, reducing systemic risk. This finding is confirmed for small banks. The authors mentioned the importance of implementing an NSFR real-time indicator that can assess adjustments in real time before the effective implementation of the Basel III guidelines in 2018. Recently, Papadamou *et al.* (2021) investigated the efficacy of banking regulation in the EU. Using dynamic panel vector auto-regression (VAR) analysis, the authors show evidence in favor of the NSFR's forecasting and prudential supervisory function, which provides an instrument for enhancing bank performance and maintaining banking sector stability.

There are few studies on the subject of the dual banking system. Ashraf *et al.* (2016) have shown that a factor affecting financial stability is an NSFR that satisfies the business model of Islamic banks. The authors examined 136 Islamic banks that operated in 30 countries between 2000 and 2013. Based on changes made by the IFSB, they have demonstrated that the size of the bank reduces the potential influence of the NFSR. Abdul-Rahman *et al.* (2017) evaluated the association between financing structure and liquidity risk during the period 1994–2014. The authors used a sample of 27 conventional banks and 27 Malaysian Islamic banks. The findings indicate that the financing structure of Islamic banks influences the risk of liquidity. The financing of the real estate sector tends to increase the exposure of Islamic banks to the risks associated with this sector, resulting in a greater exposure to liquidity risk for the Islamic banking sector. However, this type of financing has no effect on the liquidity risks of conventional banks. Finally, the authors underlined the importance of a specific liquidity risk management regulatory framework for Islamic banking institutions. The previous studies are so inconclusive, even though a unique framework is not considered.

11.3. Research Design

11.3.1. *Model specification*

The following model is developed:

$$Z\text{-score}_{i,t} = \alpha_0 + \alpha_1 Z\text{-score}_{i,t-1} + \alpha_2 \text{NSFR}_{i,t} + \alpha_3 \text{SIZE}_{i,t} + \alpha_4 \text{ROE}_{i,t} + \alpha_5 \text{NIIC}_{i,t} + \alpha_6 \text{CYCLE}_{i,t} + \mu_{i,t} + \varepsilon_{i,t}, \quad (11.1)$$

where i indicates the bank ($i = 1, \ldots, 124$) and t indicates the annual time period ($t = 2014, \ldots, 2021$).α_1 is the parameter to be estimated for the lagged endogenous variable, while $\alpha_2, \alpha_3, \alpha_4, \alpha_5$ are the parameters to be estimated as exploratory variables. $\mu_{i,t}$ is an individual-specific effect and $\mu_{i,t}$ and $\varepsilon_{i,t}$ are the error terms.

11.3.2. *Selection of variables*

11.3.2.1. *Dependent variable: Z-score*

Several studies have demonstrated the use of the Z-score as a measure of banking stability (Čihák, 2007; Chiaramonte *et al.*, 2015; Moreno *et al.*, 2021). Lepetit & Strobel (2013) have demonstrated that the Z-score may be used to evaluate the financial soundness of firms. It assesses a bank's capacity to absorb losses via capital. It consists of dividing asset returns and the equity ratio by the standard deviation of asset returns. Thus, the calculation formula is as follows:

$$Z\text{-score} = \frac{\text{ROA} + EQ/\text{TA}}{\sigma(\text{ROA})},$$

where ROA denotes the return on Assets, Eq/TA represents the equity-to-total-assets ratio, and σ(ROA) is the standard deviation of the ROA. Based on the previous literature (Laeven & Levine, 2009; Delis, 2012), the Z-score is extremely skewed. Then, we adopt the logarithmic adjustment in our empirical estimation.

11.3.2.2. *Explanatory variables*

11.3.2.2.1. The NSFR

The NSFR published in the BCBC's guidelines is measured as the ratio of available stable funding (ASF) to required stable funding (RSF) (BCBS, 2014). Previous studies have found that the probability of bankruptcy is negatively correlated with the NSFR (Hong *et al.*, 2014). Chalermchatvichien *et al.* (2014) showed that the banking sector's stability would have improved if the liquidity requirement had been applied between 2005 and 2009. Gobat *et al.* (2014) have demonstrated that the NSFR is expected to reduce the risk of excess maturity transformation in the banking industry and to promote financing stability. We computed the Net NSFR in accordance with the Basel III liquidity framework guidelines using the version of 2010 and the version of 2014. Therefore, we hypothesize the following:

H_1: The NSFR has a positive impact on financial stability.

11.3.2.2.2. The non-performing loans (NPLs)

Earlier studies argued that banks with NPLs in their portfolios avoid excessive risk taking (Shrieves & Dahl, 1992). Kim & Sohn (2017) found that banks with NPLs try reducing credit lending. These results indicate that NPLs are positively correlated with bank insolvency. This result implies that the level of NPLs may be a sign of instability in the banking system. The proxy for the NPL is the total NPLs to total loans ratio. Thus, our research hypothesis will be as follows:

H_2: The NPL has a negative impact on financial stability.

11.3.2.2.3. Diversification

Previous studies show that there is a significant relationship between financial stability and bank diversification (Sanya & Wolfe, 2011; Lee *et al.*, 2014; Ashraf *et al.*, 2016; Shim, 2019). Banks with diversified revenues are less likely to have a high probability of failure (Abuzayed *et al.*, 2018; Liang *et al.*, 2020). Shim (2013) provided empirical evidence on the benefits of diversification. He showed that banks with revenue diversification have low insolvency risk and high liquidity buffers. Köhler (2015) found that banks are more stable if they increase their shares of non-interest income, while banks that have shifted to traditional activities are less stable and become more risky in times of liquidity shortage. Kim *et al.* (2020) argue that banks should focus on traditional intermediation activities during times of crisis rather than diversifying their products and investments. The diversification is measured in terms non-interest income to total revenue. Thus, our hypothesis to be tested empirically will be the following:

H_3: The diversification has a negative impact on financial stability.

11.3.2.2.4. The size

Previous research has shown that large banks tend to maintain very high levels of liquidity to ensure that they will be able to provide liquidity if other banks are in a "lender-of-last-resort" situation. Gropp *et al.* (2011) argued that large banks are more stable because of their ability to access sophisticated risk management tools. Also, they benefit from a various activities that allow them to diversify their portfolios and, therefore, reduce their probability of failure (Shrieves & Dahl, 1992; Aggarwal & Jacques, 1998; Rime, 2001). In contrast, Schwerter (2011) suggests that the "too-big-to-fail" phenomenon would encourage large banks to take excessive risks. Thus, size is a source of financial instability. Therefore, we propose the following research hypothesis:

H_4: The size has a negative impact on financial stability.

11.3.2.2.5. Return on equity (ROE)

Most of the previous empirical literature has argued that the return on equity as a measure of profitability is associated with bank stability (Ashraf *et al.*, 2016; Le, 2020; Ben Ayed *et al.*, 2021). Indeed, banks may engage at high risk when seeking to generate higher profitability (Albaity *et al.*, 2019). However, Le (2020) found that bank stability can result in a higher profit. This might be explained by "too-safe" banks being reluctant to engage in riskier assets since they rigorously conform to regulatory standards. Consequently, they risk losing out on a chance to earn high profits as the banking industry becomes more competitive. Therefore, we propose the following research hypothesis:

H_5: The ROE has a negative impact on financial stability.

11.3.2.2.6. The GDP growth (cycle)

The business cycle is frequently used to evaluate a country's economic stability. According to Abdul-Rahman *et al.* (2017), GDP is a measure of demand for banking services (deposit taking and lending). According to Mohamad *et al.* (2013), banks have a pro-cyclical attitude toward the economic cycle. In periods of economic expansion, they increase liquidity in the financial market. This behavior offers promising results and helps banks make more revenue. As a result, when the economic situation is favorable, banks may give more liquidity (Cucinelli, 2013). Thus, our hypothesis will be as follows:

H_6: The GDP has a positive impact on financial stability.

11.3.3. *Selection of estimation technique*

In this study, we use the two-step generalized method of moments approach (GMM) developed initially by Arellano & Bond (1991) as the lag of dependent variable is among the explanatory variables (Eq. (11.1)).

11.4. Data, Preliminary Analysis, and Estimation Results

11.4.1. *Dataset*

The sample includes 124 banks operating in the MENA region during the period 2014–2021. We consider the following 11 countries: Bahrain, Egypt, Jordan, Kuwait, Saudi Arabia, Kuwait, Morocco, Oman, Qatar, Tunisia, and the United Arab Emirates. The choice of countries is motivated by the degree of compliance with prudential standards. All bank-specific information was collected from DataStream database and financial reports. Table 11.1 reports the summary statistics of the variables sorted by country.

11.4.2. *Preliminary analysis*

Table 11.2 displays the descriptive statistics of all variables by country. It shows that the average value of the NSFR is 119.3%. This value is strictly higher than 100%, which indicates that most banks have a long-term structural ratio above the minimum regulatory liquidity requirements. Based on the formula of October 2010, the NSFR ratio for selected MENA countries ranges from 90.1% (Tunisia) to 167% (Egypt). According to the Formula of December 2014, the highest value is attributed to banks in Saudi Arabia (126%), Oman (129%), and UAE (132%).

Regarding the NPL, the average in the whole sample is 0.98%. The highest value is assigned to banks in Oman (1.824). The low value of this variable (0.523%) indicates that banks in Saudi Arabia were very reluctant to deal with bad clients. The average of the variable NIICOME is 0.35%. We conclude that all banks in the sample show a high degree of diversification of the activity.

With a standard deviation of 1.518 and a mean bank size of 8.999, the sample had a low degree of dispersion. The biggest banks in

Table 11.1. Summary statistics.

Country	No. of banks	N		NSFR10	NSFR14	NPL	NIICOME	SIZE	ROE	GDP	Z3
Bahrain	18	144	Mean	1.208	1.101	0.619	0.353	8.101	0.063	2.032	3.93
			SD	0.426	0.32	0.495	0.431	2.014	0.08	2.785	1.118
Egypt	14	112	Mean	1.666	1.548	0.817	0.481	8.555	0.288	4.198	3.653
			SD	0.449	0.366	0.981	0.867	0.707	0.12	0.866	0.841
Jordan	16	128	Mean	1.254	1.101	0.812	0.219	8.122	0.124	1.814	4.039
			SD	0.259	0.109	0.771	0.0945	1.009	0.058	1.354	0.73
Kuwait	12	96	Mean	1.042	1.111	1.213	0.239	9.691	0.073	−1.095	4.623
			SD	0.385	0.075	0.862	0.098	0.991	0.038	3.945	1.097
Morocco	7	56	Mean	0.985	1.005	0.837	0.267	9.776	0.146	2.42	4.269
			SD	0.146	0.141	0.155	0.0675	0.937	0.069	3.755	1.354
Oman	8	64	Mean	1.195	1.29	1.824	0.237	8.901	0.084	1.231	4.395
			SD	0.213	0.013	3.015	0.0594	0.783	0.046	2.828	0.934
Qatar	8	64	Mean	1.042	1.12	1.018	0.174	9.958	0.098	1.443	4.266
			SD	0.246	0.246	0.565	0.617	1.419	0.118	2.844	1.203
Saudi Arabia	12	96	Mean	1.261	1.261	0.523	0.688	10.46	0.108	1.33	4.71
			SD	0.227	0.227	0.59	0.682	1.096	0.053	2.598	1.137
Tunisia	12	96	Mean	0.901	0.102	0.661	0.504	7.661	0.134	0.746	3.973
			SD	0.196	0.22	0.254	0.174	0.999	0.116	3.7	0.908
United Arab Emirates	17	136	Mean	1.156	1.32	1.314	0.28	9.743	0.054	1.899	3.712
			SD	0.18	0.2	5.33	0.0846	1.225	0.211	3.5	1.26
All	124	992	Mean	1.193	1.22	0.982	0.35	8.993	0.116	1.702	4.102
			SD	0.365	0.225	2.469	0.457	1.518	0.13	3.131	1.109

Notes: N, Mean, and SD denote the number of observations, mean, and standard deviation, respectively. NSFR10 and NSFR14 represent the ratio of liquidity according to the Basel standards of October 2010 and December 2014, respectively. NPL denotes the non-performing loans measured as the total non-performing loans to total loans ratio. NIICOME is the non-interest income to total revenue. SIZE is the log of total assets. ROE is the net income to total equity. GDP represents the economic cycle; it is measured as the growth of gross domestic product. Z3 is the Z-score that combines ROA and Eq/TA with the SD of ROA calculated over the three periods (σROA).

Table 11.2. Correlation matrix.

	Z3	NSFR	NPL	NIICOME	SIZE	ROE	GDP
Z3	1						
NSFR	−0.0949*	1					
NPL	−0.0348	−0.0103	1				
NIICOME	−0.0217	0.0947*	−0.0729	1			
SIZE	0.285***	−0.170***	−0.00959	0.148***	1		
ROE	0.179***	0.433***	−0.0189	0.138**	−0.0217	1	
GDP	0.129**	0.276***	0.0292	0.0838	−0.155***	0.423***	1

Note: Significance levels: $^{*}p < 0.05$; $^{**}p < 0.01$; $^{***}p < 0.001$.

the sample are found in Saudi Arabia, Kuwait, UAE, and Qatar. The average ROE is 0.116% with a standard deviation of 0.130%, indicating that over the 2014–2021 period, banks suffered financial distress. Most banks in the sample are profitable despite the large differences in performance among them. The most profitable banks are those in Egypt with a mean of 0.288% and a standard deviation of 0.12%. The mean value of the GDP variable is 1.7% with a standard deviation of 3.1%, indicating that there is some degree of dispersion between countries. The highest value is 4.19% (for Egypt), showing accelerated growth and improving business confidence for market participants. Finally, according to the descriptive statistics of the Z-score, the banking sectors in Saudi Arabia and Kuwait have shown the greatest levels of stability with averages of 4.71 and 4.623, respectively. However, with an average of 3.653, Egypt has the most dangerous banking sector. These results may be largely attributed to the region's political turmoil and oil price fluctuation.

Table 11.2 presents a pairwise correlation matrix for the selected variables. The correlation magnitude was low for all variables. According to Pearson (1896) and Kennedy (1998), matrix correction cannot detect the multicollinearity problem.

11.5. Estimation Results

In this section, we estimate the different specificities of our theoretical model to test our hypothesis. To this, we apply the GMM estimator, which is the most reliable method given the specificity of our sample. Table 11.3 shows the estimation results, which corroborate

Table 11.3. Estimation results.

	Model 1	Model 2
L.Z3	0.472***	0.469***
	(0.0508)	(0.002)
NSFR2010	0.520**	
	(0.263)	
NSFR2014		1.229***
		(0.431)
NPL	−0.0699**	−0.0516**
	(0.0288)	(0.0468)
NIICOME	−0.219**	−0.144***
	(0.103)	(0.174)
SIZE	−0.128	−0.265**
	(0.177)	(0.253)
ROE	3.964***	3.549***
	(0.850)	(1.279)
GDP	0.0463***	0.0906***
	(0.0115)	(0.0190)
C	2.200	5.846**
	(1.887)	(2.309)
Obs.	453	453
Hansen (p-value)	0.547	0.511
AR(2) (p-value)	0.0033	0.0031
AR(2) (p-value)	0.1387	0.1385

Note: **, and *** represent significance at 5% and 10%, respectively.

the robustness of our findings: The Sargan over-identification test (Hansen, 1982) conducted on the various specifications demonstrates the validity of the instruments. Also, the results show that there is no autocorrelation in the series of second-order residuals (AR (2)). The test statistic was equal to 13%.

Regarding models, the regression results using the previous version of the NSFR (NSFR, 2010) are shown in model (1). The regression results using the revised version of the NSFR (NSFR, 2014) are shown in model (2). Generally, the estimation results generated for models (1) and (2), using both measures of NSFR, are mostly in line with our expectations.

For models (1) and (2), the coefficient of the lagged Z3 is positive and significant across the two specifications at the 10% level. This finding confirms that the dynamic model is preferable for panel data compared to the static model. The positive signs demonstrate that the sampled banks could balance their funding and improve their stability during the study period.

The estimation results displayed in column 1 show that there is a significant relationship between the long-term structural liquidity ratio and the Z-score at the 10% level (0.520). This result was improved by adopting the NSFR 2014 (column 2). This confirms our hypothesis H_1. These results justify the efforts of the Basel committee for the implementation of a regulatory framework for liquidity, which suggests that more stable financing reduces the behavior of risk taking. The results show that the implementation of long-term liquidity ratios improves stability. This finding is consistent with the work of Diamond & Dybvig (1983) and Diamond & Rajan (2005), who revealed the systemic nature of liquidity concerns and the significant impact of contagion during the financial crisis. The FMI (2010) had emphasized the necessity of regulatory liquidity requirements in this context. According to Gobat *et al.* (2014) and Grundke & Kühn (2020), excessive maturity transformation is the main source of banking instability. Overall, our results provide evidence that banks with high insolvency risk should hold high liquidity buffers (NSFR $>$ 100%).

The results of model (1) and (2) estimates support the H_2 hypothesis at the 5% significance level. This result indicates that non-performing loans constitute a risk to financial stability. This risk could weaken the resilience of banks to a short-term distress and therefore increase the risk of bank failure. Chiaramonte & Casu (2017), Altunbas *et al.* (2017), and Cole & White (2012) have shown that excessive loan growth and non-performing loans are early indicators of bank failures. Rocha *et al.* (2011) demonstrated that loan concentrations in the real estate and construction sectors present a problem for the financial system in the MENA region. Bacchiocchi *et al.* (2022) show that periods of credit growth are usually accompanied by high rates of NPLs. Several MENA countries have experienced issues with NPLs that are above 10% during the crisis period, prompting government involvement to mitigate the negative impact of NPLs. As a result, growth in NPLs increases the likelihood of bankruptcy.

The measure of bank diversification (NIICOME) shows a negative relationship. This result supports the hypothesis that banks with diverse revenue sources are expected to be riskier than other banks (Stiroh & Rumble, 2006; Lepetit *et al.*, 2008; DeYoung & Torna, 2013). Thus, as a result, the more the bank focuses on non-interest activities, the less stable its financial situation becomes because non-interest revenues are riskier than interest revenues. This result confirms the previous work of Abuzayed *et al.* (2018) who examined the diversification characteristics of conventional and Islamic banks during the period 2001–2014. The overall conclusion shows that income or asset diversification does not improve bank stability.

ROE had a significantly positive effect on MENA banks in the sample, suggesting that an increase in earnings from equities leads banks to increase their stability and reduce the risk of bankruptcy. These results confirm the previous studies of Hong *et al.* (2014), Chiaramonte *et al.* (2015), and Mollah & Zaman (2015) who concluded that banks with higher profitability are more resilient to short-term shocks and have lower failure risk. For the variable SIZE, we find that smaller banks are more stable compared to larger banks. Large banks have a significantly lower NSFR than small banks. We confirm our hypothesis H_4. Therefore, the impact of financial shocks on small banks will be smaller in the presence of an NSFR ratio above 100%. This can be justified by the fact that small banks have fewer options to access the market and obtain liquidity. Hong *et al.* (2014) and Flannery & Hankins (2007) showed that large banks have better access to liquidity. Therefore, they seek to strengthen their financial stability and reduce the probability of default.

In terms of macroeconomic variable, the results demonstrate the effectiveness of the Basel III regulatory system, which considers the macroprudential approach and the economic cycle. Then, we confirmed our hypothesis. The estimation results show that financial stability and economic growth are proportional to a 10% significance level. This suggests that economic growth promotes the stability of MENA countries' banking systems. The findings confirm that banks are interested in increasing their capital ratios during times of economic growth. This mindset helps strengthen the bank's stability and, as a result, reduces the likelihood of failure.

11.6. Conclusion

The recent financial crisis of 2007 has demonstrated the importance of liquidity management. Indeed, the rapid decline in the financial market has revealed that liquidity falls away quickly and takes a long time to recover (BCBS, 2014). During this time, the banking system has been in a situation of panic, requiring national authorities and central banks to respond with force to reestablish market performance. To this end, the Basel Committee has continued to strengthen the liquidity risk framework. The committee published a new liquidity framework in 2010, highlighting two minimum liquidity and funding requirements. The LCR and NSFR ratios were introduced as new ratios. The first ratio aims to improve a financial institution's liquidity risk profile's short-term resilience. The NSFR ratio, on the other hand, aims to reduce banks' long-term exposure to funding risks. The Basel Committee has required financial institutions to maintain a stable funding profile to increase the resilience of the banking sector. In this context, we assess in this chapter the impact of the introduction of the structural liquidity ratio on the stability of the MENA banking sector. To do so, we selected a sample of 124 banks. We refer to the Basel regulatory framework for modeling the ratio. The study period is from 2014 to 2021. We introduce variables that characterize the banking activity to control the relationship between the financial stability and the liquidity ratio. The results highlight that the NSFR liquidity ratio has a positive impact on financial stability of the banking sector. Thus, the NSFR ratio can be considered as a metric to assess the risk profile from their maturity transformation activities. Furthermore, NPLs, diversification, bank size, and the business cycle have a negative impact on the liquidity ratio, while the ROE and business cycle have a positive impact.

These findings will be useful to authorities and policymakers seeking to understand the implications of implementing the liquidity requirement for banking behavior. They support the efforts of national authorities in the implementation of the new Basel III regulatory framework. The regulatory authorities should investigate the effect of size on financing structure adjustments, especially as a majority of the region's banking institutions are oriented toward meeting M-EBIS and I-EBIS criteria. However, one may be interested to know that the aim of financial stability would reduce economic financing and credit availability in favor of less risky government obligations. We have generally shown that the solvency issue is not the only concern for the banking institution, but so is its ability to anticipate risks and its effective liquidity management. As a result, we support the efforts of the Basel Committee on Financial Supervision to strengthen the resilience of international banking systems. However, two significant considerations should be recognized when implementing such prudential standards: (i) The first issue is about the heterogeneity of financial systems, bank business models (conventional and non-conventional), and the size of banking institutions. (ii) The second issue is that a trade-off must be made between financial stability, economic financing, and the bank's ability to respond as a supplier of liquidity.

References

Abdo, K. Y. M., Noman, A. H. M., & Hanifa, M. H. (2022). Exploring the dynamics of bank liquidity holding in Islamic and conventional banks. *International Journal of Islamic and Middle Eastern Finance and Management*, (ahead-of-print).

Abdul-Rahman, A., Said, N. L. H. M., & Sulaiman, A. A. (2017). Financing structure and liquidity risk: Lesson from Malaysian experience. *Journal of Central Banking Theory and Practice*, *6*(2), 125–148.

Abuzayed, B., Al-Fayoumi, N., & Molyneux, P. (2018). Diversification and bank stability in the GCC. *Journal of International Financial Markets, Institutions and Money*, *57*, 17–43.

Aggarwal, R. & Jacques, K. T. (1998). Assessing the impact of prompt corrective action on bank capital and risk. *Economic Policy Review*, *4*(3), 23–32.

Albaity, M., Mallek, R. S., & Noman, A. H. M. (2019). Competition and bank stability in the MENA region: The moderating effect of Islamic versus conventional banks. *Emerging Markets Review*, *38*, 310–325.

Altunbas, Y., Manganelli, S., & Marques-Ibanez, D. (2017). Realized bank risk during the great recession. *Journal of Financial Intermediation*, *32*, 29–44.

Arellano, M. & Bond, S. (1991). Some tests of specification for panel data: Monte Carlo evidence and an application to employment equations. *The Review of Economic Studies*, *58*(2), 277–297.

Ashraf, D., L'Huillier, B., & Rizwan, M. (2015). Does the implementation of a net stable funding ratio enhance the financial stability of the banking industry? An international study. https://acfrautacnz/__data/assets/pdf_file/0003/29766/B-LHuillier-V9-Does-the-implementation-of-a-NSFR enhance-the-financial-stabilitypd.

Ashraf, D., Rizwan, M. S., & L'Huillier, B. (2016). A net stable funding ratio for Islamic banks and its impact on financial stability: An international investigation. *Journal of Financial Stability*, *25*, 47–57.

Bacchiocchi, A., Bischi, G. I., & Giombini, G. (2022). Non-performing loans, expectations and banking stability: A dynamic model. *Chaos, Solitons & Fractals*, *157*, 111906.

BCBS (2009). *Strengthening the Resilience of the Banking Sector*. Basel Committee on Banking Supervision.

BCBS (2014). *Basel III: The Net Stable Funding Ratio*. Basel, Switzerland: Basel Committee on Banking Supervision, Bank for International Settlements.

Ben Ayed, W., Lamouchi, R. A., & Alawi, S. M. (2021). Does the deposit structure affect Islamic bank's maturity transformation activities? The implications of IFSB liquidity guidelines. *International Journal of Islamic and Middle Eastern Finance and Management*, *14*(3), 444–462.

Chalermchatvichien, P., Jumreornvong, S., & Jiraporn, P. (2014). Basel III, capital stability, risk-taking, ownership: Evidence from Asia. *Journal of Multinational Financial Management*, *28*, 28–46.

Cheng, W., Hermann, A. J., Coyle, K. O., Dobbins, E. L., Kachel, N. B., & Stabeno, P. J. (2012). Macro-and micro-nutrient flux to a highly productive submarine bank in the Gulf of Alaska: A model-based analysis of daily and interannual variability. *Progress in Oceanography*, *101*(1), 63–77.

Chiaramonte, L. & Casu, B. (2017). Capital and liquidity ratios and financial distress. Evidence from the European banking industry. *The British Accounting Review*, *49*(2), 138–161.

Chiaramonte, L., Poli, F., & Oriani, M. E. (2015). Are cooperative banks a lever for promoting bank stability? Evidence from the recent financial crisis in OECD countries. *European Financial Management*, *21*(3), 491–523.

Čihák, M. (2007). Systemic loss: A measure of financial stability. *Czech Journal of Economics and Finance*, *57*(1–2), 5–26.

Cole, R. A. & White, L. J. (2012). Déjà vu all over again: The causes of US commercial bank failures this time around. *Journal of Financial Services Research*, *42*(1), 5–29.

Cucinelli, D. (2013). The determinants of bank liquidity risk within the context of Euro area. *Interdisciplinary Journal of Research in Business*, *2046*, 7141.

Delis, M. D. (2012). Bank competition, financial reform, and institutions: The importance of being developed. *Journal of Development Economics*, *97*(2), 450–465.

DeYoung, R. & Torna, G. (2013). Nontraditional banking activities and bank failures during the financial crisis. *Journal of Financial Intermediation*, *22*(3), 397–421.

Diamond, D. W. & Dybvig, P. H. (1983). Bank runs, deposit insurance, and liquidity. *Journal of Political Economy*, *91*(3), 401–419.

Diamond, D. W. & Rajan, R. G. (2005). Liquidity shortages and banking crises. *The Journal of Finance*, *60*(2), 615–647.

Dietrich, A., Hess, K., & Wanzenried, G. (2014). The good and bad news about the new liquidity rules of Basel III in Western European countries. *Journal of Banking & Finance*, *44*, 13–25.

Elliot, V. & Lindblom, T. (2016). *Basel III, Liquidity Risk and Regulatory Arbitrage' in Liquidity Risk, Efficiency and New Bank Business Models*. Springer, Palgrave Macmillan, pp. 35–55.

Flannery, M. J. & Hankins, K. W. (2007). A theory of capital structure adjustment speed. Unpublished Manuscript, University of Florida, *10*(4), 26–43.

FMI (2010). Global Financial Stability Report, October 2010: Sovereigns, Funding, and Systemic Liquidity, International Monetary Fund, Washington (2010).

Gobat, J., Yanase, M., & Maloney, J. (2014). *The Net Stable Funding Ratio: Impact and Issues for Consideration*. IMF Working Paper *14*(106), 1. https://doi.org/10.5089/9781498346498.001.

Gropp, R., Hakenes, H., & Schnabel, I. (2011). Competition, risk-shifting, and public bail-out policies. *The Review of Financial Studies*, *24*(6), 2084–2120.

Grundke, P. & Kühn, A. (2020). The impact of the Basel III liquidity ratios on banks: Evidence from a simulation study. *The Quarterly Review of Economics and Finance*, *75*, 167–190.

Hansen, L. P. (1982). Large sample properties of generalized method of moments estimators. *Econometrica: Journal of the Econometric Society*, *50*, 1029–1054.

Hong, H., Huang, J.-Z., & Wu, D. (2014). The information content of Basel III liquidity risk measures. *Journal of Financial Stability*, *15*, 91–111.

IFSB (2017). *Islamic Financial Services Board*, Kuala Lumpur, Malaysia, retreived from https://www.ifsb.org/download.php?id=4419&lang=English&pg=/sec03.php.

Kennedy, P. (1998). *A Guide to Econometrics*, 6th edn., Wiley-Blackwell, Toronto, Canada, 2008.

Kim, D. & Sohn, W. (2017). The effect of bank capital on lending: Does liquidity matter? *Journal of Banking & Finance*, *77*, 95–107.

Kim, H., Batten, J. A., & Ryu, D. (2020). Financial crisis, bank diversification, and financial stability: OECD countries. *International Review of Economics & Finance*, *65*, 94–104.

King, M. R. (2013). The Basel III net stable funding ratio and bank net interest margins. *Journal of Banking & Finance*, *37*(11), 4144–4156.

Köhler, M. (2015). Which banks are more risky? The impact of business models on bank stability. *Journal of Financial Stability*, *16*, 195–212.

Laeven, L. & Levine, R. (2009). Bank governance, regulation and risk taking. *Journal of Financial Economics*, *93*(2), 259–275.

Lallour, A. & Mio, H. (2016). Do we need a stable funding ratio? Banks' funding in the global financial crisis, *Bank of England Staff Working Paper 602*.

Le, T. D. Q. (2020). The interrelationship among bank profitability, bank stability, and loan growth: Evidence from Vietnam. *Cogent Business & Management*, *7*(1), 1840488.

Lee, C.-C., Yang, S.-J., & Chang, C.-H. (2014). Non-interest income, profitability, and risk in banking industry: A cross-country analysis. *The North American Journal of Economics and Finance*, *27*, 48–67.

Lepetit, L. & Strobel, F. (2013). Bank insolvency risk and time-varying Z-score measures. *Journal of International Financial Markets, Institutions and Money*, *25*, 73–87.

Lepetit, L., Nys, E., Rous, P., & Tarazi, A. (2008). Bank income structure and risk: An empirical analysis of European banks. *Journal of Banking & Finance*, *32*(8), 1452–1467.

Liang, S., Moreira, F., & Lee, J. (2020). Diversification and bank stability. *Economics Letters*, *193*, 109312.

Ly, K. C., Chen, Z., Wang, S., & Jiang, Y. (2017). The Basel III net stable funding ratio adjustment speed and systemic risk. *Research in International Business and Finance*, *39*, 169–182.

Mohamad, A. A. S., Mohamad, M. T., & Samsudin, M. L. (2013). How Islamic banks of Malaysia managing liquidity? An emphasis on confronting economic cycles. *International Journal of Business and Social Science*, *4*(7), 253–263.

Mollah, S. & Zaman, M. (2015). Shari'ah supervision, corporate governance and performance: Conventional vs. Islamic banks. *Journal of Banking & Finance*, *58*, 418–435.

Moreno, I., Parrado-Martínez, P., & Trujillo-Ponce, A. (2021). Using the Z-score to analyze the financial soundness of insurance firms. *European Journal of Management and Business Economics*, *31*(1), 22–39.

Naceur, S. B. & Omran, M. (2011). The effects of bank regulations, competition, and financial reforms on banks' performance. *Emerging Markets Review*, *12*(1), 1–20.

Papadamou, S., Sogiakas, D., Sogiakas, V., & Toudas, K. (2021). The prudential role of Basel III liquidity provisions towards financial stability. *Journal of Forecasting*, *40*(7), 1133–1153.

Pearson, K. (1896). VII. Mathematical contributions to the theory of evolution — III. Regression, heredity, and panmixia. *Philosophical Transactions of the Royal Society of London*, *187*, 253–318.

Rime, B. (2001). Capital requirements and bank behaviour: Empirical evidence for Switzerland. *Journal of Banking & Finance*, *25*(4), 789–805.

Rocha, R. R., Arvai, Z., & Farazi, S. (2011). *Financial Access and Stability: A Road Map for the Middle East and North Africa*. MENA development report. World Bank, Washington, DC. http://documents.worldbank.org/curated/en/343771468052798123/Financial-access-andstability-a-road-map-for-the-Ch.

Sanya, S. & Wolfe, S. (2011). Can banks in emerging economies benefit from revenue diversification? *Journal of Financial Services Research*, *40*(1), 79–101.

Schwerter, S. (2011). Basel III's ability to mitigate systemic risk. *Journal of Financial Regulation and Compliance*, *19*(4), 337–354.

Shim, J. (2013). Bank capital buffer and portfolio risk: The influence of business cycle and revenue diversification. *Journal of Banking & Finance*, *37*(3), 761–772.

Shim, J. (2019). Loan portfolio diversification, market structure and bank stability. *Journal of Banking & Finance*, *104*, 103–115.

Shrieves, R. E. & Dahl, D. (1992). The relationship between risk and capital in commercial banks. *Journal of Banking & Finance*, *16*(2), 439–457.

Sidhu, A. V., Rastogi, S., Gupte, R., Rawal, A., & Agarwal, B. (2022). Net stable funding ratio (NSFR) and bank performance: A study of the Indian banks. *Journal of Risk and Financial Management*, *15*(11), 527.

Stiroh, K. J. & Rumble, A. (2006). The dark side of diversification: The case of US financial holding companies. *Journal of Banking & Finance*, *30*(8), 2131–2161.

Vazquez, F. & Federico, P. (2015). Bank funding structures and risk: Evidence from the global financial crisis. *Journal of Banking & Finance*, *61*, 1–14.

Wei, X., Gong, Y., & Wu, H.-M. (2017). The impacts of net stable funding ratio requirement on Banks' choices of debt maturity. *Journal of Banking & Finance*, *82*, 229–243.

Part 3

Macroeconomic Factors and Financial Development

https://doi.org/10.1142/9781800614734_0012

Chapter 12

Financial Accounting Disclosures and Investors' Sentiments: Perspective from UAE

Amer Alaya and Shatha Hussain

Abstract

This chapter aims to critically review the existing theoretical and empirical literature on financial accounting disclosures, investors' reactions toward bad financial news, and the moderating effect of the individual investor's sentiments (particularly the termination of loss-making projects, fluctuation of share price, and firm's image) in project-based organizations (PBOs). To achieve this, the authors have reviewed extensive research work from reputed and highly cited databases across developed and developing countries, particularly focusing on the UAE. Based on the reviewed literature, it is concluded that there is a solid connection between intention and behavior reaction in a manner that enlarges the possibility of the action to be performed. However, investors' perception of bad financial news has not been empirically examined to date through various information channels. Hence, further investigation is required to determine investors' reactions toward bad news using the dimensions determined in previous reviews.

Keywords: Financial accounting disclosures, bad financial news, investor's sentiment, project-based organizations, United Arab Emirates (UAE)

12.1. Introduction

The discipline of finance has recently witnessed a dramatic change in its application to accommodate emerging investors' management philosophies related to economic development. Using a variety of approaches, numerous studies have already examined the changes in the field (Bolaman & Mandacı, 2014; Phan & Zhou, 2014; Koseoglu, 2019) resulting in diverse and at times contradictory findings. These studies contributed to developing economies, engaging investors, enhancing thinking, enhancing stakeholder satisfaction, reducing financial market fluctuations, improving investment decision quality, achieving rational behavior, and improving the financial market performance. However, investors' perceptual reactions toward bad financial news, termination of loss-making projects, fluctuation of share market price, and firm image still need a great deal of clarification (Verma & Chandra, 2018; Yang *et al.*, 2020).

According to planned behavior theory, behavioral intention counts as a direct precursor to the upcoming action. This makes investors' reactions a familiar dependent variable in several empirical works. Most often, investors' perceptions of bad financial news, such as the termination of loss-making projects, fluctuations in market share price, and company image, are referred to in financial reports, websites, or informal channels. Among these factors are governance and disclosure awareness, information quality, trust in firms' disclosure channels, perceived benefits from the disclosure index, investment intentions, investors' judgment, perceived ease of use, perceptions of privacy and risk, system security, and disclosure policy (Clatworthy & Jones, 2003; Frankel & Li, 2004). It is indeed vital for companies to consider the best disclosure policy, the brevity of accounting, the timeliness of financial statements, and any bias in financial reporting (Gigler & Hemmer, 2001) as financial accounting disclosure significantly influences investors' reactions toward bad financial news (Al-Tamimi, 2006).

12.1.1. *An overview of the UAE's financial market sector*

Since its inception, the UAE's financial markets, especially the Dubai Financial Market (DFM) which has rapidly progressed into a principal market of the region, have always been dedicated to motivating its listed firms to adopt the best international practices of investors' relations. DFM runs as a secondary market that trades public shareholding corporations' securities, and federal or local governments' bonds, in addition to other financial instruments issued by local public institutions and mutual funds. DFM started its operations in the early 2000s and was registered on March 7, 2007 by the UAE Securities and Commodities Authority (SCA). The DFM and SCA work closely together to guard investors and deliver the best trading platform, which comprises initiatives like the delivery of margin trading and delivery versus payment (DvP) instruments. In 2010, the DFM combined its process with Nasdaq Dubai to dominate the capital markets of the region. The alliance offers investors a better selection of asset categories and smoother contact with Nasdaq Dubai and DFM-listed securities. DFM and Nasdaq Dubai are controlled separately — Nasdaq Dubai by the Dubai Financial Services Authority (DFSA) and DFM by the SCA. Nevertheless, some investors are not benefiting from such facilities, which could be due to many factors that are theoretically addressed in the literature (Al-Tammimi, 2006) but not empirically examined.

12.1.2. *The objective of the chapter*

This chapter aims to review the theoretical and empirical literature on financial accounting disclosures, investors' sentiments, and investors' reactions toward bad financial news in the context of "projectized" organizations in the UAE and fill in the literature gaps within these dimensions.

12.2. Empirical and Theoretical Literature Review

12.2.1. *Behavioral finance: The contemporary development*

The recently emerging investors' management approaches and philosophies led to a dramatic change in the methods used to investigate the discipline of finance. Numerous studies have already examined changes in the field (Koseoglu, 2019) using many different approaches, resulting in diverse and at times contradictory findings.

It is arguable whether the efficient market hypothesis (EMH) and other traditional finance theories that have dominated for a long time are sufficient to consistently and completely understand the financial markets (Chatzisarantis *et al.*, 2007). Barberis (2018) articulates the fundamentals of behavioral finance theory and highlights that it is a hugely important challenge for the research community. Koseoglu (2019) finds variations between behavioral finance and traditional finance. Further, Bolaman & Evrim Mandacı (2014) show how investor sentiments and practices vary between sectors, nations, and application areas. Due to the variations in the understanding and behavior of investors, it is vital to understand which kinds of investor sentiments dominate the literature on behavioral finance. Lovric *et al.* (2008) suggest a cognitive model of the individual investor and investment environment, which highlights the most significant results from the current literature on investor behavior and delivers a clarification on the decision-making process used by different stockholders from both an academic and a practical viewpoint. Bolaman & Evrim Mandacı (2014) consumer sentiments have a direct impact on the behavioral intent and this can consequently influence the investors' upcoming conduct (Evrim Mandaci 2014, Armitage & Conner 2001). Having reviewed the theoretical and empirical research studies on (a) making rationalistic decisions, (b) behavioral biases, and (c) attitude toward the behavior, this chapter aims to break down the studies into more specific qualities and carries out an empirical study to find out the most related items.

In the last few years, financial markets have witnessed various developments in many techniques. The developed techniques not only enhance data but also rearranged data that are warehoused in conventional databases; since then, quite a few contemporary practices for processing the data have arisen. Several novel techniques in data analysis and data mining have emerged to enhance and support the international economy, besides helping stakeholders to select the right choices and make better decisions. Numerous groundbreaking methodologies in data analysis and mining have arisen, playing a pivotal role in elevating the global economy. These methodologies not only assisted stakeholders in formulating enhanced choices and decisions but also exerted an impact on investor behaviors. Beyond the purview of these methodologies, a wide spectrum of influential factors has necessitated the creation of novel disclosure channels. For example, Albusaidi *et al.* (2017) show the importance of social media data in enhancing the outcome of investor sentiment by using the application programming interface offered by Twitter as it permits the programmer to gain access to Twitter data and analyze information and Twitter hashtags. Their findings show that Twitter users are freer to reveal their sentiments on social media than when filling out a questionnaire. The findings expose that most social media users show their opinions more spontaneously, and people return to certain hashtags. Thus, social media platforms provide an opportunity for investors to reveal their sentiments.

The emergence of new techniques that deal with data can also be linked to the emergence of new application areas in investor behavior. As a result, many investors use new social media platforms to make their investment decisions. Consequently, the field of financial markets has undergone significant developments (Hidajat, 2019). Zhou (2014) used the theory of planned behavior (TPB) as a conceptual basis for discovering elements impacting the behavioral intentions of individuals investing in financial markets. Verma & Chandra (2018) expanded the social psychological behavioral model. Phan and Rzeszutek *et al.* (2015) concentrated on the level of a tendency to behavioral biases in terms of mental accounting and the certainty effect, in addition to the sunk cost fallacy among individuals of several degrees of proficiency in investing in stock markets, to determine whether this tendency is linked to specific personality traits. Hamza & Arif (2019) further examined the impact of financial literacy and investors' personality traits on investors' choices according to the "Big 5" personality traits. Their findings indicate that financial literacy has no substantial impact on investors' choices via agreeableness, conscientiousness, and extraversion, while it negatively impacts investors' decisions via openness to experience and positively impacts their decisions via neuroticism.

However, traditional finance theories could not explain the bubbles that occur in cryptocurrencies as this incidence is linked to emotional and cognitive behavioral finance reasons, which could be linked to behavioral biases that occur in four bubble phases and could impact investment decisions. The behavioral biases that are believed to occur in four bubble phases are herding, optimism, overconfidence, confirmation bias, loss aversion, and gamblers' fallacy. Further, Hidajat (2019) empirically examined behavioral biases in the four bubble phases.

Rational decision theory indicates that investors rely on a series of logical selections from alternatives. A probable cause is that investors commonly miss information on the determination of issues. To expand the rational choice theory, Kahneman & Tversky (1979) introduced prospect theory according to which the best decisions are assessed based on reference situations. Moreover, it also explains that investors depend on a variety of heuristic principles that could be advantageous to some extent, but from the time to time result in an intense and methodical error. Despite the possibility of getting an objective evaluation of the information by investors, there are still cognitive and emotional biases in different phases of making investment decisions, which are hard to disregard. That is, despite following a series of logical selections from various investments, behavioral biases still exist in investors' brains. Further exploration of behavioral finance theories will be reviewed in the coming sections.

12.2.2. *Investors' reactions to financial markets*

Research has highlighted the significance of investor relations as an organizational phenomenon that contributes to many disciplines (Hoffmann *et al.*, 2018). Investor Relations have an essential impact on the effective delivery of organizational well-being (Bushee & Miller, 2012; Chapman *et al.*, 2019; Donati, 2020). A precise investor relation program can support the overall financial situation of the organization and permit investments to be made knowledgeably and assuredly, and with knowledge of the effect on investors' reactions. The consequent growth in investor and stakeholder interest from ideal stakeholder relationships will subsequently bring out an automatic upsurge in the organization's market value, on the condition that the organization delivers on its operative performance. Hence, it is important first to define investors' reactions, processes, tools, and systems, as these terms are being used in various ways in the literature.

12.2.3. *Perceived benefits of the disclosure index*

Investors associate the benefits perceived from the disclosure index with the belief that the disclosure index is transparent, improves communications about the firm's readiness to deal with bad news, enhances investors' confidence in the firm's integrity while dealing with bad news, and helps mitigate investment risks that are related to the firm's response to bad news (Yang *et al.*, 2020).

12.2.4. *Investment intention*

Investment intention, from a behavioral perspective, is related to the motivating factors that impact a behavior; they are signals of the degree of ease or difficulty individuals are ready to attempt, and of the volume of effort they are willing to apply to achieve the behavior (Phan & Zhou, 2014). Thus, Verma & Chandra (2018) and Alniacik *et al.* (2011), as well as others, link investors' perceptions of behavioral intention with their preferences to invest their money in a firm that voluntarily provides information about its bad news, as recommended by the IFRS and government requirements. Investors' perceptions of behavioral intention could also be linked to a firm whose disclosure index has been examined by international professional bodies and accredited auditors. Investing in a firm that voluntarily discloses information about its bad news in its disclosure index could also be preferred by investors.

12.2.5. *Investors' judgment*

Tan & Tan (2009), Phan & Zhou (2014), Haritha & Uchil (2020), and Verma & Chandra (2018) discuss that investors' judgment, which is related to comparisons between bad news and good news across firms and impacts the overreaction or underreaction of investors when making investment decisions. Furthermore, Hsu *et al.* (2014) and Yang *et al.* (2020) highlight the perceived ease of use as a factor that impacts investors who might overreact or underreact in the decision-making process if information about bad news were delivered easily.

Based on the above-reviewed literature, it could be stated that investors' reaction, a common dependent variable in several empirical studies (Phan & Zhou, 2014), reflects the intention to perform or not perform the conduct in the future. According to the planned behavior theory, behavioral or perceptual intention is a direct precursor to the upcoming action. This relationship has been evidenced and effectively accepted by several prior empirical works (Phan & Zhou, 2014; Armitage & Conner, 2001). Likewise, several empirical works state the solid connection of intention and behavior reaction in a manner that enlarges the possibility of the action to be performed. The current study is dedicated to examining the investors' reactions that are frequently noted in the existing body of knowledge as being associated with the investor's perceptions of bad financial news; these are governance and disclosure awareness, information quality, trust in firms' disclosure channels, perceived benefits of the disclosure index, investment intentions, investors' judgment, perceived ease of use, perceived privacy, and perceived risk and system security. Hence, in the following sections, further investigation has been performed to determine investors' reactions to bad news in terms of investors' perceptions of termination of loss-making projects, investors' trust toward fluctuation of share market price in financial markets, and investors' awareness of firm image.

12.3. Investors' Reactions Toward the Termination of Loss-Making Projects in Financial Markets

The project life cycle identified by the Project Management Institute (PMI) shows the significance of constantly observing a project to decide whether it is matching the aims, goals, and objectives set at the beginning (Hormozi *et al.*, 2000). Shepherd *et al.* (2014) studied the termination stage and the influence of project termination on individuals' efficiency, while Hormozi *et al.* (2000) studied the repute of the organization and the price of the organization's share; after inspection appraisal, however, the investor's perception of such decisions has not been addressed clearly. The fundamental principles of project management come into play when dealing with specific projects for singular events, such as the introduction of a new product, or when a task is exceedingly intricate, necessitating coordination among different departments. Additionally, these principles are also relevant when the project holds significant importance, as is the case with a merger exploration (Avots, 1969). Thus, a question was raised by Boehm (2000): Does the termination of a project mean project failure?

Unger *et al.* (2012) studied how the termination of loss-making and struggling projects impacts the efficiency of the portfolio and top management's critical functions in such a situation. Further, they studied its impacts on strategic fit and how the quality of the termination of bad projects is influenced by top management participation. Their results show that termination quality has a positive impact on the strategic fit. The results also show a positive but reversed unmolded association between termination quality and top management participation. It is undeniable that the termination of a loss-making project plays a positive role in enhancing the strategic fit of the organization, but Unger *et al.* (2012) do not refer to the reactions of investors toward loss-making projects. Lechler &

Thomas (2015) studied the termination decisions of new product development projects, as many studies have mainly concentrated on solo projects while inspecting the influence of official termination pronouncement procedures. Despite the large existing body of literature that improves the general comprehension of the best time to cancel a project and the related administrative consequences, there has been no discovery of the circumstantial technicalities behind the linkage between the quickness of terminating the project and the knowledge earned by people who are operating the project.

12.4. Signaling Theory and Asymmetric Information

Dissymmetric information between administration and stockholder involving the organization's activities would send signs to venture capitalists in registered real estate firms (Axelsson & Brissman, 2011). With regard to signaling theory, Axelsson & Brissman (2011) discussed that a declaration of a stock repurchasing agenda is explicated by stockholders who ensure that the organization is placing its investments in the right place, i.e., indicating that the shares are presently undervalued. Their results show an important short-term unusual earning of 1.96% at the declaration time and increased unusual earnings of 2.32% for the early days following the declaration. Based on the first stage of the theory of corporate finance, the efficient market hypothesis requires that the declaration ought to reduce the entire share price directly. Conversely, it would be sensible for stockholders to expect that the stock repurchasing agenda would be performed earlier in its whole value settlement. Signs of weak reactions were found as the study observed long-term positive share price responses to the declaration. From a stockholder's perspective, the outcomes suggest that purchasing real estate shares that declare a stock repurchasing agenda could reap affirmative unusual earnings for investment prospects for a period of 10 days to 1 year (Axelsson & Brissman, 2011).

12.5. Financial Aid, Charity, and Share Market Price

Shi *et al.* (2010) used the market response model to study the impact of financial aid given to a charity by registered corporations in China, especially after a catastrophe, on the price of shares. The findings indicate that the behavior toward the catastrophe charity by the registered corporations caused undesirable impacts to share price. Shi *et al.* (2010) suggest that registered corporations have to govern the number of payments and delay declarations of a key contribution to a different time to avert such a negative effect. Alternatively, registered corporations have to shape a perfect plan for resolutions in connection with catastrophe aids, attempting to gain investors' acceptance by persuading them that contributions to charities for catastrophes involve tactical advantages (Shi *et al.*, 2010). As material information, charity donations must be disclosed in firms' reports; but this has not been studied in terms of its perceptual effect on investors' reactions toward share market price, which is what the current study is testing via different disclosure channels.

12.6. Investors' Sentiments, Styles, and Characteristics

Most research based on investors' choices, incentives, and behavior contains divisions based on socio-demographic features like age, income, and educational degree. Such presentation tactics make the truth appear simple, by combining data about noticeable factors and thinking about investors as similar sets. By seeing an investor as a "homo economicus", namely, a logical and self-governing person who is driven by solid facts to make investment decisions, such research fails to identify all the complications that form individual behavior (Diouf *et al.*, 2016). However, Jaiyeoba *et al.* (2018) questioned eight experienced individual investors and financiers. Hence, it is recommended to adopt a mixed-methods approach or implement different audience standards; for example, a focus group debate among several participants might enhance the general understanding of the choices of investment and related behaviors of individual venture capitalists and fund executives. In summary, Jaiyeoba *et al.* (2018) have provided guidance to support venture capitalists and fund executives during their investments and decision-making processes. Following the recommendation of Jaiyeoba *et al.* (2018), the proposed study adopts a different approach to deepen our understanding of individual investors' practices, the UAE economy, and their preferences for making decisions, as well as how they moderate their emotional biases and deal with psychological impacts and other challenges. However, the current study is not examining the influence of monetary strategy choices on investors' reactions and emotions; rather, it aims to examine the dynamics of financial accounting disclosure and investors' reactions and emotions based on their perceptions of bad financial news. Hence, investors' sentiments, biases, attitudes, subjective norms, perceived behavioral control (PBC), personality traits, styles, and characteristics, along with a comparison between practices across the UAE, GCC, and international investors, are reviewed in the following sections.

12.7. Investors' Sentiments

The sentiments of investors are defined as their views and feelings toward the upcoming cash flows and related risks of their investments without having any appropriate evidence to support their judgments (Makau & Ambrose, 2018). Hence, different investors are drawn toward a certain investment due to their sentiments, which could create a bubble or a state wherein a price increase motivates the eagerness of more investors by emotional contagion from one to another, in the process spreading stories that may rationalize the price upsurges and attract more types of stakeholders. Regardless of the actual worth of investment, Rodrigue (2020) describes the four phases of a bubble, i.e., the stealth phase, the awareness phase, the mania phase, and the blow-off phase. Some kind of behavioral bias occurs in every phase of this cycle.

12.8. Financial Accounting Disclosure

Since the European Union's demand for International Financial Reporting Standards (IFRS) to be adopted by registered corporations, several nations have followed suit, expecting to earn an advantage over their competitors in an attempt to entice foreign direct investment (FDI) to support their economic progression. Alsaqqa & Sawan (2013) highlight the benefits acquired and the obstacles suffered by corporations registered in the financial markets of the UAE owing to the implementation of IFRS. They suggest a framework initiated on the recognition and evaluation of the main factors impacting corporations registered in the UAE's financial markets. The outcomes reveal that the advantages of implementing IFRS in the UAE undoubtedly exceed the challenges and expenses. Further, the results disclose that the implementation of IFRS in the UAE's financial markets has enhanced the inclusive quality criteria related to financial reportage, and therefore contributed to enticing venture capitalists to exploit and establish new investments in the financial markets of the UAE (Alsaqqa & Sawan, 2013). Nonetheless, it can be concluded that financial markets and investors have been affected positively by the adoption of IFRS. Hence, the proposed study is raising a question about the impact of financial accounting disclosure as an autonomous standard of IFRS on investors' reactions toward bad financial news disclosed in the financial reports by considering their sentiments. Many theories support the proposed study, such as behavioral finance theory, obfuscation, and impression management theories, which follow agency theory. Each theory will be discussed to support the proposed conceptual framework.

It is important to mention the work of Hassan (2012), which examined the scope of accounting disclosure as an index of corporate governance reportage in firms registered in the UAE's financial markets. It is becoming mandatory for contemporary financial organizations to disclose a good volume of information — including investment backing information — on company websites and portals (Li, 2013). The internet has turned into a complementary element of financial accounting disclosure, and the multimedia features exemplified in such websites have been revealed to impact investors' reactions (Lee *et al.*, 2008). Hassan (2012) studied the annual reports of companies listed in the UAE's financial markets; such reports are considered the main channels to disclose corporate governance materials, but it is suggested that researchers should consider additional disclosure platforms, like official statements issued to newspapers, giving information on a particular matter, company websites, and web-based reportage.

12.9. Corporate Governance Practices, Timeliness of Reporting, Transparency, and Performance

Many researchers have studied the relationship between good corporate governance practices and the timeliness of reporting, degree of disclosure, and performance. The study of Haat *et al.* (2008)

highlights the effect of good corporate governance practices on the transparency and performance of Malaysian-registered corporations. Corporate governance items have a solid forecasting influence on the performance of the corporation, primarily owing to foreign ownership debt monitoring. Nevertheless, there is a substantial negative relationship between performance and auditing quality. Their findings do not show that performance is linked with the degree of timeliness and disclosure but rather indicate that timely reporting and disclosure are not important contributing items in the association between market performance and corporate governance. However, many questions need to be answered: Are UAE corporations interested in corporate governance and transparent corporate reporting? Does corporate governance play a role in enhancing investors' decisions? And what is the impact on investors' reactions of the information disclosed by corporations that implement enhanced governance practices and transparent reporting?

12.10. Mandatory and Voluntary Disclosure

In the second phase of index design, the aspects of corporate governance disclosure were divided into mandatory and voluntary disclosure. Mandatory disclosure is required by accounting standards and requirements; this category includes financial statements such as the income statement, statement of financial position, statement of cash flow, statement of changes in equity, and notes to financial statements. In contrast, voluntary disclosure is any disclosure over mandatory disclosure that is not required by accounting standards, provided voluntarily by the company to help investors know more about the company. In addition, disclosure can be numerical (in number form or quantitative) or narrative (words) (Hussainey, 2004). Despite the strict requirements for mandatory disclosure, extra voluntary disclosure raises a company's transparency and therefore decreases information asymmetry between internal and external users of corporate governance reports. Ultimately, the fundamental aims of business governance are to enhance a company's public responsibility and increase transparency. Hence, based on a review of many studies (Haat *et al.*, 2008) as well as checking suggested items of the index against the requirements of the UAE code, the adapted index was separated into two wide-ranging groups. The first one is named "compulsory factors" and comprises factors that are compulsorily demanded by the governance code of the UAE. The second one comprises factors that are suggested by past papers; these are not demanded by the Emirati governance code but are "value-adding" factors.

A significant feature of previous governance disclosure index literature is that researchers have tried to study governance disclosure both quantitatively and qualitatively. Some scholars have used a questionnaire (e.g., Cheung *et al.*, 2007; Hussain & Mallin, 2002), whereas others have relied on a weighting/unweighting approach to determine some disclosure factors (e.g., Cheung *et al.*, 2010; Haat *et al.*, 2008). In the third phase, the significance of each factor was measured according to the source that identifies the factor. Each one of the financial accounting disclosure indices has its contextual definition and is expanded to include supplementary detailed dimensions and measurements from the review of the literature, as explained below.

12.10.1. *Transparency disclosure*

"Transparency" is considered by many academics as a key feature of effective corporate governance (Hassan, 2012; Taylor, 2000; Solomon & Solomon, 2004; Cheung *et al.*, 2010). Lately, many studies have concentrated on enhancing the quality of transparency and governance disclosure in the Asia-Pacific area. Cheung *et al.* (2007) refer to Bushman *et al.*'s (2004) definition of transparency disclosure as the obtainability of company-detailed statistics to external stakeholders and investors. The data are required for making investment decisions. The grades of transparency disclosure rest on businesses' readiness to release relevant notifications to the public. According to Article (36) of the SCA's Disclosure and Transparency Regulations, Parties and Listed Companies shall provide the Market with the following information and reports: interim financial reports (quarterly, semi-annual) reviewed by the Company's external auditor, within 45 days from the end of the specified period, signed by the Board of Directors or the person authorized to sign on its behalf. The transparency disclosure could contribute to safeguarding investors' rights, helping them to be certain that the business is being governed with investors' interests in mind. The deviation of results in prior works might come from the diverse factors being used to measure transparency disclosure. The absence of steadiness might similarly be due to the slight concentration on past works. Generally, the literature counts a single or a limited number of factors forming transparency disclosure as an alternative to complex measures. The volume of research on the links between the comprehensive practice of corporate governance and market capitalization is inadequate (Cheung *et al.*, 2007).

Information related to the company's accounting policy and legal accounting requirements, the chairman's or board of directors' statements about auditing processes, internal control function or internal audit, financial risks, risk management or any potential risks, corporate governance statement and awareness, the rating of the company by other markets, investment banks or rating agencies, matters related to the annual general meeting/statement concerning corporate social responsibility, penalties and sanctions against or by the company, and regulatory framework management are viewed as transparency indicators since their disclosure impacts investors' judgments (Cheung *et al.*, 2007, 2010; Hassan, 2012; Taylor, 2000; Solomon & Solomon, 2004). The UAE code (2007, amended 2009), in addition to many other studies (Gandía, 2008; Tsamenyi *et al.*, 2007; Haat *et al.*, 2008), emphasizes the disclosure of any legal claims, litigations, or penalties and sanctions against or by the company. It is also critical to report in which financial markets the corporation is registered and the implementation of the predominant guidelines in those financial markets. Above and beyond this, it is mandatory in the UAE code (2007, amended 2009) to provide information regarding the agenda and the wording of proposed resolutions in the annual general meeting.

12.10.2. *The role of financial accounting disclosure in investors' reactions*

Tan & Tan (2009) studied financial accounting disclosure via company and newscast internet sites, which are becoming more and more diffused, and conducted an experiment to explore factors impacting individual investors' decisions and judgments by questioning the impact of the original mistaken disclosure, which is later adjusted, on the investors' judgments of the company's chance of gaining a deal as well as the company's profitability and investing capability. However, the psychological philosophy of the power of first impressions proposes that such misrepresentation could have a continual impact on investors' choices even after it is corrected. Alternatively, internet disclosure is more effective since modifications can be done directly. Therefore, investors might often encounter the corrected version alongside the initial erroneous disclosure, mitigating the impact of the initial misrepresentation significantly.

Cybersecurity threats are remarkable obstacles as companies are vulnerable to data and further cyber-associated violations (Gao, 2017). For example, a 2017 data violation at Equifax compromised the ID of over 143 million people from the US (Gaglione, 2019). As a result, the American Institute of Certified Public Accountants (Yang *et al.*, 2020) designed an organizational-level cybersecurity disclosure framework that businesses can apply to reveal beneficial information to investors. The framework offers a mutual language that investors can use to assess a company's cybersecurity situation and the efficiency of its agenda for risk management. Yang *et al.* (2020) examined the perceptual views of non-professional investors of the framework of AICPA, how their perceptual views impact their reactions, and how issues like their perceptual views of trust, information quality, and cybersecurity awareness (CSA) impact their reactions.

Thomas *et al.* (2020) studied the strategic use of readability to obfuscate negative news in Germany. Integrating the content analysis of both printed and electronic reports, the scholars evaluated the manner and perusal of three components of the 2014 yearly reports of 30 firms listed in the DAX financial market index in Germany. Their findings show that positively phrased passages in annual reports are not substantially easier to read than negatively phrased passages. Moreover, the yearly report's readability differs based on its material importance within the report. Hence, it could be stated that managers are generally concerned with controlling the disclosed information and its impact on interested parties. This is supported by the concept of impression management (Brennan & Merkl-Davies, 2013), the incomplete revelation hypothesis (Bloomfield, 2002), and the obfuscation theory (Bayerlein & Davidson, 2012) that companies avoid undesirable news. The current study is investigating the role of investors' sentiments in the relationship between financial accounting disclosure, including readability — the textual complexity originating from the writing method (Brennan & Merkl-Davies, 2013) — and its variation within a narrative. In particular, the current study focuses on how various investors perceive companies' attempts to share negative news in a deliberately complex manner, using convoluted language to hinder easy comprehension, aiming to delay or even prevent investors from forming negative reactions and consequently maintaining firms' good reputation; this corresponds with the obfuscation hypothesis (Thoms *et al.*, 2020).

12.11. Findings and Conclusion

An extensive review of investors' reactions to bad financial news has been provided in this chapter, including termination of loss-making projects, fluctuation in share prices on the UAE's financial markets, and the image of project-based organizations. Further, this chapter has given specifics about behavioral finance, including previous research, recent developments in research, and behavioral finance theory. Among other things, it has defined investors' reactions based on their perception of trust, information quality, and risk model benefits, and provided particulars about investors' reactions to good and bad news, disclosure policy and timeliness, and their perception of the risk model. Moreover, it covers investors' reactions toward the termination of loss-making projects and their trust, investors' reactions toward fluctuation of share market price, and investors' reactions toward firm image in financial markets. Investing styles, characteristics, and sentiments have also been defined, including the four phases of a bubble, individual investor behavioral biases, attitudes toward behavior, subjective norms, perceived behavioral control (PBC), recommendations of analysts and brokerage companies, financial market proficiency, personality traits, comparisons of practices between UAE, GCC, and international investors, and corporate governance practices. Following that, the chapter reviewed the literature on the determinants of complex financial accounting disclosures and the components. Additionally, complex financial accounting disclosures and their impact on investors' reactions were discussed, in addition to signaling theory, stakeholder theory, and agency theory. Finally, the chapter summarized the key issues identified in the literature.

Drawing upon the literature reviewed above, it becomes evident that there exists a strong correlation between intention and behavioral reactions. This connection amplifies the likelihood of the intended action being carried out within the context of the UAE. Although the perceptions of investors toward bad financial news have been empirically investigated, the information disclosed in company financial reports, websites, or other formal/informal channels has not been empirically examined, namely, governance and disclosure awareness, information quality, trust in firms' disclosure channels, perceptions of the disclosure index, investment intentions, investors' judgment, perceived ease of use, perceived privacy, and perceived risk and security. It is, therefore, necessary to conduct further research to determine how investors react to bad news using the dimensions from the previous review in order to determine investors' response to bad news in the future.

References

Albusaidi, H. S., Udupi, P. K., & Dattana, V. (2017). Optimization and visualization of opinion mining and sentiments in tourism dashboard: A case of Statics Centre Abu-Dhabi (SCAD). *International Journal of Research and Innovation in Social Science (IJRISS)*, *1*(1), 8–12.

Al-Tamimi, H. A. H. (2006). Factors influencing individual investor behavior: An empirical study of the UAE financial markets. *Business Review*, *5*(2), 225–233.

Armitage, C. J. & Conner, M. (2001). Efficacy of the theory of planned behaviour: A meta-analytic review. *British Journal of Social Psychology*, *40*(4), 471–499.

Axelsson, L. & Brissman, P. (2011). Share repurchase announcements and abnormal returns for Swedish listed real estate companies. Master Thesis. KTH, School of Architecture and the Built Environment (ABE), Real Estate and Construction Management, Building and Real Estate Economics.

Barberis, N. (2018). Richard Thaler and the rise of behavioral economics. *The Scandinavian Journal of Economics*, *120*(3), 661–684.

Boehm, B. (2000). Project termination doesn't equal project failure. *Computer*, *33*(9), 94–96.

Bolaman, Ö. & Evrim Mandacı, P. (2014). Effect of investor sentiment on stock markets. *Finansal Araştırmalar ve Çalışmalar Dergisi*, *6*(11), 51–64.

Bushee, B. J. & Miller, G. S. (2012). Investor relations, firm visibility, and investor following. *Accounting Review*, *87*(3), 867–897.

Chapman, K., Miller, G. S., & White, H. D. (2019). Investor relations and information assimilation. *Accounting Review*, *94*(2), 105–131.

Chatzisarantis, N. L. D., Hagger, M. S., & Smith, B. (2007). Influences of perceived autonomy support on physical activity within the theory of planned behavior. *European Journal of Social Psychology*, *37*(5), 934–954.

Clatworthy, M. & Jones, M. J. (2003). Financial reporting of good news and bad news: Evidence from accounting narratives. *Accounting and Business Research*, *33*(3), 171–185.

Diouf, D., Hebb, T., & Touré, E. H. (2016). Exploring factors that influence social retail investors' decisions: Evidence from Desjardins fund. *Journal of Business Ethics*, *134*(1), 45–67.

Donati, E. L. (2020). *Investor Relations. Reputation Management* (4th edn.). Routledge, New York. pp. 241–258. eBook ISBN 9781351235020.

Frankel, R. & Li, X. (2004). Characteristics of a firm's information environment and the information asymmetry between insiders and outsiders. *Journal of Accounting and Economics*, *37*(2), 229–259.

Gaglione Jr, G. S. (2019). The equifax data breach: An opportunity to improve consumer protection and cybersecurity efforts in America. *Buff. L. Rev.*, *67*, 1133.

Gao, L., Calderon, T., & Tang, F. (2020). Public companies' cybersecurity risk disclosures. *International Journal of Accounting Information Systems*, *38*, 100468. https://doi.org/10.1016/j.accinf.2020.100468.

Gigler, F. B. & Hemmer, T. (2001). Conservatism, optimal disclosure policy, and the timeliness of financial reports. *Accounting Review*, *76*(4), 471–493.

Hamza, N. & Arif, I. (2019). Impact of financial literacy on investment decisions: The mediating effect of big-five personality traits model. *Market Forces College of Management Sciences*, *14*(1), 43–60.

Haritha, P. H. & Uchil, R. (2020). Impact of investor sentiment on decision-making in Indian stock market: An empirical analysis. *Journal of Advances in Management Research*, *17*(1), 66–83.

Hidajat, T. (2019). Behavioural biases in bitcoin trading. Fokus Ekonomi. *Jurnal Ilmiah Ekonomi*, *14*(2), 337–354.

Hoffmann, C. P., Tietz, S., & Hammann, K. (2018). Investor relations — a systematic literature review. *Corporate Communications: An International Journal*, *23*(3), 294–311.

Hormozi, A., McMinn, R., & Nzeogwu, O. (2000). The project life cycle: The termination phase. *SAM Advanced Management Journal*, *65*(1), 45–51.

Koseoglu, S. D. (2019). Behavioral finance vs. traditional finance. In *Behavioral Finance and Decision-Making Models*. Editorial Advisory Board, Susmita Dash, Khallikote, S. G. Deshmukh, Gaurav Kabra, Anil Kumar, Bijay Kumar Panda, Rajendra Sahu, N. K. Sharma, Parshant Singh Rana (Eds.), (pp. 1–23). IGI Global, Hershey, Pennsylvania, USA.

Lechler, T. G. & Thomas, J. L. (2015). Examining new product development project termination decision quality at the portfolio level: Consequences of dysfunctional executive advocacy. *International Journal of Project Management, 33*(7), 1452–1463.

Lovric, M., Kaymak, U., & Spronk, J. (2008). A conceptual model of investor behavior. ERIM Report Series Reference No. ERS-2008-030-F&A. https://ssrn.com/abstract=1144293.

Phan, K. C. & Zhou, J. (2014). Factors influencing individual investor behavior: An empirical study of the Vietnamese stock market. *American Journal of Business and Management, 3*(2), 77–94.

Rzeszutek, M., Szyszka, A., & Czerwonka, M. (2015). Investors' expertise, personality traits and susceptibility to behavioral biases in the decision making process. *Contemporary Economics, 9*(3), 237–352.

Shepherd, D. A., Patzelt, H., Williams, T. A., & Warnecke, D. (2014). How does project termination impact project team members? Rapid termination, 'creeping death', and learning from failure. *Journal of Management Studies, 51*(4), 513–546.

Tan, H.-T. & Tan, S.-K. (2009). Investors' reactions to management disclosure corrections: Does presentation format matter? *Contemporary Accounting Research, 26*(2), 1–43.

Thoms, C., Degenhart, A., & Wohlgemuth, K. (2020). Is bad news difficult to read? A readability analysis of differently connoted passages in the annual reports of the 30 DAX companies. *Journal of Business and Technical Communication, 34*, 157–187. https://doi.org/10.1177/1050651919892312.

Unger, B. N., Kock, A., Gemünden, H. G., & Jonas, D. (2012). Enforcing strategic fit of project portfolios by project termination: An empirical study on senior management involvement. *International Journal of Project Management, 30*(6), 675–685.

Verma, V. K. & Chandra, B. (2018). An application of theory of planned behavior to predict young Indian consumers' green hotel visit intention. *Journal of Cleaner Production, 172*, 1152–1162.

Yang, L., Lau, L., & Gan, H. (2020). Investors' perceptions of the cybersecurity risk management reporting framework. *International Journal of Accounting and Information Management, 28*(1), 167–183.

https://doi.org/10.1142/9781800614734_0013

Chapter 13

IPO Valuation, Price-Setting, and Stabilization Mechanisms in the Egyptian Capital Market

Mahmoud Otaify

Abstract

This chapter discusses the Egyptian regulatory framework of the IPO process as well as its listing on the Egyptian Exchange (EGX). We will examine the most recent IPOs executed in the Egyptian capital market during the period of 2016–2022 to identify the valuation, pricing, and stabilization mechanisms used by investment banks in light of Egyptian laws and regulations. We use descriptive analysis for the IPO structure data to implicitly identify the incentives to go public. Interestingly, all shares offered in the Egyptian IPOs during the period of concern are secondary offerings, so Egyptian IPO firms use the capital market as an exit strategy rather than to finance expansion. A discounted cash flow model and trading multiples are the techniques most applied in the IPO valuation. The book-building pricing mechanism is widely used by investment banks in the Egyptian IPO market.

Keywords: Book-building, best effort, exit strategy, going public, OPR system

13.1. Introduction

A company usually starts as a privately owned firm, and as its operations expand and investment opportunities arise, it may need funds to finance its expansion. Moreover, its retained earnings (internal financing source) may not be sufficient for funding this expansion, so it seeks external financing through two main alternatives: equity financing, through which it could issue new shares to investors in the stock market, or debt financing, through which the company may borrow long-term loans from banks (Ross *et al.*, 2020). Typically, when a privately owned company decides to sell part of its shares to investors in the stock market, it decides to go public in a process called initial public offering (IPO) — the first time the company sells shares to public investors (all types), including retail investors and institutional investors (e.g., banks, insurance companies, mutual funds, and other corporations). Alternatively, the firm may tend to maintain control and sell new shares to a specific group of institutional investors (e.g., banks and insurance banks) in a process referred to as private placement. Being a public company allows the firm to issue more shares to the existing shareholders in a process referred to as rights issue, or to all public investors in a process known as a seasoned public offering (SPO).

Once managers of the IPO-contemplating company identify incentives to go public,[1] they must weigh the advantages and disadvantages (determinants) of this decision (Pagano *et al.*, 1998; Subrahmanyam & Titman, 1999; Bancel & Mittoo, 2009; Autify, 2012). Explicitly, the advantages of going public could explain why many firms decide to do so rather than go the private placement route or borrow loans. These advantages include increasing the competitive position and creating currency (shares) for acquisition. On the other hand, the IPO decision could have disadvantages that encourage many firms to stay private, such as loss of control and confidentiality, and the risk of takeover by other companies.

The investment bank helps the issuing company decide the offering size and structure according to the company objectives, listing requirements, and market conditions. Typically, the company should determine the type of shares (primary or secondary or both) to be offered for sale in the IPO and identify the type of investors (retail and/or institutional) it targets to be its shareholders. Regarding the types of shares, the company can issue new shares (primary offering/shares) and will then receive the IPO proceeds to

[1]Going public and initial public offering are used interchangeably throughout the chapter.

finance its expansion. Alternatively, the company's initial shareholders (founders) might want to sell part of their shares (secondary shares) as an exit strategy at a favorable price. In many IPOs, the offering structure includes a primary offering and a secondary offering.

IPO pricing is a science and an art (Draho, 2004). It is a science when an investment bank applies methods such as the discounted free cash flow model (DFCF) and the relative valuation model to estimate the fair value of the company's stock. It is an art when the bank attempts to induce investors to reveal their private information about the new issue using mechanisms such as book-building, fixed price, or auction in order to set an accurate offering price.[2] Countries differ in the regulations in organizing the IPO process, so this process lasts different periods of time from country to country. However, other factors such as issue size could affect the firm's duration to finalize its IPO. Generally, a company contemplating IPO must comply with the legal requirements according to the domestic, corporate, and capital market laws that organize the domestic market's IPO process. In Egypt, the IPO process is regulated the capital market law no. 95 established in 1992 (CML95, thereafter) and its executive regulations, decrees issued by the Financial Regulatory Authority (FRA), and the listing rules of the Egyptian Exchange (EGX).

This chapter is organized as follows: Section 13.2 presents an overview of Egyptian IPO market activity; Section 13.3 describes how firms list their shares on Egyptian exchange (EGX). Section 13.4 reviews the relevant literature, while Section 13.5 describes the data and methodology used. Section 13.6 presents the analysis and discussion, and Section 13.7 concludes the chapter.

13.2. Overview of Egyptian IPO Market Activity

The number of IPOs in the Egyptian capital market has fluctuated over the period from 2016–2022,[3] from one firm in 2020 to five firms in

[2]See Draho (2004) and Iannotta (2010) who explain mechanics, characteristics, and efficiency of different price-setting mechanisms: book-building, fixed, and auction.

[3]Till the end of October 2022.

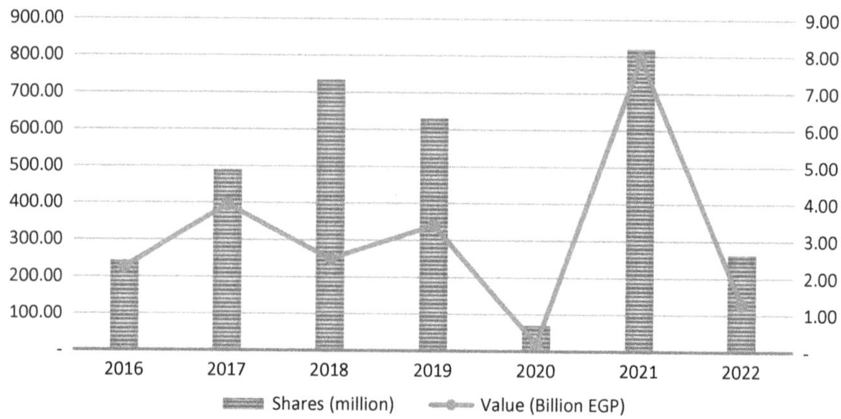

Figure 13.1. Egyptian IPO volume and value (2016–2022).

2017, reflecting that three firms went public in the Egyptian capital market per year. Figure 13.1 depicts the IPO volume and value over the period of concern, and shows its peak in 2021 when three firms went public by selling 821 million shares at EGP 7.96 billion, while just one company conducted its IPO in 2020 by selling 70 million shares at EGP 0.20 billion. On average, 465 million shares are offered annually in the Egyptian IPO market at the average value of EGP 3 billion.

13.3. Listing on Egyptian Stock Exchange

The EGX has two exchanges, the main market and the SME market (NILEX), and accordingly, it sets the rules and procedures for listing securities on each one.[4] A summary of the executive regulations to execute offering through the Egyptian stock exchange can be found at their website (EGX, 2021). However, the procedures for listing on the EGX's main market can be summarized in four main stages:

- All Egyptian and foreign companies seeking to offer securities and list them on the EGX are registered in the FRA's records. The records contain primary data about the company's name, address,

[4]For more details, see, https://www.egx.com.eg/en/How_list.aspx.

purpose, activities, ownership structure, type of securities subject for offering, main shareholders, board of directors, and type of stocks (common or preferred).

- The company then prepares for listing and provides the required documents for the listing committee at the EGX. Notably, the EGX authorizes some intermediaries as listing agents to help any company accomplish the listing procedures.[5] Otherwise, the EGX has a team ready to help companies that wish to list their shares without the listing agents' help.
- A company can issue a portion of its shares for trading on the EGX according to the prospectus approved by the FRA and published in the media. After that, the company can start executing the offering through the EGX's market operations department.
- The listing would be finalized when the offering is successfully executed and other listing requirements (number of shareholders, percentage of offered shares, and free-floating shares) are fulfilled. After that, the EGX's market operations committee would decide the start date of trading, the open price, and applicability of price limits.

In many countries, a lockup condition is not required by law, but it is usually included in the underwriting contract. However, listing on the EGX requires a lockup percentage for a specified period. In general, the lockup agreement requires the initial owners to hold their shares after going public for a specific period. In Egypt, 51% of shares owned by the initial owners and BOD, representing at least 25% of the issued shares, must be held (by initial owners and BOD) for at least 2 years after IPO, before selling some or all their shares (EGX, 2021).[6]

13.4. Literature Review

A growing body of research examines IPO decisions, pricing, and allocation as well as aftermarket performance (Ritte & Welch, 2002).

[5]You can see the Listing agents on the EGX using this link, https://www.egx.com.eg/en/ListingAgents.aspx.

[6]The lockup period was 2 years and it was changed to 6 months in 2019.

However, a few studies examine causes and effects of the IPO structure — the portion of primary shares and secondary shares in the IPO. For example, Huyghebaert & Hulle (2006) investigated firm-specific determinants of Belgian IPOs and found that young, small, highly leveraged firms are more likely to issue primary shares while large firms tend to offer secondary shares in the IPO and also tend to turn over control after going public. Brau *et al.* (2007) found a weak relationship between selling secondary shares and negative aftermarket performance. However, the selling of secondary shares by officers and directors has a negative impact on the aftermarket performance in the long run.

There have been some studies that have examined the accuracy of different valuation models in pricing IPO shares. For example, Kim & Ritter (1999) found that the price-to-forecasted-earnings (P/E) ratio of peer companies provides more accurate value than other multiples. Bonaventura & Giudici (2017) applied a reverse engineering model to examine the valuation methods used to estimate offer prices using a sample of Italian IPOs. They documented a significant difference between the forecasted future profitability and post-IPO actual results. Moreover, the aftermarket performance does not show a significant increase in the return on invested capital and in the operating performance. Ong *et al.* (2020) used Malaysian IPO data to examine the signaling role of institutional ownership in the IPO valuation. They found that book-building IPOs with larger institutional ownership tend to be fairly priced. Recently, Ong *et al.* (2021) examined the accuracy of the price multiple method in valuation of Malaysian IPOs, and found that the price multiples of IPO firms are positively related to those of five peer companies in the industry.

Many studies examine the efficiency of price-setting mechanisms in producing more information about investor interest in the IPO. Crowin & Schultz (2005) reported that as the number of co-managers increases in the underwriting syndicate, the amount of new information which could uncover the investors' interest would increase. A more significant number of underwriters could significantly decrease underpricing level because there would be much information about the market demand from different sources. Chemmanur & Krishnan (2012) examined the relationship between underwriting reputation and IPO valuation. They found support for the market power hypothesis — highly reputable underwriters could attract institutional investors, analysts, and co-managing underwriters, and consequently the heterogeneity of their beliefs will result in higher IPO valuations which will differ significantly from the intrinsic value (as opposed to the certification hypothesis). Su (2018) tested the efficiency of book-building and fixed-price mechanisms (secondary market proportional offering, SMP[7]) in the Chinese stock market. Interestingly, he found that book-building results in higher underpricing and a higher variation of short-term returns. Moreover, SMP could be better in periods of high volatility and other adverse conditions.

Chemmanur & Liu (2019) investigated the ability of fixed price and auction to extract private information about a company's intrinsic value in the IPO. Their model shows that companies prefer the fixed-price mechanism to auction mechanism, although the auction results in lower underpricing. Zhou *et al.* (2020) measured the information quality of Chinese IPO Prospectuses and its effect on underpricing. They found that a high quality of information disclosure significantly decreases the asymmetric information between IPO firms and investors, resulting in less underpricing. Ong *et al.* (2021) argued that underwriters avoid the misvaluation issue by considering the book-building mechanism. Moreover, they contended that investment banks tend to underprice the IPO firm in comparison to its peers to encourage investors to subscribe to the issue. By examining Indonesia IPO data, Hanafi (2021) reported that a larger underpricing level and greater volatility are associated with using the book-building method as compared to fixed-price IPOs. He argued that the book-building method suffers from agency conflict, contributing to its lower efficiency. Lehmann & Weber (2022) compared book-building and auction methods using Japanese IPO data. They found that auction IPOs tend to have greater price accuracy and lower underpricing than book-building IPOs.

Geranio *et al.* (2022) found two contradictory results from investigating the effect of the ongoing relationship between underwriters and institutional investors on IPO pricing. Specifically, they found that stronger relationships result in lower price adjustment, higher

[7]SMP offering only allows the existing investors who are holding shares (of any listed firms) in the secondary market to subscribe to IPO shares. The amount of IPO shares available to be subscribed by the existing investors is proportional to the market value of shares held by them in the secondary market.

underpricing, and greater agency cost, but result in higher offer prices because of lower asymmetric information in the primary market. Eom & Kang (2022) used a knowledge-based view to examine the price discovery process in Korean book-building IPOs. They documented that the quality of information provided by institutional investors significantly affects the efficacy of IPO knowledge creation. Moreover, they found that the objective component and the subjective component of the IPO knowledge creation processes affect the pricing uncertainty and underpricing in the Korean market differently. Ling *et al.* (2022) tested the effect of geographical concentration of investor base on the first-day initial returns. They found that IPO firms tend to underprice their offerings if they have smaller investor bases, to ensure full subscription.

Some studies have examined the effect of market regulations on a price-setting mechanism, especially the book-building mechanism. Sahoo (2017) investigated the role of anchor investors in creating value for the Indian IPO firms through the book-building mechanism. He found that investment of the anchor investors in the IPOs decreases underpricing and volatility. Sonu (2022) used Korean IPO data to investigate the effect of imposing more restrictions on the discretion exercised by investment banks on using the book-building method. She found that the market price discovery process tends to improve as powers of IPO pricing and allocation of shares are in the hands of the underwriters.

Few studies have examined the IPO decision in the Egyptian market. For example, Autify (2012) attempted to identify the causes of the fluctuation in number of IPOs executed by privately held corporations over the period 1998–2008 in the EGX. He argued that private companies tend to go public to fund growth, especially if they were financially distressed. On the other hand, dependence on bank loans and the high cost of information production in the stock market significantly resulted in the weak IPO activity in Egypt. Similarly, Bolbol & Omran (2005) argued that listed Egyptian firms benefited from stock market activity in obtaining more debt financing, rather than equity financing to finance their real investments.[8] This was

[8]This financing behavior for funding investments contradicts the pecking order theory, which ranks sources of finance as retained earnings first, followed by debt financing, and finally equity financing.

because these firms might avoid dilution of control and ownership. The current study aims to identify the incentives of going public, and the IPO valuation and pricing mechanisms used by investment banks in the Egyptian market.

13.5. Data and Methodology

We use a sample of 19 IPO firms over the period of 2016–2022. We review Egyptian laws and executive regulations which are related to issuing new shares to identify the IPO process and the role of the investment bank and other parties. The main sources of data include the primary data in IPO prospectuses and other related issue releases as well as secondary data of closing prices of IPO shares on the first trading day from the Egyptian exchange. We review the IPO prospectuses to identify valuation approaches, pricing mechanisms, and allocation methods used by the IPO teams. Moreover, a descriptive analysis of the IPO structure and types of target investors is used to examine the incentives to go public, and the efficiency of IPO pricing mechanisms.

13.6. Analysis and Discussion

13.6.1. *Portions of primary and secondary shares in Egyptian IPOs*

Interestingly, all shares offered in the Egyptian IPOs over the period 2016–2022 are secondary sales of the existing shares and there were no primary (new) shares, indicating that some initial shareholders want to sell part of their ownership at a favorable price by selling their shares to stock market investors through the IPO (as shown in Table 13.1). This result is consistent with empirical evidence on preference of Egyptian firms for bank loans instead of going public (Autify, 2012; Bolbol & Omran, 2005).

13.6.2. *Structure of targeted types of investors*

The exit strategy incentive to go public is supported by analyzing the structure of target investors for whom the secondary shares are

Table 13.1. Structure of primary and secondary shares in Egyptian IPOs.

Company	Offering size (Secondary shares)	
	Shares (*m*)	% of capital
Macro Group Pharmaceuticals	265	46
eFinance for Digital and Financial	418	23.50
Emerald Development and Projects Management (EMDE)	45	10.59
Taaleem Management Services	358	49
Emerald Real Estate Investment	70	28
10th of Ramadan Company for Medical Industries (Rameda)	377	49
Fawry for Banking Technology and Electronic Payments	255	36
Sarwa Capital Holding	295	47
Cairo for Investment & Real Estate Development	207	38
CI Capital Holding for Financial	225	55
B Investments Holding	5	4.28
Al Tawfeek Leasing Company	19	24
Ibnsina Pharma	269	40
Dice Sport & Casual Wear	33	62
Raya Contact Center	49	49
MM Group for Industry & International Trade	119	30
Obour Land for Food Industries	80	40
Cleopatra Hospital Company	40	25
Arabian Food Industries DOMTY	123	49

Source: Developed by the author based on IPO prospectuses.

offered, as shown in Table 13.2. The institutional tranche percentage (on average, 34.5% of capital) significantly exceeds the retail tranche (on average, 4.6% of capital) in all recent Egyptian IPOs. We could suggest two justifications for this behavior. First, the investment banks seek to guarantee full subscription of the shares offered in the IPO, especially as institution participation dominates retail trading on the EGX. Second, IPO firms want to maintain control over the ownership and avoid diluting more shares through public offering. However, statistics of the coverage ratios in public offerings

Table 13.2. Retail & institutional tranches of Egyptian IPOs (2016–2022).

Company	Public offering tranche			Private offering tranche		
	Value (EGP) million)	% of capital	# Subscription (times)	Value (EGP million)	% of capital	# Subscription (times)
Macro Group Pharmaceuticals	13.2	2.3	102	251	43.5	1.79
eFinance for Digital and Financial	25.8	1.61	61.36	392	24.5	6.8
Emerald Development and Projects Management (EMDE)	15.8	3.7	26.34	29	6.88	1.9
Taaleem Management Services	102.87	2.45	29.3	1,954	46.55	2.34
Emerald Real Estate Investment	10	1.4	17.7	192.2	26.6	1.3
10th of Ramadan Company for Medical Industries (Rameda)	87.75	2.45	36	1,667	46.55	1.17
Fawry for Banking Technology and Electronic Payments	228.5	5	30	1,420	31	16
Sarwa Capital Holding	217.2	4.7	30	1,960	42.5	11
Cairo for Investment & Real Estate Development	87	2.65	19	1.16	35.19	10
CI Capital Holding for Financial	173.7	5.5	30	1.56	49.4	6
B Investments Holding	53.7	4.28	84			
Al Tawfeek Leasing Company	31.7	6	28	95	18	40
Ibnsina Pharma	234.4	6.01	18	1,330	34.07	17
Dice Sport & Casual Wear	112	9.35	6	635	52.99	3
Raya Contact Center	80.8	4.9	10	727.6	44.09	4
MM Group for Industry & International Trade	106.2	4.5	19	601.8	25.5	9
Obour Land for Food Industries	232.3	12	2	542.1	28	7
Cleopatra Hospital Company	54	3.75	29	306	21.25	7
Arabian Food Industries DOMTY	112.7	4.9	11	1,010	44.1	1

Source: Developed by the author based on individual IPO Infographics on EGX website.

are extremely high, indicating high investor interest in new firms entering the market through IPO, which provides weak support for the first justification. In line with this, Autify (2012) argued that Egyptian firms prefer bank loans to going public, resulting in low IPO activity. Moreover, Bolbol & Omran (2005) contended that the listed Egyptian firms benefited from stock market activity to obtain more debt financing rather than equity financing to support their real investments.

13.6.3. *IPO valuation and pricing mechanisms*

Intuitively, the IPO firm has no previous trading history on the stock market, so pricing its stock is a critical stage in the IPO process. Typically, setting the offering price either too high or too low would involve a potential cost to the issuer. According to CML95 conditions, the issuing company's management must assign a financial consultant, officially known as "independent financial advisor" (IFA), to prepare a stock fair value study (FVS) according to information, notes, and assumptions provided by the company's management. On January 18, 2017, the Egyptian Financial Regulatory Authority (FRA) issued the first Egyptian standards of Financial Valuation (ESFV) as a guide for financial advisors to estimate the fair value of a company used for different purposes (IPO, follow-on offerings, merger, acquisitions, etc.).[9]

The IFA has full responsibility for selecting valuation approaches to estimate the fair value of a company's stocks. Formally, the FVS must be approved by the FRA and the issuing company's general assembly. According to decree 114 established in 2018, the FRA prohibits the underwriter from preparing the FVS for the same client (company) to underwrite or promote its shares. The investment bank would use the FVS as a preliminary price range to assess market demand for the issue.[10] This price range must be disclosed in the prospectus (decree 48 established in 2019). As shown in Table 13.3,

---

[9]See *Egyptian standards for financial valuation of enterprises* using the following link: https://www.fra.gov.eg/content/efsa_ar/PDF/ma3ayer.htm.

[10]See the list of financial advisors licensed by the FRA at: http://www.fra.gov.eg/content/efsa_ar/pool_extra_efsa/mostasharenpdf.htm.

Table 13.3. Valuation methods and pricing mechanisms used in Egyptian IPOs.

Company	DFCF (%)	Multiples (%)	Initial Price	Final offering price	Pricing mechanism
Macro Group Pharmaceuticals	70	30	5.30–6.18	4.85	Book-building
eFinance for Digital and Financial	70	30	12.5–13.98	13.98	Book-building
Emerald Development and Projects Management (EMDE)	75	25	1.28	1.28	Fixed (strike) price
Taaleem Management Services	70	30	5.48-6.02	5.75	Book-building
Emerald Real Estate Investment	50	50	2.89	2.89	Fixed Price
10th of Ramadan Company for Medical Industries (Rameda)	50	50	4.66	4.66	Fixed Price
Fawry for Banking Technology and Electronic Payments	60	40	6.46	6.46	Book-building
Sarwa Capital Holding[11]		40	8.50	7.36	Book-building
Cairo for Investment & Real Estate Development	60	40	6.30	6	Book-building
CI Capital Holding for Financial	60	40	9.27	7.7	Book-building
B Investments Holding	60	40	10.75	10.75	Book-building
Al Tawfeek Leasing Company	60	40	6.93	6.6	Book-building
Ibnsina Pharma	70	30	6.66	5.8	Book-building
Dice Sport & Casual Wear	70	30	27.10	22.6	Book-building
Raya Contact Center	60	40	17.91	16.5	Book-building
MM Group for Industry & International Trade	75	25	6.06	5.96	Book-building
Obour Land for Food Industries	60	40	9.68	9.68	Book-building
Cleopatra Hospital Company	60	40	12.16	9	Book-building
Arabian Food Industries DOMTY	60	40	11.38	9.2	Book-building

Source: Prepared by the Author using the IPO prospectuses.

[11]Sarwa Capital Holding gives a weight of 60% to the residual income method to evaluate its share.

most independent advisors use the DFCF model and trading multiples (price-to-earnings ratio and enterprise value to earnings before interest, Taxes, depreciation, and amortization) to determine the stock fair value.

The most important task of the investment bank is to set the offer price accurately. To do so, it needs to collect information about investors' interest in the issue (the art of IPO pricing). Since market participants differ between retail and institutional investors, the investment bank may include in the syndicate other investment banks as co-managers with different client bases to acquire more information about the market demand for the IPO, which in turn results in a more accurate offer price. Most investment bankers use the book-building mechanism to examine investor interest in the issue and receive their buying orders to determine the final offering price, as shown in Table 13.3. Moreover, the investment banks revised the offer price downward[12] in 11 (out of 16) IPOs to align with the orders submitted by investors, and to avoid overpricing the shares.

13.6.3.1. *Executing offering through the OPR system on the Egyptian exchange*

The Egyptian stock exchange (EGX) developed an OPR system to execute IPOs. The brokerage firms would register individual investors' orders on OPR screens during the subscription period (as predetermined in the prospectus). The exhibit shows the procedures for offering and listing new shares on the EGX (Figure 13.2). The issuing company could sign a contract with one of the listing agents that the EGX licenses to provide technical, legal, and financial consultancy to execute the IPO or SPO on EGX's private deals market or OPR. Besides, they could help companies comply with listing and disclosure rules to avoid any financial penalties.[13]

[12]As new information arrives on the market, the investors adjust their bids, and investment banks revise the offer price accordingly.

[13]Find the listing agents licensed by the EGX at: https://www.egx.com.eg/en/listingagents.aspx.

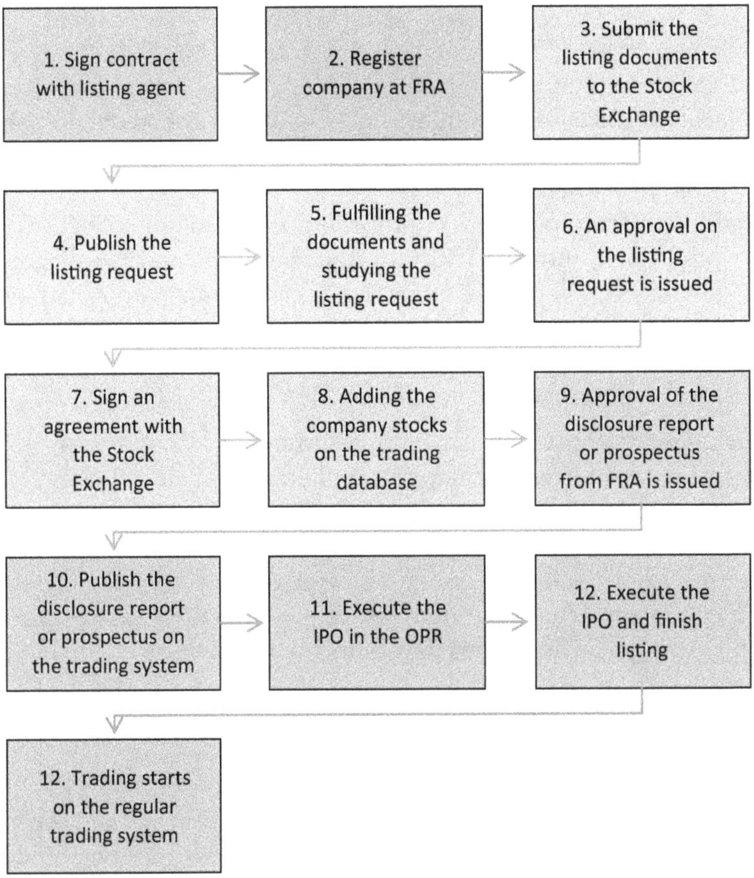

Figure 13.2. Steps to list on EGX.
Source: EGX (2021).

- Documents for Executing IPO through the OPR System (EGX, 2021):
  (a) A prospectus or public subscription note would be published after listing shares, but before executing the offering. The soundness of information included in the prospectus or note is the responsibility of the legal advisor, auditor, and financial advisor. Notably, a summary of this prospectus must be published in daily newspapers.

(b) A fair value study is conducted by the independent financial advisor (including the IFA's report, introduction, executive summary, company profile, market overview, study's assumptions for valuation, five-year projected financial statements, etc.). The soundness of this content is the responsibility of the IFA.
(c) The offering plan (including the purpose of the offering, time plan to execute the IPO through the OPR, and the ownership structure before and after the offering) must be documented by the company's legal advisor.
(d) Any additional disclosures may be included in the prospectus as per the requirements of the FRA or the EGX.

- The underwriter (Offering Manager) would send a statement to the Egyptian exchange for the private offering tranche, specifying the names and number of shares that should be distributed to each institutional investor or net worth investor.
- For secondary offering shares (Shares offered by existing shareholders in the IPO), the delivery of shares will be made through the clearing and settlement systems of the EGX.[14]

13.6.4. *Aftermarket (Post-IPO) performance and stabilization mechanism*

If the IPO shares are priced higher than their fair value (overpricing), the issuing firm may fail to sell the targeted number of shares and resort to withdrawing the issue. Conversely, if the offering is priced lower than its fair value (underpricing), the issuing firm's initial shareholders might think that they left money on the table for the new shareholders because the stock is traded at a higher price than offered. Thus, the issuing firm treats underpricing as an indirect cost of the IPO. Most IPOs in different capital markets experience underpricing, and so underpricing has become a phenomenon in the

[14]The broker will receive the buy or sell order and will then confirm with the custodian or settlement bank that the subject shares or funds required to complete the transaction are available. The broker will execute the deal at the exchange which in turn will notify the MCDR of the transaction. The MCDR will thereafter notify the broker and the custodian of the transaction and settlement will occur on a $T + 2$ basis.

IPO process. The investment bank and/or the issuer may want to underprice the issue — setting the offering share price lower than its fair value — to reduce the underwriting risk, increase investors' interest, and avoid damaging the investment bank's reputation. On the other hand, it is assumed that selecting a prestigious underwriter could reduce the uncertainty associated with the quality of the issuing company, thereby decreasing the underpricing. Aftermarket refers to the period starting with trading on the stock exchange (secondary market). Table 13.4 presents price performance on the first trading day on the Egyptian exchange for the Egyptian IPOs over the period of concern. Most IPOs experience positive change — close price exceeds the offering price, confirming the presence of the underpricing phenomenon and reflecting a greater interest in new offerings in the Egyptian IPO market.

Since the issuing firm wants to avoid the temporary drop in its share market price, it usually agrees with the investment bank to stabilize or support the price of the newly issued shares to keep them from selling below the offer price in the stock exchange for a relatively short time, e.g., 30 days. In this regard, the FRA's BOD decree # 48, established in 2019, regulates the offering manager's aftermarket stabilization mechanism that can be summarized as follows[15]:

- *The stabilization period* is 30 days after the commencement date of trading shares on the EGX.[16]
- The offering manager creates a *stabilization account* (fund) as an independent bank account in the offering manager's name to support the stock exchange's share price.
- The initial shareholders who sell their shares in the IPO must deposit the gross IPO proceeds in the *stabilization account* at least one working day before trading.
- The offering manager must submit a buy order for shares at the offering price and keep it open until the end of the stabilization period.

[15]Notably, there is no stabilization for private offering (institutional offering).

[16]Before the end date of the stabilization period by at least three working days, the offering manager must announce on the EGX screen to notify investors who want to submit sell orders to the stabilization account.

Table 13.4. Price performance of Egyptian IPOs on 1st trading day (2016–2022).

Company	1st trading day	Offering price	Close price	Change (%)
Macro Group Pharmaceuticals	10-February-2022	4.85	4.51	−7
eFinance for Digital and Financial	20-October-2021	13.98	21	50.2
Emerald Development and Projects Management (EMDE)	18-October-2021	1.28	1.58	23.4
Taaleem Management Services	7-April-2021	5.75	6.1	6.1
Emerald Real Estate Investment	26-February-2020	2.89	2.99	3.5
10th of Ramadan Company for Medical Industries (Rameda)	11-December-2019	4.66	4.44	−4.7
Fawry for Banking Technology and Electronic Payments	8-August-2019	6.46	8.48	31.3
Sarwa Capital Holding	15-October-2018	7.36	6.54	−11.1
Cairo for Investment & Real Estate Development	1-October-2018	6	7	16.7
CI Capital Holding for Financial Investments	30-April-2018	7.7	9.16	19
B Investments Holding	29-March-2018	10.75	11.82	10
Al Tawfeek Leasing Company	28-December-2017	6.6	8.13	23.2
Ibnsina Pharma	12-December-2017	5.8	6.7	15.5
Dice Sport & Casual Wear	14-November-2017	22.6	23.6	4.4
Raya Contact Center	27-April-2017	16.5	16.64	0.8
MM Group for Industry & International Trade	11-April-2017	5.96	6.45	8.2
Obour Land for Food Industries	15-December-2016	9.68	9.8	1.2
Cleopatra Hospital Company	2-June-2016	9	9.62	6.9
Arabian Food Industries DOMTY	22-March-2016	9.2	10.17	10.5

Source: Prepared by the author depending on final offering price and close prices on 1st trading dates.

- When the trading share price falls below the offering price, the new shareholders (purchasers) could submit sell orders (for their allocated shares in the offering) to the stabilization account.
- At the end of the stabilization period, the offering manager's open buy order would match investors' sell orders and be executed on the EGX.[17]
- Within five working days following the end of the stabilization period, the stabilization account will be liquidated. The purchased shares using the stabilization account or remaining funds would be returned to the initial selling shareholders proportional to their stabilization account contribution.

13.7. Conclusion

This chapter uses both primary data (prospectuses) and secondary data (stock prices) of the Egyptian firms that implemented their IPOs during the period from 2016–2022 to identify their incentive to go public, their valuation methods, the pricing mechanisms used to set the offering price, as well as aftermarket performance and stabilization mechanism with respect to Egyptian laws and regulations. The IPO structure (types of shares offered) for all firms (2016–2022) includes only secondary shares, indicating that all firms sought to go public not to raise capital, but to sell a portion of their ownership at favorable prices. This observation is supported by the greater percentages of IPO shares that are offered to institutional investors through private offering in comparison to very low percentages for retail investors, implying the desire to maintain control over the company and avoid diluting the ownership.

We reviewed 19 prospectuses and observed common valuation practices of the financial advisors and noted that they apply the discounted free cash model and relative valuation at different weights to identify the stock fair value. Thereafter, the investment banks announce the estimated fair value or a price range to investors who in turn submit their bids with quantity of shares at the desired prices. Most investment banks use the book-building mechanism to assess

[17]The offering manager should disclose all stabilization transactions to the EGX at the end of stabilization period.

investors' interest in the IPO, and adjust (upward or downward) the offering price according to the book of orders. In this regard, IPO data reveal that most offering prices are adjusted downward to avoid overpricing the issue. Moreover, by listing IPO shares on the Egyptian exchange and trading them, most IPO shares experience high demand and close at higher prices on the first trading day, indicating the presence of an underpricing phenomenon in the Egyptian IPO market. The implications of the current study can be extended in further research by examining market timing of IPOs and by conducting interviews with investment banks to identify how they could assess the investors' interest in the issue.

References

Autify, M. M. (2012). *Determinants of Initial Public Offering of Stocks, Case of Egypt (1998–2008).* MSc Thesis, Cairo.

Bancel, F. & Mittoo, U. R. (2009). Why do European firms go public? *European Financial Management, 15*(4), 844–884.

Bolbol, A. A. & Omran, M. M. (2005). Investment and the stock market: Evidence from Arab firm-level panel data. *Emerging Markets Review, 6*, 85–106.

Bonaventura, M. & Giudici, G. (2017). IPO valuation and profitability expectations: Evidence from the Italian exchange. *Eurasian Business Review, 7*, 247–266.

Brau, J. C., Li, M., & Shi, J. (2007). Do secondary shares in the IPO process have a negative effect on aftermarket performance? *Journal of Banking & Finance, 31*, 2612–2631.

CASE (2005). *CASE Yearbook.* Cairo & Alexandria Stock Exchanges.

CASE (2007). *Annual Report.* Cairo: Cairo & Alexandria Stock Exchanges.

Chemmanur, T. J. & Krishnan, K. (2012). Heterogeneous beliefs, IPO valuation, and the economic role of the underwriter in IPOs. *Financial Management, 8*, 769–811.

Chemmanur, T. J. & Liu, M. H. (2019). How should a firm go public? A dynamic model of the choice between fixed-price offerings and auctions in IPOs and privatizations. *Review of Corporate Finance Studies, 1*(1), 42–96.

Crowin, S. A. & Schultz, P. (2005). The role of IPO underwriting syndicates: Pricing, information production, and underwriter competition. *The Journal of Finance, LX*(1), 443–486.

Draho, J. (2004). *The IPO Decision: Why and How Companies Go Public.* Cheltenham: Edward Elgar.

EGX *Annual Report*. Cairo: The Egyptian Exchange (Multiple issues).

EGX (2021). How to List. Retrieved from the Egyptian Exchange. https://www.egx.com.eg/getdoc/fb763f14-82e6-4f73-8677-79c42a16a277/SMEs-Listing-Guide.aspx.

EGX (2021, March). The Egyptian Exchange. Retrieved from How to List. https://www.egx.com.eg/getdoc/ca02bf68-0b00-498f-a480-6ecca227360c/EGX-lisitng-booklet-October-2020.aspx.

Eom C., & Kang, H.-G. (2022). How does knowledge affect IPO pricing? A new approach grounded in the knowledge-based view. *Journal of Knowledge Management*, *26*(7), 1849–1867.

Geranio, M., Mazzoli, C., & Palmucci, F. (2022). Is money really left on the table? The role of regular investors in IPO pricing. *European Financial Management*, *22*, 651–692.

Hanafi, M. M. (2021). Fixed price and book building methods in an exogenous environment: Evidence from Indonesia stock market. *Research in International Business and Finance*, *58*, 101430.

Huyghebaert, N. & Hulle, C. V. (2006). Structuring the IPO: Empirical evidence on the portions of primary and secondary shares. *Journal of Corporate Finance*, *12*, 296–320.

Iannotta, G. (2010). *Investment Banking: A Guide to Underwriting and Advisory Services*. London: Springer-Verlag Berlin Heidelberg.

Kim, M. & Ritter, J. R. (1999). Valuing IPOs. *Journal of Financial Economics*, *53*, 409–437.

Klein, D. & Li, M. (2009). Factors affecting secondary share offerings in the IPO process. *The Quarterly Review of Economics and Finance*, *49*, 1194–1212.

Kucukkocaoglu, G. & Alp, O. S. (2012). IPO mechanism selection by using classification and regression trees. *Quality & Quantity*, *46*, 873–888.

Lehmann, T. & Weber, M. (2022). Auctions versus bookbuilding: The effects of IPO regulation in Japan. *The Financial Review*, *58*, 1–25.

Ling, D. C., Marcato, G., & Zheng, C. (2022). Does asset location and concentration explain REIT IPO valuation? *Real Estate Economics*, *50*, 672–706.

Ong, C. Z., Mohd-Rashid, R., & Taufil-Mohd, K. N. (2020). Do institutional investors drive the IPO valuation? *Borsa Istanbul Review*, *20*(4), 307–321.

Ong, C. Z., Mohd-Rashid, R., & Taufil-Mohd, K. N. (2021). IPO valuation using the price-multiple methods: Evidence from Malaysia. *Journal of Financial Reporting and Accounting*, *19*(4), 540–570.

Pagano, M., Panetta, F., & Zingales, L. (1998). Why do companies go public? An empirical analysis. *The Journal of Finance*, *LIII*(1), 27–64.

Ritte, J. R. & Welch, I. (2002). A review of IPO activity, pricing, and allocations. *The Journal of Finance*, *LVII*(4), 1795–1828.

Ross, S., Westerfield, R., & Jordan, B. (2020). *Essentials of Corporate Finance* (10th edn.). New York: McGraw-Hill Education.

Sahoo, S. (2017). Do anchor investors create value for initial public offerings? An empirical investigation. *IIMB Management Review*, *29*, 259–275.

Sherman, A. E. (2005). Global trends in IPO methods: Book building versus auctions with endogenous entry. *Journal of Financial Economics*, *78*, 615–649.

Sonu, C. H. (2022). Information quality and IPO underpricing: The role of underwriter pricing and allocation powers. *Pacific-Basin Finance Journal*, *75*, 101853–101889.

Su, C. (2018). The efficiency of IPO issuing mechanisms and market conditions: Evidence in China. *Review of Quantitative Finance and Accounting*, *51*, 461–495.

Subrahmanyam, A. & Titman, S. (1999). The going-public decision and the development of financial markets. *The Journal of Finance*, *LIV*(3), 1045–1082.

Zhou, K., Zhou, B., & Liu, H. (2020). IPO underpricing and information quality of prospectuses. *The Singapore Economic Review*, *65*(3), 1–19.

https://doi.org/10.1142/9781800614734_0014

Chapter 14

Exploring the Financial Development and Economic Complexity Nexus in MENA Countries: Does Corruption Matter?

Mondjeli Mwa Ndjokou Itchoko Motande, Valentine Soumtang Bime and Koumis Ngagni Agathe Cassandra

Abstract

This chapter aims to assess the effect of corruption on the relationship between financial development and economic complexity in MENA. To this end, we estimate a panel data model on 21 MENA countries between 1995 and 2020 using the double least squares method. Overall, the analysis shows significant heterogeneous results conditional on corruption. Specifically, corruption worsens the effect of financial access, and the depth and efficiency of economic complexity over the sample period. In contrast, it improves the effect of financial stability on economic complexity in the region. The results appear to be robust to an alternative estimation technique.

Keywords: Economic complexity, financial development, corruption

14.1. Introduction

The issue of economic complexity has been the focus of scientific and policy attention in recent decades because it provides an important model for understanding the key societal questions and challenges of our time (Balland *et al.*, 2022). This interest has led to a large body of literature on the levers that policymakers should use to improve the level of knowledge and technological progress in the productive structure of an economy (Romero & Gramkow, 2021; Hidalgo & Hausmann, 2009).

One strand of this literature has focused on the role of financial development, leading to controversial results (Haraguchi *et al.*, 2019; Nguyen & Su, 2021). For example, the effects of financial development as a driver of economic complexity have been documented in several studies, including Haraguchi *et al.* (2019), Nguyen & Su (2021), and Rajan & Zingales (2001). Conversely, studies such as Ewetan & Ike (2014) and Larrain (2006) show that greater financial development leads to reduced economic complexity, consistent with the Woo (1986) hypothesis. Moreover, a nonlinear U-shaped relationship has also been found (Kothakapa *et al.*, 2021). While this work has highlighted the lack of consensus around the effect of financial development on economic complexity, the reasons for this controversy, through the mediating factors, remain underexplored.

Therefore, the objective of this study is to fill this gap by assessing how corruption can affect the relationship between financial development and economic complexity. Following the work of Aram & Beji (2016), we postulate that corruption in an economy can alter the beneficial effects of financial development on economic complexity. Such an assertion can be justified because an efficient financial sector promotes entrepreneurship and encourages new players in the sector (Sharma & Paramati, 2020). This increases competition in the market. It is known that corruption is lower in countries where firms face more competition (Sharma & Paramati, 2020). By reducing their level of corruption in this way, we note that these countries will be able to increase the complexity of their export baskets. This is because good institutions, which translate into secure competitive markets, affect the relative returns to different productive economic activities. Therefore, the quality of institutions, especially the control of corruption, fundamentally determines the investments and innovative activities (Vu, 2020).

Thus, this article contributes to the economics literature on two levels. First, it highlights the heterogeneous nature of the effects of financial development on economic complexity in the specific case of the MENA region, which can be explained by institutional quality, including corruption. Indeed, it has been shown that this variable is likely to affect economic development, of which economic complexity is a part (Chong & Calderon, 2000), and also influence financial development (Pagano & Volpin, 2005; Wiliamson, 1975). The advantage is to see which variable is most relevant to the institutional environment of MENA economies and therefore to formulate appropriate economic policies.

Second, unlike previous work, this study emphasizes the importance of financial development as a lever of economic complexity by using a multidimensional approach to measure financial development in terms of depth, access, stability, and efficiency financial.[1] The advantage is to see which variable is most relevant in MENA and therefore to formulate the most appropriate economic policies. To the best of our knowledge, this is the first study that highlights the effect of corruption in the relationship between financial development and economic complexity using a dimensional analysis in the MENA region, where the situation is more problematic and the problem is more accentuated by corruption.

Indeed, the factual analysis[2] shows that the level of economic complexity in MENA is low. In fact, it was around −1.14 according to *Atlas of economic complexity* during the 1995–2020 period. Moreover, data show that with regard to corruption, financial development, and economic complexity in MENA, there can be three types of situations in general. We can have countries such as Libya with a low level of financial development (16.63) and a high level of corruption (−1.60) but a low level of economic complexity (−0.78). Next to this, we also have countries with a high level of financial development (96.27), a high level of corruption (−0.27), and still a low level of economic complexity (−0.33) such as Morocco. Finally, we have countries like Jordan that have a high level of financial development (83.14), with rather a low level of corruption and a high level of economic complexity.

The remainder of the article is organized as follows: Section 14.2 discusses the literature review, Section 14.3 describes the methodology,

[1]We distinguish between the dimensions of accessibility (which reflects the ability of individuals and firms to access financial services), efficiency (which captures the ability of institutions to provide good-quality, low-cost financial services), and depth (which represents the size and liquidity of financial markets), as distinguished by Svirydzenka (2016), and stability (which is the resilience of banks to economic shocks).

[2]Based on the Economic Complexity Atlas (2020) database for economic complexity, ICRG (2020) for corruption, and the Global Financial Development Index (2021) for financial development.

Section 14.4 discusses the results, Section 14.5 describes the effects of corruption, Section 14.6 takes account of a concurrent estimation technique, and Section 14.7 presents the conclusion.

14.2. Literature Review

14.2.1. *Theoretical anchoring*

The basic relationship between financial development and economic complexity has been the subject of theoretical controversy. Indeed, Mckinnon (1973) and Shaw (1973) have shown that finance through financial development has an effect on development in general. In fact, financial development makes more financing available to economic agents to engage in productive activities in order to increase the complexity of their economies. Bencivenga and Smith's (1991) study has highlighted how the creation and growth of financial institutions lead to a positive effect on growth. Indeed, financial intermediaries play a central role in allocating capital to its best possible use. The work of Guiso *et al.* (2004) supports this by finding that the level of financial development of a country impacts its ability to grow.

However, the work of Woo (1986) challenges the opinion of Mckinnon (1973) and Shaw (1973) by demonstrating that two patterns are possible in this relationship through the notions of financial development and economic growth in particular. On the one hand, they find that economic growth induces the expansion of the financial system. This is called "demand leading". The absence of financial growth is a manifestation of the absence of demand for financial services. On the other hand, the expansion of the financial system precedes the demand for services. By channeling scarce income sources from savers to investments at relative rates of return, the financial sector precedes and induces real growth. This pattern is called "supply leading".

14.2.2. *Financial development and economic complexity: A review of the literature*

Empirical analysis of the effect of corruption on the relationship between financial development and economic complexity is done in this study in a sequential manner, that is, first, to show the relationship between financial development and economic complexity and, second, to show the limits of this relationship and the interaction with corruption.

The relationship between financial development and economic complexity yielded several results depending on the region studied, the estimation technique, and the variables used. First, we observe a positive link. In particular, we start from work by Nguyen & Su (2021) who find a positive link between financial development and economic complexity, using a panel of institutional indicators (financial institutions and financial markets). They add that financial institutions have a stronger effect than financial markets. Next, Nguyen *et al.* (2020) conduct an analysis of 52 economies, 32 high income and 20 middle income. The authors find that the effect of development on economic complexity is positive in the short run for financing reasons. However, in the long run, it has a negative effect due to an overly large financial sector that does not necessarily promote sophistication of operations and business production. Also, Nieminen (2020) shows in his work that financial development influences export performance because exporters need external financing and face credit constraints. He conducts a firm-level analysis of over 60 countries and confirms that access to domestic financial services contributes positively to export diversification.

Chu's (2019) study examines the effect of financial development on economic sophistication using a panel of 94 high- and middle-income countries between 1968 and 2015 with the GMM method, and finds that financial development through banking sector and stock market development has a positive effect on economic sophistication. Also, the effect of financial development through domestic credit on export diversification was studied by Fosu & Abass (2019). The authors work over the period 1962–2010 with 80 countries, 62 of which are developing countries and 29 African countries. Using GMMs, they show the importance of domestic credit for African countries while its role is marginal in developing countries. Other authors have focused on this relationship, but specifically in Nigeria (Adeola & Evans, 2017). Indeed, they conduct an analysis between 1981 and 2014 with the fully modified least squares (FMOLS) method and conclude that financial development has a positive effect on economic diversification. However, this effect is not significant.

Second, the negative effect of financial development on economic sophistication has also been raised by work such as Moore & Mirzaei (2016), with UNIDO industry-level data for a panel of 82 countries finding that the crisis has led to a decline in the production of sophisticated products. However, the effect is more pronounced for industries that are traditionally dependent on external financing services. Also, Ewetan & Ike (2014) show that financial development through the ratio of money supply to GDP has a negative effect on sophisticated products. They conduct an analysis from 1981 to 2011 with time series data with a multivariate VAR model and a vector error correction model.

Finally, we also note an "inverted U" relationship with the work of Kathakapa *et al.* (2021). They use the system-based GMM estimation method for the period 1970–2014 with a dynamic panel model to analyze the relationship between financial development and industrialization (which is the lower stage to economic complexity) in the context of low- and high-income countries. The authors show that financial development has a negative effect on industrialization up to a certain point.

Looking for the causes of such contradictions and in the light of past empirical work, the divergence of results can be explained by the measure of financial development used. Indeed, we note that some authors used domestic credit (Nieminen, 2020) and others even the money supply ratio (Ewetan & Ike, 2014). Moreover, this controversy can also be explained by the consideration of the institutional aspect, especially corruption. Indeed, corruption through the fact that it can facilitate the obtaining of credit by individuals will encourage private sector agents to benefit from credits and the latter will use these credits to improve their complex activities, which are very profitable (Altunbaş & Thornton, 2012; Vu, 2022).

14.3. Methodology

This section identifies the model used, the different variables chosen, and the estimation technique used in this study.

14.3.1. *Model specification*

In order to examine the effect of corruption on the relationship between financial development and economic complexity, our model is specified as follows:

$$\begin{aligned}\mathrm{ECI}_{it} &= \beta_0 + \beta_1\mathrm{FD}_{it} + \beta_2\mathrm{Corrupt}_{it}\\ &\quad + \beta_3\mathrm{DF}_{it}\#\mathrm{Corrupt}_{it} + Z_{it} + \mu_i + \delta_t + \varepsilon_{it}, \qquad (14.1)\end{aligned}$$

with i and t being the country and the year, respectively; μ and δ are the country fixed effects and the year fixed effects, respectively; β is the coefficient; ε is the error term; ECI is the economic complexity; Z is the vector of control variables; FD is the financial development; *Corrupt* is the level of corruption; and $\mathrm{FD}_{it}\#\mathrm{Corrupt}_{it}$ represents the combined effect of financial development and corruption.

This study is conducted for the period 1995–2020 for 21 MENA countries. The different data for this work are taken from WDI (2020), ICRG (2020), Altas of economic complexity (2020), and Global financial development index (2020).

14.3.2. *Variables*

14.3.2.1. *Measuring economic complexity*

We measure economic complexity using Hidalgo & Hausmann's (2009) Economic Complexity Index (ECI). The idea is that an economy that is complex in terms of the products it produces and exports is an economy that has a developed secondary sector (Gala *et al.*, 2018; Pugliese *et al.*, 2014). Also, the economic complexity atlas notes that manufactured goods are clearly characterized as more complex goods (Gala *et al.*, 2018). Economic complexity is an indicator that measures both the sophistication of an economy and its productive structure. According to the authors (Hidalgo *et al.*, 2007), economies grow by improving the products they produce and export. Growth is measured by economic diversity and ubiquity.

Economic diversity refers to the number of products produced by a country. Note that the productivity of a country lies in the diversity of its available non-tradable "capabilities" (Hidalgo & Hausmann, 2009). The ubiquity of a product here represents the number of countries that export that product (Hidalgo & Hausmann, 2009). Products that are exported by few economies (i.e., products with low ubiquity) seem to have more difficulties in gathering the necessary capacities.

Let's define a matrix called M_{ab} and postulate that an element of this matrix equals 1 if country a exports product b with a revealed comparative advantage (RCA > 1) and 0 otherwise. Then, diversity and ubiquity can be computed by adding the rows and columns of the matrix together:

$$\text{Diversity} = k_{a,o} = \sum_{b} M_{ab}. \tag{14.2}$$

$$\text{Ubiquity} = k_{b,o} = \sum_{a} M_{ab}. \tag{14.3}$$

By generalizing, this allows us to measure economic complexity as follows:

$$\text{ECI} = \frac{k^{-} - avg(k^{-})}{\sigma(k^{-})}. \tag{14.4}$$

14.3.2.2. *Measuring financial development*

We want to use a good indicator of financial development to capture its effect on economic complexity. However, this is a difficult task as the literature raises a number of indicators that capture the level of financial development.[3] It should be noted here that financial development is a multidimensional concept (Svirydzenka, 2016; De Haan & Sturm, 2017). To this end, and according to the International Monetary Fund database, we distinguish the dimension of financial accessibility (FAI) which reflects the ability of individuals and firms to access financial services. We also use financial efficiency (FEI) which captures the ability of institutions to provide good-quality and low-cost financial services and financial depth (FDI)

[3]Bittencourt *et al.* (2019) use the ratio of nominal stock market wealth per capita to nominal personal income per capita as a variable. Also, other studies, including those by which Jauch and Watzka (2016), De Haan and Sturm (2017), have used variables such as M2/GDP, liquid liabilities, and credits among others.

(which represents the size and liquidity of financial markets) as distinguished by Svirydzenka (2016). To this, we add the stability dimension (which is the resilience of banks to economic shocks), which is not taken into account by this author.[4]

Also, our work relies on only banking or institutional sector data. This choice is justified by the argument that, for authors such as Zhang & Naceur (2019), the development of the banking system is more important for developing countries than the stock market system. Also, the International Monetary Fund (2019) finds that the banking system provides better risk sharing than the stock markets.

14.3.2.3. *Measuring corruption*

The consideration of corruption in the relationship between financial development and economic complexity is important because the institutional environment is fundamental to achieving a given level of economic complexity. Indeed, according to the work of Aram & Beji (2016), the effect of financial development on economic complexity could be influenced by the institutional environment. In line with the work of Mijiyawa (2017), the inclusion of institutional variables in the model is therefore crucial, especially with regard to corruption. To this end, the authors show that institutions with corruption at a high level in a country are likely to encourage several market failures (Kocenda & Poghosyan, 2018; Pellegrini, 2011), and government actions in order to resolve them will be less successful. This study uses political corruption as a variable of corruption.

14.3.2.4. *Control variables*

This model takes into account several control variables including natural resources, economic growth, trade openness, and population. Natural resources are measured by the benefits derived from natural resources relative to GDP (Camargo & Gala, 2017). Note that an economy that specializes in the primary sector is more volatile and

[4]Note that in the paper, the different dimensions of financial development refer to FAI, FDI, FEI, and BankZscore.

vulnerable to shocks. According to the literature, natural resources have an inverse relationship with economic complexity.

Another control variable used in our model is economic growth measured by the growth rate of GDP per capita (Albeaik *et al.*, 2017). It is often used to assess development levels across countries (Rodrik, 2013). The expected effect according to the literature is the positive sign. The literature also identifies trade openness as an important variable (Baltagi *et al.*, 2009). It is measured by the sum of exports and imports of goods and services relative to GDP. The more an economy trades with the outside world, the more complex it becomes. The expected sign here is positive according to the literature.

Population is also an important variable in that it captures the size of the domestic market. It is measured by the growth rate of the total population (Hidalgo & Hausmann, 2009). The expected sign here is positive. FDI also seems relevant as an explanatory factor for structural transformation. Indeed, FDI can affect structural transformation in the sense that it allows the creation of new productive capacities that contribute to a large diversification (Hausmann & Rodrik, 2003). The expected sign is positive.

14.3.3. *Estimation technique*

In order to achieve the abovementioned objective, this chapter uses the double least squares (IV-2SLS) method of Basmann (1957) and Theil & Nagar (1961). This choice is justified because it allows us to correct the endogenous bias inherent in panel data. Indeed, although the study focuses upstream on the effect of financial development on economic complexity, reverse causality is possible (Khan *et al.*, 2020). In addition, some control variables clearly identify financial development and economic complexity. For example, there is a relationship between financial development and growth on the one hand (Ibrahim & Alagidede, 2018) and between growth and the complexity index on the other hand (Ahmed *et al.*, 2022; Zhu *et al.*, 2017). It is then necessary to use instrumental variable techniques to correct for this bias.

This method consists in assigning at least one instrumental variable to each variable suspected of suffering from endogeneity bias. The instrumental variable is a variable that is correlated with the source variable of endogeneity, but which is not correlated with the error term or the dependent variable. In the case of double least squares, in addition to the instrumental variables that are exogenous to the model, it is also possible to use the lagged variables of the endogenous variables as instruments, since these are assumed to be endogenous reference variables as instruments, since they are assumed to be uncorrelated with the residuals.

14.4. Results

This section presents first the descriptive statistics, second the scatterplot analysis, and third the results of the effect of financial development on economic complexity and those of the interaction with corruption in this relationship.

14.4.1. *Descriptive statistics*

According to the descriptive statistics, we note that the economic complexity variable varies from −2.77 to 0.69 for an average of 0.49 in the MENA countries. As for the financial development variables, the table of descriptive statistics shows that these variables generally vary around 0 and 0.88, for a maximum average of 23.03. For the different control variables, population is the variable with the highest number of observations with a maximum level of 17.7 and a minimum of −4.53. As for education, it varies between 23.36 and 128.46. Corruption varies very little (−1.86 and 1.56) with an average of −0.41. Economic growth is a variable that varies quite widely (from −62.07 to 123.13) with a mean of 3.36 and a standard deviation of 8.45. Trade openness and natural resources have respective averages of 83.62 and 16.61. They vary between 0.78 and 347.99 for trade openness and between 0.001 and 67.91 for natural resources (see Table 14A).

Also, for the following scatter plots analysis on economic complexity, financial development, and corruption (see Figure 14.1), the graphs show us that the different dimensions of financial development affect the economic complexity index differently according to the different levels of corruption in MENA region. The analysis of dispersions does not allow us to conclude a priori how corruption may affects the effect of financial development on the economic

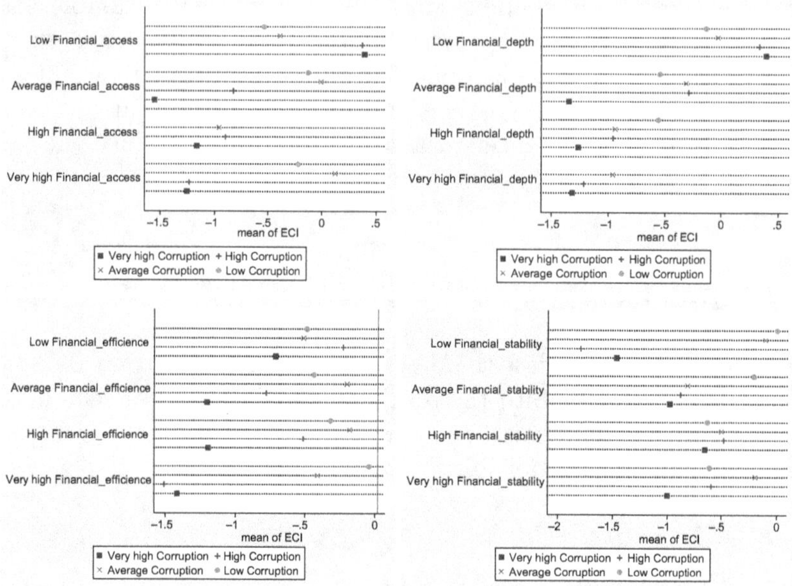

Figure 14.1. Financial development and complexity economic in MENA by level of corruption.

complexity index. The mixed analysis of these scatters then legitimizes the econometric analysis.

14.4.2. *Effect of financial development on economic complexity in MENA*

Table 14.1 highlights the relationship between the dimensions of financial development and economic complexity in MENA countries using the double least squares method. We present the results on the effect of financial development on the one hand and the effect of control variables on the other. The columns from 1 to 4 represent the effect of depth, efficiency, stability, and financial access on economic complexity, respectively.

14.4.3. *Effect of financial development*

The analysis in Table 14.1 generally leads to two effects. First, we observe that access and financial depth improve the level of economic

Table 14.1. Effect of financial development on the economic complexity index in MENA.

	(1)	(2)	(3)	(4)
	ECI	ECI	ECI	ECI
Population	0.020**	0.025***	0.012	0.010
	(0.010)	(0.009)	(0.009)	(0.009)
Economic growth	−0.006	−0.005	0.004	−0.006
	(0.005)	(0.005)	(0.006)	(0.005)
Trade openness	−0.000	0.006***	0.005***	0.005***
	(0.001)	(0.001)	(0.001)	(0.001)
Natural resources	−0.011***	−0.022***	−0.019***	−0.023***
	(0.003)	(0.002)	(0.003)	(0.003)
Foreign direct investments	−0.001	−0.006	−0.008	−0.004
	(0.009)	(0.012)	(0.012)	(0.009)
Financial depth index	3.194***			
	(0.528)			
Financial efficiency index		−0.783**		
		(0.307)		
BankZscore			0.000	
			(0.002)	
Financial access index				1.454***
				(0.232)
Constant	−0.776***	−0.095	−0.518***	−0.840***
	(0.090)	(0.252)	(0.112)	(0.097)
Obs.	**225**	**225**	**263**	**225**
R-squared	**0.470**	**0.388**	**0.263**	**0.461**
Hansen	**0.549**	**0.761**	**0.619**	**0.282**

Notes: Values in parentheses are standard deviations corrected for heteroskedasticity. $^{**}p < 0.05$ and $^{***}p < 0.01$ represent the significance levels of the different coefficients at 5% and 1%, respectively.

complexity in MENA countries. Specifically, when access to financial services and financial depth increase by 1%, economic complexity increases by 1.454% and 3.194%, respectively. These results are significant at the 1% level and can lead to two conclusions.

One, the coefficient on financial access implies that financial inclusion significantly boosts economic complexity in the region. This result can be explained by the fact that when agents have access to financial services, it allows them to have the financing to acquire equipment to produce products that other countries do not have. Two, the coefficient on financial depth also tells us that financial depth increases economic complexity. The fact that the banking system in MENA countries has a high level of development provides agents with several tools to facilitate credit.

Second, the regressions show that financial efficiency rather has a negative effect on economic complexity in MENA countries. Indeed, when financial efficiency increases by 1%, economic complexity decreases by 0.783%. This result may reflect the fact that banks are less efficient in this region, which discourages economic complexity. This can be explained by the fact that banks cannot grant the minimum amount of credit to their clients and, therefore, they cannot obtain the technologies to make their products more complex.

14.4.4. *Effect of control variables*

Consistent with the effect of the control variables, the analyses show that population and trade openness have a positive effect on economic complexity and natural resources have a negative effect.

With respect to population and trade openness, Table 14.1 shows that they increase economic complexity by 0.020% and 0.025% in models (1) and (2), respectively, and by 0.006, 0.005, and 0.005% in models (2), (3), and (4), respectively. As for the population, this result can be explained in the sense that in MENA economies, the increase in population allows one to really educate this population. Thus, it will direct people's knowledge to the sectors that allow them to make their economies more complex. Being educated enough for these sectors, the population will turn to knowledge-intensive activities such as industry and innovation, activities that lead to economic complexity.

This result is contrary to the work of Lapatinas (2019). With respect to trade openness, we note that the more commercially open a MENA economy is, the more sophisticated its products are. This result can be explained in that trade openness allows economies to import foreign products that are more sophisticated than local products. Economies can then model the composition and manufacture of these products, which they will then reproduce themselves, making their production more complex. This result is consistent with the work of Nguyen *et al.* (2020).

However, natural resources are significantly (at 1%) and negatively related in each model to economic complexity in MENA countries (−0.011%; −0.022%; −0.019%; and −0.023%). Indeed, this result can be explained in the sense that products from natural resources cannot be complexified. They come from the primary sector, which is known to be the least complex sector. Thus, as the natural resources of an economy increase, the products of that economy become less complex. This result is consistent with the work of Camargo *et al.* (2017).

14.5. Effect of Corruption on the Relationship Between Financial Development and Economic Complexity in MENA

Table 14.2 shows the effect of corruption on the relationship between financial development and economic complexity in MENA countries. Columns 1 to 4 represent the interaction between corruption and financial development, taking into account each of its dimensions (financial depth, efficiency, stability, and access, respectively) on economic complexity. The variables Financial depth index#Corruption, Financial access index #Corruption, Financial efficiency index #Corruption, and BankZscore#Corruption represent the interaction between corruption and financial depth, access, efficiency, and stability, respectively.

Table 14.2 shows the effect of corruption on the relationship between financial development and economic complexity in MENA countries. Three effects can be noted in general. First, corruption reduces the effect of financial access and depth on economic complexity. The coefficients associated with these dimensions are positive while those associated with their interactions are negative. These results lead to the conclusion that corruption in MENA reduces the effect of financial accessibility and financial depth on ECI by 2.273% and 3.802%, respectively. The rationale for this result is that low levels of corruption control reduce the magnitude of financial access and financial depth in terms of economic complexity. Our results are consistent with the predictions of Chong & Calderon (2000) that in countries with low institutional quality, policies to boost economic performance fail. Indeed, they put forward the prediction that poor

Table 14.2. Effect of corruption on the relationship between financial development and economic complexity in MENA.

	(1)	(2)	(3)	(4)
	ECI	ECI	ECI	ECI
Corruption	0.657***	0.831***	1.567***	−0.182
	(0.072)	(0.097)	(0.474)	(0.182)
Population	−0.004	0.006	−0.001	−0.011
	(0.009)	(0.008)	(0.011)	(0.010)
Economic growth	−0.006***	−0.006**	−0.006	−0.001
	(0.002)	(0.002)	(0.003)	(0.003)
Trade openness	0.002	0.002	0.002	0.003**
	(0.001)	(0.001)	(0.001)	(0.001)
Natural resources	−0.014***	−0.020***	−0.022***	−0.021***
	(0.003)	(0.002)	(0.002)	(0.003)
Foreign direct investment	−0.001	−0.007	0.012	0.009
	(0.007)	(0.008)	(0.011)	(0.012)
Financial depth index	2.000***			
	(0.416)			
Financial depth index × Corruption	−3.802***			
	(0.383)			
Financial access index		0.682***		
		(0.213)		
Financial access index × Corruption		−2.273***		
		(0.287)		
Financial efficiency index			−0.645**	
			(0.307)	
Financial efficiency index × Corruption			−1.795***	
			(0.633)	
BankZscore				−0.003
				(0.002)
BankZscore × Corruption				0.022***
				(0.006)
Constant	−0.499***	−0.200	0.271	−0.184
	(0.117)	(0.136)	(0.236)	(0.144)
Obs.	**219**	**219**	**219**	**229**
R-squared	**0.586**	**0.564**	**0.473**	**0.417**
Hansen	**0.387**	**0.246**	**0.847**	**0.807**

Notes: Values in parentheses are standard deviations corrected for heteroskedasticity. $^{**}p < 0.05$ and $^{***}p < 0.01$ represent the significance levels of the different coefficients at 5% and 1%.

countries with low levels of development will remain trapped in the primary sector unless a sound and credible institutional climate is established.

Second, we find that corruption positively affects the relationship between financial efficiency and economic complexity. This is justified by the fact that the coefficient of the direct effect is negative, and thus the coefficient of the interaction is also negative (−1.795%). Thus, corruption reduces the negative effect of financial efficiency on economic complexity. Indeed, this result can be analyzed in the sense that since banks do not facilitate the mechanisms for granting credit, individuals are sometimes obliged to *bribe* the competent authorities in order to simplify the mechanisms for granting credit. Thus, the effect of financial efficiency on economic complexity will be reduced in MENA countries through corruption.

Third, this table also shows that financial stability only has an effect on economic complexity when the effect is through corruption. We note that while the direct effect of financial stability is not significant, the coefficient associated with the "BankZscore#corruption" interaction was significant and positive at 0.022%.

14.6. Taking into Account a Concurrent Estimation Technique

To test the robustness of our results, this study performs a quantile regression analysis. The double least squares approach focuses on the average effect of economic complexity, but the relevance of our results may be questioned because the effect of different dimensions of financial development may vary across different intervals of economic complexity.

Thus, quantile regressions derived from the work of Koenker & Bassett (1978) provide an answer to this shortcoming. Indeed, it is an estimation technique that allows us to take into account the effect of one variable on another at different points of its distribution. So, this study analyzes the effect of the dimensions of financial development at different intervals of the distribution of the economic complexity index (10th, 25th, 50th, 75th, and 95th quantile). This method may be better than the double least squares method in that the estimate of the mean may sometimes be biased in the case where censored data exist. QR regression studies the effect of a covariance on the entire distribution of the dependent variable, instead of focusing on its conditional average. Thus, by considering the effect of one variable on all points in the distribution of another variable, this method analyzes dimensional effects according to the magnitude of the relationship (Mignamissi & Mouhamed, 2022; Xu 2019; Dufrenot *et al.*, 2010). Low (high) quantiles thus reflect low (high) strength. The quantile estimator is obtained by minimizing the following equation for any the θth quantile ($0 < \theta < 1$):

$$\min_{\beta \in R^K} \left[\sum_{i \in \{i: y_i \geq x'\beta\}} \theta |y_i - x_i'\beta| + \sum_{i \in \{i: y_i \prec x'\beta\}} (1-\theta)|y_i - x_i'\beta| \right], \tag{14.5}$$

where y_i is the education inequality index of country i, β is the vector of parameters to be estimated, and x_i is a $K-1$ vector of explanatory variables.

Tables 14.3 and 14.4 present the effect of financial development on different intervals of economic complexity and the effect of corruption in the relationship.

In the following tables, column 1 represents the baseline analysis, and columns 2–5 represent the regressions for the 10th, 25th, 50th, 75th, and 95th quantile, respectively. We note that the quantile regression analysis shows us that the positive and significant effect of access and depth is stable throughout the distribution of economic complexity. For financial efficiency, we find that its effect is positive and significant between the 10th and 25th quantile. Its effect is consistent with the baseline result from the 75th to the 95th quantile because at the 50th, the effect is negative and not significant.

Table 14.4 presents the effect of corruption in the financial development on different intervals of economic complexity nexus. Column 1 reports the baseline analysis, and columns 2–5 report the regressions for the 10th, 25th, 50th, 75th, and 95th quantile, respectively. We note that the quantile regression analysis does not change our basic results. Indeed, analysis shows that the effect of corruption on the relationship between financial development and economic complexity does not vary along the distribution of economic

Table 14.3. Financial development and economic complexity in MENA by quantiles.

	(1)	(2)	(3)	(4)	(5)	(6)
	2SLS	Q10	Q25	Q50	Q75	Q95
Financial depth index	3.194***	4.193***	4.362***	2.300***	2.342***	2.793***
	(0.528)	(0.785)	(0.654)	(0.669)	(0.552)	(0.527)
Control variables	**Yes**	**Yes**	**Yes**	**Yes**	**Yes**	**Yes**
Obs.	**225**	**327**	**327**	**327**	**327**	**327**
R-squared/Pseudo R-squared	**0.470**	**0.309**	**0.290**	**0.223**	**0.199**	**0.150**
Financial access index	1.454***	2.046***	2.239***	1.904***	1.334***	1.622***
	(0.232)	(0.467)	(0.302)	(0.257)	(0.206)	(0.242)
Control variables	Yes	**Yes**	**Yes**	**Yes**	**Yes**	**Yes**
Obs.	**225**	**327**	**327**	**327**	**327**	**327**
R-squared/Pseudo R-squared	**0.461**	**0.276**	**0.310**	**0.277**	**0.266**	**0.202**
Financial efficiency index	−0.783**	1.800***	1.658***	−0.269	−0.742***	−0.887***
	(0.783)	(0.418)	(0.403)	(0.324)	(0.269)	(0.273)
Control variables	**Yes**	**Yes**	**Yes**	**Yes**	**Yes**	**Yes**
Obs.	**225**	**327**	**327**	**327**	**327**	**327**
R-squared/Pseudo R-squared	**0.388**	**0.254**	**0.215**	**0.185**	**0.196**	**0.146**
BankZscore	0.000	0.005	0.006	−0.001	−0.001	−0.001
	(0.002)	(0.005)	(0.005)	(0.003)	(0.003)	(0.003)
Control variables	**Yes**	**Yes**	**Yes**	**Yes**	**Yes**	**Yes**
Obs.	**263**	**293**	**293**	**293**	**293**	**293**
R-squared/Pseudo R-squared	**0.263**	**0.219**	**0.214**	**0.217**	**0.190**	**0.086**

Notes: Values in parentheses are standard deviations corrected for heteroskedasticity. $^{**}p < 0.05$; and $^{***}p < 0.01$ represent the significance levels of the different coefficients at 10%, 5%, and 1%.

Table 14.4. Corruption, financial development, and economic complexity in MENA by quantiles.

	(1)	(2)	(3)	(4)	(5)	(6)
	2SLS	ECI	ECI	ECI	ECI	ECI
Financial depth index × Corruption	−3.802***	−5.642***	−4.116***	−3.600***	−3.790***	−3.690***
	(0.383)	(1.176)	(0.867)	(0.734)	(0.701)	(0.610)
Control variables	**Yes**	**Yes**	**Yes**	**Yes**	**Yes**	**Yes**
Obs.	**219**	**281**	**281**	**281**	**281**	**281**
R-squared/Pseudo R-squared	**0.586**	**0.382**	**0.369**	**0.342**	**0.318**	**0.271**
Financial access index × Corruption	−2.273***	−2.047***	−1.951***	−1.677***	−1.717***	−2.596***
	(0.287)	(0.736)	(0.525)	(0.461)	(0.415)	(0.515)
Control variables	**Yes**	**Yes**	**Yes**	**Yes**	**Yes**	**Yes**
Obs.	**219**	**281**	**281**	**281**	**281**	**281**
R-squared/Pseudo R-squared	**0.564**	**0.356**	**0.377**	**0.338**	**0.308**	**0.242**
Financial efficiency index × Corruption	−0.645**	−1.838**	−1.268*	−2.415***	−3.098***	−1.814***
	(0.307)	(0.727)	(0.646)	(0.682)	(0.414)	(0.656)
Control variables	**Yes**	**Yes**	**Yes**	**Yes**	**Yes**	**Yes**
Obs.	**219**	**281**	**281**	**281**	**281**	**281**
R-squared/Pseudo R-squared	**0.473**	**0.355**	**0.312**	**0.248**	**0.260**	**0.188**
BankZscore × Corruption	−0.003	0.027***	0.019**	0.019***	0.019***	0.027***
	(0.002)	(0.010)	(0.009)	(0.007)	(0.007)	(0.007)
Control variables	**Yes**	**Yes**	**Yes**	**Yes**	**Yes**	**Yes**
Obs.	**229**	**270**	**270**	**270**	**270**	**270**
R-squared/Pseudo R-squared	**0.417**	0.311	**0.304**	**0.260**	**0.216**	**0.133**

Notes: Values in parentheses are standard deviations corrected for heteroskedasticity. $^{*}p < 0.10$; $^{**}p < 0.05$; and $^{***}p < 0.01$ represent the significance levels of the different coefficients at 10%, 5%, and 1%.

complexity in MENA. Consequently, whatever the level of economic complexity retained, the effect of corruption on the relationship between the three dimensions of financial development-access, efficiency, and financial depth-on economic complexity remains the same. Corruption mitigates the positive effect of financial development on economic complexity in MENA.

14.7. Conclusion and Policy Implications

The objective of this study is to assess the role of corruption in the relationship between financial development and economic complexity in 21 MENA countries over the period 1995–2020. To do so, our empirical strategy is based on the double least squares method. The results show that in MENA countries, there is a conditional relationship between financial development and economic complexity driven by the level of corruption. In general, corruption worsens the effect of financial development on economic complexity over the study period. Specifically, it decreases the effect of financial access, depth, and efficiency; in contrast, it improves the effect of financial stability on economic complexity in the region.

In light of these findings, the financial system, in the quest to promote economic complexity, needs to be embedded in a sound institutional framework combined with a drive to improve its performance in terms of financial service delivery. Specifically, the first recommendation calls on MENA authorities to improve the rule of law to better regulate contracts and enable effective implementation of redistributive policies. The second recommendation suggests that governments improve their capacity to formulate and implement policies and regulations, on one hand, and their capacity to effectively implement their stated programs, on the other hand. Increased stability will tend to improve the business climate and make investment attractive. While these results underscore the crucial role of institutional quality, it must be recognized that in MENA countries there is significant cultural dominance and transmission of circumstances. In contrast to this study, future studies could explore the relationship between financial development and economic complexity by taking cultural aspects into account.

Appendix

Table 14A. Descriptive statistics.

Variable	Obs.	Mean	Std. dev.	Minimum	Maximum
Economic complexity	390	−0.498265	0.6545088	−2.778437	0.696947
Financial depth index	456	0.1268772	0.1001172	0.0129599	0.4717021
Financial access index	456	0.1898268	0.154804	0	0.5201409
Financial efficiency index	456	0.6398093	0.1620707	0.1189775	0.8805239
Z-score	351	23.03758	12.38903	0.0244457	66.63377
Education	367	96.34998	17.69257	23.36354	128.4603
Corruption	420	−0.4104822	0.7475259	−1.868714	1.567186
Population	519	2.782549	2.387465	−4.533415	17.51221
Economic growth	468	3.36321	8.456321	−62.07592	123.1396
Trade	455	83.62317	44.19826	0.7846308	347.9965
Natural resources	499	16.61987	16.5784	0.0010569	67.91786

Table 14B. Table of correlation.

	ECI	FDI	FAI	FEI	BankZscore	Education	Corruption	Population	Growth	Trade openness	Natural resources
ECI	1.0000										
FDI	0.6203	1.0000									
FAI	0.3454	0.3068	1.0000								
FEI	0.0205	0.3604	0.1680	1.0000							
BankZscore	0.1265	0.2724	0.2807	−0.0548	1.0000						
Education	0.1042	0.0510	0.2808	0.0945	−0.0913	1.0000					
Corruption	0.3274	0.4763	0.5896	0.1311	0.1564	0.2689	1.0000				
Population	0.0288	0.1486	0.2647	0.0597	0.0318	0.0493	0.4412	1.0000			
Growth	−0.0693	0.0120	0.0535	0.0299	0.0407	0.0241	0.1206	0.2177	1.0000		
Trade openness	0.1786	0.5055	0.2598	0.2813	0.0423	−0.0838	0.4199	0.1817	0.1213	1.0000	
Natural resources	−0.4759	−0.2699	0.3170	0.1186	−0.1050	0.2244	0.2097	0.2198	0.1094	0.1169	1.000

Looking at the correlation between the variables of interest, Table 14B in the appendices highlights a positive correlation between economic complexity and the dimensions of financial development on one hand, and between economic complexity and corruption on the other hand.

References

Adeola, O. & Evans, O. (2017). Financial inclusion, financial development, and economic diversification in Nigeria. *Journal of Developing Areas, 51*(3), 1–15.

Ahmed, Z., Adebayo, T. S., Udemba, E. N., Murshed, M., & Kirikkaleli, D. (2022). Effects of economic complexity, economic growth, and renewable energy technology budgets on ecological footprint: The role of democratic accountability. *Environmental Science and Pollution Research, 29*(4), 24925–24940.

Albeaik, S., Kaltenberg, M., Alsaleh, M., & Hidalgo, C. A. (2017). Measuring the knowledge intensity of economies with an improved measure of economic complexity. arXiv preprint arXiv:1707.05826.

Altunbaş, Y. & Thornton, J. (2012). Does financial development reduce corruption? *Economics Letters, 114*(1), 221–223.

Aram, B. & Beji, S. (2016). The determinants of industrialization: Empirical evidence for Africa. *European Scientific Journal, 12*(10), 220–240.

Baltagi, B. H., Demetriades, P. O., & Law, S. H. (2009). Financial development and openness: Evidence from panel data. *Journal of Development Economics, 89*(2), 285–296.

Basmann, R. L. (1957). A generalized classical method of linear estimation of coefficients in a structural equation. *Econometrica: Journal of the Econometric Society, 25*(1), 77–83.

Bencivenga, V. & Smith, B. D. (1991). Financial intermediation and endogenous growth. *Review of Economic Studies, 58*(2), 195–209.

Bittencourt, M., Chang S., Gupta, R., & Miller, S. M. (2019). Does financial development affect income inequality in the US States? *Journal of Policy Modeling, 41*(6), 1043–1056.

Camargo, J. S. M. D. & Gala, P. (2017). The resource curse reloaded: Revisiting the Dutch disease with economic complexity analysis, *Real-World Economics Review, 81*(1), 118–134.

Chu, L. K. (2019). The effects of financial development on economic sophistication: Evidence from panel data. *Applied Economics Letters, 27*(4), 1–5.

Chong, A. & Calderón, C. (2000). Causality and feedback between institutional measures and economic growth. *Economics and Politics*, *1*(1), 69–81.

De Haan, J. & Sturm, J. E. (2017). Finance and income inequality: A review and new evidence. *European Journal of Political Economy*, *50*, 171–195.

Dufrenot, G., Mignon, V., & Tsangarides, C. (2010). The trade-growth nexus in the developing countries: A quantile regression approach. *Review of World Economics*, *146*(4), 731–761.

Ewetan, O. O. & Ike, D. N. (2014). Does financial sector development promote industrialization in Nigeria? *International Journal of Research in Social Sciences*, *4*(1), 17–25.

Fosu, A. K. & Abass, A. F. (2019). Domestic credit and export diversification: Africa from a global perspective. *Journal of African Business*, *20*(1), 160–179.

Gala, P., Camargo, G., Rocha, I., & Magacho, G. (2018). Sophisticated jobs matter for economic complexity: An empirical analysis based on input-output matrices and employment data. *Structural Change and Economic Dynamics*, *45*(2), 1–8.

Guiso, L., Sapienza, P., & Zingales, L. (2004). Does local financial development matter? *Quarterly Journal of Economics*, *119*(3), 929–969.

Haraguchi, N., Martorano, B., & Sanfilippo, M. (2019). What factors drive successful industrialization? Evidence and implications for developing countries. *Structural Change and Economic Dynamics*, *49*(2), 266–276.

Hausmann, R. & Rodrik, D. (2003). Economic development as self-discovery. *Journal of Development Economics*, *72*(4), 603–633.

Hidalgo, C. A. & Hausmann, R. (2009). The building blocks of economic complexity. *Proceedings of the National Academy of Sciences*, *106*(26), 10570–10575.

Hidalgo, C. A., Klinger, B., Barabási, A.-L., & Hausmann, R. (2007). The product space conditions the development of nations. *Science*, *317*(5837), 482–487.

Ibrahim, M. & Alagidede, P. (2018). Effect of financial development on economic growth in sub-Saharan Africa. *Journal of Policy Modelling*, *40*(4), 1104–1125.

Jauch, S. & Watzka, S. (2016). Financial development and income inequality: A panel data approach. *Empirical Economics*, *51*(1), 291–314.

Kathakapa, G., Bhupartirajuset, S., & Siroki, R. A. (2021). Revisiting the link between financial development and industrialization: Evidence from low- and middle-income countries. *Annals of Finance*, *17*(4), 215–230.

Khan, H., Khan, U., & Khan, M. A. (2020). Causal nexus between economic complexity and FDI: Empirical evidence from time series analysis. *The Chinese Economy, 53*(1), 374–394.

Kocenda, E. & Poghosyan, K. (2018). Export sophistication, a dynamic panel data approach. *Emerging Markets Finance and Trade, 54*(2), 2799–2814.

Koenker, R. & Bassett, G. (1978). Regression quantiles. *Journal of the Econometric Society, 46*(1), 33–50.

Larrain, B. (2006). Do banks affect the level and composition of industrial volatility? *Journal of Finance, 61*(4), 1897–1925.

Lapatinas, A. (2019). The effect of the internet on economic sophistication: An empirical analysis. *Economics Letters, 174*(1), 35–38.

McKinnon, R. (1973). *Financial Deepening in Economic Development.* Washington: Brookings Institution.

Mignamissi, D. & Mouhamed, M. N. (2022). Dimensional and dynamic effects of common currency on trade: The case of the African franc zone. *The Journal of International Trade and Economic Development, 31*(2), 1243–1280.

Mijiyawa, A. (2017). Drivers of structural transformation: The case of the manufacturing sector in Africa. *World Development, 99*, 141–159.

Moore, T. & Mirzaei, A. (2016). The impact of global financial crisis on industrygrowth. *Manchester School, 84*(2), 159–180.

Nguyen, C. P. & Su, T. D. (2021). Financing the economy: The multidimensional influences of financial development on economic complexity. *Journal of International Development, 33*(2), 644–684.

Nguyen, C. P., Schinckus, C., & Su, T. D. (2020). The drivers of economic complexity. *International Economics, 164*(4), 140–150.

Nieminen, M. (2020). Multidimensional financial development, exporter behavior and export diversification. *Economic Modelling, 93*(4), 1–12.

Rajan, R. G. & Zingales, L. (2001). Financial systems industrial structure and growth. *Oxford Review of Economic Policy, 17*(4), 467–482.

Rodrik, D. (2013). Unconditional convergence in manufacturing. *Quarterly Journal of Economics, 128*(1), 165–204.

Romero, J. P. & Gramkow, C. (2021). Economic complexity and greenhouse gas emissions. *World Development, 139*(1), 1–18.

Pagano, M. & Volpin, P. F. (2005). The political economy of corporate governance. *American Economic Review, 95*(4), 1005–1030.

Pugliese, E., Chiarotti, G. L., Zaccaria, A., & Pietronero, L. (2014). The discernment of heterogeneous country industrialization patterns through economic complexity. *Universita Politecnica Della Marche, Dipartimento di Economia Quaderno di Ricerca, 327*(1), 1–8.

Shaw, E. (1973). *Financial Deepening in Economic Development.* London: Oxford University Press.

Svirydzenka, K. (2016). *Introducing a new broad-based index of financial development.* International Monetary Fund, Washington DC.

Woo, S. J. (1986). Financial development and economic growth: International evidence. *Economic Development and Cultural Change*, *34*(2), 333–346.

Zhang, R. & Naceur, S. B. (2019). Financial development, inequality, and poverty: Some international evidence. *International Review of Economics and Finance*, *61*(2), 1–6.

Zhu, S. & Li, R. (2017). Economic complexity, human capital and economic growth: Empirical research based on cross-country panel data. *Applied Economics*, *49*(38), 3815–3828.

https://doi.org/10.1142/9781800614734_0015

Chapter 15

Determinants of Financial Inclusion: Evidence from the MENA Region

Rachida El Yamani

Abstract

The financial crisis, the accumulation of sovereign debt, shocks to commodity prices, and pandemics are just a few of the recent economic crises that have affected the world and had a major effect on economic activities. In this context, the financial sector must fully contribute to encouraging economic growth in order to achieve equitable economic growth and reduce poverty. To that end, access to affordable and secure financial services is crucial. The main goal of financial inclusion, which allows people to take advantage of saving and investing opportunities, is to provide basic financial services to society's poor and excluded groups. This study aims to identify the factors that promote financial inclusion in the MENA region. It specifically examines the impact of GDP per capita, the money supply as a percentage of GDP, the number of internet users as a percentage of the population, and consumer price inflation. The International Monetary Fund and the Global Development Indicators provided the secondary data for the study, which covers the period 2004–2020. The dynamic panel was conducted using Stata 17 software to obtain the coefficients of such variables that affect the levels of financial inclusion in six MENA countries. The results reveal that income level, measured by GDP per capita, financial sector development, measured by the money supply, and the number of internet users all have positive effects on financial inclusion in the MENA region, while consumer price inflation has no impact. The Financial Inclusion Index (FII), according to Sarma's (2008) approach, has not been employed in any relevant studies, despite the theoretical and empirical literature offering a range of perspectives on which factor can determine financial inclusion. This study uses this index to measure financial inclusion and then applies dynamic panel estimation to identify the factors that promote financial inclusion in MENA countries. Consequently, this chapter strives to enrich the literature by comprehending the determinants of financial inclusion in the MENA region, covering the period 2004–2020.

Keywords: Financial system, financial inclusion, MENA region, dynamic panel approach

15.1. Introduction

According to 2017 statistics, the World Bank estimates that 77% of the world's population is excluded from any financial services. Moreover, the financial services offered are problematic because they are tailored to the region and the local needs. For example, there are still unbanked people in developing economies and underbanked people in developed economies.

Currently, financial inclusion (FI) has become a priority for governments and non-governmental organizations. At the local level, the governments of several countries are partnering with the ecosystem to expand access to the financial system. At the global level, the World Bank Group, the United Nations, and the International Monetary Fund are all focused on FI determinants.

Furthermore, there is no uniform definition of the FI concept among researchers. For example, Sarma's (2008) definition emphasizes the ease of access to financial services and their availability and affordability. The author considers the use of financial services as an important aspect of FI. That aims to guarantee access to basic and formal financial services for the entire population, especially the low-income population (Ozili, 2018). In addition to access to formal financial systems, recent definitions include the use, quality, and cost of financial services provided by these systems (Demirgüç-Kunt *et al.*, 2018; Morgan & Long, 2020). Also, various international organizations (the United Nations, the World Bank, the International Monetary Fund, etc.) have proposed definitions of FI, some of which are more comprehensive than others.

To promote equitable economic growth and reduce poverty, it is essential to increase the vulnerable population's ability to access secure and affordable financial services (Pazarbasioglu *et al.*, 2020). Access to and use of basic financial services by the vulnerable and marginalized in society will increase access to savings and investment opportunities that can help raise incomes and improve living standards. Access to basic financial services can reduce the amount of money circulating outside formal financial channels and support small and medium-sized companies, which often face constraints in accessing finance. For this reason, many countries have recognized the importance of investing in creating the infrastructure and conditions necessary to ensure access to financial services for all populations (Pazarbasioglu *et al.*, 2020).

FI has received the attention of policymakers and researchers for four reasons. First, FI is a long-term strategy that helps achieve the United Nations Sustainable Development Goals (Demirguc-Kunt *et al.*, 2018). Second, FI can promote financial stability in many economies (Vo *et al.*, 2021). Third, FI can help to reduce the poverty level (Neaime & Gaysset, 2018). Finally, FI brings other socio-economic advantages (Sarma & Pais, 2011; Kim *et al.*, 2018; Ozili, 2021). Moreover, the question of how to build inclusive financial systems is a challenge, and this is particularly important in developing and emerging economies, where financial services penetration rates are relatively low. In this context, governments in these countries have launched several initiatives, including the development of FI strategies. These strategies aim to foster FI by expanding access to all financial services for all people in society.

The MENA region is one of the weakest regions in the world in terms of FI (Demirguc-Kunt *et al.*, 2015) and also one of the regions with the highest gender gap in terms of access to and use of formal financial services. In fact, a majority of the governments in the region have taken a number of actions to increase FI. The measurement of the FI level, however, is a very major issue that has not been fully addressed in MENA countries.

In order to assess the effectiveness of political initiatives in favor of the FI, a credible and precise measurement of the FI level is required. This study uses a synthetic index that combines different aspects of financial inclusion into one index. This index will be used to identify the factors that can increase FI in MENA countries and assess changes in FI levels over time in various countries. This study aims to characterize the concept of FI and identify its determinant factors in MENA countries.

15.2. Background

According to Demirguc-Kunt *et al.* (2015), the MENA region has one of the lowest levels of financial inclusion (FI) and one of the biggest gender disparities in access to and use of formal financial services. In fact, a majority of the governments in the region's economy have taken significant steps to improve their FI. Neaime & Gaysset (2018) looked at the effects of FI on poverty and income inequality in eight MENA economies from 2002 to 2015. The results confirmed the hypothesis that, while FI reduces income inequality, it has no impact on poverty levels because of high inflation, trade openness, and the large population in this region.

Naceur *et al.* (2017) examined the relationship between FI and the services provided by Islamic banks and found that access to these services has not grown as rapidly as predicted. Pearce (2011) evaluated the state of FI in MENA economies and recommended (i) the establishment of a regulatory framework that governs access to financing through banks; (ii) the creation of a regulatory environment for the use of cell phone technology and agents; (iii) the creation of a financial company model for leasing and microcredit; (iv) the encouragement of loyal competition among financial service providers; and (v) the removal of barriers to promote the use of Islamic financial services and accreditation.

In order to assess FI levels in those countries, we calculated the composite financial inclusion index (FII), based on Sarma's (2008) approach, for a sample of six middle-income economies in the MENA region for which data are available: Algeria, Djibouti, Egypt, Jordan, Lebanon, and Morocco. The International Monetary Fund is the source of all data relating to FI indicators. The progression of the Financial Inclusion Index in the six MENA countries between 2004 and 2020 is shown in Figure 15.1. The findings indicate low-to-moderate FI levels in these countries, which is consistent with the existing literature (Demirguc-Kunt *et al.*, 2015). It demonstrates the major differences across countries in comparison with other countries: Lebanon has the highest FI level; however, since 2012, it has been steadily declining. Jordan has also failed to raise its FI level, indicating an important decline. This decline in the FI level in both countries was most likely caused by the Syrian crisis and the ensuing migration of refugees. It is important to remember that a country's

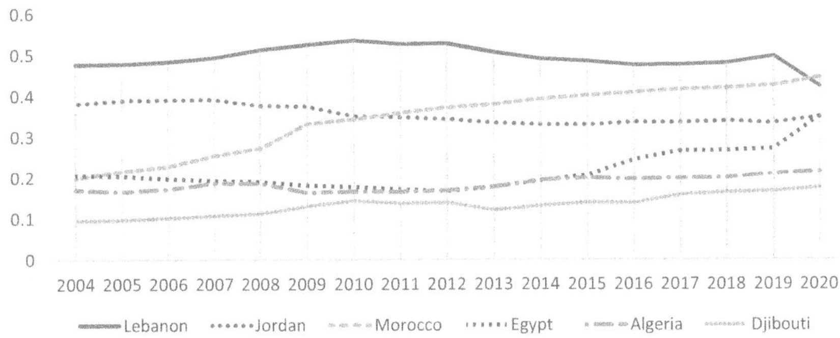

Figure 15.1. Evolution of FII in MENA countries from 2004 to 2020.
Source: Compiled by the author from Financial Access Survey (FAS) data, 2021. International Monetary Fund website.

FI suffers from macroeconomic and political volatility. People in this situation strongly prefer fiat money due to a lack of trust in the financial system, which limits the intensity and use of financial services (such as bank accounts and deposits). Djiboti, which has the lowest FI level, can be found at the bottom of the graph. Elsewhere, Morocco, Egypt, and a small part of Algeria have shown a slow evolution in FI level. Its development in Morocco is a result of the public and monetary authorities' initiatives to increase public access to and use of financial services. In fact, Bank Al-Maghrib, the financial sector's actors, the government agencies, and others are continuing to make efforts to reach an impressive FI level.

Using the summary index, we can classify these six economies from the MENA region according to their average FII, as shown in Table 15.1.

In general, a financial inclusion index below 0.3 reflects low FI, between 0.3 and 0.5 is moderate, and above 0.5 indicates a high financial inclusion level (Sarma, 2008). Thus, we have classified countries into two major groups:

The first one is composed of economies with an intermediate level of financial inclusion ($0.3 \leq \text{FII} \leq 0.5$). These are Lebanon (0.492), Jordan (0.354), and Morocco (0.344). Indeed, with the financial systems of these three countries being relatively well developed, this classification is to be expected. Also, a significant number of international and sub-regional bank branches are located in these

Table 15.1. Average financial inclusion index across the dataset's countries (2004–2020).

S.No.	Country	Average of FII
1	Lebanon	0.49242135
2	Jordan	0.35382233
3	Morocco	0.343876939
4	Egypt	0.215071702
5	Algeria	0.183794394
6	Djibouti	0.132292276

Source: The Financial Access Survey (FAS), 2021, from the website of the International Monetary Fund.

countries. The second group consists of countries with a low level of FII (FII < 0.30). In our case, we have Egypt (0.215), Algeria (0.184), and Djibouti (0.132).

Therefore, it is crucial that each of these countries increases its investment in the diversity of its financial sectors. Finding the factors that promote FI will be crucial.

15.3. Theoretical Literature Review

To reduce poverty, emerging economies give high priority to the financial sector's development. The financial system is essential for increasing access to the use of financial services, which raises the living standards of the underprivileged by mobilizing savings, encouraging efficient resource allocation, and enabling payments (Evans, 2018). To promote sustainable economic growth, authorities have recently turned their attention from research on financial development to research on FI. FI has grown in importance for many countries all over the world, and an expanding collection of research has examined its causes and advantages.

In the theoretical literature, there are several indicators that probably promote FI. These indicators can generally be divided into five categories.

15.3.1. *Supply-side and demand-side factors*

The literature argues that supply side and demand side, for financial services, can explain the FI level. The cost of holding a bank account depends on a variety of commissions and fees (Allen *et al.*, 2016), including interest charges on paid accounts, on the offer side. As a result, the cost of using credit is the main factor. Also, the cost of financial services is directly related to the level of competition between banks, which is influenced by banking concentration (Adil & Jalil, 2020; Markose *et al.*, 2022). On the other hand, use of and access to financial services depend on the banking infrastructure and its density (branches, ATMs). The authors have shown that one of the main barriers to accessing financial services is the low density of banking institutions.

As for the demand for financial services, it depends not only on the average per capita income of the country but also on the distribution of income within the economy. Yangdol & Sarma (2019) showed that narrowing the gaps in access to credit and deposits between the poor and non-poor was associated with higher levels. Thus, a lower GDP per capita explains the low level of FI.

15.3.2. *Institutional factors*

Regarding the institutional context, Anthony-Orji *et al.* (2019) indicate that insufficient institutional quality is at the root of the low FI level. In fact, to promote FI levels, the government and policymakers should give more importance not only to the financial and economic factors but also to the institutional factors, such as governance quality, fighting corruption, and the legal protection of investors' property rights.

15.3.3. *Structural and political factors*

Due to the functions and characteristics of the financial sector, there are two types of constraints that limit its development. The size of the financial market is determined by a number of structural factors, including population size and density, per capita income, and the degree of economic informality. These factors collectively fall under the first category. The level of macroeconomic stability and the enabling legal and institutional framework are examples of policy factors in the second category that may increase or decrease the risks and costs of providing financial services and, as a result, affect how financial activity develops in a nation (Naceur *et al.*, 2017).

15.3.4. *Individual characteristics factors*

Using Honohan's (2008) access factors, Park & Mercado (2015) argued that FI is driven by higher per capita income. Using macroeconomic data sourced from the World Bank, the authors calculated FI indicators for 37 Asian countries. Their results are consistent with those of a similar study conducted by Demirgüç-Kunt & Klapper (2013), who analyzed FI in several economies. They concluded that deeper financial services penetration is associated with higher income. Consequently, the empirical findings confirmed the positive effect of income level on FI level.

The level of a household's education is a major challenge, despite the existence of a significant relationship between education level and FI level (Awad & Eid, 2018). It was concluded that the consumption of financial services increases linearly with the level of education.

15.3.5. *Technological factors*

Banking is a large part of financial services and is at the core of FI in each country. In fact, FI goes beyond physical branches, as ICT (information and communication technology) is revolutionizing access to and use of banking services. Chatterjee (2020) argued that successful experiences of FI in developing economies are due to the use of ICT-based banking services. Thus, the authors revealed that ICT applications, like internet penetration and mobile phones, influence access to and use of financial services provided by the banking system, which can be an important factor in promoting financial inclusion.

15.4. Empirical Literature Review

According to several empirical studies, the evidence on the indicators that determine FI is inconsistent and varies by country, methodology, and particularly the measurement of FI.

Based on a cross-sectional approach, Sarma & Pais (2011) argued that cell phone and internet use, income, income inequality, and adult literacy are the main determinants of FI. According to the authors, the main determinants of financial exclusion are low GDP per capita, low literacy, and low connectivity.

Allen *et al.* (2014) found that FI in Africa is significantly associated with population density, and financial innovations like mobile banking can also help to overcome infrastructure challenges and improve financial access in some African economies.

Using a dynamic panel data approach for the data from 2005 to 2014, Evans (2015) outlined the main indicators that increase FI in Africa. The finding showed that money supply (as a percentage of GDP), GDP per capita, literacy, internet access, and the presence of Islamic banks are the main factors that promote the FI process in Africa. In addition, inflation, interest rates on deposits, and population seizing have insignificant effects on the FI level. Furthermore, David *et al.* (2018) defined the indicators that determine FI. The results, from an Error Correction Model (ECM) with secondary data from 1990 to 2016, revealed that GDP per capita, money supply, credit, and the number of internet users are the main determinants of FI in Nigeria. Thus, a country's FI level will be higher if its GDP per capita is higher, its financial system is more developed, and it uses the internet more frequently.

When Evans (2018) analyzed the link between cell phones, the internet, and FI in Africa, the author found that cell phones and the internet have increased access to basic financial services, which helps accelerate the FI process. On the other hand, Kabakova & Plaksenkov (2018) studied the indicators that promote FI in developing economies and showed that economic, political, and socio-demographic factors are the main determinants of FI level in these economies.

Through social cohesion, Okello Candiya Bongomin *et al.* (2018) reported that social networks have increased the FI level in rural Uganda. Addressing the issue centered on the gender approach and the level of wealth, Fungáčová & Weill (2015) showed that those most likely to be financially included in China are older, wealthier, and more educated men. In addition, they indicated that, compared to men, women have a low probability of accessing formal financial services versus a high probability of accessing informal financial services. Their results showed, too, that income and education levels influence the choice between formal and informal credit. Also, financial inclusion was attracting the attention of policymakers in many African economies. Zins & Weill (2016) identified several factors that increase FI in 37 African economies. The authors found that being male, more educated, wealthier, and older are linked to a high FI level in these African economies.

For Awad & Eid (2018), the more important factors that promote FI in Central Africa and West Africa are income, age, gender, employment status, education, household size, residence area, and degree of trust in financial institutions. Qamruzzaman and Wei (2019) showed that FI has been achieved through financial innovations; the authors reveal that innovative financial services can help promote FI levels in South Asian countries.

15.5. Research Design

This study aims to identify the factors that determine FI in six MENA economies.

15.5.1. *Data and variables*

To identify the determinants of FI in the MENA region, a dynamic panel data analysis was performed using annual data covering the period 2004–2020 for six (06) countries representing MENA economies, namely, Algeria, Djibouti, Egypt, Jordan, Lebanon, and Morocco. The data were sourced from the International Monetary Fund (IMF) for FI indicators and the World Development Indicators (WDI) database for explanatory indicators.

As for the measurement of FI, the literature identifies two groups of researchers. The first group uses the number of depositors with commercial banks per 1,000 adults (Čihák *et al.*, 2012; Evans, 2015; Naceur *et al.*, 2017; David *et al.*, 2018). The second group of researchers turned to the construction of a financial inclusion index (FII) by introducing several indicators following the construction procedure established by Sarma (2008, 2012) and used by other researchers (Qamruzzaman & Wei, 2019; Otekunrin *et al.*, 2021).

Constructing the FII has the obvious benefit of enabling cross-country comparisons and offering a more rigorous characterization of FI, taking into account several characteristics.

In this study, FI was measured according to the indexing procedure developed by Sarma (2008) (details on the construction of FII are provided in the Appendix 15A), which was inspired by the methodology for calculating the Human Development Index (HDI). Like the HDI, the Financial Inclusion Index (FII) summarizes, in a single indicator, all the information provided by several indicators. Indeed, based on the FII, countries could be ranked according to their FI level. It not only facilitates cross-country comparisons but also comparisons over time, especially for the purpose of evaluating actions to promote FI.

According to the literature review, the most identified determinants of FI (Table 15.2) are GDP per capita, money supply (% of GDP), number of internet users (% of population), and consumer price inflation.

Table 15.2. Variables and their measurement.

Explanatory variables	Explication	Expected signs	References
GDPC is annual percentage growth rate of GDP per capita (is the proxy for income level)	A high income level positively influences the level of financial inclusion.	Positive	Sarma & Pais (2011), Evans (2015), David *et al.* (2018)
M2/GDP is money supply (% of GDP) (is the proxy for financial development)	The financial development promotes financial inclusion, though financing of the economy.	Positive	Evans (2015), David *et al.* (2018)
Number of internet users (% of population)	The digitalization of financial services through digital technology (including internet and cell phones) encourages users to benefit from accessing financial services, especially banking services that are offered remotely.	Positive	Sarma & Pais (2011), Evans (2015), David *et al.* (2018)
Consumer price inflation	Consumer price inflation should dampen financial development if it makes it harder to contract credit. Consumer price inflation could also inhibit deposits in the formal financial system for fear of not being able to recover them quickly enough.	Negative	Allen *et al.* (2014), Evans (2015)

Source: Established by us based on literature review.

15.5.2. *Dynamic panel data approach*

Denbel *et al.* (2016) examined how the money supply affected economic growth while taking into account the endogeneity issue that was discovered during the causality test. Ndoricimpa (2017) stated the impact of inflation on economic growth. Alexandrov *et al.* (2021) confirmed the impact of the money supply on inflation.

The generalized method of moments (GMM) approach was performed to overcome the endogeneity problem, namely, the dynamic panel estimation using the Arellano–Bond method and the system dynamic panel estimation method. Our specification includes a lagged financial inclusion index as an exploratory variable.

This study uses dynamic panel data regression in the following form:

$$Y_{it} = \alpha_{it} + \delta_{1i}\, Y_{it-1} + \alpha_{1i}\, \beta' X_{it} + \varepsilon_{it}, \tag{15.1}$$

$$\varepsilon_{it} = \mu_{it} + \vartheta_{it}, \tag{15.2}$$

where

Y_{it}: the response of the individual i in the time t;
δ: the coefficient vector of Y_{it-1};
Y_{it-1}: the lagged 1 of the endogenous variable Y_{it};
$\beta'(\beta_1, \beta_2, \ldots, \beta_k)$: the slope coefficient vector of size $1 \times k$, where k is the number of explanatory variable;
X_{it}: the exogenous variables for individual i at time t;
α_{it}: the intercept coefficient for individual i at time t;
ε_{it}: the error term in time t.

It should be noted that a logarithmic transformation has been carried out on some variables to ensure the accuracy and robustness of the estimates.

The model is specified as follows:

$$\begin{aligned}\text{FINC}_{it} = \alpha_{it} + \beta_{1i} Y_{it-1} + \beta_{2i}\, \text{GDPC}_{it} + \beta_{3i}\, \text{LM2}_{it} \\ + \beta_{4i}\, \text{LIUSERS}_{it} + \beta_{5i}\, \text{INF}_{it} + \varepsilon_{it},\end{aligned} \tag{15.3}$$

$i = 1, \ldots, 6$ and $t = 1, \ldots, 17$ with $N = 6$ countries and $T = 17$ years, $n = N \times T = 102$, where FINC_{it} is the financial inclusion index for country i in year t; GDPC_{it} is GDP per capita growth rate (% annual) for country i in year t; LM2_{it} is the logarithm of money supply (% of GDP) for country i in year t; LIUSERS_{it} is the logarithm of number of internet users (% of population) for country i in year t; and INF_{it} is consumer price inflation for country i in year t.

α_{it} refers to intercepts for individual i. $\beta_{1i}; \beta_{2i}; \beta_{3i}; \beta_{4i}; \beta_{5i}$ are explanatory variables' coefficients, and ε_{it} is the error term of individual i at year t.

15.6. Results

Table 15.3 shows descriptive statistics for the overall sample, consisting of all six countries in the MENA region over the period from 2004 to 2020, for a total of 102 observations.

According to the statistic descriptive of the dependent variable (FINC), it has a fairly low mean and standard deviation with values of 0.2869 and 0.1297, respectively. The value ranges from at least 0.095 to at most 0.5343. We are also led to assume that, unlike the other exogenous variables, the consumer price inflation deviation is the most important. This means that consumer price inflation in six countries in the MENA region is very volatile.

According to Table 15.4, all variables are stationary at the second difference except for FINC, which is stationary at the first difference.

We will move on to the Granger test established by Dumitrescu & Hurlin (2012) to investigate the causal relationships between financial inclusion index (FINC) volatility and the explanatory variables.

Table 15.5 shows that, according to the Z-bar and Z-bar tilde statistics, with the first lag, GDPC, LM2, LIUSERS, and INF cause FINC volatility, in the Granger sense, for the countries under study.

Table 15.3. Descriptive statistics.

Variable	Obs.	Mean	Std. dev.	Minimum	Maximum
FINC	102	0.2868798	0.1297194	0.0953073	0.534355
GDPC	102	1.329095	3.885497	−21.116	9.13666
LM2	102	4.669014	0.4340306	3.985788	5.570055
LIUSERS	102	3.23391	1.019221	−0.2467741	4.432249
INF	102	114.6304	40.698	55.07544	303.1311

Table 15.4. Results of unit root test (Im, Pesaran, Shin).

Variable	At level	1st difference	2nd difference	Decision
FINC	2.83011	−1.28199*	—	I(1)
GDPC	1.02021	−0.39772	−3.02041**	I(2)
LM2	−0.68206	−1.21034	−3.18208***	I(2)
LIUSERS	0.82538	−1.23757	−3.05085***	I(2)
INF	1.55949	−0.19771	−1.51704*	I(2)

Notes: ***, ** and * represent, respectively, significance at 1%, 5% and 10% level.

Table 15.5. Granger's non-causality test.

Direction of causality relationship	Statistics		p-value
GDPC → FINC	Z-bar	6.8593	**0.0000**
	Z-bar tilde	4.7957	**0.0000**
FINC → GDPC	Z-bar	2.0813	**0.0374**
	Z-bar tilde	1.2944	0.1955
LM2 → FINC	Z-bar	3.5718	**0.0004**
	Z-bar tilde	2.3866	**0.0170**
FINC → LM2	Z-bar	1.8987	**0.0576**
	Z-bar tilde	1.1606	0.2458
LIUSERS → FINC	Z-bar	6.0156	**0.0000**
	Z-bar tilde	4.1774	**0.0000**
FINC → LIUSERS	Z-bar	2.3744	**0.0176**
	Z-bar tilde	1.5092	0.1313
INF → FINC	Z-bar	6.5272	**0.0000**
	Z-bar tilde	4.5523	**0.0000**
FINC → INF	Z-bar	0.3778	0.7056
	Z-bar tilde	0.0461	0.9632
INF → GDPC	Z-bar	2.5506	**0.0108**
	Z-bar tilde	1.6383	0.1014

Note: Significant p-values at 0.05 are made bold.

In order to obtain reliable estimators, dynamic panel data regression was performed with FINC (−1) included as an instrumental variable.

The dynamic panel data regression results, using the dynamic panel estimation using the Arellano–Bond method and the system dynamic panel estimation method, are synthesized in Table 15.6, which shows the main factors that promote the FI level in the MENA region.

Table 15.6. The factors that determine financial inclusion in MENA economies: GMM Estimation.

	Dependent variable: Financial inclusion index	
Variables	Arellano–Bond dynamic panel data estimation	System dynamic panel data estimation
FINC(−1)	0.5430404	0.6089062
	(0.2747069)**	(0.0700974)***
GDPC	0.0009439	0.0019075
	(0.0005324)*	(0.0003803)***
LM2	0.0838899	0.0815541
	(0.0198888)***	(0.0161403)***
LIUSERS	0.0158535	0.0145115
	(0.0047013)**	(0.003301)***
INF	−0.0001868	−0.0000772
	(0.0001048)*	(0.000056)
Constant	−0.2906328	−0.3075137
	(0.1027985)**	(0.0640711)***
Wald χ^2 (5)	85.71	1108.05
p-value $> \chi^2$	0.000	0.000

Notes: In parentheses are standard errors. ***, **, and * represent, respectively, 1%, 5%, and 10% significance levels, respectively.

The p-values of χ^2 for the FINC variable in the Arellano–Bond method and the system dynamic panel estimation method are 0.000. Therefore, both of the models are valid, so at least one of the exogenous variables is statistically significant. Thus, the Z-test was performed to test the significance of each parameter.

15.7. Discussion

In this research, we retain the results of system dynamic panel data estimation since this approach uses both lagged and differenced variables as instruments to estimate the model parameters. As expected, the lagged financial inclusion index's coefficient is significant at the 1% level. It shows a value of 0.60, which confirms the hypothesis that financial inclusion persists with any change in the specification. The GDP per capita coefficient is 0.019 and is found to be significant at the 1% level with a positive sign, which is consistent with the results found by Sarma & Pais (2011), Zins & Weill (2016), Awad *et al.*

(2018), and David *et al.* (2018). This means that high income levels are conducive to increasing the FI level in the studied countries; as individuals' income increases, they are more likely to be financially included. In this sense, financial exclusion is primarily a problem for people with low incomes. These people face great difficulties in accessing and benefiting from formal financial services. In this case, we can deduce that improvement in income levels and living conditions is essential to promoting financial inclusion.

The coefficient of money supply (in % of GDP) is statistically significant with a significant sign; this result is consistent with the literature. Evans (2015) found that money supply, as a proxy for financial development, promotes financial inclusion in African economies, and David *et al.* (2018) confirm that the continued increase in money supply will certainly improve the process of FI in Nigeria.

The coefficient of internet users' numbers is significant and positive. The literature reveals that intensive internet use affects positively financial inclusion. In this regard, Sarma & Pais (2011), Evans (2015), and David *et al.* (2018) have shown that access to the Internet is a factor favoring the evolution of the digital economy. The proliferation of digital banking services is an important development for financial inclusion in developing economies because it reaches many poor people and even those in remote locations, reducing the cost.

The only variable that is not significant is the inflation rate. This variable is not statistically significant, despite showing the expected sign. This finding is consistent with the result found by Evans (2015).

15.8. Conclusion

In conclusion, it should be recalled that the goal of our contribution was to determine the factors that promote FI levels in MENA economies. Admittedly, the concept of FI has never had a universal definition among international organizations, although the objective has always been common. Indeed, efforts at financial inclusion to ensure access to and use of basic financial services by the entire population are necessary in order to improve their standard of living.

Recently, FI has received increasing attention from international institutions, financial sector regulators, and governments. This trend reflects an increased awareness of the crucial role of FI in promoting inclusive growth and achieving sustainable development goals, including reducing poverty and disparities in the population. Although the FI climate in the MENA region has improved, it still remains fragile on average, with the exception of the Gulf countries.

Moreover, over the past decade, many actions have been implemented by the various actors in the financial sector to promote access to financial services. However, this progress hardly masks the persistence of certain challenges that remain to be met.

The results of our research indicate that income level, financial system development, and internet use are the main determinants of FI evolution. Furthermore, the results provide some insight into the economic and social development levels of the countries studied. There are several concrete actions that need to be taken to strengthen the FI process of disadvantaged (poor and low-income) people. Indeed, financial institutions (commercial banks, microfinance institutions) should provide financial services adapted to this population's needs at reasonable costs in order to improve their FI.

Nonetheless, the dominance of the informal sector is a major factor in the studied countries' FI delays. However, in the countries under study, the delay in terms of FI mainly depends on the dominance of the informal market. In this case, government policies to increase social inclusion and the integration of the informal sector into the formal economy can promote the potential for FI.

Finally, it is important to note that FI can only be achieved and optimized when it allows vulnerable populations to access formal financial services upstream, beginning with opening an account to enable access to credit and insurance. To guarantee that the business and public sectors' commitment to promoting FI is explicit, strong, and sustained over time, it is imperative to continue developing FI plans. Even though the road to FI may be long, the benefits of development may significantly change people's lives in the MENA region.

Appendix 15A. Details of Financial Inclusion Index Construction

Sarma's (2008) index was constructed on the basis of three dimensions, namely, banking penetration, availability, and use.

- The first dimension is banking penetration:

This dimension concerns the use of financial services available and provided by formal financial institutions. In addition, financial system penetration (p) is measured by the proportion of people with a bank account in a financial institution (Sarma, 2008). Thus, if every person in a nation has a bank account, the value of this indicator would be 1. However, the Global Findex database does not publish data on the number of people who have had a bank account for a long period of time.

- The second dimension is financial services availability:

Availability (a) is another characteristic of an inclusive financial sector. It is represented by the number of commercial bank branches (a_1) per 100,000 adults and the number of ATMs (a_2) per 100,000 adults. There is no denying the crucial role of ATMs in increasing access to banking services in many economies. They have great importance in economies due to their efficiency and flexibility, allowing customers to benefit from services without going through their branches. This dimension encompasses all the procedures that the formal financial sector uses to provide its financial services to the population.

- The third dimension is financial services use:

This dimension focuses more on the intensity and permanence of the use of financial services or products. Indeed, the use of financial services can take many forms, including details about the regularity, duration, use, or frequency. So, this dimension includes information on deposits, credits, payments, remittances, and transfers. But the unavailability of data to measure all these different forms causes a problem. To measure this dimension, in our study, the volume of deposits and credit as a percentage of GDP were used (Sarma, 2008, 2012).

According to Sarma (2008), the IFI is calculated using the three dimensions mentioned above. The starting point is to calculate the sub-indices of the different dimensions according to the following formula:

$$di = \frac{A_i - m_i}{M_i - m_i}, \tag{15A.1}$$

where d_i is the value of the dimension i, A_i is its current value, m_i is its minimum value, M_i is its maximum value, and the formula must guarantee that d_i is between 0 and 1, when the value of d_i is higher, which means that the country's achievements in this dimension are also higher.

Thus, since several indicators can be used to calculate each dimension, the dimension index is obtained by taking the average of its indices.

If we consider n dimensions, each country i will be described by a point $D_i = (d_1, d_2, d_3, \ldots, d_n)$ on the Cartesian space of dimension n.

Thus, the point $O(0, 0, 0, \ldots, 0)$ refers to the bad situation and the point $L(1, 1, 1, \ldots, 1)$ refers to the best one, for each n dimensional space.

For each country, the financial inclusion index (FII) was calculated as the normalized Euclidean distance inverse between the ideal situation in Cartesian space $(d_1, d_2, d_3, \ldots, d_n)$, i.e., $(1, 1, 1, \ldots, 1)$ and the least ideal one, i.e., $(0, 0, 0, \ldots, 0)$. Let be:

$$\text{IFI} = 1 - \frac{\sqrt{(1-d_1)^2 + (1-d_2)^2 + (1-d_3)^2 + \cdots + (1-d_n)^2}}{\sqrt{n}}. \tag{15A.2}$$

The numerator of the fraction, in Eq. (15A.2), is the Euclidean distance between the point D_i and the ideal point L. Normalize by $\sqrt{n}$ and subtract by 1; we find the normalized inverse distance.

Normalization allows the index to take a value between 0 and 1 and the inverse distance is considered so that a high IFI describes high financial inclusion.

The lower bounds (m_i) of all dimensions are equal to 0.

The upper bounds (M_i) are determined empirically by Sarma (2015).

For banking penetration, the upper limit is 2500, which represents more than the full scope of financial services.

The availability dimension consists of two indicators, namely, the number of commercial bank branches (a_1) (with an upper limit, $Ma_1 = 60$) and the number of ATMs (a_2) $(Ma_2 = 120)$. Availability is then defined according to the equation $\left(\frac{2}{3}a_1 + \frac{1}{3}a_2\right)$.

The final dimension of the Sarma (2008) index is usage, represented by private sector domestic deposits and credit as a percentage of GDP; its upper bound is 300.

References

Adil, F. & Jalil, A. (2020). Determining the financial inclusion output of banking sector of Pakistan — Supply-side analysis. *Economies*, *8*(2), 42. https://doi.org/10.3390/economies8020042.

Alexandrov, D. G., Valinurova, L. S., Kostromin, P. A., Zenkina, E. V., & Egorov, V. G. (2021). Metrics for assessing the effect of household income and the money supply on inflation. *Montenegrin Journal of Economics*, *17*(4), 147–154.

Allen, F., Carletti, E., Cull, R., Qian, J. Q., Senbet, L., & Valenzuela, P. (2014). The African financial development and financial inclusion gaps. *Journal of African Economies*, *23*(5), 614–642. https://doi.org/10.1093/jae/eju015.

Allen, F., Demirguc-Kunt, A., Klapper, L., & Peria, M. S. M. (2016). The foundations of financial inclusion: Understanding ownership and use of formal accounts. *Journal of financial Intermediation*, *27*, 1–30. https://doi.org/10.1016/j.jfi.2015.12.003.

Anthony-Orji, O. I., Orji, A., Ogbuabor, J. E., & Nwosu, E. O. (2019). Do financial stability and institutional quality have impact on financial inclusion in developing economies? A new evidence from Nigeria. *International Journal of Sustainable Economy*, *11*(1), 18–40. https://doi.org/10.1504/IJSE.2019.09654.1.

Awad, M. M. & Eid, N. H. (2018). Financial inclusion in the MENA region: A case study on Egypt. *Journal of Economics and Finance*, *9*(1). DOI: 10.9790/5933-0901021125.

Chatterjee, A. (2020). Financial inclusion, information and communication technology diffusion, and economic growth: A panel data analysis. *Information Technology for Development*, *26*(3), 607–635. https://doi.org/10.1080/02681102.2020.1734770.

Čihák, M., Demirgüç-Kunt, A., Feyen, E., & Levine, R. (2012). Benchmarking financial systems around the world. *World Bank Policy Research Working Paper*, (6175).

David, O. O., Oluseyi, A. S., & Emmanuel, A. (2018). Empirical analysis of the determinants of financial inclusion in Nigeria: 1990–2016. *Journal of Finance and Economics*, *6*(1), 19–25. DOI: 10.12691/jfe-6-1-3.

Demirgüç-Kunt, A. & Klapper, L. (2013). Measuring financial inclusion: Explaining variation in use of financial services across and within countries. *Brookings Papers on Economic Activity*, *2013*(1), 279–340. https://muse.jhu.edu/article/524137/summary.

Demirgüç-Kunt, A., Klapper, L. F., Singer, D., & Van Oudheusden, P. (2015). The global findex database 2014: Measuring financial inclusion around the world. *World Bank Policy Research Working Paper*, (7255). https://ssrn.com/abstract=2594973.

Demirguc-Kunt, A., Klapper, L., Singer, D., & Ansar, S. (2018). *The Global Findex Database 2017: Measuring Financial Inclusion and the Fintech Revolution.* World Bank Publications, http://documents.worldbank.org/curated/en/332881525873182837/The-Global-Findex-Database-2017-.

Denbel, F. S., Ayen, Y. W., & Regasa, T. A. (2016). The relationship between inflation, money supply and economic growth in Ethiopia: Co integration and Causality Analysis. *International Journal of Scientific and Research Publications*, *6*(1), 556–565.

Dumitrescu, E. I. & Hurlin, C. (2012). Testing for Granger non-causality in heterogeneous panels. *Economic Modelling*, *29*(4), 1450–1460. https://doi.org/10.1016/j.econmod.2012.02.014.

Evans, O. (2015). The Effects of Economic and Financial Development on Financial Inclusion in Africa. Published in: *Review of Economics and Development Studies*, *1*(1), 17–25.

Evans, O. (2018). Connecting the poor: The internet, mobile phones and financial inclusion in Africa. *Digital Policy, Regulation and Governance.* https://doi.org/10.1108/DPRG-04-2018-0018.

Fungáčová, Z. & Weill, L. (2015). Understanding financial inclusion in China. *China Economic Review*, *34*, 196–206. https://doi.org/10.1016/j.chieco.2014.12.004.

Kabakova, O. & Plaksenkov, E. (2018). Analysis of factors affecting financial inclusion: Ecosystem view. *Journal of Business Research*, *89*, 198–205. https://doi.org/10.1016/j.jbusres.2018.01.066.

Kim, D. W., Yu, J. S., & Hassan, M. K. (2018). Financial inclusion and economic growth in OIC countries. *Research in International Business and Finance*, *43*, 1–14. https://doi.org/10.1016/j.ribaf.2017.07.178.

Markose, S., Arun, T., & Ozili, P. (2022). Financial inclusion, at what cost?: Quantification of economic viability of a supply side roll out. *The European Journal of Finance*, *28*(1), 3–29. https://doi.org/10.1080/1351847X.2020.1821740.

Morgan, P. J. & Long, T. Q. (2020). Financial literacy, financial inclusion, and savings behavior in Laos. *Journal of Asian Economics*, *68*, 101197. https://doi.org/10.1016/j.asieco.2020.101197.

Naceur, S. B., Barajas, A., & Massara, A. (2017). Can Islamic banking increase financial inclusion? In *Handbook of Empirical Research on Islam and Economic Life* (pp. 213–252). Edward Elgar Publishing. https://doi.org/10.4337/9781784710736.00017.

Ndoricimpa, A. (2017). Threshold effects of inflation on economic growth: Is Africa different? *International Economic Journal*, *31*(4), 599–620. https://doi.org/10.1080/10168737.2017.1380679.

Neaime, S. & Gaysset, I. (2018). Financial inclusion and stability in MENA: Evidence from poverty and inequality. *Finance Research Letters*, *24*, 230–237. https://doi.org/10.1016/j.frl.2017.09.007.

Okello Candiya Bongomin, G., Ntayi, J. M., Munene, J. C., & Malinga, C. A. (2018). Mobile money and financial inclusion in sub-Saharan Africa: The moderating role of social networks. *Journal of African Business*, *19*(3), 361–384. https://doi.org/10.1080/15228916.2017.1416214.

Otekunrin, A. O., Chinoda, T., & Matowanyika, K. (2021). The nexus between economic growth, financial development, financial inclusion and financial innovation in Africa. *Asian Economic and Financial Review*, *11*(8), 672–681. https://doi.org/10.18488/journal.aefr.2021.118.672.681.

Ozili, P. K. (2018). Impact of digital finance on financial inclusion and stability. *Borsa Istanbul Review*, *18*(4), 329–340. https://doi.org/10.1016/j.bir.2017.12.003.

Ozili, P. K. (2021). Financial inclusion research around the world: A review. In *Forum for Social Economics* (Vol. 50, No. 4, pp. 457–479). Routledge. https://doi.org/10.1080/07360932.2020.1715238.

Park, C. Y. & Mercado, R. (2015). Financial inclusion, poverty, and income inequality in developing Asia. *Asian Development Bank Economics Working Paper Series*, (426). http://dx.doi.org/10.2139/ssrn.2558936.

Pazarbasioglu, C., Mora, A. G., Uttamchandani, M., Natarajan, H., Feyen, E., & Saal, M. (2020). Digital financial services. *World Bank*, 54. https://pubdocs.worldbank.org/en/230281588169110691/Digital-Financial-Services.pdf.

Qamruzzaman, M. & Wei, J. (2019). Financial innovation and financial inclusion nexus in South Asian countries: Evidence from symmetric and asymmetric panel investigation. *International Journal of Financial Studies*, *7*(4), 61. https://doi.org/10.3390/ijfs7040061.

Sarma, M. (2008). Index of financial inclusion (No. 215). Working Paper. https://www.econstor.eu/handle/10419/176233.

Sarma, M. (2012). Index of financial inclusion — A measure of financial sector inclusiveness. Centre for International Trade and Development, School of International Studies Working Paper Jawaharlal Nehru University. Delhi, India.

Sarma, M. & Pais, J. (2011). Financial inclusion and development. *Journal of International Development, 23*(5), 613–628. https://doi.org/10.1002/jid.1698.

Vo, D. H., Nguyen, N. T., & Van, L. T. H. (2021). Financial inclusion and stability in the Asian region using bank-level data. *Borsa Istanbul Review, 21*(1), 36–43. https://doi.org/10.1016/j.bir.2020.06.003.

Yangdol, R. & Sarma, M. (2019). Demand-side factors for financial inclusion: A cross-country empirical analysis. *International Studies, 56*(2–3), 163–185. https://doi.org/10.1177/00208817198492.

Zins, A. & Weill, L. (2016). The determinants of financial inclusion in Africa. *Review of Development Finance, 6*(1), 46–57. https://doi.org/10.1016/j.rdf.2016.05.001.

https://doi.org/10.1142/9781800614734_bmatter

Index

www.ingramcontent.com/pod-product-compliance
Lightning Source LLC
LaVergne TN
LVHW011658200926
848484LV00004B/989